Max Planck Series on Asian Intellectual Property Law

Volume 13

Editor
Reto Hilty
Director
Max Planck Institute for Patent, Copyright and Competition Law

Over the last few decades, intellectual property law has assumed an increasingly vital role in the expansion of the Internet and the rapid pace of technological innovation. Intellectual property law has therefore grown into one of the world's biggest and fastest-growing fields of law. As the relative value of intellectual property increases in the global economy, the development of intellectual property rights in Asia has been nothing less than dramatic in the last couple of years. Spurred by the TRIPS Agreement, most Asian countries have completely overhauled their intellectual property systems. This formal adaptation of intellectual property law to international standards is now followed by a period in which Asia is re-conceptualizing the way that it thinks about intellectual property law, its administration, and enforcement. Thus, Asia is emerging as a potent force in reshaping the global intellectual property landscape.

The Max Planck Institute for Intellectual Property has pioneered intellectual property research and education in Asia since 1975. It has not only been involved in fundamental research on intellectual property law, but also in drafting legislation both on the Institute's own account, and in cooperation with projects funded by the European Union, WIPO, the World Bank, UNDP, and others. Cooperation agreements have been concluded with institutions in Japan, Korea, Taiwan, and Thailand. The Max Planck Institute is further renowned for its conferences and workshops on Asian intellectual property law and its state-of-the-art research facilities. It annually welcomes more than 40 students, guest researchers, and distinguished expert lawyers from Asia thereby deepening the international dialogue on intellectual property policy.

The Max Planck Series on Asian Intellectual Property Law aims at providing expert coverage of intellectual property rights, their administration and enforcement in Asian jurisdictions for both academic and practising lawyers. Particular attention is given to the non-English speaking countries of Asia where reliable information is often difficult to come by. The series includes both country-specific reports and comparative studies on current problems of interest.

The titles published in this series are listed in the back of this volume.

Kluwer Law International

The Protection of Trade Secrets in China

SHAN Hailing

Professor of Law
East China University of Political Science and Law
Shanghai, China

Wolters Kluwer
Law & Business

AUSTIN BOSTON CHICAGO NEW YORK THE NETHERLANDS

Published by:
Kluwer Law International
PO Box 316
2400 AH Alphen aan den Rijn
The Netherlands
Website: www.Kluwerlaw.com

sold and distributed in North, Central and South America by:
Aspen Publishers, Inc.
7201 McKinney Circle
Frederick, MD 21704
United States of America
Email: customer.care@aspenpubl.com

sold and distributed in all other countries by:
Turpin Distribution Services Ltd.
Stratton Business Park
Pegasus Drive, Biggleswade
Bedfordshire SG18 8TQ
United Kingdom
Email: Kluwerlaw@turpin-distribution.com

ISBN 978-90-411-2758-7

Summary of Contents

Table of Contents

Preface

When the world entered the Information Age, the strength and potential for the development of a nation's economy came to be measured by the capability of its industrial economy to protect trade secrets. The industrial capability of an economy is supported by knowledge and by intellectual property, among which secret knowledge and confidential information play an important role. Along with economic development, trade has broken the constraints of territorial boundaries and has expanded beyond the limits of time and space. In particular, now that information has become a kind of commodity, it has become a common phenomenon that the protection and the battle for possession of information have evolved into heated international competition within industries.

The right to trade secrets is a civil right in law. Trade secrets are important intangible assets and resources within an economy and are powerful competitive tools within markets. Trade secrets are highly valued by many international organizations including those that are members of the World Trade Organization. The World Trade Organization Agreement on Trade-Related Aspects of Intellectual Property Rights (the TRIPS Agreement) defines trade secrets as 'undisclosed information,' a term which illustrates the high level and broad scope of protection of information in the domain of modern economies. Currently, trade secret protection is an important legislative issue in many countries. Under the regulations contained in the TRIPS Agreement, there has been a trend toward unifying the definition of trade secrets, their constitutive requirements, and their scope of protection under the law in different countries and more and more countries have promulgated new law or have improved their current laws in order to better protect trade secrets. Traditional civil remedies seek to protect trade secrets from infringement, and criminal punishment is sometimes meted out for serious acts of infringement as well. These measures are implemented for the purpose of maintaining basic commercial ethics and for protecting property rights as well as for encouraging research and innovation on the part of enterprises and individuals.

In China, promulgation of trade secret legislation and research on the legal science of trade secrets began in the 1990s. Progress toward the establishment and development of a trade secret protection system in China has maintained a momentum similar to that of its economic growth and social reform. With unexpected speed and on an impressive scale, China has gone through a process of 'marketization', urbanization, diversification of economic ownership, and globalization, achieving results that have attracted the attention of the world. However, with a booming private economy and the improvement of technology and scientific research as well as of the labour market in China, the number of trade secret disputes occurring has increased to the highest level in Chinese history. In addition, with more and more Chinese employees frequently changing jobs, the relationship between employees and employers has become very fragile. Trade secret disputes involving employment relationships now account for a large proportion of causes of action involving trade secrets which are heard by the courts in China.

According to statistics published on the China IPR Judgment and Decisions website[1] regarding various categories of disputes heard between 2001 and 2005, a high percentage (32.93%) involved the infringement of operating confidential information while cases involving co-existence of infringement of trade secrets and a duty of non-competition comprised 25.61% of the total. Infringement of technical confidential information comprised 21.95% and causes of action involving infringement due to disclosure by employees accounted for 34.15%. The greatest percentage of disputes, however, entailed misappropriation by third parties acting alone or in league with employees of plaintiffs (40.24%).

In a span of only twenty years, a legal system has been created in China for the protection of trade secrets using international treaties as its foundation, the Law against Unfair Competition at its centre, and the Contract Law, the Labour Law, and the Criminal Law as component provisions, a feat which is unique in the history of the development of contemporary legal systems. In recent years, discussion and study of legislative and judicial issues regarding trade secret protection have continued within Chinese academic and judicial circles. The majority of this activity has focused on the introduction into the Chinese legal system of specific provisions found in the law of various other countries and the review of the current situation in China regarding trade secret protection. In recent years as well, the courts in China have conducted research into trial practice regarding trade secrets and related policies and legal issues. At the annual National Conference on Intellectual Property Right Trials, the resolution of disputes involving trade secrets is always an important issue. In addition, the Supreme People's Court has drafted a judicial interpretation of the Law against

1. <http://ipr.chinacourt.org>, 10 January 2007. The data used to compile the Statistics of Trade Secrets Cases originated from 82 cases heard in courts in Beijing, Shanghai, and Jiangsu Provinces from 2001 to 2005.

Unfair Competition that includes guidelines for the hearing of trade secret lawsuits and in November 2005 it published a draft at www.Chinacourt.org to solicit public opinion. In March 2006, the Supreme People's Court opened the China IPR Judgments and Decisions website and plans to eventually publish all of its decisions, some of which concern disputes regarding intellectual property rights, on the Internet. While actively cooperating with strategic research on intellectual property rights being conducted at the state level for improving the national intellectual property right system, the Supreme People's Court is also conducting research into improving the judicial protection system for intellectual property rights, which includes remedial judicial systems. The measures so far taken by the courts and the legislature in China have created an environment for the continuing improvement of trade secret protection.

This book consists of five parts. Part One, History and Development of Trade Secret Law in China, contains an overview of the historical evolution of trade secret protection in China, describes the present situation and the future trend in the science of trade secret law in China, and draws a clear picture of the development track and of the basic framework of China's current trade secret laws by summarizing present research achievements within academic circles.

Part Two, Legislation on the Protection of Trade Secrets in Chinese Law, is a general introduction to current Chinese trade secret law vis-à-vis a comparison with legal provisions contained in international and regional treaties and in the law of certain foreign countries. This section looks at the legal framework for the protection of trade secrets, and addresses core issues such as legal definitions and constitutive elements of trade secrets, as well as differences between trade secrets and other forms of intellectual property in Chinese Law.

Part Three, titled Remedies for Infringement and Administrative Protection of Trade Secrets, is devoted to determining what constitutes infringement of a trade secret, classifies types of infringement, and looks at elements of infringement in terms of Chinese law. It also contains an introduction to the theoretical foundation for a system of legal protection in the view of Chinese scholars of jurisprudence. Civil remedies, criminal punishment, and administrative penalties for the enforcement of the protection of trade secrets are examined with a focus on a comparison between China and certain other countries regarding the characteristics of civil remedies and criminal penalties for trade secret infringement within their respective jurisdictions. Trade secret protection mechanisms currently in place in China are compared with the legal provisions contained in international treaties as well as in the legal systems of certain other countries.

In Part Four, Employment Relations and Trade Secret Protection, the main factors that affect the protection of trade secrets in employment relationships in China are analyzed with regard to the ongoing transformation of the Chinese employment system. This includes labour force allocation and the marketization of labour forces, and the conflict between rights and private interests and the public interest in trade secret protection. Finally, issues of confidentiality agreements, non-competition agreements, and applicable laws are examined.

In Part Five, developing trends in global trade secret protection legislation and judicial practice are taken into consideration in an effort to propose an effective means for raising the level of trade secret protection and for perfecting mechanisms for the implementation of trade secret law in China. More specifically, with reference to the situation on the ground in China, proposals for improving several specific aspects of the Chinese legal system regarding employment relationships are put forth.

To conclude this preface, a word of sincere thanks is more than due. I would like to thank Professor Johan Erauw, Professor Willy van Eechkoutte and Professor Paul Torremans of Gent University in Belgium. All of them encouraged and supported me to do profound comparative research on the issue of trade secret protection in employment relationships, which forms the main content of this book. They also carefully read my original manuscript and provided highly valuable suggestions, which were of great importance in improving the quality of the book. Equally, I wish to thank Professor Cao Jianming for his guidance and advice in my research and in the preparation of this book. In the preparation and editing of the English-language edition of the book, Mr. Guy Bernfeld was of great help in formulating and improving the text. In this regard, I would also like to thank my friend Ms. Lu Lihua. Lastly, my heartfelt thanks to my family, who have always encouraged and supported me in my studies, my work and my aspirations.

Foreword by Prof. Dr. Johan Erauw

It is a pleasure to be associated with this work by Professor SHAN Hailing. She is a scholar of private international law relationships and in that capacity has published international work before this book, namely a book on tort law in China. In China she is a well-established author and commentator of conflicts-of-law. Her work on the topic of intellectual property rights and on the protection of trade secrets or know-how in particular goes back some time. She dutifully collected all the materials on the subject of know-how in employment relationships and over a period of five years has gone through all the phases of a doctoral dissertation, which she deposited at the Gent University in September of 2007 and which brought her the doctoral title in January 2008 after a spirited and most highly acclaimed oral defence in Gent.

This book is indeed a by-product of the dissertation effort and it brings the practical elements thereof together in a concentrated version. She worked through this self-imposed task besides her regular and heavy teaching-load at the East China University of Political Science and Law (Shanghai), where she is a much-liked professor who drives young students to enthusiastic work, while she transfers to them her strong interest and her great energy. She makes the study of international law a pleasure for them and shows them the way to respect for the rule of law and respect for the practical business orientation of university training in the law.

This book is commendable for several reasons: it is well-researched and well-written; it is insightful and offers views of intriguing developments in China – linked as this topic is, to the labour organization and its rapid and profound changes. Chinese law has sought to find a new balance between the social aspects of providing protection of acquired knowledge and experience of the worker and giving increasing value to intangible assets for the employer, such as for trade secrets. Indeed we saw the increasing acceptance of innovation as a market value taken into account, as the law became more often confronted with challenges caused by quick technological progress (home-grown as well as licensed-in). The increased sensibility in regard to intellectual property rights is illustrated throughout this development. Ms SHAN reports on the changed perceptions and places this in the context of the broader Chinese law on contracts and on torts and the administrative law plus the criminal law. She also reflects regularly on international standards as she compares the legal developments of her country with the theories and practise of others countries. That gives the foreign reader a useful frame of reference.

SHAN Hailing has written a book that enriches the law of intellectual property for China and that places the new legislation (with so many facets to it) in those matters of trade secret protection, next to the search for remedies in either civil law, administrative law or in criminal law, in order to draw her conclusions for a better protection of know-how in Chinese labour relationships. Within the civil law her focus is on the traditional worker-employer relationship and on how this was permeated by views on the protection of the assets of the employer – thus on private property and on compensation for damage done. She describes changes that will attract the attention of any scholar and practitioner of the Chinese legal scene as well as of the social scene in general. In her own preface she claims those changes to be no less than dramatic within the given timeframe. Her having been a 'child' of the Maoist revolution (or young student then), whereby students were sent out to do the communal work; she is one in touch with the fundamental nature of the changes in the new China and she is one to convince others of the legal nature of this new perspective. She has in the meantime become a legal scholar with a broad view and exemplary knowledge of many sectors of the law. She depicts the sectors of civil law, torts and contracts and the theories and opinions imbedded there; she describes administrative remedies and other sanctions under the law; she is also knowledgeable of the aspects of procedural law and of labour arbitration boards. She ends up showing to practitioners how to obtain protection or how to provide it; depending on the viewpoint. She wrote an inspired proposal for a new and improved synthesis of the rules on trade secret protection.

Her new book will be helpful in consultation practice as well as in litigation. I trust it will be useful to those who seek insight and who may want to put the described developments into perspective. It will also be a help for the entrepreneurs and their advisors who seek the more precise indications to assure a suitable protection of their know-how and who want to make the fitting arrangements with their employees or who might be placed before litigation over issues of this nature.

This book is based on rich information sources that are: in the first place the laws and regulations of China, of its many hierarchical rule-makers – including through the court system; and that further are the doctrinal sources flowing from a quickly developing world of bountiful academic and practical commentary. Ms SHAN has furthermore obtained useful information on the court practise and that also commends this work.

During her work on this treatise on labour law and trades secrets, we organized together, late in 2004, at the East China University of Shanghai, a conference on Intellectual property and TRIPS compliance in China, with the collaboration of the President of that university. In those days SHAN Hailing brought a first report on her topic[1] – and I remember her spirited talk in front of such dignitaries as of the Supreme Court of the People's Republic and I remember how she firmly held the attention of those present and how she whipped the simultaneous translator into an excellent performance. It is with fond memories of that day that I can safely say this author will keep you, reader and user, focussed and well-informed.

Professor SHAN's book on trade secret protection in China should find praise and success as a further step in the steady development of a qualitative, academic legal commentary for China and even as one further step in the development of the law of China itself.

Prof. Dr. Johan Erauw
Director of the Institute for Private International Law – University of Gent and Adjunct professor at the Washington College of Law, American University, Washington DC.

1. H. SHAN, 'Protection of know-how in Chinese enterprises and employment relationships', in: *Intellectual property and TRIPS Compliance in China – Chinese and European perspectives* (P. Torremans, H. SHAN and J. Erauw, editors), Series: New horizons in intellectual property, Cheltenham (UK) and Northampton (USA), Edward Elgar, 2007, pages 153–174.

Foreword by Prof. Willy van Eeckhoutte

The title of this book, which is the revised commercial edition of a Phd thesis Professor SHAN Hailing defended with great success at the Ghent University, doesn't immediately disclose the very important part the book devotes to employment law. As a matter of fact, Part IV of the book comprises almost a work on it own on the very topical matter of the interaction between trade secret protection and the protection of workers in employment relationships.

I want to focus on the qualities of this part of the book, which are many and substantial.

First and most important there is the comprehensive approach of the subject.

The legal treatment of the issue of protection of trade secrets in the context of an employment relationship is of course determined by the way in which the status of workers is conceived in society and more specifically under the law. Hence Professor SHAN Hailing judiciously spends an introductory chapter on the evolution of Chinese law with respect to employment relations. Following on from that she demonstrates the topic is not merely a legal question, but also one with ethical, economic and political dimensions.

The main item, viz. the actual discussion of how Chinese employment law deals with the protection of trade secrets, is the subject of two consistently written chapters on the different situations of the time employment is still going on and the period after employment came to an end. This part of the book concludes with a chapter on a topic of utmost importance, being the settlement of disputes concerning trade secrets in employment relations with a cross-border element.

As the other parts of the book, Part IV contains a lot of comparative material and an accurately selected scientific apparatus. It is fluently written and, as has been shown above, well structured.

The work is balanced, but also critical. The author certainly cannot be accused of being noncommittal. She does not just discuss carefully the pros and cons of every topic she deals with, but always gives us her own opinion, based on solid arguments.

I had the privilege and the pleasure to be the author's copromoter when she prepared the doctoral thesis from which this book originates. I must say I am very satisfied with this ultimate result. Professor SHAN Hailing has done a wonderful job for which she deserves esteem and admiration.

The many personal conclusions of this promising scholar and her concrete, creative and innovative proposals for the adaptation of the law will prove to be for a longer time and for many people a copious source of inspiration.

Willy van Eeckhoutte
Professor of Employment and Labour Law
University of Ghent, Belgium
Member of the Bar of the Supreme Court of Belgium

Part I
History and Development of Trade Secret Protection Law in China

Chapter 1
Historical Evolution of the Science of Law on Trade Secrets in China

I. FROM FOLK SECRETS TO STATE SECRETS (PRIOR TO 1978)

Folk trade secrets sprang from the wealth of traditional skills that have historically existed in China. Secret knowledge of formulas and techniques has been the pride of Chinese culture down through the ages. For example, the porcelain-making skills of Jingde Town, the ingredients in Guizhou Maotai, the techniques for the manufacture of Anhui rice paper, secrets of the cultivation of Fujian narcissus, as well as of traditional Chinese medicine and acupuncture can be considered business secrets having rather high economic value and affording competitive advantages in domestic and foreign markets. For centuries, however, folk secrets have depended on the discretion of the secret holders themselves rather than on legal protection. In 1889, Emperor Guangxu issued the Regulations on Rewarding Vitalization of Industry to promote the protection of inventions and creations including business secrets, yet these regulations were never actually implemented due to historical reasons.[1]

Since the establishment of the People's Republic of China in 1949, however, the central government has issued a series of rules and regulations to protect business secrets, the main subjects of which are technical secrets, scientific invention, and discovery. These regulations include:

The Provisional Regulations for Maintaining State Secrets, promulgated by the Government Administrative Council (predecessor of the State Council) (1951);

The Regulations on the Issue of Science and Technology Secrets; issued by the Central Committee of the CPC (1958);

1. Lu Heyun, *On Trade Secret Law* (Hubei People's Press, 2000), p. 303.

The Proposals for Science and Technology Exchange and Maintaining Confidentiality, jointly formulated by the China Security Committee, the State Scientific Committee, the Engineering Office of National Defence, the Scientific Committee of National Defence, and the State Economic Committee as well as other authorities (1965);

The Regulations for Maintaining Confidentiality of Science and Technology, formulated by the Security Committee of the Central Committee of Communist Party of China (1978).

The type of information protected by these rules and regulations included mainly scientific invention and discovery[2] as well as technical secrets and traditional skills related to technology,[3] and the term 'trade secret' appears nowhere in the language of that legislation.

During this period in Chinese history, trade secrets were confined to being classified only as one important type of State secret and by that measure alone they acquired the status of State secrets[4] and were protected by state administrative measures. The purpose of the State in protecting trade secrets was the same as that for protecting other state secrets: 'To prevent spies, counter-revolutionaries, and saboteurs at home and abroad from scouting, stealing, or selling State secrets and to prevent various persons from disclosing or losing them'.[5] The State was against the creation of technology-based monopolies and constraint of the use of technology,[6] within and between enterprises, but rather encouraged 'academic and technical exchanges so that the results of advanced experience and science and technology could be widely applied'.[7] Consequently, there existed no obligation to confidentiality within enterprises or between them with the result that anyone could use trade secrets free of charge. This peculiar system of protection of trade secrets was in line with China's political and economic system at that time.

Not long after the establishment of the People's Republic of China in 1949, the Chinese government set about creating a new economic system that was centralized and unified, based on State ownership of the means of production and on an economic and industrial structure dominated by socialist public ownership with a central planning system at its core. Through confiscation of bureaucratic capital the State established a leading position of ownership in the domestic economy.

---

2. See Article 2 of the *Provisional Regulations for Maintaining State Secrets* promulgated by the Government Administration Council (1951) (present State Council).
3. See *Regulations for Maintaining Confidentiality of Science and Technology* formulated by Security Committee of the Central Committee of the Communist Party of China (1978).
4. See Article 2 of the *Provisional Regulations for Maintaining State Secrets* promulgated by the Government Administrative Council (1951). The article specifies that the basic scope of State secrets includes science inventions and discoveries.
5. *Ibid.* See Article 1.
6. See *Proposals for Science and Technology Exchange and Maintaining Confidentiality* (1965) jointly formulated by the China Security Committee, the State Scientific Committee, the Engineering Office of National Defence, the Scientific Committee of National Defence, and the State Economic Committee, as well as other authorities.
7. See Regulations on the Issue of Science of and Technology Secrets issued by the Central Committee of the CPC (1958).

Through a process of land reform, landlord ownership was transformed into collective ownership. From 1949 to 1960, the State completed socialist reforms in agriculture, handcraft industries and 'capitalist handicraft' and instituted socialist public ownership whereby the State became the dominant owner of all means of production. In 1956 China began implementation of the first five-year plan of national economic development, (i.e., carrying out the planned purchase and planned supply of grain, executing direct planning and deciding on the allocation of goods and materials to all industrial enterprises and determining the means of communication and transportation.) The State imposed a monopoly over income and spending and assumed decision making over storage, distribution and allocation of financial means as well as over credit loans and salaries. In this way, a centralized and unified economic system with central planning came into being. Under this economic system, the State and the administrative organs under its authority protected trade secrets through a unified system of administrative measures and they were its sole beneficiaries.

In 1958, the Chinese government made a series of major mistakes regarding economic policy. For example, with regard to ownership, it tried to create an entirely State-directed economy and distribution system that would be owned by the People in order to establish egalitarianism. The implementation of these policies nearly extinguished all individual economic activity, which was called at that time the 'remaining private ownership'. The State protected neither inventions nor the creations of employees. The rules were 'All scientific and technological achievements belong to the State' and 'Any domestic enterprise may make full use of them so long as it is required for their work'.[8]

After 1962, the central government promulgated a series of labour regulations, including the Proposals for Science and Technology Exchange and Maintaining Confidentiality, with a view to adjusting its strategy for national economic growth. However, the Cultural Revolution that followed thrust China into a catastrophe wherein the state turned from first ignoring the rule of law to totally discarding it. In the process, the nascent trade secret protection system was abandoned along with the entire legal system.

II. FROM STATE SECRETS TO TRADE SECRETS: THE RUDIMENTS OF CHINA'S TRADE SECRET LAW (1978 TO 1993)

In December 1978, the CPC convened the Third Plenary Session of the Eleventh Central Committee. In formulating strategic policy for constructing socialist modernization, it took on the task of perfecting socialist democracy and strengthening

8. See Regulations on the Issue of Science and Technology Secrets issued by the Central Committee of the CPC (1958).

the socialist legal system.[9] In 1982, an amendment was added to the Constitution of the PRC stating that the Constitution would be the fundamental law of the State and would have supreme legal authority. All State organs, the armed forces, and all political parties and institutions were to adopt the Constitution as the basic standard of conduct.[10] The Constitution was placed above all political parties including the CPC and all State organs were to be led by it. This was a revolutionary recognition of the legal system by the CPC and by all the people of China. The Constitution dictated that the legal system was to become a pillar in the creation of the 'new' China.

From 1978 to the end of 1990, the National People's Congress and its Standing Committee formulated and modified laws, making more than two-hundred decisions on relevant legal issues. During this period, over three-hundred administrative regulations were formulated by the State Council.[11] Among them were approximately seventy laws and regulations concerning trade secret protection. This was, however, only an initial stage in the establishment of an independent system of trade secret protection in China.

Features of the system of trade secret protection of the period 1978 to the end of 1990:

(1) Initial broad use of the legal term 'trade secret'.

Since the 1980s, the understanding of what constitutes a trade secret in China has become broader. In addition to protecting confidential information, also protected by law are: inventions; discoveries, traditional technical secrets, technical data such as mapping results,[12] prescriptions for protected types of traditional Chinese medicines, technological methods,[13] various historical records in all written forms as well as in illustrations, audio and visual recordings[14] and non-patented technology.[15]

9. According to the understanding at that time, the term 'socialist democratic politics' referred to democratic politics based on socialist public ownership of the means of production. It was to guarantee that most people would enjoy wide-ranging democratic rights, that the socialist economic system would be maintained' and was to embody the equal relationship among the People and a correct relationship between individuals and society, and practice the organizational principles of democratic centralism.
10. See the Preface and Article 5 of the Constitution of the People's Republic of China (1982).
11. <www.chinalawinfo.com>, 1 January 2008.
12. According to the *Mapping Law of the People's Republic of China* effective 1 July 1993, mapping results fall under the scope of intellectual property rights and a fee shall be charged for their use (Article 20).
13. See Articles 13 and 14 of the *Regulations on the Protection of Traditional Chinese Medicines* promulgated by Order No.106 of the State Council on 14 October 1992.
14. See Article 2 of the *Archives Law of the People's Republic of China* promulgated in 1987 and modified in 1996.
15. See Articles 7, 32, 39, and 41 of the *Technology Contract Law of the People's Republic of China* (Expired) adopted at the twenty-first meeting of the Standing Committee of the sixth NPC on 23 June 1987 putting forward the concept of 'non-patented technology results'. Article 6 of the *Rules for Implementation of the Technology Contract Law of the People's Republic of China* (Expired) issued by the State Science and Technology Committee and approved by the State Council in 1989, delimited non-patented technology by providing that non-patented technology

On 9 April 1991 the Civil Procedure Law of the People's Republic of China was promulgated. Article 66 of the Law provided that 'Evidence that involves State secrets, trade secrets, and personal privacy shall be kept confidential. If it needs to be presented in court, such evidence shall not be presented in an open court session'. This was the first time that the legal term 'trade secrets' was used in Chinese law.

In 1992, the Supreme People's Court of the PRC issued the Proposals on Several Problems of Enforcing the Civil Procedure Law of the People's Republic of China that included a judicial interpretation of the meaning of the term 'trade secrets'. Trade secrets, it said, mainly referred to:

> [t]echnological secrets and commercial intelligence and information. For example, industrial and trade secrets that interested parties are unwilling to make public such as production skills, formulas, business contacts or purchase and sales channels.[16]

According to this interpretation, trade secrets included not only technical secrets but also business information that the parties concerned were reluctant to reveal.

Although the interpretation of the Proposals regarding trade secrets was a bit rough from today's viewpoint, it was meaningful in the development of China's trade secret protection system at the time. It was the most authoritative judicial interpretation of the concept of trade secrets in the historical context of that time and it was an important basis upon which China's courts, at all levels, and was able to make decisions in trade secrets disputes.[17] It also established a solid foundation for future legislation regarding trade secrets.

---

contained in the law included technical achievements and technical achievements which were not yet the subject of an existing application for patent, technical achievements that had not been granted patent, and technical achievements prescribed in the *Patent Law* that are not patentable.

16. See Article 154 of the Provisions of the Supreme People's Court regarding Several Issues Concerning the Application of the Civil Procedure Law of the People's Republic of China promulgated by the Supreme People's Court on 14 July 1992.
17. In China, 'judicial interpretation' refers to the guidelines drafted by the Supreme People's Court *that* provide interpretations on concrete problems of applying law in judicial practice. In 1981, the Standing Committee of the National People's Congress made a series of rules in the form of the Decision on Strengthening Legal Interpretation Work and provided that 'The application of laws and rules in the trial practice of all courts shall be interpreted by the Supreme People's Court. Application of laws and rules in the field of prosecutory work of all procuratorates shall be interpreted by the Supreme People's Procuratorate'. Judicial interpretation of the Supreme People's Court is, according to the rules regarding the application of law and judicial practice in China, binding on the trial activities of the courts, and actually has become a source of law in China. This was confirmed in the Provisions on Judicial Interpretation of the Supreme People's Court issued by the Supreme People's Court in 1997. This provision confirms definitively that: 'Judicial interpretations issued by the Supreme People's Court shall be discussed and adopted by the judicial committee; judicial interpretations issued by the Supreme People's Court shall have force of law; and in order to formulate and issue such judicial interpretations, the Supreme People's Court shall follow procedures such as putting the issues on record, drafting, approval and modification of drafts for adoption and publication. A judicial interpretation is effective as of the date it is issued publicly. In cases where a new law is promulgated and where formerly existing law is modified or repealed or new judicial interpretations are made, the former shall lose its legal force'.

(2) Trade secrets were gradually separated from state secrets.

As mentioned above, in China, trade secrets had for a long time assumed the nature of state secrets. However, the establishment of the market economy in China and the modification of the Constitution altered the common understanding of the nature of trade secrets.

The 1982 Constitution laid the legal foundation for China's reform and policy of opening up.[18] Yet, as the Constitution was amended at the beginning of that period of reform, the state economic system and the structure established by it still contained major deficiencies[19] and neither could not meet nor safeguard the real demand for economic growth. For instance, the appearance of a greater number of Sino-foreign joint ventures and wholly foreign-funded enterprises posed a problem to the legal position of private enterprises in China. The emergence of varied forms of economic operations, including individual enterprises, private enterprises, Sino-foreign joint ventures, cooperative enterprises, and wholly foreign-funded enterprises cast doubt on the allocation process and administrative management under the planned economy system. Consequently, in 1988, and again in 1993, the National People's Congress modified the 1982 Constitution by enacting the proposals of its delegates. The modified Constitution replaced the 'State with a planned economy on the basis of public ownership' described in the former Constitution with a 'socialist market economy' and confirmed that China practiced a market economy system endorsed by its Constitution.[20] Meanwhile, it also provided that individual economic activities operating within the limits prescribed by law were a complement to the socialist public economy and that the state would protect the lawful rights and interests of the private sector economy,[21] thus confirming the legal legitimacy of the private sector economy in China for the first time.

A market economy is a competitive economic system that requires a guaranteed rule of law to underpin it. The law must ensure equal legal protection of private citizens in the conduct of economic activity and it must ensure fair competition in the operation of markets. To that end, in 1982 China promulgated the first Trademark Law. In 1984 came the Patent Law followed by the General

18. Yin Xiaohu, *The Road to Constitutionalism in the New China* (Shanghai Jiao Tong University Press, 2000), p. 193.
19. See Article 6 of the 1982 Constitution which provides: 'The basis of the socialist economic system of the People's Republic of China is socialist public ownership of the means of production; that is, ownership by all the people and collective ownership of the labour masses. Here, the State-run economy is a socialist economy owned by all the people and collective ownership of the labour masses is the main economic form in rural areas of China'. Article 15 provides 'the State practices a planned economy based on socialist public ownership. The State shall guarantee that the national economy will develop in proper proportion through a comprehensive balance of planned economy and the auxiliary role of market regulation'. This set up a national economic system with the planned economy as its basis, complemented by market regulations.
20. See Article 15 of the Amendment to the Constitution (1993).
21. See Article 11 of the Amendment to the Constitution (1988).

Principles of Civil Law of the PRC in 1986, the Law of the PRC on Technology Contracts in 1987, and the Copyright Law in 1990. The promulgation of these laws formed a basic legal framework for the protection of intellectual property rights in China. When protection of patents, trademarks, and copyrights as three forms of intellectual property was introduced, more attention began to be paid to the nature of trade secrets as property and it was realized that the protection of trade secrets was different from the protection of state secrets in purpose, in means, and in method.

The Law of the PRC on Technology Contracts (the Technology Contracts Law), which became effective 1 November 1987, for the first time employed such concepts as 'unpatented technical achievements' and 'unpatented technology transfers' and contained provisions regarding relevant content.[22] For example, clause three of Article 32 provides that:

> The right to use unpatented technological know-how achieved through a contract commissioning development work or cooperative development, the right to transfer it, and the methods of distributing benefits from it shall be stipulated by the parties to the contract. In the absence of contractual stipulations, each party shall have the right to use and transfer the technical know-how, except that the party undertaking research and development under a commission development contract may not transfer the results of said research and development to a third party before delivering them to the commissioning party.

Although this law does not employ terms such as technical secrets and trade secrets, unpatented technology here obviously refers mainly to what is understood to be confidential technical information. The Technology Contracts Law subsequently protected technical secrets in the form of contract and was also the first substantive law to contain clauses protecting technical secrets or trade secrets in China. The Implementation Rules of Technology Contract Law issued on 15 March 1989 defined unpatented technology as technical achievements that have not been the subject of an application or that have not been granted patent or that, under the Patent Law, cannot be granted patent.[23] This definition basically extended the category of technical secrets to include unpatented technology.

In September 1988, the Law on Protecting State Secrets of the People's Republic of China was promulgated and adopted by the Seventh Standing Committee of the National People's Congress. For the first time, the Law provided a clear definition of State secrets: 'State secrets shall be matters that have a vital bearing on State security and the national interest and, as specified by legal

22. See Articles 7, 32, 39, 41 of the Technology Contract Law of the People's Republic of China (1987) (Expired).
23. See Article 34 of the Rules for Implementation of Technology Contract Law of the People's Republic of China (1992) (Expired).

procedure, are entrusted to a limited number of people for a given period of time'.[24] These items included secrets of science and technology,[25] but such secrets qualified as State secrets only when their disclosure might cause such consequences as reducing the economic, scientific, or technological power of the state.[26] The Civil Procedure Law of the PRC, as modified in 1991, used the legal term 'trade secrets' twice.[27] The Proposals on Several Problems of Enforcing the Civil Procedure Law of the PRC issued by the Supreme Court of the PRC, defined trade secrets as secrets of industry and commerce including technological secrets, business operations information (e.g., manufacturing skill or formulas), business contacts and channels for purchasing and selling. All of these secrets constitute information that the holder is unwilling to make public.[28] The Civil Procedure Law of the PRC provided the first definition of trade secrets. Taken together, all of the abovementioned legislation demonstrated the status of trade secrets as an independent legal subject in China.

(3) Trade secrets mainly depended on the protection of 'public law'.

Although the understanding of trade secrets deepened during the period discussed above, legal protection of trade secrets still depended on 'public law' such as the Law on Protecting State Secrets of the People's Republic of China and the Criminal Law. The idea that the nature of trade secrets made them subject to private law required further development and the legal concept of trade secrets needed to be more clearly defined in legislation.

24. See Article 2 of the Law of Law on Protecting State Secrets of the People's Republic of China (1989). In accordance with the provisions of Article 2, State secrets shall include the following:
Secrets concerning major policy decisions on State affairs;
Secrets in the building of the national defence and in the activities of the armed forces;
Secrets in diplomatic activities and in activities related to foreign countries as well as secrets to be maintained as commitments to foreign countries;
Secrets in national economic and social development;
Secrets concerning science and technology;
Secrets concerning activities for safeguarding State security and the investigation of criminal offences;
Other matters that are classified as State secrets by the State security department.
25. *Ibid.* See Article 8.
26. See Article 4 of the Implementation Method on Law on Protecting State Secrets of the People's Republic of China issued by Order No.1 of the State Security Bureau on 25 May 1990 and approved by the State Council on 25 April 1990.
27. See Article 66, 120 of the Civil Procedure Law of the People's Republic of China (1991).
28. See Article 154 of the Provisions of the Supreme People's Court about Several Issues Concerning the Application of the Civil Procedure Law of the People's Republic of China promulgated by the Supreme People's Court on 14 July 1992.

III. A NEW DEVELOPMENT PHASE: THE ESTABLISHMENT OF AN ADVANCED TRADE SECRET PROTECTION SYSTEM IN CHINA (1993 TO 1998)

As described in the previous section, in the increasingly competitive environment in China, more enterprises depended on trade secrets to gain profit and competitive advantage. The technological and operational secrets of enterprises had become important elements of their very existence as well as development. Meanwhile, motivated by the drive for profits, the phenomena of illegal use and the outright stealing of trade secrets became increasingly common. In addition, the reform of the economic system was bringing about change in China's labour and employment system. In 1983 the State Council promulgated the Provisions on Reasonable Mobility of Science and Technology Personnel, which allowed persons employed in those fields to 'go to work in such units that can give full play to their professional skill'.[29] In 1986 the State Council promulgated the Provisional Rules for Adopting the Labour Contract System in State-run Enterprises, and the Provisions on Employing Workers inside State-run Enterprises. These laws required state-run enterprises to hire from the public labour market[30] and to establish and enforce a labour contract system. The rules had the effect of shifting government management of labour to a free market system by means of uniform contractual arrangements through a centralized allotment of the labour force under the planned economy. The establishment of a labour market permitted and stimulated the mobility of personnel in China and ensured the freedom of individuals to choose their own careers. However, the number of trade secret disputes consequently increased and became a hot topic affecting a greater number of people. Among the many trade secret disputes that arose, some concerned infringement on the trade secrets rights of enterprises and others concerned damage to the employment rights of employees or their freedom to choose their own careers. In order to regulate market competition and to restrict unfair competition in the form of trade secret infringement, and in order to promote the development of unpatented technology and technological know-how, a better protection system for trade secrets needed to evolve in China.

In 1987, the State Council proposed for the first time the formulation of a national law against unfair competition. In 1992 the Law against Unfair Competition prohibiting certain practices was listed in the legislative plan of the Standing Committee of the NPC. In the following year, through the efforts of experts and academics, the PRC Draft Law against Unfair Competition was completed (following three revisions) and was adopted at the Third Meeting of the Standing Committee of the Eighth NPC on 2 September 1993, making it the first specific law against unfair competition in Chinese history.

---

29. See Provisions on Reasonable Mobility of Science and Technology Personnel promulgated by the State Council in 1983.
30. See Articles 4 and 5 of the Provisions on Employing Workers Inside State-run Enterprises issued by the State Council on 12 July 1986.

The Law against Unfair Competition required that, in market transactions, a business operator must follow the principles of freedom of contract, equality, fairness, honesty, and credibility and must observe generally recognized business ethics.[31] The unfair competition mentioned in this law referred to the acts of business operators that violated provisions of the law and which infringed upon the lawful rights and interests of other business operators and disturbed the socio-economic order.[32] In addition to a general description of infringement, Chapter 2 of the Law against Unfair Competition also enumerated eleven acts of unfair competition, including acts considered to be infringement upon trade secrets. The Law against Unfair Competition also contains certain provisions concerning the legal responsibility for acts of infringement of trade secrets. Moreover, Article 10 defined what constitutes a trade secret:

> A trade secret is any technological information or information regarding business operations that is unknown to the public which may create business interest or profit for its legal owners, and which is maintained in secrecy by its legal owners.

Following the promulgation of the Law against Unfair Competition, on 25 November 1995 the State Industrial and Commercial Administrative Bureau issued the Several Rules on Forbidding the Infringement of Trade Secrets to concretely implement the regulations regarding trade secrets contained in that law.

The Law against Unfair Competition was the most important and specific law for the protection of trade secrets ever to be promulgated in China. It took the trade secret protection system a step further and, from its introduction, trade secrets were granted legal protection as a private right. The Law provides that only those legal persons and other economic organizations or individuals who deal with commercial businesses or profitable services (referred to as 'managers' in the Law against Unfair Competition) are subject to the rules concerning infringement of trade secrets.[33] In a certain sense, the law restricts its own scope of application. In practice, in addition to managers other very important parties are concerned with trade secrets. Employees of enterprises that have contractual rights and obligations in exploiting technology or who have an obligation of confidentiality might also commit acts of infringement of trade secrets.

On 6 July 1994 the first labour law in China came into being. It promoted labour reform and contained provisions regarding trade secret protection clauses in labour contracts. On 15 March 1999 a new PRC Contract Law was adopted by the Ninth National People's Congress (1999 Contract Law). The 1999 Contract Law, which became effective on 1 October 1999, prescribes trade secret protection during the creation and performance of contracts, as well as following their termination. In addition to the 1999 Contract Law, in certain other laws (e.g., the Company Law, the Audit Law, the Commercial Banking Law, and the Attorney's

31. See Article 2 (1) Law against Unfair Competition (1993).
32. *Ibid.* See Article 2 (2)
33. See Article 2 (3) Law against Unfair Competition (1993).

Law which were formulated by the National People's Congress and its standing Committee between 1994 and the present) there are corresponding provisions regarding non-competition as well as obligations regarding state secrets and the trade secrets of companies. Further, the Criminal Law of the PRC, as amended by the Fifth Session of the Eighth National People's Congress on 14 March 1997, created the new criminal offence of trade secret infringement in order to punish acts of serious infringement.

On 11 December 2001 China joined the WTO and began to meet the obligations contained in that agreement, including the obligation to protect undisclosed information as provided in the TRIPS Agreement.[34]

China initiated a legal program in 1998, when it was negotiating entry into the WTO, to amend certain laws and to abolish certain other laws, regulations, and rules in order to comply with the WTO rules. Prior to May 2002, China had already amended approximately fifty laws and administrative regulations, including the Patent Law (2000), the Trademark Law (2001), and the Copyright Law (2001), and had abolished nearly 532 statutes including certain laws, administrative regulations, and rules.[35] The program was completed in 2003. The completion of this work illustrated that China was serious about establishing a legal system in accordance with the obligations of the treaty.

In summary it can be said that, motivated by economic policy incentives and inspired by international treaties, China has established a legal framework for the protection of trade secrets based upon international treaties with the Law against Unfair Competition as its centrepiece in addition to the regulations contained in the PRC Constitution, the Contract Law, the Labour Law, and the Criminal Law.

---

34. See Article 39 of *TRIPS Agreement*, </www.wto.org/>, 17 August 2006.
35. Wang Xuebi, 'We have established a basic legal system in accordance with principles contained in the WTO Agreement' (11 December 2002) *Renmin Ribao*, 6.

Chapter 2

Present Situation and Trends in the Science of Law on Trade Secrets in China

Globally, there has been swift development of modern scientific technology as well as an increasingly tight integration of economic activities. Information and information management are of unprecedented importance in socio-economic development. If it can be said that in the nineteenth century the overall national strength of a country rested on its gold reserves, it can be said that in the twenty-first century the overall national strength of a country rests on the degree to which intellectual property rights are enjoyed by its population and its corporations.

The wide scope of the protection of the law regarding trade secrets and the rights inherent under it compensate for certain remaining gaps and flaws within the body of intellectual property protection. More advanced legal systems pay special attention to the protection of trade secrets and China attaches great importance to it as well. It has been a major research task within legal circles in China to work out a strategy for a timely and efficient design of an appropriate framework for the protection of trade secrets. Reform and innovation have been, and are, challenging. Detailed regulations and standardization are needed in order for China to participate in intense international competition.

Looking back over the entire process of the rise and development of the science of law regarding trade secrets in China for more than ten years, one finds the basic characteristics of its development to be its late start, the advanced starting point from which it began, the strong international role models that exist in present times and global integration.

I. A LATE START BUT AN ADVANCED STARTING POINT

The first law regarding trademarks, the Rules for the Registration of Trademarks for Trial Implementation was published in 1904 during the Qing Dynasty. The first law regarding copyright, the Law of the Great Qing Dynasty on Copyright, and the first law regarding patents, Provisional Rules for the Encouragement of Handicraft Articles, came into being in 1910 and 1912 respectively. In 1944, while the temporary Chinese government promulgated the Law on Patents, comprised of four chapters and 133 articles, it never became effective in mainland China and consequently research regarding intellectual property remained nearly non-existent. Professor Guo Shoukang, of the People's University of China, graduated from Beijing University in 1948 and in 1984 was a member of the drafting group for the Law of the People's Republic of China on Patents. Looking back at the history of intellectual property education and research in China, he wrote:

> During the whole four-year period of study at university, I never heard or saw legal terms like 'intellectual property' or 'industrial property', not in the classes of professors nor on the pages of teaching materials, periodicals, or reference documents.[1]

It was not until the 1980s that the basic framework of an intellectual property law system was set up in China and it was not until the early 1990s that, nearly half a century later than in Western countries, Chinese academics began to be familiar with and to apply the legal concept of trade secret protection.

Published in 1994 by the China Patent Document Publishing House, *Legal Protection of Trade Secrets*, a treatise written by Prof. Zhang Ruiyu,[2] a researcher at the Institute of Law of the Chinese Academy of Social Sciences and a director of the Research Committee for Intellectual Property in China, was the first comprehensive and systematic analysis of trade secret protection. In the book, which substantially laid the foundation for the initiation of the systematic research of trade secret protection in China, a relatively elaborative discourse is held regarding matters protected by trade secret law and the conditions necessary for the existence of a trade secret, as well as on liability for torts, solutions of tort cases, trade secret management for modern enterprises, characteristics of rights relating to trade secrets and other general matters. Relevant cases were also listed and analyzed.

---

1. Guo Shoukang, 'Memories of Teaching and Research of Intellectual Property Law in China Since The Opening to the Outside World', in *The Intellectual Property System in China*, Liu Chuntian (ed.), (Beijing, Patent Document Publishing House, 1998), p.199.
2. He was engaged in researching and teaching the science of law for a long period of time. He has published very many writings which, besides the books listed in the first line and the sixth line of table 1, include research treatises such as *Patent Law and Practice, A Complete Collection of Analyses of Cases of the People's Republic of China* (The section including cases on patent), and *200 Subjects on the Application and Protection of Trade Secrets.* In addition, Professor Zhang Ruiyu translated *Detailed Explanation of the Management of Trade Secrets* and *Multimedia and Copyright* that were published in 1997.

From 1995 to 2005 several other books were published, among which *The Science of Law on Trade Secrets* (1999) by Zhang Ruiyu, *Principles of the Law on the Protection of Trade Secrets* (1999) by Kong Xiangjun, and *A Talk about Laws on Trade Secrets* (2000) by Lu Heyun of the Law Department of the College of Politics and Law of Central China Normal University are the three most influential.

Since 2001, Kong Xiangjun[3] has been an associate chief judge of the administrative division of the Supreme Court of the People's Republic of China. For many years engaged in the administration and enforcement of laws against unfair competition and monopoly, he has done well in integrating theory with practice in his writings. In his book, *Principles of Law on the Protection of Trade Secrets*, he sets forth the basic principles of trade secret law citing a great number of laws and foreign cases including detailed research into trade secret law, as well as administrative rules in China, relevant judicial interpretation, and domestic court cases.[4]

In 2000, Professor Lu Heyun, together with Liu Li (an assistant professor in the art department of Hubei Institute of Education), Xu Zhaoxian (an assistant professor in the management department of Wuhan University of Science and Technology), and Liu Hua (an assistant professor in the law department at the College of Politics and Law of the Central China Normal University), together wrote the treatise *A Talk about Trade Secret Law*. The 421-page book is divided into four sections regarding trade secret law. In the book, traditional methods of analysis are used in the study of, among other issues, the properties of trade secrets, the basic legal principles of legislation, protective measures at home and abroad, and relief for civil and criminal actions. In addition, methods of economic analysis are applied to the science of law regarding trade secrets, the treatment of trade secret property rights, and the relationship between trade secrets and economic growth.

During the period between 1996 and 2005, much research related to trade secret protection was published in China, among which, it is estimated by the author, there are up to twenty-three representative books. The subject matter of these writings includes, among other topics, anti-unfair competition, protection of intellectual property, the relationship between WTO and the Chinese legal system, as well as legal matters regarding the Internet. In most cases, the matter of trade secret protection is an important part of each of these writings, providing abundant commentary on the science of Chinese law regarding trade secrets.[5]

China has increased the speed at which it is creating and promulgating intellectual property law and regulations and has done well considering the

---

3. He is a student of Professor Jiang Ping, a famous professor of the science of civil law at China University of Political Science and Law, and the first post-doctor of civil and commercial law in Mainland China. From 1996 to 2001, he was engaged in the enforcement of laws against unfair competition and monopoly in the Fair Business Section of the State Bureau of Industry and Commerce of China and was a professor at a number of colleges and universities such as the China University of Political Science and Law. He holds the degree of Honorary Doctor from the University of Ghent.
4. See Appendix 1.
5. See Appendix 2.

relatively short time within which it established an intellectual property system and the considerable indifference of its citizens to intellectual property protection. It has devoted a major effort to the development of educational literature regarding intellectual property protection and has set up research organizations and learned societies at the state and local level as well as at colleges and universities.

In 1984, upon authorization by the State Ministry of Civil Affairs, the China Intellectual Property Society, the most authoritative academic organization for intellectual property research in China, came into existence in Beijing. The Society is supported by the State Intellectual Property Office of the People's Republic of China and its members are from famous organizations and units that are fairly authoritative and influential in intellectual property, legal, scientific, and technological circles, as well as from private and state-owned enterprises. Its honorary chairman is Ren Jianxin, the vice chairman of the Standing Committee of the CPPCC National Committee and its director is Jiang Ying, former commissioner of the State Intellectual Property Office. Mostly, it undertakes research on major intellectual property-related topics of the state and the unit responsible for its operation; organizes annual meetings, seminars, and other academic exchange activities at home and abroad on intellectual property; disseminates and publicizes information regarding intellectual property; devises planning for intellectual property research and provides expert opinion on IPR infringement and ownership decisions as well as patent-related technical analysis and appraisals. In addition, it conducts training of intellectual property personnel and is responsible for editing and publishing the influential nationally-distributed magazine *Intellectual Property*. The Society currently maintains more than thirty local and industrial branches in locations across the country.

In 1985, following authorization and funding by the Ministry of Education of the People's Republic of China (formerly the State Education Commission), the China Intellectual Property Society of Colleges and Universities (the CIPSCU), the first academic body to be engaged in intellectual property research in educational circles in China, formally came into existence. CIPSCU members are divided into two categories between which group members are mainly colleges and universities and a small number of government departments and enterprises. Individual members are mainly professors and researchers engaged in intellectual property education and research and a small number are functionaries and enterprise staff members. In the order of importance among the aims of the CIPSCU is, first, the development of academic activities, the study of the intellectual property protection system within the context of conditions in China, and the provision of advisory opinions regarding the establishment by the state of appropriate intellectual property laws, rules, regulations, courses and policies; second is the conduct of research into the intellectual property protection system within colleges and universities, and the provision of advisory opinions regarding matters of intellectual property protection; third is the organization of conventions for academic and working exchanges between academics and researchers at colleges and universities in the intellectual property aspect, and the conduct of academic exchanges in the area of foreign trade in order to raise the academic and working level of Chinese intellectual property researchers and professors; fourth is the collection, translation, and introduction of updates domestically and abroad in order to provide information to various colleges, universities, and their researchers to help decide the direction of new research; and fifth is helping to establish a direct relationship between enterprises and intellectual property organizations at colleges and universities for facilitating the development and implementation of achievements in scientific research there. Since its establishment, the CIPSCU has basically relied on funds provided by the government and with the development of scientific research, its main source of funds has been contributions from individuals and enterprises and the membership dues of its members.

Since coming into existence twenty-one years ago, the organizational scale of the CIPSCU has expanded year by year, the scope of its research has become increasingly broad, and the level of its research has been elevated. It has grown to include 175 group members from an initial 30, among which 158 are colleges and universities, and has attracted more than 300 individual members, training and bringing up a multitude engaged in intellectual property instruction and research at colleges and universities that possess both theoretical knowledge of and practical experience with intellectual property. The CIPSCU has been actively initiating intellectual property research projects and it has undertaken many major state-sponsored research projects. So far, it has convened eight annual academic conferences and has published eight collections of papers. During its annual meetings, it stages exhibitions of and arranges talks regarding achievements in scientific research at colleges and universities, and promotes communication between colleges, universities and enterprises.

At the same time, colleges and universities in China have established organizations like intellectual property training and research centres and intellectual property institutes such as the Intellectual Property Training and Research Centre of the People's University of China established in 1986, the Intellectual Property Institute of Beijing University established in 1993, the Intellectual Property Research Centre of Fudan University, the Intellectual Property Research Centre of Wuhan University, and the Intellectual Property Institute of East China University of Politics and Law established in 2003. Intellectual property law has come to be regarded as a compulsory subject in the colleges and universities of China. An educational system for undergraduates, masters and doctors for developing intellectual property professionals has been gradually formed, and a new flock of intellectual property professionals are year by year being steadily introduced into society.

Moreover, the Chinese Academy of Social Sciences Centre for Intellectual Property Research (established in 1994), the Chinese National Foundation for Social Sciences and the Chinese National Foundation for Natural Sciences provide financial aid and facilitate research regarding intellectual property issues. This has spurred an unprecedented increase in academic research, and an array of essays and articles of relatively high level have been published, (e.g., Research on Legal Matters on the Protection of Trade Secrets in China, Legal Matters in Assessing the Value of Intellectual Property, and Problems Faced by the Intellectual Property

System in the Twenty-first Century and China's Solutions).[6] In fact, a series of problems regarding the intellectual property system that China faces in the twenty-first century have been listed as topics for discussion and research for Chinese jurisprudence academics. These problems include: the relationship between the development of digital technology, the Internet, and intellectual property protection; the relationship between biological technology and intellectual property protection; the relationship between intellectual property protection and international competition; the issue of international intellectual property protection; the issue of intellectual property protection for certain cultural heritages such as traditional Chinese medicine and literary and artistic folk works.

It has taken only twenty years for China to construct an edifice of intellectual property protection (including trade secrets) on a nearly barren legal landscape. Throughout this period, Chinese legal practitioners and professors have focused their research on the establishment of an intellectual property system of law and the drafting and formulation of intellectual property law in China. At the same time, they have actively participated in related activities with international organizations and have strengthened relationships and cooperation with countries all over the world in the field of intellectual property. In conclusion, it can be said that the intellectual property protection system in China was begun at a rather advanced level in its initial stages, vis-à-vis international standards.

II. CHARACTERISTICS OF THE TIMES

The reform and opening up that was initiated at the end of the 1970s catapulted China into the global marketplace. With the opening of a commercial gateway into China, Western technology, capital and concepts of law in line with the modern market economy flooded in. China began the reconstruction of its legal system with unprecedented resolve and courage for the sake of its own development as well as to meet the demands of the international marketplace, making outstanding achievements, in particular through the setting up of an intellectual property protection system. In reviewing the World Intellectual Property Organization's past twenty years of cooperation with China, Dr Arpad Bogsch, former director-general of the Organization of Intellectual Property, points out that 'China had accomplished all this at a speed unmatched in the history of intellectual property protection'.[7]

6. See National Planning Office of Philosophy and Social Science website. <www.npopss-cn.gov.cn>, 25 July 2006.
7. Central People's Government of PRC, 'Status Quo of Intellectual Property Protection in China' <www.gov.cn/zwgk/2005–05/27/content_1605.htm>, 1 January 2008.

While continuously strengthening its intellectual property system, China has also made impressive progress in the area of trade secret protection. Within the context of its domestic conditions and international development, China has formulated new legislation and has improved its existing laws, rules, and regulations on trade secret protection. Consequently, a legal system for the protection of trade secrets with Chinese characteristics that integrates administrative protection, as well as civil and criminal remedies, has evolved. Its scope and level of protection is gradually improving to meet international standards. Trade secrets, still an unfamiliar term in 1993, have become a hot issue as a result of the implementation of the Law against Unfair Competition.

However, it must be said that China, like most developing countries that are anxious to develop their national economies, has been forced to come to terms with intellectual property protection as a consequence of importing advanced technologies and capital from developed Western countries and, through arduous effort and at great cost, to accelerate the opening of markets for, among other things, domestic finance, raw materials for production of commodities, human resources, and manufacture of heavy equipment. One clear example is the three-year-long IPR dispute with the United States that took place from 1988 to 1991. In April 1988, the United States attempted to apply the special '301' provisions of its trade law to China for obstruction of IPR claims because China had failed to fulfil the provisions of the Agreement on Trade Relations Between the United States of America and the People's Republic of China (1980) which stated that US patents, trademarks, and copyrights must be protected in a manner similar to that by which the US protects those of others. By that time, China had implemented its new Trademark Law (1982), had promulgated the Patent Law (1984), and had joined the Paris Convention for the Protection of Industrial Property (1967). However, it remained for China to strengthen protection of computer software, pharmaceuticals, chemicals, and other commodities of foreign origin. As a result, China became more active in the promulgation of new legislative measures although it was said that there was a gap between the letter of the law and its effective enforcement.

China entered into the Madrid Agreement Concerning the International Registration of Marks in July 1989 and promulgated the Copyright Law in September 1990 in preparation for publication of regulations for the protection of intellectual property concerning computer software. It promised to modify the term and scope of protection of its patent law and joined the Berne Convention to further expand copyright protection. After many years of negotiation, the Memorandum of Understanding between the Government of the People's Republic of China and the Government of the United States of America for the Protection of Intellectual Property (1992) was ratified by the two countries.

According to the memorandum, China promised to enter into relevant international treaties, to make corresponding amendments and additions to its domestic laws, to sign and promulgate laws related to anti-unfair competition and to strengthen trade secret protection. Specifically, in order to ensure effective prevention of unfair competition as provided for in Article 10 of the Paris

Convention for the Protection of Industrial Property,[8] the Chinese government pledged to prevent trade secrets from being disclosed, acquired, or used by others without the consent of the trade secret owners in a manner contrary to honest commercial practices including the acquisition, use, or disclosure of trade secrets by third parties who know, or have reasonable grounds to know, that such practices were involved in the acquisition of that information. Also, pursuant to the memorandum, the United States promised to terminate an investigation initiated pursuant to the special 301 provisions and to remove China's designation as a priority foreign country (i.e., a country that fails to provide 'adequate' protection for IPR of the United States).[9] Thus, the IPR dispute between the two countries was finally resolved, and 'trade secrets' appeared for the first time as a legal term in an official document in mainland China. Shortly afterward, China promulgated its Law against Unfair Competition which included provisions consistent with the doctrines of trade secret protection contained in existing treaties as well as with constitutive elements and concepts of the legal protection of trade secrets. Chinese academics believed that the agreement reached through Sino-American negotiation strongly promoted the importance of the establishment of China's trade secret system.[10]

A system of protection for intellectual property, including trade secret protection, is a legal guarantee that fosters human creativity and strengthens the competitive power of a nation. Simon Kznets, winner of the 1971 Nobel Prize for Economics, believed that innovation in knowledge and technology was a precondition for economic growth in any historical era but that it was only a necessary condition and was not, in itself, sufficient to create that growth. If technology was to be employed efficiently and widely and, indeed, if economic progress was to be stimulated by such use, institutional and ideological adjustments needed to be made to affect the proper use of innovation generated by the

---

8. In 1991, the governments of China and the US published the Memorandum of Understanding between the Government of the People's Republic of China and the Government of the United States of America on the Protection of Intellectual Property in the spirit of cooperation embodied in the bilateral Agreement on Trade Relations and consistent with the principles of the relevant international agreements. Article 4 of the Memorandum provides: '1. For the purpose of ensuring effective protection against unfair competition as provided for in Article 10 of the Paris Convention for the Protection of Industrial Property, the Chinese Government will prevent trade secrets from being disclosed to, acquired by, or used by others without the consent of the trade secret owner in a manner contrary to honest commercial practices including the acquisition, use or disclosure of trade secrets by third parties who knew, or had reasonable grounds to know, that such practices were involved in their acquisition of such information. 2. The term of protection for trade secrets shall continue so long as the conditions for protection are met. 3. The competent authorities of the Chinese Government will submit the bill necessary to provide the levels of protection specified in this Article to its legislative body by 1 July 1993 and will exert its best efforts to enact and implement this bill before 1 January 1994'. <www.mac.doc.gov/tcc/data/commerce_html/tcc_2/PRCIntellectual_(3).html>, 16 August 2006.
9. *Ibid.* See Article 7.
10. Kong Xiangjun, Application and Perfection of the Law against Unfair competition Law (Beijing, Law Press, 1995), p. 395.

expanding inventory of human knowledge.[11] Douglas North, another Nobel Prize winner, attaching greater importance to the role of such systems, believed that an effective mechanism for property right protection containing managerial innovation and proper incentive for individuals was a decisive factor in facilitating economic growth. He believed, as well, that the growth of the global economy was not the result of the Industrial Revolution, but rather rested on institutional mechanisms, in particular legal mechanisms for the determination of property ownership. Thus, he concluded, an efficient mechanism for the determination of property rights must be established in order to make rate of yield per capita approximately equal to that of the society as a whole so as to motivate people to become engaged in activities that will comply with the needs of that society. It would have been impossible for modern industry to develop if there had been no guarantee of the right to personal property and income augmented by appropriate support systems and consistent incentives.[12] The reasonableness of this hypothesis is reflected in the history of the development of the Chinese economy since 1978. It is commonly accepted that, since that time, China has progressed at a very rapid pace economically, socially, and culturally.

In 2001, the GNP of China reached 1.1586 trillion US dollars (USD) which when measured in real dollars was nine times that in 1978, representing an annual average increase of 9.5% and ranking China among countries with the most rapidly-growing economies. China has made an important historic leap from a relatively backwards society to one of increasing wealth by:

(a) Introducing a system of market operation:

The highly centralized planned economy pursued in the 1980s laid a foundation for development following reform and opening up, but it was not meeting the needs of commodity production or the law of value. It hindered the sustainable development of productive forces and restricted the national enthusiasm for developing a market economy. Following the introduction of a system of market operation, enterprises became participants in production, exchange (e.g., price, modes of exchange, channels of exchange) and investment. In addition, distribution was no longer decided through state planning but by markets, the vitality of which is the impetus for the development of productive forces;

(b) Establishing a new basic economic system to meet the needs of the development of productive forces with the public-owned economy as the principal player and various other economies developing together with it:

Under this new economic system, distribution depended upon the demands of the market. While accounting for a smaller portion of the market, the public-owned economy has played a dominant role. For example, in 2001 state-owned

11. <www.nobel.se/economics/laureates/1971/kuznets-lecture.html>, 8 August 2006. Also see *A Collection of Speeches of Nobel Prize Winners* (Chinese version) (People's Publishing House of Inner Mongolia, 1998), p.61.

12. <www.nobel.se/economics/laureates/1993/north-lecture.html>, 8 August 2006. Also see *Ibid.* p.534.

enterprises and state-owned holding enterprises accounted for only 0.3% of all industrial enterprises nationwide but their total assets accounted for 59.2%, their sales accounted for 41.9%, their profits accounted for 49.4% and their tax payments accounted for 67%. As for non-public-owned enterprises, their contribution to the national economy has increased to nearly one third from less than 1%. Consequently, the production value of private enterprises has grown to three times that of the China's total GDP in 1978;

(c) Giving attention to the changing industrial structure so as to enable the quality of its economic to keep pace with modernization.

The production value of large-scale enterprises accounts for 44.7%, among which eleven rank in the top 500 enterprises worldwide. The proportion of contribution of small and mid-size enterprises to the economy has reached two thirds;

(d) Accelerating technological progress and promoting the science of management.

With the rate of contribution of technological progress rising to 33% from 10%, the quality of the economy has been gradually enhanced, the economic structure has been continuously improved, and consumption of natural resources has been increasingly reduced;

(e) Increasing return on investment (ROI) and efficiency of investment: Commercialization of investment and high ROI has enhanced the efficiency of investment that has become the basis of economic production and development.

With bank deposits amounting to USD 966 billion, a fair majority of disposable income has been converted into a productive financial resource for the further development of the economy;

(f) Enhancing the quality and skills of the labour force:

The Chinese labour force accounts for 26.5% of the worldwide labour force and its skilled labour force accounts for 17.5% of skilled labour worldwide. As for the rate of literacy of adults and access to primary education, China ranks highest in both among developing countries. The number of professional technicians in Chinese state-owned enterprises has exceeded twenty million. Every year in China, there are more than thirty-thousand major achievements in scientific research and patents on more than fifty-thousand creations and inventions are applied for; and

(g) Becoming more open to the outside world:

In the areas of investment capital, technology, managerial experience, expansion of markets and other aspects, China has benefited from opening to the outside world. For example, from 1979 to 2000 China actually utilized 518.9 billion US dollars in foreign capital accounting for forty percent of the total capital invested in developing countries and approximately ten percent of the total capital invested in fixed assets in China. In the same period, the value of China's imports and exports was sixth in the world.[13]

---

13. China Statistical Yearbook, vol. 1979–2000. <www.stats.gov.cn/english/statisticaldata/yearlydata/>, 1 January 2008.

As discussed above, Chinese rules and regulations for trade secret protection did not originate with the Law against Unfair Competition alone, nor were they the result of international pressure. They evolved from laws, rules, and regulations related to the exchange of technology and were the result of the need to establish a legal protection system in China on speaking terms with its market economy.

Constitutional amendments adopted in 1988 and 1993 provided the legal basis for China to establish a quasi-market economy. By doing so, competitive mechanisms were introduced into the areas of production, manufacturing, and distribution and there was a sharp drive toward innovation. Suddenly, new forces emerged out of enterprises of all types including those that were state-owned.[14] With the development of the market economy, trade secrets were rapidly increasing in number and came to have greater importance in the field of technology trade in the form of technology transfer and licensing. Trade secrets also began to play a more important role in facilitating technological progress and economic growth as well as in changing modes of economic growth. However, in reality, there were still many problems with trade secret protection. Firstly, a greater variety of individuals were infringing on trade secret rights. In addition to business owners engaged in unfair competition, many individuals, especially employees, were also involved. Modes of tort were becoming increasingly complicated, and the means of illegal acquisition, disclosure, and use of trade secrets had become increasingly diverse. Secondly, more tort cases regarding infringement of trade secrets were coming before the courts, and the number was increasing year by year. During the period from January to June 1996, the number of trade secret infringement cases increased by 150% compared with the same period in 1992.[15] Thirdly, damages caused by trade secret infringement can be grave. As a result of the commission of torts involving trade secrets, many enterprises were pushed to the brink of bankruptcy, and among them state-owned enterprises suffered most. Consequently, the loss of trade secrets had become an important element in the loss of state-owned assets. Fourthly, it had become difficult for the judicial system to handle trade secret cases in a timely manner and in accordance with the law. It was a relatively frequent phenomenon that the courts accepted cases which never went to trial and, even if they did, were difficult for judges to decide.[16] The main reason for the problem was that the law in operation at that time did not specify trade secret protection as an important part of the civil system of law. That is to say, there was still no law by which many special problems regarding the development, use and protection of

---

14. It is believed that 1988 was the golden year for China's private economy. By the end of that year, there were over 1000 individual economic enterprises and 200,000 private enterprises all over China, and the number of workers employed by those enterprises reached 24.8 million. See Ma Licheng and Ling Zhijun, reporters for 'People's Daily', *Confrontation – Records of the Third Ideological Emancipation of Modern China* (Beijing, Today's China Publishing House, 1998), p.256.
15. See Explanation on *Law of the People's Republic of China on Trade Secrets Protection* (draft submitted for examination) by State Economic & Trade Commission.
16. See Explanation on *Law of the People's Republic of China on Trade Secrets Protection* (draft submitted for examination) by State Economic & Trade Commission.

trade secrets could be addressed nor was there an effective system for the remedy of trade secret infringement.[17] The pace of the promulgation of trade secret law was accelerated to be conducive to the earnest protection of the legitimate rights and interests of trade secret owners, the maintenance of economic order, the public interest, the momentum of economic growth, increasing openness to the outside world and facilitation of the sound development of a market economy.

As noted by Professor Zhang Ruiyu:

> From the beginning, in 1987, when we protected IPR with the civil law and when technology contract claims were based on the Technology Contract Law, to 1993 when the infringement of technical secrets and business secrets became prohibited, a process of development was taking place. This process was undertaken to meet not only international requirements but also, and more importantly, to promote domestic development. In pursuing its policy of reform and opening up, the protection of trade secrets in China was inevitable. As the legal practice of trade secret protection continues to evolve in China, it will surely make important contributions to trade secret protection worldwide.[18]

III. THREE MAJOR TRENDS OF DEVELOPMENT

A. Increasingly Wide Scope of Protection

Historically, the concept of trade secret protection in China began relatively late but, the scope of that trade secret protection has tended to continue to become broader, as has legislation in various other countries as well as within certain international treaties, and the emergence of new sciences and the application of new technologies have hastened that trend.

In the 1980s, the concept of 'exclusivity' was defined in the Regulations of the PRC for the Administration of Technology Acquisition Contracts, and a definition of 'technical secrets' was specified in the Technology Contract Law. In 1991, the term 'trade secret' was used as a legal term for the first time in the Civil Procedure Law of the PRC. According to a judicial interpretation of the Supreme Court of the PRC, the term trade secret refers mainly to technical secrets, business information, and the like, including technical processes, methods of production, trading contacts, channels of purchase and sale and other industrial and commercial secrets that interested parties are not willing to disclose. In 1993, the Law against Unfair Competition defined a trade secret as technical or business information that is not known in the public domain which can bring economic benefit to the owner of the

17. See *Law of the People's Republic of China on Trade Secrets Protection* (draft submitted for examination), by State Economic & Trade Commission.
18. Zhang Ruiyu, *Science of Law on Trade Secrets* (Beijing, China Legal System Publishing House, 1999), p.30.

information, that is practical, and for the protection of which the owner has adopted secrecy measures. The State Industrial and Commercial Administrative Bureau, in promulgating the Law against Unfair Competition, asserted that technical and managerial information includes designs, procedures, directions for products, process technologies, know-how, client lists, information regarding supply of goods, strategy for production and sale, sealed tenders (in the submission of tenders or invitations to bid) and the content of bidding documents (in the submission of tenders or invitations to bid). Thus it can be seen that during a short period of several years China underwent a process of development in the scope of trade secret protection. First industrial technology, then know-how, followed by industrial and commercial secrets, and finally trade secrets. The concept of trade secrets in the Law against Unfair Competition includes industrial technology and technical secrets, as well as industrial and commercial secrets as contained in the provisions of former laws, and basically conforms to the international trend in definition and scope. However, Chinese law places stricter demands on what constitutes a trade secret than does TRIPS or other relevant laws of the United States or other countries.

B. Strengthened Protection

With the advent of the Information Age, the information industry has grown vigorously to become a mainstay of any advanced society. This has caused more attention to be paid to various technologies as well as to business and cultural information, including traditional intellectual property and trade secrets. By 1994, information had become such an important business asset that the Uruguay Round of TRIPS focused its attention on issues regarding intellectual property, departing from its former emphasis on tariffs. Since then, the protection of intellectual property (including trade secrets), standing side by side with protection of ‘trade in goods’ and ‘trade in services’ has become one of the three major principles of WTO. More extensive attention has been paid to trade secrets by various countries in the world because in developed Western countries a trade secret can mean extremely big profits and have a high market value. There has even been a tendency for trade secrets to surpass patents, trademarks, copyrights and other traditional IPR as the focus of legal establishments in those countries.[19] At the same time, the globalization of the economies, the high-degree of development of media technology, and the creation of the Internet may have made the dissemination of information more convenient but secrecy has become more difficult as well. Consequently, China has had to periodically revise its laws, rules and regulations in order to strengthen trade secret protection.

In the Draft of the Trade Secret Law of the PRC, submitted for revision by the State Economic and Trade Commission of the PRC in 1996, countermeasures were

---

19. Tang Haibin, *How to Protect Trade Secrets in the US* (Beijing, Law Press, 1999), pp.12–13.

proposed which included, among others: determining the nature of trade secrets from the perspective of property rights and IPR, establishing a special law on trade secrets and strengthening trade secret protection through a combination of civil, administrative, criminal and other regulations.

The Draft of the Trade Secret Law of the PRC is composed of five chapters:

- Chapter 1 General Provisions:
  Includes a definition for and content of trade secrets and the aim and principles of the Trade Secret Law;
- Chapter 2 Rights and Interests of Trade Secret Holders:
  Specifies ownership of trade secrets;
- Chapter 3 Protection of Trade Secrets:
  Prescribes the obligation of confidentiality and the protection of trade secrets by employees and counterparties in the conduct of business activities as well as by state organs and their personnel. This chapter also discusses covenants of non-competition with ex-employers;
- Chapter 4 Legal Liability:
  Prescribes civil liability for infringing upon the trade secrets of others, including liability for breach of contract and tort liability, the forms in which liability for breach of contract and tort liability are borne and the method for calculating monetary damages. This chapter also discusses the interests of trade secret holders and of third parties acting in good faith. Chapter 4 also contains general principles of administrative liability and criminal liability for infringement of business secrets;
- Chapter 5 Supplementary Provisions:
  Contains a definition for reverse engineering and covenants not to compete and provides that when state security or important state interests are involved, technological information and operational information which has been deemed a state secret must be handled according to relevant principles of existing state law.

At present, the Draft of the Trade Secret Law of the PRC remains under discussion and examination.

C. The Trend toward Internationalization and Globalization

By the end of the twentieth century, every major country had established its own legal system for the protection of trade secrets which laid the foundation for the internationalization of trade secret protection. In the latter half of the century, certain bilateral and multilateral international agreements as well as treaties drafted by international organizations addressed trade secret protection. More notable is that, driven by certain countries (in particular the United States) and through the efforts of international organizations, the TRIPS Agreement brought trade secrets into the intellectual property system and provided protection for such information. Given the broad membership of the WTO, trade secret protection has become global, corresponding to the great trend toward the proliferation of intellectual property and the globalization of economies. Considering the sweep of its legislation and the revision of its existing law regarding trade secret protection, it can be said that China has certainly made great strides in conforming to international rules for trade secret protection and to meeting the expectations of WTO.

China has undergone a process of development from having no protection to providing substantive protection of trade secrets; from careless protection to careful protection; from narrow scope of protection to wide scope of protection; from protection by domestic law to protection by bilateral treaties, multilateral treaties and global conventions.

Part II

Legislation on the Protection of Trade Secrets in Chinese Law

Chapter 1

The Legal Framework for the Protection of Trade Secrets in China

The value of protecting trade secrets has been recognized by international society. Many countries define the legal status of trade secrets through domestic legislation. Some international organizations, particularly the World Trade Organization, have issued substantive uniform rules regarding trade secret protection on the basis of practice and legislation of each member country, and have made great effort to improve trade secret protection worldwide.

However, how is the law applied when dealing with trade secret disputes? Within existing international legislative practice exists a very complex and challenging problem. Most countries have not issued specific trade secret regulations and so rules that can be applied to disputes of this nature can only be found in related laws or precedent. For example, certain countries within the European Union have a long history of trade secret protection. The French Penal Code of 1848 provided punishment for theft of trade secrets. The German Act against Unfair Competition (1909) contained provisions for punishment of violations of trade secrets. Regarding domestic legislation, however, European countries have mostly employed a dispersed form of legislation, and include trade secret regulations in their civil codes, commercial codes, or other separate regulations, and have not issued a special code or a single regulation for domestic trade secret protection. Most countries consider infringement of trade secrets to be simply unethical and immoral and have addressed the concept and characteristics of trade secrets by issuing laws against unfair competition and by creating regulations that provide penalties for certain activities which violate trade secrets.[1] Many countries,

1. Such as Articles 4, 17, 18, and 20 of the German Act against Unfair Competition (1909); Article 15 of the Swiss Federal Law on Unfair Competition of 19 December 1986 (consolidated version, status as of 10 December 2002) [Art. 4 (c) induces employees, agents or ancillaries to betray or

however, regulate special issues regarding employment, such as covenants not to compete or the obligation of employees to maintain secrecy both during employment and following termination, through civil law or labour law.[2] The commercial law in some countries contains regulations for protecting commercial secrets.[3] Most countries punish serious violations of trade secret protection under their criminal laws.[4]

In this context, there are some differences between legislative forms in China and other countries. It seems that there exist different understandings about trade secrets, for example regarding the legal attributes of trade secrets.

I. EXISTING JURISPRUDENCE IN CHINA ON THE PROTECTION OF TRADE SECRETS

Existing Chinese laws can be divided into those which have been approved and adopted by the National People's Congress (the NPC) and the Standing

---

pry into the manufacturing or trading secrets of their employer or principal; Art. 6. shall be deemed to have committed an act of unfair competition, anyone who, in particular, exploits or discloses manufacturing or trading secrets he has discovered or of which he has obtained undue knowledge in some other manner; Art.15. Safeguarding of industrial or business secrets (in civil law proceedings). N.B. The definition of industrial and business secrets has been developed by case law; it corresponds to that set out in Art. 39(1) of the TRIPS Agreement.]; Section 11 of the Austrian Federal Act against Unfair Competition of 1984 (*Bundesgesetz gegen den unlauteren Wettbewerb 1984 – UWG*) (Disclosure of Business or Trade Secrets. Misuses of Entrusted Documents), Article 10 of the Marketing Act of Denmark (regulating the marketing of products by enterprises, includes in its §10, a specific rule on the protection of an employer's trade secrets against improper use by employees); Articles 13 and 14 of the *Law on Unfair Competition of Spain* (1991) (Law 3/1991 of 10 January 1991) (Article 13. Practices of unfair competition include the infringement of industrial and commercial secrets). <www.wipo.int/clea/en/index.jsp>, 16 August 2006.

2. Such as Articles 13 and 14 of the 1921 Salaried Employees Act of Austria (Angestelltengesetz), Article 17 of the 1978 Law on Contracts of Employment of Belgium (Loi relative aux contrats de travail), Article 4 of the 1980 Basic Employment Law of Spain. <www.ilo.org/dyn/natlex/natlex_browse.home?p_lang=en> and <www.eurofound.eu.int/emire/emire.html>, 18 August, 2006. Also see Pete Burgess (General editor), Contracts and Terms and Conditions of Employment (London Institute of Personnel and Development, 1995).
3. Such as Section 14 of the Act governing Economic Interest Grouping of Spain (1991) (Liability of Managers), Article 20 of the Danish Private Companies Act (*Bekendtgørelse af lov om anpartsselskaber*) (2000) and Section 25 of the Limited Liability Company Act of Austria (GmbH-Gesetz) and section 84 paragraph 1 of the Stock Corporation Act of Austria (Aktiengesetz) (1965) (a company may claim damages from a director for unlawful acts).
4. Such as Article 20 of the *Hungarian Penal Code* (1999), Article 162 of the Swiss *Penal Code* (Schweizerisches Strafgesetzbuch vom 21. December 1937), Articles 121–124 and Article 301 of the *Austrian Penal Code* (Strafgesetzbuch, 1974), Articles 272–273 of the *Dutch Penal Code* (1881, amended 1994)), Article 309 and Article 461 of the *Belgian Penal Code* (1999), Article 497 and Article 499 of the *Spanish Penal Code* and Articles 622–623 of the *Italian Penal Code* (*Codice Penale*) (1930) <http://wings.buffalo.edu/law/bclc/resource.htm> (19 August 2006).

Committee of the National People's Congress (the SCNPC), administrative laws and regulations of the State Council (state laws); local regulations promulgated by the various people's congresses of the provinces, major cities, and special economic zones and their respective standing committees (local regulations); and departmental rules implemented by ministries and commissions, the People's Bank of China, and the Auditing Administration under the State Council as well as agencies directly under the control of the State Council (departmental rules). There were more than 130 important laws and regulations relating to the protection of trade secrets (including technological secrets) promulgated and implemented in China during the period from 1985 to 2002, among which twenty-four were state laws, fifteen were administrative laws and regulations of the State Council, seventy-six were departmental regulations of the State Council, and fifteen were local regulations, all of which constitute the source of law for current trade secret protection in China.

A. State Laws

The first Chinese law regarding the protection of trade secrets was the Law of the People's Republic of China on Technology Contracts (effective 1 November 1987 and repealed 1 October 1999 which employed the concept of 'unpatented technology'[5] and which applied only to contracts for technology development, technology transfer, technology consultation and technological services concluded between Chinese corporations, between Chinese corporations and Chinese citizens, and between Chinese citizens.[6] It mainly protected know-how not fundamentally related to confidential business information or other trade secrets and therefore played a fairly limited role in trade secret protection.

The Law on Protecting State Secrets of the People's Republic of China (the LPSS) became effective on 1 May 1989 and methods for the concrete implementation of the LPSS were published in Order No.1 issued by the State Secrets Bureau in May 1990 following approval by the State Council. The LPSS was applicable to all secret matters in the area of scientific technology related to national security and interests.[7]

5. See articles 34 to 40 of the Law of the People's Republic of China on Technology Contracts.
6. *Ibid.* See article 2.
7. See Article 8 of the Law on Protecting State Secrets of the People's Republic of China (1988).

Figure 1. Hierarchical Structure of the Chinese Legal System on Trade Secrets

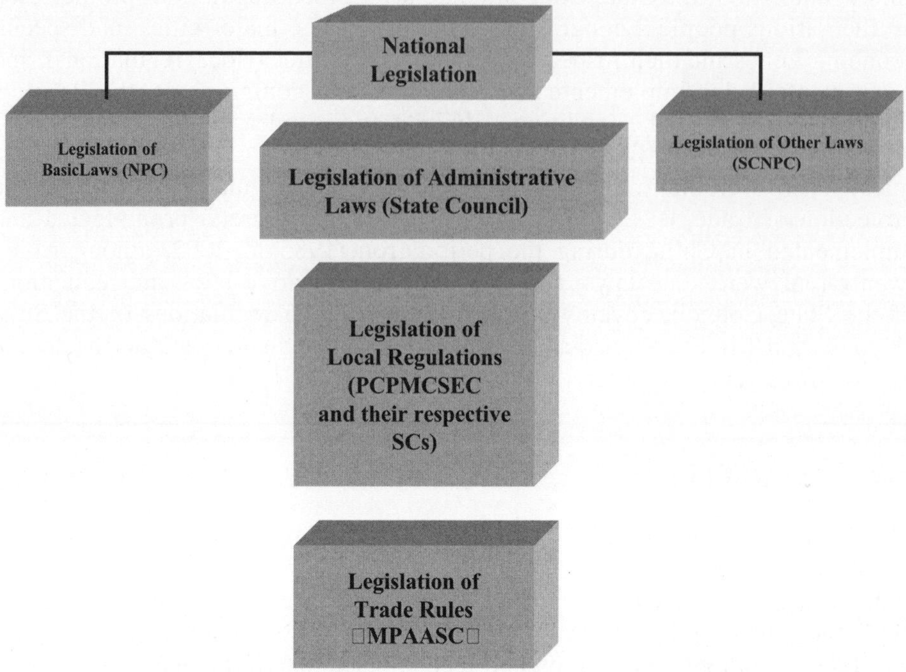

Hierarchical structure is drawn according to level of legislation.

Article 60 of the Law of the People's Republic of China on Science and Technological Progress (effective 2 July 1993) provides that:

> Anyone who encroaches upon another person's copyright, patent right, right of discovery, right of invention, or right of scientific and technological achievements by means of plagiarism, alteration, or imitation, or who illegally acquires technical secrets, shall be dealt with in accordance with relevant provisions of the law.

Chapter 3 of the Labour Law of the People's Republic of China (effective 1 January 1995) titled 'Labour Contracts and Collective Contracts' provides that: 'Parties to a labour contract can reach agreements in the contract on matters concerning the keeping of the trade secrets of the employer'.[8]

In the Criminal Law of the People's Republic of China (CL1997) effective 1 October 1997, the phrase 'crimes of infringing trade secrets' was added,[9] which provides that 'Whoever commits any of the following acts of infringing on business secrets and thus causes heavy losses to their owner shall be sentenced to a

8. See Article 22 of the Labour Law of the People's Republic of China (1994).
9. See Article 219 of the Criminal Law of the People's Republic of China.

fixed-term of imprisonment of not more than three years, criminal detention, and/or imposition of a fine:

(1) obtaining an owner's business secrets by stealing, enticement, coercion or by any other illegitimate means;
(2) disclosing, using or allowing another to use business secrets obtained from the owner by any means mentioned in the preceding paragraph or
(3) in violation of the agreement to an owner's demand for maintaining business secrets, disclosing, using or allowing another person to use the business secrets he or she has knowledge of. If the losses to a holder are particularly serious, defendants may be sentenced to a fixed-term of imprisonment of not less than three years but not more than seven years and may also be fined.

The Contract Law of the People's Republic of China became effective on 1 October 1999 and, at the same time, the Economic Contract Law, the Foreign Economic Contract Law, and the Law of Technology Contracts were repealed. To better meet the needs of China's developing market economy, the Contract Law contained new provisions regarding obligations of contract secrecy emphasizing principles of equity, free will, fairness, good faith and legality[10] and used foreign legislation as a model for Chinese practice. According to the provisions of the Contract Law:

> A business secret the parties learn in concluding a contract shall not be disclosed or unfairly used, no matter whether the contract is established or not. A party who causes another party to suffer losses due to disclosing or unfairly using said business secret shall be liable for damages.[11]

Parties must abide by the principle of good faith and perform the obligations of notice, assistance, maintaining confidentiality and the like based on the character and purpose of the contract and in compliance with fair business practices.[12] Chapter 18 of the Contract Law contains special provisions for technology contracts. Vis-à-vis trade secret protection, it incorporates the main content of the former Law of Technology Contracts allowing secrecy provisions to be included in technology contracts and obligates transferors and transferees in contracts concerning technology transfers to maintain confidentiality. In addition, the Contract Law contains rules regarding choice of applicable law. It provides that parties to a contract involving foreign elements may choose the law governing the settlement of contractual disputes with the exception of those prohibited by other existing law. If the parties concerned decline to choose, then the laws of the country that is most closely related to the subject contract will be applied.[13]

---

10. See Articles 3 to 6 of the Contract Law of the People's Republic of China (1999).
11. *Ibid.* See Article 43.
12. *Ibid.* See Article 60.
13. *Ibid.* See Article 126.

B. Administrative Law and Regulations of the State Council

The Detailed Rules and Regulations for the Implementation of the Regulation on Administration of Technology Import Contracts of the People's Republic of China (the 'DRR'), jointly promulgated by the State Council and the Ministry of Foreign Trade and Economic Cooperation and effective 20 January 1988, was repealed by the PRC Regulations on the Management of Technology Import and Export which became effective 1 January 2002.[14] Article 13 of the DRR provides that:

> A recipient shall undertake the obligation to keep confidential the technical secrets of certain know-how and relevant information provided or imparted by a supplier in accordance with the scope and term of confidentiality stipulated in the technology import contract. The term of confidentiality shall not exceed the period of validity of said contract. The recipient shall be relieved of any obligation to confidentiality if the technical secrets of the imported technical know-how or relevant information are made public during the term of confidentiality not owing to the recipient. If it is specified in the technology import contract that the supplier is required to provide products developed by or improved versions of the imported technology to the recipient during the contract validity period, the recipient may continue to bear the obligation to keep confidential the technical secrets of the developed products or improved versions of the technology after the validity of the said contract has lapsed. However, the additional term of confidentiality (that overlaps the original term) shall not be longer than the term of confidentiality previously approved in the technology import contract and the additional term of confidentiality shall become effective on the date the developed products or improved versions of the technology are provided to the recipient.

Article 4 of Chapter 1 titled 'General Provisions' of the Regulations of the People's Republic of China on Customs Investigations and Inspections (promulgated by the State Council and effective 3 January 1997) provides that customs personnel must, when executing customs inspections, be objective and fair, seek truth from facts, be honest in performing their official duties, must keep confidential trade secrets of persons they inspect and must not violate the legitimate rights and interests of persons that are subject to said inspection.

The Regulations on the Protection of Traditional Arts and Crafts, effective 20 May 1997, was promulgated by the State Council in order to develop and protect Chinese traditional arts and crafts. The Regulations expressly provided that enterprises that produce traditional arts and crafts must establish and implement systems for the protection of secrets regarding traditional arts and crafts and must concretely strengthen the management of traditional arts and crafts. Whoever engages in the

---

14. This new regulation provides only that a recipient shall undertake the obligation to keep confidential the un-disclosed portion of technology provided by a supplier in accordance with the scope and duration of confidentiality stipulated in the contract. See Article 3 of the Regulations of the People's Republic of China on the Management of Technology Import and Export.

production of traditional arts and crafts must abide by the provisions of relevant state law and not divulge technological secrets or other trade secrets that they may know.[15]

Figure 2. Statistical Ratios of Legislation on the Protection of Trade Secrets in China (1987–2005)

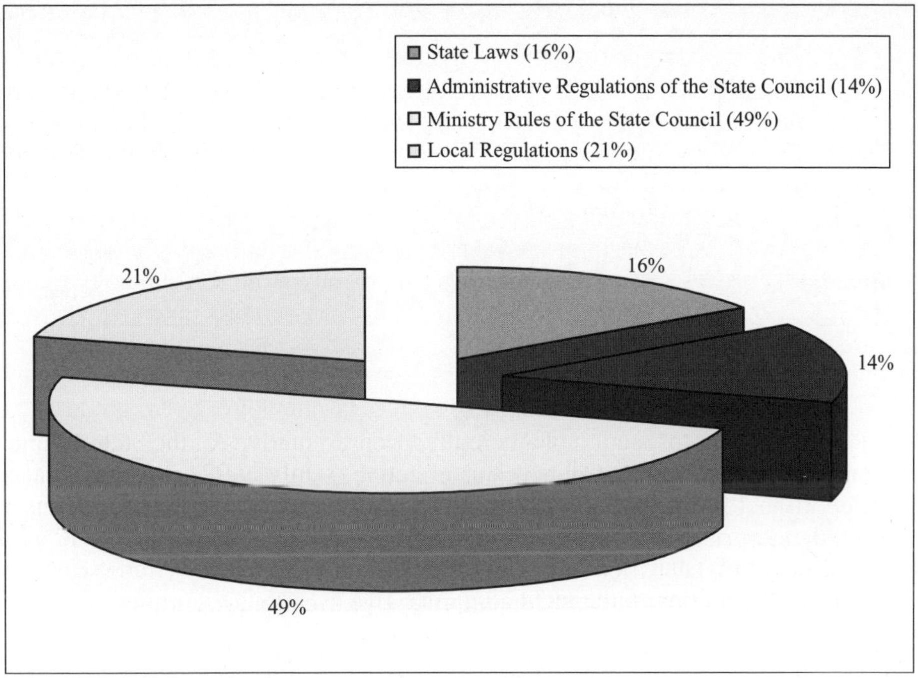

The Regulations on Export Control of Military Items of the People's Republic of China (promulgated by the State Council and the Central Military Commission of the People's Republic of China on 22 October 1997) provides that:

> Military trading companies, as required by the regulations of the national military export control authorities, shall faithfully submit documents and files related to their military export activities. The national military export control authorities shall maintain commercial confidentiality and safeguard the legitimate rights and interests of military trading companies.[16]

---

15. See Article 18 of the Regulations on the Protection of Traditional Arts and Crafts (1997).
16. See Article 11 of the Regulations on Export Control of Military Items of the People's Republic of China (1997).

Graph 1. Graph of Chinese Legislation on Protection of Trade Secrets by Year (1987–2005)

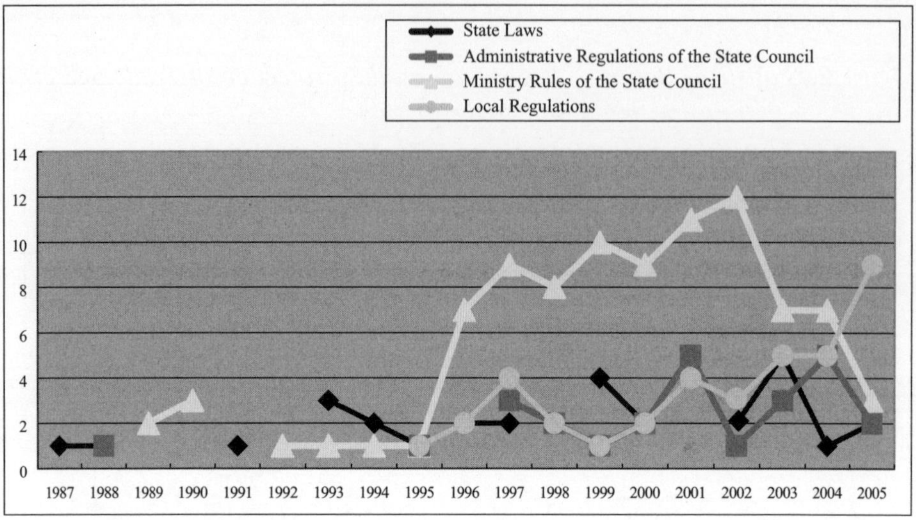

The Regulations on Inspection of Accredited Representatives of the State Council (promulgated by the State Council and effective 3 July 1998) stipulate that no certified inspector nor any aid to certified inspectors may divulge trade secrets of inspected enterprises that they may come to know or possess during the process of inspection,[17] that certified inspectors and their aids who divulge trade secrets of inspected enterprises will be issued administrative sanctions according to law and that, in cases deemed serious enough to constitute a crime, criminal responsibility will be affixed according to law.[18]

The Provisional Regulations on the Board of Supervisors of state-owned Enterprises and the Provisional Regulations on the Boards of Priority State-owned Financial Institutions were promulgated by the State Council and became effective 15 March 2000. Both provisional regulations provide that every member of a board of supervisors must keep confidential the content of inspection reports and may not divulge the trade secrets of enterprises[19]and/or of state-owned financial institutions.[20]

The Provisional Regulations on the Management of the Futures Business were promulgated by the State Council and became effective 1 September 1999. Article 43 of Chapter 4 of the Regulations titled 'Basic Rules of the Futures Business'

17. See Article 21 of the Regulations on Inspection of Accredited Representatives of the State Council (1998).
18. *Ibid.* See Article 24.
19. See Article 22 of the Provisional Regulations on the Board of Supervisors of State-owned Enterprises (2000).
20. *Ibid.*

provides that divulging trade secrets related to the futures business is not permitted in delivery warehouses, that disciplinary action will be taken against personnel of any futures exchange who divulge state secrets and trade secrets of members or clients of the exchange that they have access to during their service in the exchange or during their service in member units of the exchange within a year after leaving their employment and that criminal penalties will be imposed in cases deemed so serious as to constitute a crime.[21] In addition, where personnel of the CSRC divulge state secrets and/or trade secrets of members and clients and/or resort to deception for personal gain, commit dereliction of duty, abuse their power, or accept bribes and where such cases are serious enough as to constitute a crime, criminal penalties will be imposed. If a case is not deemed serious enough to constitute a crime, administrative punishment will be meted out according to law.[22]

C. MINISTRY RULES OF THE STATE COUNCIL

The Provisional Regulations on the Resignation of Personnel in Specific Technical Fields and Managerial Personnel of Institutions Owned by the Whole People (promulgated by the State Personnel Bureau and effective 8 September 1990) emphasize that personnel that have resigned are prohibited from removing without permission the results of scientific research, inside information, equipment and so on of their original units.[23] The Provisional Regulations also provide the procedure for resignation of persons in charge as well as for key members in the operation of priority scientific research projects of the state and in the provinces (as well as in municipalities and in autonomous regions) and for personnel engaged in work related to state secrets.[24] The Rules on the Procedure for Hearing Administrative Punishment of Labour (approved by the PRC Ministry of Labour and effective 1 October 1996) provides that hearing chairmen are subject to an obligation to keep confidential state secrets, trade secrets and private affairs related to cases.[25] In addition, hearings wherein state secrets, trade secrets, or personal privacy are involved are not permitted to be held openly.[26]

The Notice on the Strengthening of the Protection of Trade Secrets of State-owned Enterprises (promulgated by the General Office of the State Economic and Trade Commission of the PRC and effective 2 July 1997) provides that state-owned enterprises must arrange for the protection of technological and business information on a case-by-case basis. state-owned enterprises must, after weighing the advantages and disadvantages of each, choose a proper form for the

21. See Article 66 of the Provisional Regulations on the Management of Futures Business (1999).
22. *Ibid.* See Article 68.
23. See Article 14 of the Provisional Regulations on the Resignation of Personnel in Specific Technical Fields and Managerial Personnel of Institutions Owned by the Whole People (1990).
24. *Ibid.* See Article 7.
25. See Article 7 of the Rules on the Procedure of Hearing of Administrative Punishment of Labour (1996).
26. *Ibid.* See Article 12.

protection of intellectual property and for the protection of relevant information. They must, for information that meets the standard for protection as trade secrets, correctly define the scope of those trade secrets and must regard them as important intellectual property in the course of the management of enterprise assets. They must also, when defining the scope of their trade secrets, determine the various levels of those trade secrets in accordance with their importance and adopt practical protective measures in a timely manner so as to prevent them from being stolen, divulged, or deciphered. They must establish or designate special full-time or part-time personnel that are particularly responsible for the management of trade secrets, (e.g., departments of legal affairs or corporate counsels of enterprises). They must notify their employees in writing that they are obligated to maintain confidentiality and must affirm the fact that their employees have been trained in the keeping of trade secrets. They may, according to their actual circumstances, establish the following systems for the management of trade secrets: methods for controlling the creation and determination of trade secrets; methods for controlling the use and destruction of trade secrets; methods for controlling the level and duration of the secrecy of trade secrets; methods for controlling the keeping of trade secrets by employees; methods for reward and punishment regarding the management of trade secrets; methods for maintaining secrecy during reception of visitors; methods for the maintenance of secrecy of work in vital areas; secrecy rules regarding conferences; and rules for the management of facsimile printers, computers, and communications apparatus. If it is found that the legitimate rights and interests of state-owned enterprises regarding their trade secrets have been infringed upon, relevant cases must be settled in a timely manner through an administrative or judicial process.[27]

The Several Proposals for the Strengthening of the Management of Technological Secrets in the Flow of Scientific and Technological Personnel (promulgated by the State Science and Technology Commission of the PRC and effective 2 July 1997) expressly provides policy limits and measures for technical management in the movement of scientific and technological personnel. The Several Proposals define technological secrets owned by an enterprise as technological information which the enterprise possesses through development and/or other legal means, which have not been made publicly available, which can bring economic benefit and/or competitive advantage to the enterprise, which are practical, for which the enterprise has adopted secrecy measures, and which include but are not limited to design drawings (including drafts), experimental results and records, technological processes, ingredients and formulas, samples, data and computer programs. Technological secrets can include technological plans that have specific and integrated technological content and that constitute a product, a process, a material (or improvements on said product, process, or material), as well as partially technological essential elements of a certain product, process or material. Departing scientific and technology personnel may not reveal to new employers, transfer

27. See Article 2 of Notice on the Strengthening of the Protection of Trade Secrets of State-owned Enterprises (1997).

to third persons, or use by themselves in unlawful ways technological secrets that they may have come to possess during their original employment that are owned by their original employers (including technological achievements tied to a project which they themselves have conducted or in which they have participated).[28] Enterprises and institutions must be attentive to the management of scientific and technological personnel that conduct state scientific and technological projects and/or important scientific research tasks of an enterprise. Certain scientific and technological personnel who have been enlisted for construction project tasks that have been certified as major state scientific or technological projects, or who have been chosen to be members of relevant cooperative research project teams, who request transfers or who resign prior to the completion of said scientific or technological tasks and who might possibly divulge technological secrets related to those projects and/or scientific research tasks (thereby threatening the security and interests of the nation) are generally not permitted to transfer or to resign. Personnel who leave their positions without authorization and bring about economic loss to the state or to their original employer or who divulge technological secrets will incur civil liability, and the employer of said personnel will bear joint and several liability for payment of compensation according to law.[29] Security measures that must be adopted by enterprises and institutions in order to avoid such liability include the conclusion of confidentiality agreements, establishment of security systems, adoption of security technologies, installation of reasonable security equipment and adoption of other reasonable security methods. Relevant security measures must be clear, definite and explicit and must concretely establish the scope, form and duration of secrecy. Security measures for technological secrets owned by the enterprise should also include punishment for leaking of those secrets. Scientific and technological personnel may freely use technological information for which an enterprise has not implemented proper security measures, or the content of which has been made available to the public. Scientific and technological personnel may sign written agreements with their employers regarding the use and transfer of technological secrets and technological achievements and those agreements must stipulate the scope, mode, and conditions of the voluntary use of those technological secrets and technological achievements.[30] Enterprises and institutions may, in accordance with provisions of relevant law, sign agreements regarding the confidentiality of technological secrets with their scientific and technological personnel, with administrative staff, with persons who may learn technological secrets in the course of business and with other persons related to the business. A confidentiality agreement may be combined with a labour employment contract or with an intellectual property ownership agreement into one contract, each of which may be separately signed. Scientific and technological personnel in

---

28. See Article 2 of the Several Proposals on the Strengthening of the Management of Technological Secrets in the Flow of Science and Technology Personnel (1997).
29. *Ibid.* See Article 3.
30. See Article 5 of the Several Proposals on the Strengthening of the Management of Technological Secrets in the Flow of Science and Technology Personnel (1997).

the performance of their obligation to maintain confidentiality are entitled to receive remuneration and bonuses for being engaged in technological development activities and have the right to request alteration or termination of confidentiality agreements if their employers refuse to pay said remuneration and bonuses without reasonable grounds.[31] An employer may, through consultations with administrative, scientific and technological personnel who are essential to its technological and economic interests, include non-competition clauses in labour employment contracts, intellectual property right ownership agreements and confidentiality agreements stipulating that relevant personnel may not, within a certain period of time after their leaving said employer, hold posts within other enterprises that produce goods of the same kind, engage in businesses that compete with those of the original employer or that share other interests with the original employer, or engage for themselves in the production of goods of the same kind or in the operation of businesses that compete with those of the original employer. If agreements of this kind are entered into, employers must pay a certain amount of compensation to relevant personnel and the non-competition period may not exceed three years. Employers and employees have the right to appeal to an arbitration panel or to bring an action before the people's courts in disputes regarding non-competition. Where employers are fully aware that personnel are obligated to confidentiality or non-competition agreements with their previous employers and intentionally employ these personnel in order to acquire technological secrets, said employers shall bear civil liability.[32] Scientific and technological personnel and other relevant personnel who, after leaving their original employer, achieve new technological results or technological innovations on the basis of technological secrets that they have come to know or have had access to during their previous employment, and that are owned by said new employer, have the right to apply and use those new technological results and technological innovations. However, if scientific and technological personnel seek to exploit technological secrets that are owned by their previous employer and for which they are obligated to maintain confidentiality, they must receive the consent of said previous employer and pay royalties to that employer. If they have not received the consent of their previous employer or if they have no evidence proving that disputed technological content is the result of new technological results or of technological innovation that they themselves have developed, then they and their current employer may be subject to civil or criminal liability.[33]

The Provisional Methods for the Management of Holders of Projects Concerning Confidential State Technologies (jointly promulgated by the State Science and Technology Commission of the PRC and the State Secrets Bureau and effective 4 January 1998) provides that supervisors at various levels responsible

31. *Ibid.* See Article 6.
32. See Article 7 of the Several Proposals on the Strengthening of the Management of Technological Secrets in the Flow of Science and Technology Personnel (1997).
33. See Article 8 of the Several Proposals on the Strengthening of the Management of Technological Secrets in the Flow of Science and Technology Personnel (1997).

for science and technology and supervisors at various levels responsible for secret information are charged with guiding, supervising, and examining secret information of the project contractors concerning confidential state-owned technologies.[34] These contractors must establish a management department for the protection of scientific and technological secrets for which their executives are responsible, and full-time and part-time managerial personnel must be provided to that department. These departments are responsible for establishing systems for the protection of scientific and technological secrets of their enterprises, for organizing secret works for scientific and technological projects of their enterprises, for conducting instruction regarding the protection of scientific and technological secrets, and for reporting at regular intervals to the supervisor responsible for security at the same level as well as to departments at higher levels responsible for the protection of scientific and technological secrets.[35] These holders must precisely determine the main protected scope of projects, information involved, content of secrecy, and crucial places where relevant information is kept and relevant technologies are used. All confidential information must be marked with their level of secrecy and the term of confidentiality in accordance with the law and they must be strictly referenced in rules made by their holders.[36] These holders must define the scope of confidential projects to which certain personnel have access and those personnel must be examined and approved by holders. In addition, the holders must sign confidentiality agreements with said personnel.[37] Where changes occur to a holder as a result of reorganization, the original holder and the new holder must continue to maintain confidentiality in accordance with the original level of secrecy so as to secure state-owned confidential technologies from infringement.[38]

D. Local Regulations

The Regulations of Shenzhen SEZ on the Protection of Technological Secrets of Enterprises (the Shenzhen Regulations) were promulgated by the Standing Committee of the People's Congress of Shenzhen City and became effective 3 November 1995. The promulgation of these regulations preceded that of the Several Rules on the Prohibition of Infringement of Trade Secrets (the Several Rules) by the State Administration for Industry and Commerce by twenty days. It was the first to protect trade secrets in the form of local legislation, playing an important guiding role in the protection of trade secrets of enterprises. Many successive local laws and regulations have continued to use basic provisions

34. See Article 4 of the Provisional Methods for the Management of Holders of Projects Concerning Confidential State Technologies (1998).
35. *Ibid.* See Article 5.
36. *Ibid.* See Article 6.
37. See Article 7 of the Provisional Methods for the Management of Holders of Projects Concerning Confidential State Technologies (1998).
38. *Ibid.* See Article 8.

established in the Several Rules. The Shenzen Regulations expanded on the general principles of the Law against Unfair Competition regarding the prohibition of acts which infringe on trade secrets and concretely and systematically defined technological secrets, legal responsibility regarding infringement management of technological secrets of enterprises, and non-competition agreements. They elaborated on other detailed rules for implementation as well, enabling Chinese legislation on the protection of trade secrets and relevant practice to take a step forward. The Shenzhen Regulations provided that technology and technological information include designs, processes, data, ingredients and formulas, know-how and other media that may be physical, chemical, or biological in form.[39] Where there are many developers that independently develop the same technological secret, each of them can freely use, transfer and disclose that technological secret.[40] Where an enterprise requests that its employees guard its technological secrets, it must sign confidentiality agreements with these employees whose obligation to maintain said confidentiality would end when their employment is terminated if there were no clear and definite confidentiality agreement or other relevant written agreement.[41]

During the term of a confidentiality agreement, employees must strictly abide by the rules of secrecy of an enterprise, are not permitted to divulge technological secrets of the enterprise to other persons, and they are not permitted to use the technological secrets in production or operational activities without the written consent of the enterprise that legally owns the technological secrets.[42] An enterprise may sign non-competition agreements with its employees that know or could possibly know its technological secrets, stipulating that they are not permitted to hold posts in other enterprises that produce products of the same kind that compete with its own products. If agreements of this type are entered into, the employer must pay those employees a certain amount of compensation.[43] The non-competition period may not exceed three years and the compensation stipulated in the agreement must be no less than two thirds of the total remuneration that the employee earned for the year prior to leaving the enterprise.[44] Whosoever infringes on the technological secrets of an enterprise and in doing so causes damage to that enterprise will be subject to payment of damages and will bear other civil liability as well as reasonable costs incurred by the infringed enterprise for investigating the tort committed upon its legitimate rights and interests.[45] According to the Shenzhen Regulations, the department of Shenzhen city in charge of science and technology has the right to order the immediate cessation

39. See Article 5 of the Regulations of Shenzhen SEZ on the Protection of Technological Secrets of Enterprises (1995).
40. *Ibid.* See Article 6.
41. *Ibid.* See Article 9.
42. *Ibid.* See Article 11.
43. *Ibid.* See Article 14.
44. *Ibid.* See Article 17.
45. *Ibid.* See Article 25.

and, on a case by case basis, impose a fine of thirty-thousand to one-hundred and fifty thousand yuan renmibi (CNY) for the following torts:

(a) A person that undertakes an obligation to maintain confidentiality for technological secrets discloses and uses said secrets without the written consent of the legitimate owner of those secrets;
(b) A person that undertakes an obligation of non-competition with an enterprise holds a post in another enterprise that produces goods of the same kind that compete with those of the original enterprise, or a person engages in production and related business of the original enterprise that compete with that of the original enterprise without the prior written consent of the legitimate owner of the technological secrets; or
(c) An enterprise employs a person who, said enterprise is fully aware, has undertaken an obligation of non-competition with another enterprise and who, according to that obligation, is not permitted to hold a post in that enterprise.[46]

The Shenzhen Regulations go on to state that where technological secrets are acquired through fraud, theft, persuasion through bribery, coercion, subornation or by any other improper means, the department of the city in charge of science and technology can order the immediate cessation of the infringement, the restitution of documents and equipment related to said acquisition and can impose a fine of CNY fifty-thousand to five-hundred thousand.[47] Where technological secrets are acquired through improper means and are disclosed, used or transferred, the department of the city of Shenzhen in charge of science and technology can order the immediate cessation of infringement and restitution of documents and equipment related to said acquisition, and can impose a fine of CNY one-hundred thousand to one million.[48] Where an enterprise is fully aware or should have been aware that a technological secret is being disclosed as the result of a breach of a confidentiality agreement or was acquired through improper means, and the enterprise accepts, uses or discloses to others said secret, relevant agreements of transfer shall be deemed invalid, the enterprise shall be subject to payment of compensation, and the department of the city in charge of science and technology shall seal equipment and documents related to the secret and impose a fine of CNY three-hundred thousand to five-hundred thousand.[49]

The Regulations of Zhuhai City on the Protection of Technological Secrets of Enterprises (the Zhuhai Regulations, adopted by the Standing Committee of the People's Congress of Zhuhai City on 10 July 1997) provide that the administrative department of science and technology of Zhuhai city is the department in charge of the protection of technological secrets of enterprises and is responsible for directing and supervising the protection of technological secrets of enterprises, for investigating and prosecuting conduct violating the Zhuhai Regulations and for

46. *Ibid.* See Article 27.
47. *Ibid.* See Article 28.
48. *Ibid.* See Article 29.
49. *Ibid.* See Article 30.

assisting arbitral agencies and judicial offices in identifying technical matters in cases where technological secrets of enterprises have been infringed.[50] Technological secrets deemed legally owned by an enterprise include those acquired through transfer of technology, transmission of technological information, technological cooperation or by other legitimate means, including through independent development and research or commissioned development and research.[51] An enterprise may, according to how its economic interests, development or survival are affected, independently determine different levels of technological secrets: e.g., AAA, AA, or A.[52] An enterprise must, according to the level of secrecy involved, determine various classifications of sites related to technological secrets, to scientific research, handling of official business, production or other purposes, and must adopt security measures to ensure that technological secrets are not leaked.[53] The duration of the term of non-competition for various personnel generally will be from two to five years according to, among other things, the level of the technological secrets involved, the level of security clearance of a specific position, and special training received. If the duration of a term of non-competition exceeds five years, it must be approved by the administrative department of science and technology of Zhuhai city. If there is no relevant provision in a non-competition agreement, the term of non-competition will be two years.[54] An enterprise may, according to the life cycle, maturity and potential value of a technology, as well as the market demand of a product manufactured based on that technology, independently determine the term of secrecy for its technological secrets. Where a term of secrecy has not been specifically determined, it is ten years.

The Regulations of Guangdong Province for the Protection of Technological Secrets (the Guangdong Regulations adopted by the seventh meeting of the ninth Standing Committee of the People's Congress of Guangdong Province and effective 1998) provides that administrative departments of science and technology of the people's government at various levels together with administrative departments of industry and commerce at similar levels are responsible for the organization and the implementation of the Guangdong Regulations.[55] Where a technological secret is formed through contract or commissioned research and development, its ownership will be determined in a manner agreed upon in writing by the parties concerned. If there is no agreement regarding the manner of determining ownership, all parties concerned will have the right to use or transfer said secret. However, for technological secrets that are formed through commissioned research and development, researchers and developers are not permitted to transfer

50. See Article 7 Regulations of Zhuhai City on the Protection of Technological Secrets of Enterprises (1997).
51. *Ibid.* See Article 3.
52. *Ibid.* See Article 9.
53. *Ibid.* See Article 13.
54. *Ibid.* See Article 20.
55. See Article 4 of the Regulations of Guangdong Province on the Protection of Technological Secrets (1999).

such secrets to a third party before delivering it to the client.[56] An enterprise must clearly identify its technological secrets by affixing corresponding labels on technological documents. As for models, samples, data, ingredients and formulas, technological processes and other items to which labels cannot be affixed, other identification methods must be used.[57] An enterprise may sign non-competition agreements with persons that know its technological secrets, and the duration of validity of said agreements may not exceed three years.[58] Where there is a dispute regarding an agreement on the protection of technological secrets, the parties concerned may, in accordance with arbitral clauses in the agreement or in accordance with a written arbitral agreement reached thereafter, appeal for arbitration. If there is no arbitral agreement or other relevant clause in writing, the parties concerned may lodge a complaint with a people's court.[59]

In Article 15 of Chapter 2 of the Regulations of the Shanghai Municipality against Unfair Competition (the Shanghai Regulations promulgated by the Standing Committee of the People's Congress of the Shanghai Municipality and effective 1 December 1995) titled 'Unfair Competitive Behaviour,' additional remarks are included regarding the scope of technological or business information that has been deemed a trade secret. The Shanghai Regulations state that such information includes, but is not limited to, ingredients and formulas, technological processes, know-how, designs, management methods, marketing strategies, customer information and sources of supply.

The Regulations of the Shanghai Municipality on Labour Contracts (the Shanghai Labour Regulations promulgated by the Standing Committee of the People's Congress of the Shanghai Municipality and effective 1 May 2002) is the newest local legislation in China for the regulation of labour relations. The Shanghai Labour Regulations are applicable not only to labour relationships between government agencies, government-sponsored institutions, and social organizations within the administrative divisions of the Shanghai Municipality and their employees, but are also applicable to labour relationships between enterprises and individual economic organizations within those divisions and their employees. Chapter two of the Shanghai Labour Regulations titled 'Conclusion of Employment Contracts' states that:

> Parties to a labour contract may agree upon clauses regarding confidentiality or may enter into separate confidentiality agreements. When a business secret becomes public knowledge, such confidentiality clauses and agreements will automatically become void. If an employee is to be obligated to maintain the confidentiality of the business secrets of their employer, the parties to a labour contract may agree upon an advance notice period in the labour contract or in a confidentiality agreement for employees requesting early termination

56. *Ibid.* See Article 5.
57. *Ibid.* See Article 8.
58. *Ibid.* See Article 13.
59. *Ibid.* See Article 24.

> of their employment contracts. Said advance notice period, however, may not exceed six months. During this period, the employer may take appropriate measures to declassify its business secrets.

In addition, the Shanghai Labour Regulations state that:

> If an employee is obligated to maintain the confidentiality of the business secrets of his employer, the parties concerned may agree upon non-competition clauses in a labour contract or confidentiality agreement to provide that when the labour contract is terminated, the employee will receive compensation. Said scope of non-competition shall be limited in that an employee may not, within a certain period of time following his termination, engage in any business for himself or on behalf of other business operators that compete with that of the original employer. The term of non-competition is subject to the terms of the employment contract between the parties, but shall not exceed three years with the exception, however, of provisions contained in the law or regulations of the PRC. If the parties enter into an agreement of non-competition in an employment contract, they may not include an agreement on an advance notice period for the employee in the event of early termination of the contract.

The Regulations of the Beijing Municipality on the Talent Market (the Beijing Regulations approved by the Standing Committee of the People's Congress of the Beijing Municipality and effective 1 January 1998) provide that a job applicant or one accepting an offer of employment must, upon leaving their previous employment, deal in good faith regarding contract agreements they have signed with said previous employer.[60] Where a job applicant or one accepting an offer of employment early terminates an employment contract with their previous employer and divulges trade secrets or technological secrets of that employer or infringes upon intellectual property rights of that employer and has caused damages to that employer, they will bear relevant civil liability in accordance with the Beijing Regulations and criminal charges shall be brought in cases where the damages caused are so serious as to constitute a crime.[61]

The Regulations of the Beijing Municipality on the Technology Market (approved by the Standing Committee of the People's Congress of the Beijing Municipality and effective 1 November 2002) provide that a business broker must maintain the confidential technological information of his clients according to confidentiality agreements reached with his clients.[62] Offices for registration of technology contracts and their staffs are obligated to maintain confidentiality of state-owned technology contracts as well as of trade secrets of parties concerned.[63]

---

60. See Article 25 of the Regulations of the Beijing Municipality on the Talent Market (1998).
61. *Ibid.* See Article 28.
62. See Article 16 of the Regulations of the Beijing Municipality on the Technology Market (2002).
63. *Ibid.* See Article 30.

II. CHARACTERISTICS OF THE EXISTING CHINESE SYSTEM FOR THE PROTECTION OF TRADE SECRETS

Through investigation of the existing Chinese system for the protection of trade secrets, with the help of classification statistics and graphic analysis, the following characteristics can be clearly identified:

First, Chinese legislation regarding the protection of trade secrets is contained within the framework of the legal system regarding unfair competition, and has elements of both public and private law.

The Law against Unfair Competition aims to maintain fair competition in the marketplace and to protect the rights and interests of operators and consumers by prohibiting acts of unfair competition, including infringement of trade secrets.[64] At the same time, in order to realize this aim, the Law against Unfair Competition establishes civil and administrative penalties and creates a legal system within which administrative bodies are responsible for law enforcement while judicial bodies are responsible for adjudication. Pursuant to the Law against Unfair Competition, law enforcement agencies are obliged to adopt proper measures to prevent acts of unfair competition including infringement of trade secrets.[65] They may take the initiative to investigate and prosecute acts of unfair competition and order cessation of illegal acts, and may impose administrative penalties such as fines and confiscation of illegal gains. Aggrieved persons can lodge complaints with administrative bodies and request that they investigate and fix the administrative responsibilities of parties concerned. However, if aggrieved persons wish to obtain compensation for damages they must also file civil actions with the people's courts.

That the State actively interferes with unfair competition is an important characteristic of the Chinese legal system for the protection of trade secrets. From 1987 to 2002, China implemented a total of ninety-one administrative rules and regulations of various kinds, accounting for 70% of the total legislation implemented during that period.

Second, the content of local law and regulations is more extensive. In accordance with provisions of the Law on Legislation of the PRC, the People's Congresses and their respective Standing Committees are entitled to establish local law and regulations.[66] Following promulgation of the Law against Unfair Competition, nearly twenty local People's Congresses in Shanghai, Beijing and Shenzhen as in well as in other municipalities promulgated local laws against unfair competition. These local regulations are more concrete in content and more extensive in their scope of application. For one thing, the scope of their subject matter was expanded. Perpetrators of acts of unfair competition as identified in the Law against Unfair

64. See Article 1 of the Law against Unfair Competition of the People's Republic of China (1993).
65. *Ibid.* See Article 3.
66. See Article 63 of the Law of the People's Republic of China on Legislation (2000).

Competition can be corporations, individuals that engage in commodity trading, for-profit enterprises, and other economic entities, viz., business operators.[67] Many local laws and regulations have expanded the scope of the subject matter of the Law against Unfair Competition enabling it to be applied to entities and individuals other than business operators that engage in activities related to market competition. For example, Article 2 of the Regulations of the Shanghai Municipality against Unfair Competition provide that any corporation, individual, or other economic entity that engages in the production of goods, the sale of goods, or the provision of profitable services as well as any administrative body or authorized organization that engages in administrative management must abide by said Regulations. Article 2 of the Regulations of Henan Province against Unfair Competition (the Henan Regulations) provide that any organization or individual other than business operators that engages in activities related to market competition must also abide by the Henan Regulations. In addition, punitive administrative measures were added. The Law against Unfair Competition does not contain punitive measures for the protection of trade secrets yet many local laws and regulations, in accordance with the requirements of local law enforcement, have strengthened punitive administrative measures in their own jurisdictions. These measures can include sequestration or attachment, sealing up and freezing of assets. For example, the Henan Regulations provide in item 3 of clause 1 in Article 27 that where it is found that an examinee has an obvious intent to displace, hide, or destroy examined property or where there is obvious evidence of such intent, relevant property may be sealed up, attached or frozen, and be disposed of within a stipulated period.

Moreover, provisions contained in the Law against Unfair Competition for the protection of trade secrets are couched in general principles. For example, it included only the principles of free will, equality and equity and promoted honesty and trustworthiness. Further, its provisions regarding the definition of trade secrets, types of infringement upon trade secrets, liability of payment of compensation for injury and other matters are expressed as general principles. Yet during a period of ten years following its promulgation, there have been nearly 130 state laws, administrative laws and regulations, departmental rules and regulations as well as local laws and regulations that have come into force that contain specific provisions regarding various trade-secret related matters (i.e., elements and scope of trade secrets; administrative, civil and criminal penalties for acts of infringement upon trade secrets; burden of proof; duty of non-competition; and the obligation of confidentiality of skilled workers of enterprises and institutions).

---

67. *Ibid.* See Article 2.

Chapter 2
Legal Definition and Elements of Trade Secrets

The elements of a trade secret include inherent characteristics of information that render it eligible for protection, a major criterion for determining whether business information is entitled to legal protection. It is acknowledged that different countries employ different sources of law for the protection of trade secrets, but some countries have no legal definition of trade secrets contained in their domestic law. It can been found, however, that, whether they contain a legal definition of trade secrets or not, existing regulations in most countries are very similar regarding the legal understanding of what a trade secret is and, in practice, there is a trend towards a unanimous opinion on the inherent characteristics of trade secrets. In 1994, the TRIPS Agreement defined a legally protected trade secret in the context of 'information not made known to thc public'[1] and its signing heralded the advent of a common basic principle for the protection of trade secrets in the international community.

Chinese legal academics have been puzzled by the question of how to precisely define trade secrets, which has caused contention among them regarding which no consensus has currently been reached.[2] Nevertheless, over a long period of judicial practice, consensus has been reached within legal circles in China regarding the elements of trade secrets. Judicial scholars place emphasis on the idea that, in order to be legally protected, business information must be confidential and have a certain commercial value, and that its holder must employ proper

1. See §39.2 of the TRIPS Agreement. See <ww.wto.org/>, (5 January 2008).
2. More people in China think that a trade secret is constituted by three or four elements. Scholars such as Zhang Yuri and Kong Xiangjun think that trade secrets are constituted by confidentiality, value, manageability and novelty. Other academics think that trade secrets are constituted by confidentiality, value and manageability.

measures to maintain its secrecy. In China, the elements of what constitutes legally protected subject matter are generally defined in PRC legislation.

I. VALUE OF TRADE SECRETS

Among countries with trade secret protection systems, some aim to maintain fair competition in the market, some to protect private property and some to encourage technological advancement and the application of trade secrets. Under all of these systems, however, trade secrets must have a certain value or such protection is meaningless. Therefore, that a trade secret must have value has become a generally accepted basic principle within the legislation of all countries and international organizations of the world and, by this principle, they have formulated normative terminology, for example:

> [i]ndependent economic value, actual or potential, derived from not being generally known to, and not being readily ascertainable through proper means by, the public' (the United States);[3] '[t]echnical or business information useful in commercial activities'(Japan);[4] '[a]ctual or potential commercial value' (NAFTA);[5] '[i]ndependent economic value, useful in operating activities' (South Korea);[6] '[p]rovided with the commercial value' (TRIPS).

Yet, what is the commercial value of a trade secret? And what is the standard for determining that commercial value?

Upon observing the impact of trade secrets on certain national economies the answers to these questions are constantly being developed and expanded. For example, in the United States, the Restatement (First) of Torts (1939) stipulates that:

> A trade secret may consist of any formula, pattern, device or compilation of information which is used in one's business and which gives one an opportunity to obtain an advantage over competitors who do not know or use it.

However, with economic and technological development, many works still in the process of research and development as well as unusable technological and operational information (i.e., negative information) often become the type of information for which there is intense competition. Such scientific research and negative information are the fruit of human labour and are ingredients essential to the

---

3. See Section 1839 of the *Economic Espionage Act*, (1996) (US).
4. See §2.4 of the Unfair Competition Prevention Law of Japan (1993). < www.wipo.int/clea/docs_new/en/jp/jp005en.html >, 6 January 2008.
5. See §1711.1.2 of NAFTA. <www.nafta-sec-alena.org/DefaultSite/index_e.aspx?CategoryId=42>, 6 January 2008.
6. See Article 2 of the *Korea Unfair Competition Protection and Trade Secret Protection Law*, Law No. 911, Promulgated on 30 December 1961. As last amended by Law No. 6421, 3 February 2001. < www.wipo.int/clea/docs_new/pdf/en/kr/kr038en.pdf >, 6 January 2008.

realization of end products. Once obtained by competitors, this type of information can help them to avoid detours in development, to conserve human resources, material and financial investment in the development and research of similar products and to gain a competitive advantage in the marketplace. Therefore, one cannot underestimate the potential commercial value of this type of information. If the law protects only information that is 'in use' and pays attention only to the actual commercial value of such information, it will unreasonably limit the scope of the subject matter protected by trade secret law,[7] leaving much information with extremely high potential commercial value legally unprotected and ultimately reducing enthusiasm for invention and creativity. Consequently, the American Uniform Trade Secrets Act (1985), in order to adapt to this new legal environment concerning trade secret protection, suggested that a trade secret is information that 'derives independent economic value, actual or potential'.[8] However, it is not so easy to define the 'independent economic value' of a trade secret because valuable information is often created in the course of commercial activity by combining information already generally known with information in which a holder has invested a certain amount of resources. The result can bring the holder competitive advantage over others in the marketplace. In order to protect this kind of information, the American Law Institute put forward in the Restatement (Third) of Unfair Competition (1995) that:

> A trade secret is any information that can be used in the operation of a business or other enterprise and that is sufficiently valuable and secret to afford an actual or potential economic advantage over others.

However, the Third Restatement goes on to say, 'That advantage need not be great. It is sufficient if the secret provides an advantage that is more than trivial'.[9] Thus, the American understanding of the value of a trade secret has undergone a process from 'actual' competitive advantage to 'actual or potential independent economic value' to 'actual or potential economic advantage'. This process of changing terminology reflects the ever-increasing importance of business information in economic life.

It is a characteristic of Chinese law in comparison with that of other countries to emphasize not only the commercial value, but also the practicality of a trade secret. The first directly involves the mode and range of relief as well as other rights to which a holder is entitled when his rights are infringed upon, and the latter determines if a trade secret exists.

Certain Chinese academics are of the opinion that 'commercial value' of a trade secret means that the current or future use of the trade secret will bring actual economic benefit to its owner. The most substantial manifestation of commercial value is that the use of the trade secret will bestow a competitive edge on its owner,

---

7. See §39 of the Restatement of Unfair Competition, 1995, (US), comment e.
8. See Section One of *Uniform Trade Secrets Act*, 1985, (US).
9. See §39 of the *Restatement of Unfair Competition*, 1995, (US), comment e. Also see Edwin Fraumann and Joseph Koletar, 'Trade Secret Safeguards' (1999) 43 *Security Management*, 64.

(i.e., market dominance among competitors).[10] The 'practicality' of a trade secret means that it is objectively useful (i.e., business information that can be used to improve the level of technology, to increase labour productivity or to upgrade the quality of products) and that is conducive to the enhancement of the performance of an operation or the management of an enterprise as well as to the reduction of its expenses. Practicality also means that the information is specific and definite and can be put into practice in production or operation. In order to merit legal protection, information must be transformed into a specific plan or pattern that can be used. The law does not protect simple ideas, general principles or abstract concepts because their owners are usually still at a stage of exploration and have not developed practicable information. If this type of information were to be given legal protection, the scope of protected trade secrets would undoubtedly be infinitely broad.[11] Practicality is also manifest in the fact that trade secrets can be imparted to others. A trade secret can be removed from the direct control of its original owner by another who is then able to realize its economic value through direct or indirect dealings.[12]

However, having now achieved a greater understanding of business information and negative information, Chinese academics and the judicial community have called into question the requirement for trade secrets to have an element of practicality. This approach leaves the abovementioned type of information in a no-man's-land regarding legal protection. In this connection, in 1995 the State Administration for Industry and Commerce of the People's Republic of China promulgated the Several Rules on Forbidding the Infringement of Trade Secrets, further expounding on the value of trade secrets and determining that a trade secret is any information that 'can bring its holder economic benefit or competitive advantage, whether actual or potential'.[13]

How then is the competitive advantage, whether actual or potential, of a certain piece of information to be ascertained? It is very difficult to quantify the economic value of information due to the complexity of business information and of markets themselves and so there is presently no written law that contains specific rules on this. Only those principles and methods offered for reference herein that are based on precedent and actual judicial decisions have so far been implemented in the area of trade secret protection. For example, there are three generally accepted methods for determining the value of business information in American precedents:

(a) the market analysis approach, which determines the commercial value of information according to its content and its impact on the market;

10. Zhang Yuri, 200 Subjects on the Application and Protection of Trade Secrets (Beijing, People's Publishing House, 1996), p.36.
11. Zhang Yuri, *Science of Law on Trade Secrets* (Beijing, China Legal System Publishing House, 1999), p.157, and Kong Xiangjun, *Principles of the Law on the Protection of Trade Secret* (Beijing, China Legal System Publishing House, 1999), pp.48–49.
12. Li Jun, *The Era of Trade Secrets* (Beijing, Jincheng Publishing House, 1998), p.16.
13. See Article 2 of *Several Rules on Forbidding the Infringement of Trade Secrets* promulgated by the State Administration for Industry and Commerce of the People's Republic of China in 1995.

(b) the cost analysis approach, which determines the commercial value of information according to the resources invested in it by its owner and the precautions taken by its owner to protect its secrecy;
(c) the income analysis approach, which determines the economic value of information according to the licensing fee others are willing to pay to acquire it.[14]

In Chinese legal practice, factors in accordance with which value is determined can be expanded to include the following:

(a) Real value and potential value. Real information that can be directly used as well as information that is still in the process of being researched, is in trial production, or that is still in development and has potential value can constitute a trade secret;
(b) Valuable information, whether positive or negative, can constitute a trade secret. Positive information, for instance, can include information that is directly useful to production, sales, scientific research, development or business activities. Negative information is that which can contribute to cost savings or that which can enhance managerial efficiency such as reports of aborted experiments, lists of customers or design drawings; and
(c) Valuable information, whether of sustainable usefulness or of short duration, can be a trade secret.[15]

In 2003, the Beijing City Haidian District People's Court hearing the unfair competition dispute of *Beijing Hezong Science and Technology Co., Ltd v. Beijing Kunze Science and Technology Development Co., Ltd, Guo Maowen, Lee Hourong, Shen Yongzhi and Lee Shuxiang*, held that as a company operating power transmission and distribution equipment, Hezong had quite an extensive customer list. The customers of Hezong were mainly local electricity bureaus and therefore the names, addresses, names of legal representatives and phone numbers of the customers should not have naturally constituted a trade secret. However, specific commercial information such as that regarding the requirements of customers including the equipment used by customers, equipment that might possibly be used by customers, specific customer needs and quotations for equipment for specific customers created during the conduct of business with them becomes valuable confidential information as a result of the labour expended by the holder. As the customer lists of Hezong had the aforementioned characteristics, the court held, they were eligible for protection as trade secrets.[16]

---

14. See §757 of the *Restatement of Torts*, 1993, (US), comment e.
15. *Ibid.* Kong Xiangjun, pp.47–48.
16. (2003) Hai Min Chu Zi No. 11034. Published on Beijing Court Net. <http://bjgy.chinacourt.org/public/detail.php?id=11623&k_title=商业秘密&k_content=商业秘密&k_author=>, 5 January 2008.

II. CONFIDENTIALITY OF TRADE SECRETS

The language used in the legal statutes of many countries regarding the criteria for confidentiality of trade secrets contains terms such as 'not generally known,'[17] 'not disclosed'[18] and the like. It can be deduced from such language that a trade secret is entitled to legal protection and its confidentiality is meaningful in establishing the commercial value of business information and enabling its holder to attain a competitive advantage in the marketplace.[19] According to the principles of property law, parties can only claim that confidential business information is their property if it has not entered into the public domain because public information does not belong to anyone exclusively and, consequently, there is no benefit to be gained through the transfer of such information. Thus, public information has no value and cannot be considered a trade secret.[20]

Confidentiality has become an essential element of trade secrets and has become a premise for their legal protection in various countries. Yet, what constitutes confidentiality? And what is the standard for deciding whether certain information exists in a state of confidentiality? In answering these questions, the basic principles of the laws of various countries are similar but, in practice, the standards and methods for determination contained in those laws are slightly different.

We can draw the conclusion that international conventions and domestic legislation use 'not generally known' or 'not made publicly available' as the common standard for deciding the confidentiality of information.[21] In 1948, the British Court of Appeals hearing the case of *Saltman Engineering Co., Ltd v. Campbell Engineering* defined the confidentiality of information in this way:

> The information, to be confidential, must, I apprehend, apart from contract have the necessary quality of confidentiality about it; namely, it must not be something which is public property and public knowledge.[22]

When business information is made publicly available, the public can find and freely access it and once that business information becomes 'public property and public knowledge', its confidentiality is lost.

Therefore, the key standard adopted by legislation, including TRIPS, to judge whether a certain piece of information has been made publicly available is the possibility that or the degree of difficulty by which members of the public may legally obtain the information. Confidential information is of this nature. Practically,

---

17. See Article 10 of the *Law against Unfair Competition* of the People's Republic of China and Article 2 of the *Unfair Competition Prevention Law* of Japan. < www.wipo.int/clea/docs_new/en/jp/jp005en.html >, 6 January 2008.
18. See Article 39 of *TRIPS*. < www.wto.org/ >, 6 January 2008.
19. Roger M. Milgrim, *Milgrim on Trade Secrets* (New York, Matthew Bender, 1984), pp.2–31.
20. *Ibid.*
21. *Ibid.*
22. [1948] 65 R. P. C. 203 at 215; See also John Hull, *Commercial Secrecy: Law and Practice* (London, Sweet & Maxwell, 1998), p.50.

it is very difficult for anyone but the holder of confidential information to obtain it legally and only through exerting certain effort such as by investing a certain amount of time, material and human resources can a non-owner of the information find and access it. In general, business information already published or obtained at public occasions such as academic conferences is no longer clothed in confidentiality.

With regard to the confidentiality of trade secrets, the legislation in many countries emphasizes that the number of members of the public that know a trade secret is certainly not the only criteria for determining confidentiality.[23] Even if there are only a rather small number of persons that know a certain piece of business information owned by others, the confidentiality of that information will be lost when among this number is experts or professionals in the very industry to which the information belongs.

In addition, there is a common understanding among countries with regards to the idea that the confidentiality of a trade secret is not absolute but relative.[24] For example, regulations in the European Union hold that know-how is considered confidential if the public is not familiar with it and if it is not easy for the public to obtain and understand it.[25] In Comment f of Section 39 of the Restatement (Third) of the Law against Unfair Competition it is asserted that:

> A piece of information that constitutes a trade secret must be confidential, but it is not required to be absolutely confidential. In accordance with the rules referred to in this section, a trade secret is only required to bring its holder economic benefit, whether actual or potential.

So, if the legal means (illegal means are not included) stated in Section 40 of the Third Restatement through which others are able to obtain information are difficult or expensive, said information meets the requirements of confidentiality.

A more incisive explanation is contained in the TRIPS Agreement with regard to confidentiality, which states that undisclosed information is 'a secret in a certain sense,' viz. generally, the information as the precise configuration or integration of a whole or any part of the whole is not known or easily acquired by persons in the fields relevant to the information.[26]

In judicial practice, the characteristic of relative confidentiality of a trade secret is affirmed by precedent. For example, the court in *Peabody v. Norfork* (1868) cited that a trade secret '[d]oes not lose its confidentially through disclosure to agents or servants without whose assistance it could not be made

23. *Ibid.* p.52.
24. It seemed that the American courts judged some cases in the early history of the United States from the viewpoint of 'absolute secret'. Roger M. Milgrim, *Milgrim on Trade Secrets* (New York, Matthew Bender, 1984), pp.2–130.
25. See Article 10 of Commission Regulation (EC) No. 240/96 of 31 January 1996 on the application of Article 85(3) of the Treaty to certain Categories of Technology Transfer Agreements. <http://eur-lex.europa.eu/LexUriServ/LexUriServ.do?uri=CELEX:31996R0240:EN:HTML>, 5 January 2007.
26. See §39.2 of the *TRIPS Agreement*, <www.wto.org>, 5 January 2008.

of any value'.[27] In 1904, the Supreme Court of Pennsylvania, in *Pressed Steel Car Co. v. Standard Steel Car Co.* held that a trade secret could be accessed by the public in a certain form:

> A certain amount of publicity is unavoidable in any manufactory, but an unlocked door is not an invitation to the passerby or to the servant of the household to help himself. Neither does a manufacturer abandon his or her property in a design by delivering it or a copy to another for a restricted purpose, nor by a limited publication. His or her property rights will be protected in such cases, and he or she will be protected against a breach of trust, confidence, or contract, and in particular, will he or she be protected against a breach of the confidence existing between employer and employee.[28]

In the conduct of production, operations and commercial transactions, limited openness or disclosure of a piece of business information is often absolutely necessary. For example, an employer may need to disclose confidential business information to its employees to a certain extent as required by their work; during business negotiations, the holder of confidential information will inevitably need to disclose some of its business information to its associates; and, as may be required in the course of business, parties may need to disclose confidential business information to their agents. In such situations, protecting valuable information would be impossible without the protection afforded by the concept of relative secrecy.[29] In addition, anyone can obtain a trade secret already owned by others through reverse engineering, self-development or research without infringing on the trade secret rights of others.[30]

Although the TRIPS Agreement, as well as the trade secret laws of certain countries, places emphasis on the quality of confidentiality of business information, rules for the determination of confidentiality are basic in principle. Luckily, in countries in which the Continental Law system is applied as well as in those where the Common Law system is used, legal precedent is an important source of law for the handling of disputes regarding trade secrets. Principles put forward by certain courts have enriched and helped to develop written legislation regarding trade secrets, providing an important legal basis for reaching judicial decisions in cases regarding trade secret protection For example, the extent to which information is known outside a trade secret holder's business, the extent to which information is known by employees and others involved in the holder's business, the extent of measures taken by a holder to protect the secrecy of information and the ease or difficulty with which information can be properly acquired or duplicated by others.[31]

27. *Peabody v. Norfolk* 98 Mass. 452, 461, 96 AM. Dec. 664 (1868).
28. *Pressed Steel Car Co. v. Standard Steel Car Co.* 210 Pa. 464, 60A. 4 (1904).
29. John Hull, *Commercial Secrecy: Law and Practice* (London, Sweet & Maxwell, 1998), p.53.
30. Reverse engineering will be discussed in Part IV.
31. *Restatement (First) of Torts*, 1939, (US), §757, comment b.

In China, certain academics are of the opinion that confidentiality is one of the most important characteristics of business information if it is to be deemed a trade secret and notably differentiates trade secrets from other intellectual property rights. Confidential information in Chinese law and regulations is described as information that is 'not something that can be obtained directly through public channels'.[32] The value of trade secrets is maintained through confidentiality and once the information is made public it will entirely or partially lose its intrinsic value.[33] Confidentiality is relative and is not absolute. For example, even if confidential information is deemed to be a trade secret and has not been disclosed within a particular field, it does not mean that only the legal owner of said information has knowledge of it.[34]

In Chinese judicial practice, confidentiality of business information is determined from two aspects:

> One is the subjective standard – that a trade secret holder must be aware that the technical information, business information or commercial information he holds and uses is not known to the public and has economic value and that he has adopted measures to properly maintain its confidentiality. The other is the objective standard – that a trade secret has not actually been made available to the public and is not known in the public domain.[35]

In 2004, the Beijing No. 2 Intermediate People's Court hearing the trade secret dispute of *Beijing City Sifang Special Oil Factory v. Beijing Huate Luboil Co., Ltd and Lee Xinmin* held that technical information 'not known to the public' is 'non-publicly-known technical information', which means that neither the information as a whole nor certain technical content of the information is generally known or is difficult to be obtained by ordinary technical personnel in the field. In judicial practice, in the following situations technical information will be deemed to have entered the public domain and to have lost its secrecy:

(1) The information is published in public journals;
(2) Related products are publicly sold or exhibited and the technical information can be directly and easily obtained from the products;
(3) The technical information is generally known to and possessed by ordinary technical personnel in the field.[36]

---

32. See Article 2 of Several Rules on Forbidding the Infringement of Trade Secrets of the State Administration for Industry and Commerce of the People's Republic of China; and Article 51 of the Rules on Some Issues on Hearing Cases of Scientific and Technological Disputes promulgated by the Supreme People's Court of the People's Republic of China on 2 April 1995.
33. Lu Heyun, *A Talk about Laws on Trade Secrets* (Bao Din, Hubei People's Publishing House, 2000), p.43.
34. Kong Xiangjun, *Principles of the Law on the Protection of Trade Secrets* (Beijing, China Legal System Publishing House, 1999), p.42.
35. Deng Shemin, 'Initial Exploration of the Concept of Trade Secret' (2002) 2 *Intellectual Property*, 29 *et seq*.
36. (2004) Er Zhong Min Chu Zi No. 9726. Published on Beijing Court Net.

    <http://bjgy.chinacourt.org/public/detail.php?id=11623&k_title=商业秘密&k_content=商业秘密&k_author=>, 5 January 2008.

In China, criteria considered in determining the confidentiality of information are as follows:

(a) The scope of the public domain:
The right of the public to know certain information is restricted in the course of commerce;
(b) The degree of difficulty in acquiring the information:
A trade secret consists of information that cannot be easily acquired by others because it will endow its holder with an advantage over its competitors. Technical information that can be discovered through reverse engineering or in some other manner, or business information that can be acquired without a certain amount of effort is generally not considered to be confidential information; and
(c) Proper measures.

Secret information is no longer considered secret if its owner is not aware of the secrecy of the information or if the information becomes known to the public as a result of the carelessness of its owner. Therefore, whether the owner is aware of said requirement of secrecy and has actually adopted secrecy measures are important factors for determining the confidentiality of information.[37]

However, there is no specific legal definition of 'public domain' and, because the Chinese legal system is not based on precedent, the determination of the confidentiality of business information has caused a bottleneck in legal practice. Similarly, the vague understanding of confidentiality which currently exists in China is also a principle cause of disputes regarding trade secrets.

III. MANAGEABILITY OF TRADE SECRETS

'Manageability' refers to the secrecy measures adopted by a holder to prevent the disclosure of its confidential business information.[38] Much international legislation, including the TRIPS Agreement and certain other domestic legislation, stipulates that business information is not eligible for legal protection unless its owners adopt proper and reasonable secrecy measures to prevent it from entering into the public domain.[39]

Emphasizing the manageability of trade secrets is meaningful in ascertaining that a holder considers business information to be secret, requiring a holder to maintain the confidentiality of business information and to prevent it from entering the public domain, and is frequently used as an important basis by judges in

37. Liu Aizhen, 'How to Determine the Confidentiality of Trade Secrets' (1999) 8 *People's Justice* (published by the Supreme People's Court), 21 *et seq.*
38. Zhang Yuri, *Science of Law on Trade Secrets* (Beijing, China Legal System Publishing House, 1999), p.168, and Kong Xiangjun, *Principles of the Law on the Protection of Trade Secrets* (Beijing, China Legal System Publishing House,1999), p.49.
39. See Paragraph 2, Article 39 of the *TRIPS Agreement*, < www.wto.org>, 5 January 2008.

relevant cases in deciding whether misappropriation of a trade secret has occurred. If a party does not regard its business information as confidential and does not adopt proper and reasonable measures to protect it, it will be unnecessary for the law to protect it.

In order for it to merit legal protection the manageability of business information is also an important requirement, but it is impossible for a holder to keep it perfectly safe only through the adoption of security measures. The level of the security measures adopted by a holder of a trade secret bears closely on its character and type, the degree of difficulty one has in imitating it, the intrinsic value of the information and the economic strength of its holder. A law can only stipulate these measures in principle but cannot unify nor standardize them. Consequently, when a law stipulates the obligation of confidentiality of a holder of business information, it primarily emphasizes the appropriateness and reasonableness of such confidentiality, (i.e., as long as the measures adopted by a holder for maintaining confidentiality meet the requirements of the specific circumstances, they are deemed reasonable and the information is eligible for legal protection).[40] For example, Article 39 of the TRIPS Agreement requires that secret information is 'subject to reasonable steps under the circumstances by the person lawfully in control of the information to keep it secret'.

Reasonableness is a common element required by legislation of trade secrets and their use in various countries. But what standard of 'reasonableness' does the law require? Many countries use reasonableness as an important basis for determining whether the security measures adopted by holders are sufficient to prevent confidential business information from entering into the public domain.[41] At the same time, relevant law specifically forbids 'misappropriation of trade secrets' and lists 'violations of trade secret law' in order to limit the responsibility of holders, viz. if confidential business information is obtained through illegal means, this does not necessarily mean that its holder has been careless in keeping it confidential.

The United States has a rich judicial history regarding the reasonableness of security measures. In this regard, *Du Pont de Nemours & Co. v. Christopher* is an oft-cited case.[42] In 1970, E.I. du Pont de Nemours & Company, Inc (DuPont) began constructing workshops and installing equipment in preparation for establishing a line for the production of methanol by a new process. At the time, certain production facilities were located in the open air within workshops without roofs. One day, Dupont employees noticed that an airplane was circling over the plant and immediately began an investigation to determine why. Soon afterwards, the investigation disclosed that the aircraft was involved in a photographic expedition and that the Christopher brothers were the photographers. DuPont contacted the

---

40. In the past, some courts of the United States might phrase the requirement more stringently to suggest that secrecy should be protected as far as possible but, at present, whether interested parties have met their duty to secrecy is decided on the basis of the actual circumstances. See Roger M. Milgrim, *Milgrim on Trade Secrets*, (Matthew Bender, New York, 1984), p. 2–37.
41. See V of this Chapter.
42. *Du Pont de nemour & Co, v. Christopher* 431 F. 2d 1012 (1970)

Christophers and asked them to reveal the name of the person or corporation that had commissioned the photographs. The Christophers refused to disclose the information or to turn over the photographs citing their client's desire to remain anonymous. Having reached a dead end in the investigation, DuPont subsequently filed suit against the Christophers alleging that since the area photographed by them included the plant designed to produce methanol by a secret process and because the plant was still under construction and parts of the process were exposed to view from above the construction area, that they had wrongfully obtained photographs revealing DuPont's trade secrets which they then sold to the anonymous third party. Photographs of the area, DuPont alleged, would enable a skilled person to deduce their secret process for making methanol. DuPont thus contended that the Christophers had wrongfully appropriated DuPont trade secrets by taking the photographs and delivering them to an undisclosed third party. The Christophers argued at trial that they committed no 'actionable wrong' in photographing the DuPont facility and passing the photographs on to their client because they conducted all of their activities in public airspace, violated no government aviation standard, did not breach any confidential relationship and did not engage in any fraudulent or illegal conduct. In short, the Christophers argued that for an appropriation of trade secrets to be wrongful there must be a trespass, a breach of a confidential relationship or other illegal conduct. The court ultimately held that:

> Perhaps ordinary fences and roofs must be built to shut out incursive eyes, but we need not require the discoverer of a trade secret to guard against the unanticipated, the undetectable or the unpreventable methods of espionage now available. Reasonable precautions against predatory eyes we may require, but an impenetrable fortress is an unreasonable requirement, and we are not disposed to burden industrial inventors with such a duty in order to protect the fruits of their efforts. 'Improper' will always be a word of many nuances, determined by time, place, and circumstances.

Furthermore, *Syntex Opthalmics Inc. v. Novicky* (1982) established that even if there was fault in implementing security measures which provided an opportunity for others to take advantage, this did not disturb the constitution of an act of infringement of a trade secret. In that case, there was evidence presented proving that the plaintiff did not always adhere to certain recommended security precautions for maintaining confidentiality, such as stamping sensitive documents 'confidential', and that such documents were occasionally left unlocked within the research and development area. The court held that, on the whole, the plaintiff took extensive precautions to protect the integrity of its secrets and that the slackness of the company could not be taken as a legal excuse or reason for the employees to violate their obligation to confidentiality and, thus, decided in favour of the plaintiff.[43]

43. *Syntex Ophthalmics, Inc. et al. v. Novicky et al.* 214 U.S.P.Q. 272. (US).

The Restatement (Third) of the Law against Unfair Competition elaborated on the precautions to be taken in order to maintain the confidentiality of trade secrets. It held that reasonable precautions that should be implemented to maintain confidentiality may take many forms including, among them, physical security designed to prevent unauthorized access, procedures intended to limit disclosure based upon the 'need to know' and measures that emphasize the confidential nature of the information to a recipient such as nondisclosure agreements, labels and restrictive legends.[44]

These cases and the elaboration aforementioned have been cited in many Chinese books and in some academic theses. The Law against Unfair Competition states, with respect to manageability, that a trade secret must be something for which 'its holder takes precautions to maintain its secrecy',[45] The Several Rules on Forbidding the Infringement of Trade Secrets of the State Administration for Industry and Commerce further interprets precautions taken in order to maintain secrecy to include those taken 'to conclude secrecy agreements, to establish security systems and to adopt other reasonable security measures'.[46] Certain local regulations also detail more specific security measures. For example, the Regulations of the Shenzhen Special Economic Zone for the Protection of the Technical Secrets of Enterprises interprets security measures to include enterprises legally owning technical secrets signing confidentiality agreements with their employees and with persons related to their operations who need to know said secrets for business reasons, issuing written rules of confidentiality and making them known specifically to relevant employees and operational personnel and adopting effective control measures with respect to the maintenance, use and transfer of their secrets.[47] The Regulations of Zhuhai City for the Protection of the Technical Secrets of Enterprises also contain stipulations with respect to security measures, including that an enterprise has specified the level of its security and the scope its technical secrets, an enterprise has signed confidentiality agreements with each of its employees who know or might come to know technical secrets of the enterprise as well as with persons related to the enterprise or has issued written rules of confidentiality which are to be signed by relevant employees and persons as evidence of their recognition of said rules and that an enterprise has adopted reasonable and effective controls for the maintenance, use and transfer of its technical secrets.[48]

44. See §39 of the Restatement (Third) of Unfair Competition, 1995, (US), comment g, Precautions to Maintain Secrecy.
45. See Article 10 of the Law against Unfair Competition of the People's Republic of China (1993).
46. See Article 2 of the Several Rules on Forbidding the Infringement of Trade Secrets of the State Administration for Industry and Commerce of the People's Republic of China (1995).
47. See Article 4 of the Regulations of the Shenzhen Special Economic Zone on the Protection of Technical Secrets of Enterprises (1995).
48. See Article 4 of the Regulations of Zhuhai City on the Protection of Technical Secrets of Enterprises (1997).

However, in practice the issue of the reasonableness of security measures is undoubtedly a complicated one, and only on the basis of existing actual circumstances can reasonableness be determined.

IV. SCOPE OF PROTECTION OF TRADE SECRETS

How a particular country's law views trade secrets determines the scope of protection of confidential business information in that country. Furthermore the definition of the scope of protection of trade secrets is integral to the direction of the policies of a country with respect to the protection of intellectual property rights and the national interest. Too broad a scope means less public information. Too narrow a scope is detrimental to the adequate protection of intellectual property rights and will affect the enthusiasm of the public for investing in new technologies, new sciences and other new and developing industries. Consequently, because different countries have different legislative processes the scope of legal protection in a particular country may often vary in different periods of its history. For example, in the United States precedents for the protection of trade secrets in its early history are relatively limited. Existing case law of the time dealt mainly with the protection of technical information as property. A leading case on the issue was *Salomon v. Hertz et al* (1886). The facts of the case are that Hertz was an employee of Salomon. After leaving his employment, Hertz disclosed to a third party the trade secrets of Salomon regarding the manufacture of leather. The court of first instance granted an injunction on behalf of Salomon restraining Hertz from disclosing, and rival manufacturers from using, said secrets. The court also prohibited Hertz and others from making known to anyone from where or from whom Salomon purchased its materials, to whom it sold its goods and the price at which the goods were bought and sold. On appeal, the Appeals Court of the State of New Jersey enjoined Hertz from disclosing confidential technical information but did not restrain Hertz from disclosing business information which included where Salomon bought its raw materials and to whom it sold its manufactured goods.[49] In 1905, however, the Supreme Court of the United States, in *Chicago Board of Trade of the City of Chicago v. Christe Grain and Stock Co.* included business secrets within the scope of legal protection. The case involved the continuous quotation of prices on the sale of grains and other commodities for future delivery. The plaintiff collected prices and other relevant business information regarding the sale of various grains. The defendant, a company that obtained said quotations through improper means and illegally transferred them for profit, was sanctioned by injunction of the Court.[50] This was the first instance in the history of American jurisprudence wherein a court held that confidential business information was entitled to legal protection.

49. *Salomon v. Hertz et al.* 40 N. J. Eq. 400, 2 A. 379 (1886).
50. *Chicago Board of Trade v. Christe Grain and Stock Co.*198 U.S. 236 (1905).

The Restatement (First) of the Law of Torts issued by the American Law Institute contained the scope of protection of trade secrets. The First Restatement listed subject matter that was entitled to the protection of trade secret law but placed emphasis on the 'use' of trade secrets, limiting the scope of their legal protection.[51] In the United States in 1985, the Uniform Trade Secrets Act classified subject matter that was entitled to trade secret protection based on its characteristics and scope of content. The Uniform Trade Secrets Act concluded that information is deemed a trade secret and legally protected if it is confidential, novel or valuable and if its holder takes measures to maintain its secrecy. The Uniform Trade Secrets Act abandoned the requirement of 'continuous use' and extended the protective scope of trade secret law to include business information which had not yet been used for lack of opportunity and business information that had been acquired through the course of long-term and expensive research and testing but for which no useful application had yet been found. In 1996, the American Law Institute published the Restatement (Third) of Unfair Competition, which summarized the judicial practices of the American courts over the course of many years and used for reference the research results of academics. The Third Restatement incorporated the provisions of the Uniform Trade Secrets Act and even included a section titled 'The Definition of a Trade Secret', which contained a comprehensive explanation of the scope of protection of trade secrets. In the comments contained in the Third Restatement, trade secrets were divided into two major categories – technical secrets and operating secrets – and the status of business secrets within the context of trade secret law was specifically mentioned.[52] Also in 1996, the first federal trade secret law of the United States, the Economic Espionage Act, included all forms and types of financial, business, scientific, technical, economic or engineering information that is confidential, valuable and manageable within the scope of trade secrets. It can be seen then that the protection of confidential intellectual property in the United States has evolved from the initial protection of technical secrets with obvious characteristics of property to the protection of business secrets with not so obvious characteristics of property. Thus, it can be said that the scope of protection in the United States has become broader over time.

Similar to that in the United States, legislation and practice in many other countries in recent years indicate that the protective scope of trade secret law is becoming gradually broader, and a great deal of previously unprotected subject matter is increasingly being included within the scope of legal protection. These include: secret information with a very short life span, secret information that is scattered and non-systematic, and secret information that is negative. The TRIPS Agreement broadly defines 'protective scope' to include undisclosed information. Thus, generally, any information that is related to production or operations can be deemed a trade secret as long as it contains the elements of a trade secret.

In China, too, the scope of trade secret protection is constantly being broadened. The Law against Unfair Competition, contained the first legislative

---

51. See §757 of *Restatement (First) of Torts*, 1939, (US), comment b.
52. See §39 of Restatement (Third) of Unfair Competition, 1995, (US), comment d, Subject Matter.

definition of trade secrets, stipulating in section 10.3 that the term 'trade secrets' as contained in the law refers to technical or operating information which is not generally known, which can bring economic benefit to its holder, which is practical and for which its holder has taken precautions to maintain its secrecy'. Pursuant to section 10.3 and according to the function of confidential information, trade secrets can be divided into technical information and business information. These two main categories basically cover the spectrum of trade secrets. The Several Rules on Forbidding the Infringement of Trade Secrets contains additional remarks on the scope of trade secret protection, specifying that:

> Technical information and business information include designs, programs, formulas of products, processes, managerial skills, lists of customers, information regarding suppliers of goods, production and marketing strategies, base amount of a tender in public bidding, content of bid documents and other information.[53]

The Advices on Strengthening the Protection of Trade Secrets of State-owned Enterprises of the State Economic and Trade Commission of the People's Republic of China promulgated in 1997 holds that:

> The term 'trade secret' refers primarily to processes, skills, technologies, ingredients and formulas, data, programs, designs, lists of customers, information on suppliers of goods, bidding documents and other technical and operating information.[54]

In addition, the Several Opinions on Strengthening the Management of Technical Secrets in the Flow of Scientific and Technical Staff, also promulgated in 1997 by the State Science and Technology Commission of the People's Republic of China, specifies that:

> Technical secrets owned by an enterprise include, but are not limited to, design papers (including draft drawings), experimental results and records, technologies, ingredients and formulas, samples, data and computer programs.

The Several Opinions also state that:

> Technical information can consist of original engineering plans for industrial products, technology, and materials with specific integrated technical content, as well as of the revisions of said engineering plans and technical elements of a particular product or technological material.[55]

53. See Article 2 of the Several Rules on Forbidding the Infringement of Trade Secrets of the State Administration for Industry and Commerce of the People's Republic of China (1995).
54. See Article 1 of the Advice on Strengthening the Protection of Trade Secrets of State-owned *Enterprises* of the State Economic and Trade Commission of the People's Republic of China (1997).
55. See Article 2 of the Several Opinions on Strengthening the Management of Technical Secrets in the Flow of Scientific and Technical Staff of the State Science and Technology Commission of the People's Republic of China (1997).

At the same time, certain economic development zones in China, in accordance with state legislation, have promulgated their own local regulations containing stipulations on the scope of the protection of trade secrets. For example, the 1995 Regulations of the Shenzhen Special Economic Zone for the Protection of Technical Secrets of Enterprises state that:

> The technologies and technical information referred to in these regulations include designs, technologies, data, ingredients and formulas, know-how and other information in physical, chemical, or biological form.[56]

The 1997 Regulations of Zhuhai City for the Protection of Technical Secrets of Enterprises, state that the term 'technical secrets' refers to non-patented technologies and technical information including designs, technologies, data, ingredients and formulas, know-how and other information in physical, chemical or biological form.[57] The Law against Unfair Competition, however, emphasizes that trade secrets, in order to merit legal protection, should have the element of 'practicality' thus limiting the protective scope of Chinese trade secret law.

V. BRIEF SUMMARY

Each element of a trade secret is different from, yet connected to, the other. Business information that is not confidential is not valuable, and business information that is both valuable and confidential is undisputedly manageable. The precautions taken to maintain the secrecy of information can be considered evidence of its value and confidential nature.[58] However, subject matter that is protected by trade secret law includes information that is intangible, diverse and changeable, presenting challenges to international legislation regarding protection of trade secrets. Likewise, certain well-known academics in China hold that it is very difficult to formulate a legal definition of trade secrets. The law can provide rules and guidance in principle but only practice can enhance the impact of trade secret law and promote its development.

56. See Article 5 of the Regulations of the Shenzhen Special Economic Zone on the Protection of Technical Secrets of Enterprises (1995).
57. See Article 3 of the Regulations of Zhuhai City on the Protection of Technical Secrets of Enterprises, (1997).
58. See §39 of the Restatement (Third) of Unfair Competition, 1995, (US), comment g.

Chapter 3
Differences between Trade Secrets and Traditional IPR

A comparison of trade secrets and traditional intellectual property rights (e.g., trademark rights, patent rights and copyrights) is required in order to grasp precisely the legal characteristics of trade secrets and will aid in the improvement of the existing system of legal protection. Consequently, Chinese law school academics have focused their efforts on research of this type.

I. TRADE SECRETS AND PATENTS

Chinese legal circles, over a long period of judicial practice, have reached a consensus on the relationship between trade secret law and patent law. Both protect technical information, but trade secrets and patents are very different:

(a) A patent is an exclusive right conferred on a patentee for a reasonable period of time in return for said patentee making publicly available to society the knowledge on which an invention is based. This is the manner in which patent rights protect inventions. A trade secret is protected by means of secrecy of a holder's own accord for the purpose of preventing others from acquiring it through misappropriation, thereby ensuring his competitive advantage;

(b) Trade secrets and patents must meet different requirements as to their degree of novelty and creativeness. A patent is subject to a special requirement regarding its novelty, creativeness and practicality, but novelty and creativeness, to a certain extent, are sufficient in order for technical information and business information to be considered trade secrets. Moreover, while a patent must be published, a trade secret requires only confidentiality.

(c) Once having acquired a patent right, a patentee enjoys that right exclusively. A patentee can use or assign a patent and retains the right to prevent others from developing, forging, or using that patent for the legal duration of the patent. This is not the case with trade secrets. The owner of a trade secret can preserve its permanent right of exclusivity to that trade secret so long as confidentiality is maintained. However, once the trade secret is disclosed, that exclusivity will be lost. In addition, the owner of a trade secret may not prevent others from acquiring that trade secret by legitimate means such as through independent development or reverse engineering.

(d) It is necessary for a patentee to complete administrative registration procedures which are relatively complicated before acquiring a patent right. The scope of a patent right is relatively specific, so it is easy for a patentee to produce evidence of its ownership during litigation. By contrast, a trade secret does not need to be registered in order to be protected by law but relies on the owner taking proper measures to maintain its secrecy.[1]

II. TRADE SECRETS AND TRADEMARKS

Certain Chinese academics are of the opinion that trade secret rights and trademark rights are similar in that they are both designed to protect intellectual property, but there are still obvious differences between the types of property to which they apply and between the procedures necessary for gaining those rights:

(a) The manner in which they were originally acquired:
Trademark registration is essential for the acquisition of a trademark right and involves attribution of the trademark right. This form of administrative authorization procedure is not necessary to the constitution of trade secret rights, which will automatically come into being so long as the technical or business information meets the legal definition of a trade secret.

(b) A trademark is a symbol used to protect goods and to differentiate the source of those goods, namely written language or images or a combination of written language and images. Thus, the scope of protection for trademark rights is limited. A trade secret right protects technical and business information and its protective scope is quite broad.

(c) A trademark right is an exclusive right limited by time and region, and provides an exclusive right to use within the period and scope specified by law. Regarding trade secrets, however, it is possible for those rights not to be limited by time and region so long as the owner adopts proper security measures. The exclusivity of a trade secret right is relative. Any other party that acquires the same or similar trade secret through legal means can become a legitimate holder of that trade secret. Therefore, a single trade secret can have multiple rights holders simultaneously.

---

1. Kong Xiangjun, *Principles of the Law on the Protection of Trade Secrets* (Beijing, China Legal System Publishing House, 1999), pp.23–24.

Table 1. Comparison of Trade Secrets and Patents in the Protection of Technology

Aspects for Comparison	**Is it required that the technology be made publicly available?**	**Requirement for the level of creativity and novelty**	**Cost of protection**	**Duration of protection**	**Possibility of forfeiture of protection**	**Date of commencement of protection**	**Is it exclusive?**
Patent	Yes	Very high	High	20 years	Low	Date of application	Yes
Trade secret	No	Unspecified	Low	Possibly longer	Relatively high	Date of Innovation	No
Aspects for Comparison	**Attorney fees**	**Is it protected under criminal law?**	**Procedure**	**Licensing**	**International protection**	**Is there a risk?**	**Scope of subjects**
Patent	High	Yes	Application, examination, and declaring	Longer	Determined by international convention or bilateral agreement	No	Narrow
Trade secret	High	Yes	Agreement or other measures	Longer	Determined by international convention or bilateral agreement	Yes	Wide

Source: ***High and New Technologies and the Law regarding Intellectual Property*****, Author Chen Chuanfu, published by the Publishing House of Wuhan University, (2000 edition) page 254.**

(d) The conditions under which the two rights are protected are different:
A trade secret, due to the nature of its confidentiality, is information that is not publicly available. The exclusivity established through secrecy is critical for the creation of the value of information. Once the information is disclosed or is known in the public domain, it breaches the legal requirement for it to be considered a trade secret. The function of a trademark is to indicate the source of a commodity or a service. Visibility is a basic condition for the acquisition of a trademark right. Therefore, the confidentiality of a trade secret and the visibility of a trademark are important differences between the conditions under which they merit protection.

(e) The durability of the two rights is different.

Generally, once a trademark right is established through registration and a holder has the intent to maintain that right, its existence is not easily shaken. Consequently, the mode for protecting confidential information must be chosen carefully because trade secret exclusivity is established through the maintenance of confidentiality and once confidentiality is destroyed that right will be lost.[2]

Table 2. Main Differences between Trade Secrets and Traditional Intellectual Property Rights[3]

	Patent Right	Copyright	Trademark Right	Trade Secret Right
Subject of Civil Rights	Single	Single	Single	Possibly many
Protected Subject Matter	Inventions and creations	Writing	Trademarks	Technical and managerial information
Scope	Narrow	Narrow	Narrow	Broad
Term	twenty years	Author's natural life plus fifty years	Possibly limitless	Possibly limitless
Exclusivity	Yes	Yes (for independent creations)	Yes	No
Registration required	Yes	No	Yes	No

2. Lu Heyun, *A Talk about Laws on Trade Secrets* (Bao Din, Hubei People's Publishing House, 2000), pp.118–119.
3. *Ibid.* at p.119.

III. TRADE SECRETS AND COPYRIGHTS

Trade secrets and copyrighted material are products of the human spirit, and so it is possible that a creation arising from one's intellectual activities may enjoy the right of copyright owing to its originality as well as the right to be protected by trade secret law due to the nature of its secrecy. There remain, however, differences between them:

(a) The subject matter of the two rights is different. The subject matter of a copyright can include literary, musical, dramatic and artistic works, as well as computer programs, maps and technical drawings.[4] Subject matter of trade secrets, however, consists of technical, business and other information that afford its owner a competitive advantage in the marketplace.
(b) Copyright protects only expressions of ideas, not the ideas themselves.
    Trade secret rights, on the other hand, can prevent unauthorized use of a new concept that is considered legally protected information.
(c) 'Originality' is one of the most basic requirements for copyright, while the basic requirements for trade secrets are 'confidentiality, value and secrecy.
(d) The valid term for protection of copyrights and trade secrets is different as well. In China, copyright protection lasts, as a general rule, for the life of the creator plus fifty years while there is no fixed term for trade secret protection, which exists as long as confidentiality is maintained.[5]

---

4. Tao Ran and Jun Hua, Questions and Answers on Practical Affairs about the Copyright Law of the People's Republic of China (Beijing, Law Press, Beijing, 2002). p.154.
5. Zhang Naigen and Lu Fei (eds.), *Intellectual Economy and the Intellectual Property Law* (Shanghai, Publishing House of Fudan University,) (2000), at pp.308–309.

Part III
Remedies for Infringement

Chapter 1
The Theoretical Foundations for a System of Legal Protection in China

According to the definition of 'legal remedy' in the *Oxford Companion to American Law*, a remedy is 'a correction, rectification or redress for unreasonable conduct having already occurred or having already caused injury, harm, loss or damage'.[1] In the opinion of its authors, parties are legally endowed with two categories of rights and entrusted with two categories of obligations. An example of the first category is the right to receive delivery of purchased goods or to receive payment for goods sold. An example of the second category is the right to enforce delivery of goods by another or to enforce payment of compensation for the non-delivery of goods by another. Likewise, this includes the right to enforce payment for goods by another or to enforce compensation for the refusal to accept or take goods by another. The remedial rights included in the second category cannot become effective unless the first category of rights is not met. The term 'legal right' refers to the right to impel another to perform their obligations or to seek remedy for the non-performance or improper performance of those obligations. Accordingly, a remedy is sought by one party against another for redressing or mitigating consequences caused by non-performance of another's obligations.[2]

With the appearance of the trade secret protection system, corresponding legal protective mechanisms have been gradually formulated and developed in various countries for protecting the basic rights and interests of trade secret holders. However, legal protective measures which have been adopted differ from one

1. David Walker, *The Oxford Companion to American Law* (Beijing, Law Press, 2003), p.958. Also, a 'remedy' is 'the means by which a right is enforced or the violation of a right is prevented, redressed or compensated'. See Bryan A. Garner (ed.) *Black's Law Dictionary* (US, West Publishing Co., 2004), p.1320.
2. David M.Walker, *The Oxford Companion to American Law* (Beijing, Law Press, 2003), p.958. Originally published in English by Oxford University Press in 1980.

country to another. Some countries place emphasis on civil remedy while others have established criminal and administrative penalties for infringement of trade secrets. This is due to differences among the legal systems of different countries, and is also a result of different understandings of the nature of trade secrets and the application of different theories of trade secret protection.

Many academics and judges in China have formulated various theories for regulating relationships involving trade secrets with respect to the formation and development of trade secret protection regimes. These include, among others, theories based on the Contract Law, the Law against Unfair Competition, and civil law as well as tort law regarding illegal gains and confidential relationships. All of these theories seek to elaborate on the justification for and effectiveness of trade secret protection from different research perspectives. They expound on the nature of trade secrets and the jurisprudential basis on which different countries form their regimes for trade secret protection. These theories portray an awareness of the nature of trade secrets and reflect changes in the social and economic status of trade secrets. The genesis of theory and the application of precedent are driven by certain policy and interest considerations.

Without doubt, these current theories have served as significant driving forces in the establishment and improvement of contemporary trade secret protection regimes. Among these theories, property right theory and confidential relations theory most accurately reflect the nature of trade secrets and have exerted the greatest influence on the formation of trade secret regimes. Upon entering the Information Age, these two theories have been much favoured by Western countries and are well recognized by academics for their role in promoting the validity and effectiveness of the operation of trade secret protection regimes, making them the main theories for regulating relationships involving trade secrets.

It is a characteristic of Chinese jurisprudence to place emphasis on theoretical analysis in the areas of trade secret protection. Chinese legal academics have been puzzled by the question of what should be the theoretical foundation for regulating relationships involving trade secrets. Nevertheless, following a period of long and careful study of Western judicial practice, those within Chinese legal circles have reached a consensus on the formation and development of the underlying theories of trade secret protection. Therefore, the author feels it is necessary here to address the opinions of academicians in this aspect before introducing the legal protection system in China.

I. SEEKING PROTECTION UNDER CONTRACT AND TORT LAW

It was not until early in the nineteenth century that the value of trade secrets became evident. As companies were predominantly family operated prior to the nineteenth century, trade secrets were naturally protected because they were shared only among family members. Consequently, disclosure of family-held trade secrets was prevented through the use of only minimal safeguards. In earlier times, the relationship of employer and employee was that of master and apprentice. The master was responsible for training and mentoring the apprentice who, as repayment, worked for the former without pay and maintained the confidentiality of all trade secrets obtained during the apprenticeship. For the sake of regulating the relationship between master and apprentice and to balance the rights and obligations between them, the then-relevant law organized apprenticeships in such a manner as to ensure that an employer was able to recover the cost of training employees. However, those laws did not limit the occupational choices of dismissed employees who were able to use their acquired skills elsewhere. For example, The Statute of Apprentice enacted in England in 1562 limited the term of apprenticeship to a maximum of seven years in order not only to guarantee the interests of employers but also to prevent employers from exploiting employees and to ensure that workers received greater benefit through market competition by finding new employment or by creating their own enterprises.[3] Toward the end of the eighteenth century, however, the master-apprentice system began to change in some Western countries.

At the end of the eighteenth century and into the beginning of the nineteenth century, the Industrial Revolution began in England and soon spread to other Western countries. Regarded as one of the three most significant developments in human history, the Industrial Revolution influenced all societies, including their economics, their politics and their social systems. The extensive mechanization of production systems through industrialization resulted in a shift from home-based manufacturing by hand to the large-scale production carried on by factories. As a result, capital was accumulated mainly by business enterprises. In the post-modern economy following the Industrial Revolution, the management of production played a dominant role in the activities of various economic organizations and the development of scientific technology became a mechanism for sustained technical and organizational creativity.[4]

It was inevitable that the Industrial Revolution would change employment relationships as it changed all other social relationships.

First of all, from the viewpoint of employers, the expansion of the scale of business and the development of scientific technology posed a challenge to family-style operations and management. In order to realize maximum economic benefit, an enterprise needed more technically trained workers and required the assistance of professionals who could participate in its operation and management.

Secondly, from the viewpoint of employees, with the popularization and expansion of the educational system more ordinary citizens were given the opportunity to become educated and to be hired by an enterprise based on their professional knowledge. Within these enterprises, the status and function of educated employees was different from that of the apprentice. For one thing, they were more independent.

---

3. See Restatement (Third) of Unfair Competition, 1995, (US) §42, comment d.
4. *The Concise Encyclopaedia Britannica* (Beijing, Chinese Great Encyclopaedia Publishing House, 1985), p.417.

Thirdly, economic development relied on scientific technology which intensified competition in the marketplace. Consequently, in addition to focusing on the acquisition of material resources, more attention was paid to technological innovation and achievement as well as to skilled workers who had a grasp of new technologies. Thus, a more intensely competitive labour market was born. These developments expedited the creation of the modern system for the protection of trade secrets.

Early trade secret disputes were mainly caused by two types of activities: employees obtaining benefit through disclosure to a third party or through using technical secrets such as ingredients or elements of production or design drawings developed by their employers; and third parties gaining advantage over market competition by inducing employees of competing enterprises to disclose technical secrets such as elements of production or of design drawings developed by their employers. When settling disputes arising from these two kinds of actions, the courts, in early judicial practice, for the most part invoked traditional principles of law.[5]

At that time, the settlement by the courts of disputes caused by the disclosure or use of trade secrets by employees was based on employment contracts and by invoking principles of contract law. In their employment contracts, employers generally included confidentiality agreements and stipulations on the use and disclosure of their trade secrets. The stipulations contained in these types of contracts were used as the basis for the courts to decide whether an employee had undertaken an obligation of confidentiality. Once an employee had violated a confidentiality agreement, he became liable for breach of contract. In addition to the explicit agreements contained in employment contracts, the courts in certain countries held that employees undertook an obligation of confidentiality to their employers in accordance with the principle of implied contracts. If an employer could prove that implied consent of the parties on both sides existed, it could be presumed that an agreement restricting the use of trade secrets existed between the parties. Therefore, even in the absence of an express contract, or even given the existence of a disputed express contract, the owner of a trade secret could seek legal remedy based on implied contract.

Regarding actions of third parties who induce employees to disclose the trade secrets of their employers, employers could, in accordance with the 'enticement doctrine' of tort law, bring an action for damages against a party who interfered with the performance of the contractual obligations of their employees.[6]

However, whether based on express or implied contracts, implied consent between employees and their employers was considered the foundation of the obligation of employee confidentiality. The enticement doctrine was applied on the basis that a third party had interfered with the performance of an employee's contractual obligations. Very obviously, in early judicial practice, attention was

5. Robert G. Bone, 'A New Look at Trade Secret Law: Doctrine in Search of Justification' (1998) 86 *California Law Review*, 255.
6. See *Restatement (Second) of Torts*, 1979, (US), §766, comment C.

paid to the wrongful actions of parties and focus was not on the protection of the trade secret itself. This was due to the fact that, at the time, there was a limited understanding of infringing activities and of trade secrets themselves. It was considered that the issue of trade secret protection was based mainly on good faith and on the moral value of work. It was also held that the purpose of the legal protection of trade secrets was the maintenance of contractual relationships and professional ethics.[7]

With the continuing advancement of industrialization however, the importance of knowledge to economic development was enhanced. At the same time, with the increased popularity of education, knowledgeable employees increased in number. Their independence and legally protected employment rights posed a challenge to the traditional system of trade secret protection. With the steadily increasing number of trade secret disputes, the traditional legal system was becoming less effective in resolving issues arising from those disputes. Confusion created the following types of problems:

(a) Whether employers should be able to prevent their former employees from using or disclosing trade secrets they obtained during their tenure of employment.
(b) Whether employees should continue to be obligated to confidentiality by their former employers following termination of their contractual relationship.
(c) Whether third parties should be restrained from acquiring trade secrets from dismissed employees.
(d) Whether a party should be allowed to use trade secrets obtained from the public domain such as through newspapers or magazines.
(e) Whether a party should permitted to use or disclose trade secrets obtained during negotiations regarding commercial transactions.
(f) Whether a party should be permitted to use or to disclose trade secrets obtained through reverse engineering.

In the pursuit of resolution of the abovementioned issues, the purpose of trade secret protection and the nature of trade secrets were reconsidered. Theories regarding confidential relationships and property rights vis-à-vis trade secret protection were advanced, laying the theoretical foundation for the establishment of the modern system for trade secret protection.

II. FOCUSING ON THE CONFIDENTIAL RELATIONSHIP

In the history of development of the trade secret protection system, it can be concluded that one of the purposes of trade secret protection was to encourage

7. Catherine L. Fisk, 'Working Knowledge: Trade Secrets, Restrictive Covenants in Employment and the Rise of Corporate Intellectual Property, 1800–1920' (2001) 51 *Hastings Law Journal*, 447.

loyalty and good faith as well as professional ethics.[8] One important reason for this was that, in general, trade secret disputes occurred between two interested parties who enjoyed a special relationship. For example, a trade secret dispute might occur between an employer and employee, between an agent and principal, or between two interested parties to a commercial transaction. Though a third party might have no special relationship with the interested parties, they often obtained the trade secrets of another party through the aforementioned interested parties. Among these parties, the principles of loyalty and good faith were the basis of their normal relationships, and these principles have become an important basis of the law regulating confidentiality obligations of interested parties between themselves.

According to the principles of loyalty and good faith, agents, employees and other recipients of trade secrets must be honest in their purpose, show faithfulness to their duty and obligations, observe reasonable commercial standards of fair dealing in a given trade or business and must have no intent to defraud or to seek unconscionable advantage.[9] In 1895, the British courts heard the case of *Robb v. Green* in which the defendant Green had held the post of manager in the company of the plaintiff Robb. During his work there, Green made private copies of customer lists. When he left the company, he set up his own business and used the lists obtained from the company in the conduct of that business. Consequently, the plaintiff filed an action with the court requesting that the defendant be restrained from using the lists and be ordered to pay compensation for losses incurred by the plaintiff. The court of appeals pointed out in its decision that:

> Because it is a thing which must necessarily have been in view of both parties when they entered into the contract, it is impossible to suppose that a master would have put a servant into a confidential position of this kind, unless he thought that the servant would be bound to use good faith towards him or that the servant would not know, when he entered into that position, that the master would rely on his observance of good faith in the confidential relationship between them.[10]

Very obviously, the appeals court thought that loyalty and good faith were the foundation of the employment relationship between parties. So it can be said that *Robb v. Green*, and similarly *Lamb v. Evans*,[11] began the practice in British law of regulating the confidentiality obligations of parties in accordance with the principles of loyalty and good faith.[12]

Similarly, in modern times in the United States, the Restatement (Second) of Agency holds that agents must undertake an obligation of loyalty to their principals

---

8. John Hull, *Commercial Secrecy: Law and Practice* (London, Sweet & Maxwell, 1998), p.2.
9. Bryan A. Garner (ed.), *Black's Law Dictionary* (US, West Publishing Co., 1999), p.701.
10. *Robb v. Green* [1895] 2 Q.B. per Lord Esher MR, p.317. Quoted from John Hull, *Commercial Secrecy: Law and Practice* (London, Sweet & Maxwell, 1998), p.191.
11. *Lamb v. Evans* [1893] 1 Ch. (Eng.) 218.
12. John Hull, *Commercial Secrecy: Law and Practice* (London, Sweet & Maxwell, London,1998), p.190.

and that the former are obliged to act in the interest of and to protect the rights of the latter. According to the Second Restatement, legal liability is incurred if an agent breaches its obligation of loyalty and works for its own interests.[13] One of the specific consequences of the obligation of loyalty is that agents have a responsibility not to use or disclose the confidential information of their clients and that legal liability incurs if they do so without authorization.[14]

A great number of academics have for a long time paid much attention to these special relationships while researching theories for the protection of trade secrets. Many hold the opinion that the obligations of loyalty and good faith contained in the law of equity are the basis for determining if an employee has an obligation to maintain the confidentiality of the trade secrets of his employer in the absence of a confidentiality agreement in their employment contract or when there is no cause to presume the existence of an implied contract.[15] However, there are two different theories regarding the nature of legally regulated confidentiality obligations. Some scholars believe that confidentiality is an implied or presumed contractual obligation constituted in law. This is the 'quasi-contract' theory. According to this theory, it is legally presumed that an employment relationship, or any another confidential relationship that involves trade secrets, contains an implied promise of good faith by and between the parties. Thus the law in many countries, for example the United States, imposes an obligation of loyalty upon parties entering into employment or confidential relationships with trade secret holders and affirms that this obligation of loyalty continues to exist even after said employment relationship or other confidential relationship has ended. The difference between a quasi-contract and an implied contract in fact is that in a quasi-contract the parties need not prove implied consent and may presume the existence of a contractual relationship between parties based on objective phenomena. The quasi-contract theory provides a theoretical basis for the court to presume an obligation of confidentiality of a party while also providing a legal basis for a party to seek remedy under contract law.

Other academics are of the opinion that an obligation of confidentiality of a party is an operation of law arising from the confidential relationship between the interested parties.[16] This form of confidential relationship can be established based on a contract between parties. Where there is no express contract or implied contract in fact, special relationships such as employment and agency relationships, established based on good faith, become an important element for the court to construct an obligation of confidentiality. This is known the theory of confidential

13. See Restatement (Second) of Agency, 1958, (US) §403, 404, 407.
14. *Ibid.* See §395.
15. John Hull, *Commercial Secrecy: Law and Practice* (London, Sweet & Maxwell, 1998), p.105.
16. In the majority of decisions, in the absence of express contracts American courts tend to support the concept of 'confidential relationship'. See Roger M. Milgrim, *Milgrim on Trade Secrets* (Matthew Bender, New York) (1984), at p.4-02. In addition, in British judicial practice, judges do not pay attention to the attributes of the information itself but to the relationship between the interested parties (consensual link) See Paul Torremans and John Holyoak, *Intellectual Property Law* (London, Butterworth, 2001), Chapter 28.

relationship. According to this theory, a party breaching an implied promise or an obligation to warrant secrecy bears tortious liability and an injured party may be entitled to relief in accordance with tort law. In 1939, the American Law Institute pointed out in the Restatement (First) of Torts, that a person who discloses or uses the trade secrets of another without permission to do so is liable to the other if their disclosure or use of said trade secrets constitutes a breach of confidence reposed in him by the other in disclosing the secret to him.[17]

The difference between quasi-contract theory and confidential relationship theory lies in the nature of the legal liability of parties. The former includes liability for breach of contract, and the latter, tortious liability. Thus, the differences between the two theories extend to include the limitation of actions, legal procedure and especially extent of compensation. However, the two theories are similar in that the obligation of confidentiality undertaken by a party is an operation of law and thus a legal obligation as well. Nevertheless, express or implied promises between parties relating to trade secret protection supersede the obligation of confidentiality which exists as an operation of law.[18] Roger M. Milgrim notes in his work that:

> The overlapping of the characterization of a relationship as 'confidential' and the characterization of the duty neither to use nor to disclose trade secrets as 'implied' has led to decisions in which relief is transported by a Centaurian-like creature, half confidential relationship, half implied contract.[19]

What then is the purpose of the law in creating this form of obligation? What nature of rights will be protected? Most Western academics hold that the protection of trade secrets by operation of law began in the middle of the nineteenth century.[20] As mentioned previously, more trade secret disputes in which the defendants were mostly former employees or commercial partners of the plaintiffs occurred during that period of time. Most often, when disputes occurred, there was no express contractual relationship or implied contract in fact between a defendant and a plaintiff. However, there usually existed a special relationship between them, and it was based on this relationship that a defendant was able to obtain the trade secrets developed by the plaintiff. Therefore, at that time, safeguarding good faith and professional ethics became an important purpose of the law for determining the obligation of confidentiality of parties.

In conclusion, it can be said that both quasi-contract theory and confidential relationship theory are used to determine the obligation of confidentiality based on

---

17. See Restatement (First) of Torts, 1939, (US) §757.
18. Roger M. Milgrim, *Milgrim on Trade Secrets* (NY, Matthew Bender, 1984), pp.4-1.
19. *Ibid.*
20. Many famous cases generally recognized as the earliest appliers of the quasi-contract principle for determining the secrecy obligation of an interested party occurred during the period from the middle of the nineteenth century to the beginning of the twentieth century. For example, *Merryweather v. Moore* (1892) and *Robb v. Green* (1895) heard by the British Court; *Cincinnati Bell Foundry Co. v. Dodds*, (1887), *Eastman Co. v. Reichenbach* (1892), *E. I. Du pontde Nemours powder Co. v. Masland* (1917), and the like heard by the American Courts.

the special relationship of trust between parties and the nature of their actions and that these two theories are extensions of the traditional theory of tort, bringing with them the traditional limitations of tort theory. For example, according to these theories, property right-related disputes occurring during the transfer of trade secrets cannot be resolved. In addition, the constitution of a tort is based on the occurrence of harmful consequences. Thus, because in practice once technical secrets are leaked or divulged they cannot be recovered, a trade secret holder should urgently seek effective relief upon perceiving a threat to its trade secrets in order to protect the value of those trade secrets. Injunctive relief is one such effective means provided in rem.

III. REMEDIES FOUND IN PROPERTY LAW

The protection of trade secrets by operation of law was established during a period when it was acknowledged that trade secrets were a form of property.

Peabody v. Norfolk (1868) is generally acknowledged to be the most well-known case among early trade secret dispute cases in the United States. In that case, Francis Peabody, the plaintiff, invented a new process and equipment with which raw material for gunnysack production could be extracted from jute. He subsequently built a factory and hired Norfolk, the defendant, as his machinist. In order to protect his trade secrets, Peabody signed a confidentiality agreement with the defendant stipulating that the latter was not allowed to use or to disclose the secret process. Before long, the defendant terminated his employment relationship with the plaintiff, joined the company of James Cook, the third party to the case, and used the secret process of the plaintiff. Peabody, relying on the principles of contract law and the traditional law of tort, filed a petition with the court requesting that the court issue an injunction prohibiting the new factory from using the process he had invented. However, the plaintiff and the third party advanced the point of view, firstly, that the agreement between Norfolk and Peabody constituted constraint of trade, secondly, that as the plaintiff's factory was so large, no information was secret and, thirdly, that there was no confidentiality agreement between James Cook, the third party, and the plaintiff. In addition, Norfolk had joined the company of the third party voluntarily, so the third party should not bear legal liability.[21] Very obviously, the problems reflected in these viewpoints cannot be explained in the context of traditional legal theories. However, the court held that an employer had a right to the trade secrets developed by it stating:

> It is the policy of the law, for the benefit of the public, to encourage and to protect invention and commercial enterprise. If a man establishes a business and makes it valuable by his skill and attention, the good will of that business is recognized by the law as property.[22]

---

21. *Peabody v. Norfolk* (1868) 98 Mass 455.
22. *Ibid.* See p.457.

The court concluded that, whether a proper subject for a patent or not, if one invented or discovered and kept secret a process of manufacture, that he did not have an exclusive right to it against the public interest, or against the interests of those who in good faith might acquire knowledge of it, but that it was his property, which the law would protect against one, who in violation of contract and through breach of confidence, undertook to apply it to his own use or to disclose it to third persons.[23]

Very obviously, the court's point of view in the Peabody case countered the position taken by the defendants. Holding secret information to be property meant that the unauthorized use of the confidential information of others was an illegal act, so that even a third party who had no contractual relationship with the holder was not permitted to abuse the confidential information of others. In addition, this provided a theoretical foundation of law based on equity for a court to grant injunctive relief when necessary to provide an adequate and complete remedy to protect property rights under risk of violation.

With trade secret protection now anchored in property law, the owner of an enterprise became the right-holder of his trade secrets and was entitled to the protection bestowed on him by law, just like a patent inventor, a trademark owner or a copyright owner. This right is imbued with all the powers and functions of possessing, using, profiting from and disposing of property. When a trade secret is infringed, the right-holder of a trade secret may, in accordance with tort law, take action against the infringing party for remedy. The holder may also, in accordance with contract law, investigate and fix liability for breach of contract by illegal users or disclosers. A government prosecutor may even, in accordance with criminal law, impose criminal punishment upon on those who steal trade secrets in order to deter the intent to infringe on trade secrets and to protect the legal interests of trade secret owners.

The acknowledgement of the nature of trade secrets as property was an important development in the understanding of trade secrets and indicated by the end of the nineteenth century and the beginning of the twentieth century that the status of trade secrets in economic activities was becoming increasingly enhanced, and that trade secrets were an impetus for the economic development of Western countries. It also indicated that the economic value of trade secrets was gaining social recognition and it was acknowledged that trade secrets, like other intangible property, were assets that deserved to be protected by law. Furthermore it brought the recognition that trade secrets were commercial and transferable and the effort invested by an enterprise owner to acquire trade secrets was recognized by society. More importantly, with the deepening understanding of the nature of trade secrets, the trade secret protection policies of various countries began to change. Safeguarding business ethics was no longer the main focus of lawmakers but rather research and innovation that would propel the development of the trade secret business were encouraged.[24]

---

23. *Ibid.* See p.452.
24. Jay Dratler, Jr, and Danielle Conway-Jones, *Intellectual Property Law: Commercial Creative and Industrial Property* (NY, Law Publishing Company, 1991) volume 1, Chapter 4.

In *Cincinnati Bell Foundry Co. v. Dodds* (1887), before the US Superior Court of Cincinnati, Ohio[25] and *Elaterite Paint and Mfg. Co. v. S. E. Frost Co.* (1908), before the Supreme Court of the State of Minnesota, the doctrine of trade secrets as property was adopted.[26] In other early trade secret cases in England, such as *Prince Albert v. Strange* (1849) and *Morison v. Moat* (1851), the property right theory was applied and the request by plaintiff for the protection of its trade secrets was granted. In 1916, the court in *Herbert Morris Ltd v. Saxelby* held that '[t]rade secrets may not be taken away by a servant; they are his master's property'.[27] The nature of trade secrets as property, as confirmed in those early cases, has in modern judicial practice become broadly accepted.[28]

However, even though the court relied on the protection of trade secrets as property in the Peabody case, there remained then, as now, unanswered questions when traditional property theory is used to define the protection of trade secrets. In the traditional opinion, a property right is a right existing in any thing, and includes the right of its possession, use, loan, assignment, exhaustion or consumption.[29] Property rights are based on the actual possession that is the basis of property ownership, and a person enjoys the property right to a thing through actual control of it by exclusive possession or by excluding the unauthorized use of it by others.[30] However, a trade secret is an intangible thing. It can exist in a person's mind and one can use it without possessing it. Consequently, the creator of a trade secret can in no way achieve the exclusive right to it. At the same time, the value of a trade secret lies in its confidentiality. It is not entitled to legal protection or exclusivity simply through registration, or authorization or by other measures such as patent or trademark. Therefore, when property theory was advanced to make the case for protection in the area of trade secrets, there were dissenting voices heard within legal circles and in judicial practice. Many academics and judges doubted that trade secrets had the nature of property.[31] Some even thought that the discussion regarding trade secrets as property was meaningless because most trade secret disputes were related to employment relationships. For example, US Supreme Court Justice Oliver Wendell Holmes in *E.I. duPont deNemours Co. v. Masland* in 1917 held that:

> The word 'property' as applied to trademarks and trade secrets is an unanalyzed expression of certain secondary consequences of the primary fact that the law makes some rudimentary requirements of good faith. Whether the

---

25. *Cincinnati Bell Foundry Co. v. Dodds* 10 Ohio Dec. Reprint 154 (Super. Ct. 1887)
26. *Elaterite Paint & Mfg. Co. v. S. E. Frost Co.*, 105 Minn. 239, 117 N. W. 388 (1908)
27. Quoted from John Hull, *Commercial Secrecy: Law and Practice* (London, Sweet & Maxwell, 1998), p.39.
28. See *Restatement (Third) of Unfair Competition*, 1995, (US) §42, Reporters' Note, comment b. See also Roger M. Milgrim, *Milgrim on Trade Secrets* (NY, Matthew Bender, 1984), pp.1–7.
29. *The Concise Encyclopaedia Britannica* (Beijing, Encyclopaedia of China Publishing House, 1985), p. 913.
30. Neel Chatteriee, 'Should Trade Secret Appropriation Be Criminalized?', (1997) 19 *Hastings Communications and Entertainment Law Journal*, 865.
31. Roger M. Milgrim, *Milgrim on Trade Secrets* (NY, Matthew Bender, 1984), pp.1–2.

> plaintiffs have any valuable secret or not, the defendant knows the fact, whatever it is, through a special confidence that he or she accepted. The property may be denied, but the confidentiality cannot be denied. Therefore, the starting point for the present matter is not property or due process of law, but that the defendant stood in confidential relations with the plaintiffs.[32]

Much labour and financial investment is devoted to the creation of trade secrets, but the economic and social value of a trade secret cannot be realized but through being used or transferred to another party. Consequently, only when creators of trade secrets are legally endowed with property rights can it be efficiently ensured that they will profit from the ownership of said trade secrets. In this way, they will be encouraged to devote themselves to innovation. Certain American academics cite the theory of natural law of John Locke, the British philosopher and jurist who lived in the seventeenth century (1632–1704), for his analysis of intangibles as property.

Three hundred years ago, Locke propounded the theory that the investment of a person's labour can form the foundation for ownership of property. He believed that 'No one ought to harm another in his life, liberty or possessions', so that every human being '[h]as property in his own person and in the labour of his body and the work of his hands'. He believed that when a person takes things from the 'common plenitude, as in drawing water from a river or picking fruit from a tree, he or she joins his or her labour to that thing' and that, therefore, a person creates property in the things taken from the natural environment by his or her labour, provided there is enough left for others. Thus, it can be concluded that people are under a duty not to 'take away' anything containing the labour of another person. John Locke's theory is often used by parties to support their viewpoint that they are entitled to the rights to their inventions and creations as property. At the same time, Locke's theories have influenced the formation and development of the theory of intellectual property and the protection of trade secrets.[33]

After the 1950s, property right theory was widely accepted and many countries came to regard trade secrets as a type of intellectual property or a type of legally protected intangible property. For example, in Japan and in Taiwan most academics agreed that trade secrets derived from human intellectual labour and thus were a type of intangible property.[34] At present, the status of intellectual property theory is unshakeable in intellectual property legal circles. In addition to relevant agreements established by the ICC and WIPO in the 1960s and 1970s, in the 1990s more than 100 members and applicant countries of the WTO signed the TRIPS Agreement during the Uruguay round of negotiation. At that time, trade

---

32. *E.I. du Pont deNemours Co. v. Masland*, 244 U.S. 100, 102 (1917) (US).
33. Wendy J. Gordon, 'A Property Right in Self-Expression: Equality and Individualism in the Natural Law of Intellectual Property' (1993) 102 Yale L.J. 1533, 1540.
34. Yamakuqi, *Infringements upon Business Secrets and Punishments thereon* (ジュリスト No.962, 1990), pp.46–48, quoted from Xu Yuling, *The Protection of the Business Secret* (Taiwan Sanmin Publishing House, 1993), p.43.

secrets were brought under the umbrella of intellectual property protection and special stipulations were included for 'the protection of undisclosed information'.

In the final analysis, however, trade secrets are different from other intellectual property. They are not provided with the exclusivity of a jus in re. It is a paradox that parties can possess trade secrets identical to those of the original holder of those secrets. An original trade secret holder cannot defend against the unauthorized use of its trade secrets if said secrets have been legally acquired by others. Consequently, the new challenge for legal academics in the latter part of the twentieth century was how to establish a perfected system of protection according to the characteristics of trade secrets by combining the existing theories mentioned above.

IV. COMBINING VARIOUS REMEDIES

Generally, every existing theory has its limitations. Trade secrets are unique and it is difficult to establish effective mechanisms for protecting them through application of traditional legal theories. During the twentieth century, with the nature of trade secrets as property generally recognized and particularly with the ongoing development of market economies, the protection of trade secrets in modern economic society became increasingly more important. The purpose of trade secret protection is no longer confined to the maintenance of good faith and business ethics. Legal protection has also become an important guarantee for encouraging innovation, for regulating trade secret disclosure and for clarifying the rules for using know-how between employees and employers, between agents and clients and between other interested parties, thereby facilitating efficient and reasonable use of trade secrets among them.[35]

Consequently, legal scholars are becoming increasingly aware that the system for the legal protection of trade secrets must be established on the basis of many different types of theories such as property right theory, contract theory and tort theory. All theories should be unified for the purpose of creating a flexible and diversified legal protection system so as to achieve a viable regime for trade secret protection.[36]

One of the most important developments in trade secret protection theory is the proper integration and effective linking of property right theory and confidential relations theory. The concept of trade secrets as a property has gradually come to be recognized, and the protection of trade secrets as special property relies on the concept of confidential relationships. Confidential relationship theory was created to validate the legal protection of trade secrets in one certain aspect and evolved into a primary tool for academics and judges to refute property right theory. With the deepening awareness of the importance of trade secrets has come a change in the role of confidential relations theory. The features of trade secrets and the

35. See *Restatement (Third) of Unfair Competition*, 1995, (US), §42, Reporters' Note, comment a.
36. John Hull, *Commercial Secrecy: Law and Practice* (London, Sweet & Maxwell, 1998), p.121.

special relationship between parties to trade secret disputes, as revealed by confidential relations theory, serve as a theoretical basis for countries to improve their legal regimes for the regulation of the protection of trade secrets.

The uniqueness and value of a trade secret lie in its confidentiality, which remains a precondition to it being entitled to protection as property. If a trade secret were to be made known to the public, it would bring no competitive advantage to its owner and would create no benefit for its owner. For instance, infringement of trade secrets for the purpose of competition or for gaining personal benefit can only follow from breaching the confidentiality of a holder. The court in *Werckmeister v. American Lithographic Co.* (1904) vividly compared the character of information to an animal. Only when information is captured can it be possessed, otherwise it belongs to the public. Trade secrets, the court held, could be found and 'captured' and so the owner creates the exclusive right to a trade secret by maintaining its secrecy.[37] Therefore, the court concluded, the confidentiality of trade secrets is a prerequisite for maintaining the property right to a trade secret.

Professor Milgrim, when comparing various theories of trade secret protection concluded that the owner of a trade secret has a property right to it which permits him to use and disclose the secret in certain situations without forfeiting his right of ownership to it. One of those situations is use and disclosure pursuant to contractual protection; another, in the context of a relationship in which the trade secret is protected by operation of law. Milgrim outlined the basic framework for trade secret protection regime in the US.[38]

The Restatement (First) of Torts epitomizes the judicial practice of states and courts at different levels. Summarizing the fundamental principles for the protection of trade secrets in sections 757 to 759, the First Restatement is the first document in US history to systematically set forth the definition, constituting elements and tortious acts of trade secret infringement. As a model law, the First Restatement naturally did not have binding force. However, in 1939, it served as a source for trade secret legislation of many US states. The fundamental principles established thereunder greatly influenced the practice of trade secret protection in the US and became a major source for the influential Uniform Trade Secrets Act.

In light of the types of infringement on trade secrets listed in the First Restatement,[39] the special nature of trade secrets was taken into full consideration, incorporating both property right theory and confidential relations theory for the creation of legal obligations to protect trade secrets. It is clear that the definition of trade secrets contained in the First Restatement attributes the elements of value and secrecy to information protected under the law. Meanwhile, the special relationship between parties is relied on in the determination of infringement, for which

37. *Werckmeister v. American Lithographic Co.*, 134 Fed. 321 (2d Cir. 1904), quoted from Robert G Bone, 'A New Look at Trade Secret Law: Doctrine in Search of Justification', (1998) *86 Calif. L. Rev*, note 71.
38. Roger M. Milgrim, *Milgrim on Trade Secrets* (NY, Matthew Bender, 1984), p.4-4.
39. See Chapter 2 of this Part.

civil liability must be assumed, with the violation of confidentiality as an important criterion for judging whether the act of a party is 'justifiable' or not.

Some Continental Law countries in Europe define the concepts and features of a trade secret through formulation of laws against unfair competition in order to regulate trade secret infringement that damages market competition, and the legal liability thereof. In terms of legal definition and type of infringement, these countries require a subjective element, (i.e., a use intended for the purpose of competition or for harming the holder, or for individual or third party benefit). The emphasis is on legal protection and safety of a transaction. With respect to determination of any misconduct of the parties, however, the special relationship between the parties is an important consideration.

An analysis of the formation and development of modern trade secret protection regimes in Western countries clearly reveals that the proper and effective operation of their protection regimes has benefited from the continued improvement in property right theory and confidential relations theory and is complemented by domestic trade secret law, laws against unfair competition, contract law, criminal law and other legal instruments.

On the one hand, trade secret law seeks to offer remedies when the interests of a trade secret holder are infringed upon. The right holder may file an action with a court to prohibit an infringer from using or disclosing its trade secrets and to hold the infringer liable for compensation, based either on the grounds of an express confidentiality agreement or a de facto implied confidentiality agreement or, in the absence of such contractual agreement, on the grounds of confidential rights and obligations created under law.

On the other hand, trade secret law safeguards the expectation of confidentiality. In order to prevent parties from taking advantage of their own or another's special relationship with a contracting holder to obtain a trade secret through apparently legitimate means and from unauthorized use or disclosure of such trade secret for illegal gains, the law may, on the basis of confidential relations theory, protect the interest of the trade secret holder by preventing a potential infringer from directly or indirectly infringing on another party's trade secret.

Chapter 2
Civil Law Remedies for Infringement of Trade Secrets

A civil remedy is anything a court can do for a litigant who has been wronged or whose rights are about to be infringed.[1] The purpose of invoking civil remedies, in various countries, is mostly based on the following considerations:

(a) compensation of plaintiffs for losses that they have incurred;
(b) prevention of the occurrence of damage;
(c) punishment of acts of infringement.

The two most common remedies are the awarding of damages to plaintiffs to compensate for losses and injunction to block a defendant's infringement or to undo the consequences of its infringement.[2] Specifically, forms of civil remedies include: compensation, injunction, restitution, punitive damages and other ancillary remedies.

However, civil law remedies for trade secret infringement are quite complicated, as trade secrets can be easily disseminated and transferred and are prone to lose their confidential nature upon entering the public domain. A trade secret is a type of intangible asset, the status of which is preserved by virtue of taking measures to ensure confidentiality. In the event of infringement of a trade secret, failure to take timely measures often leads to consequences such as difficulty in furnishing evidence and in investigating facts, as well as to disclosure of the trade secret, all of which poses a great threat to the interests of a trade secret holder. Therefore, apart from applicable contractual remedies, the most effective remedial measures that can be taken against trade secret infringement are payment of damages and

---

1. Douglas Laycock, *Modern American Remedies: Cases and Materials* (Beijing, CITIC Publishing House, 2003), p.1. Originally published by Aspen Publishers, Inc.
2. *Ibid.*

injunction. The first can remedy losses incurred to a right holder as a result of the loss of trade secrets, while the latter protects undisclosed trade secrets from further damage. Injunction can also punish an infringer by prohibiting him from using an infringed trade secret, thereby eliminating his competitive edge in the market.

In respect of civil remedies for infringement of trade secrets, the Common Law system is quite typical in a certain sense. More unique is injunctive relief, which plays an important role in protecting intellectual property rights, including trade secrets. Providing relief for holders of trade secrets is a necessary means to ensuring that they eventually realize their substantive rights, which is an important goal of civil actions. Injunctive relief is new to China's civil remedy system and is not yet widely applied to trade secret infringement. Generally, in the event of infringement, a victim is able only to protect its rights by resorting to compensatory remedies under Chinese law. Certain civil remedies, however, possess some of the same characteristics of an injunction.

I. DETERMINING WHAT CONSTITUTES INFRINGEMENT OF A TRADE SECRET

The Law against Unfair Competition lists four types of torts against trade secrets:

(a) obtaining trade secrets of a party that has rights in such secrets through theft, enticement by promises of gain, duress or by other unfair methods;
(b) disclosing, using or allowing others to use trade secrets of a party that has rights in such secrets where they were obtained by any of the methods set forth in preceding item (a);
(c) disclosing, using or allowing others to use trade secrets in one's possession, where doing so is in breach of an agreement or is contrary to the confidentiality requirements of the party that has rights in the trade secrets;
(d) third parties that obtain, use or divulge trade secrets of others that they are well aware or ought to be aware have been acquired by any of the methods set forth in the preceding items (a), (b) and (c) shall be deemed to have infringed trade secrets.[3]

As one can see, based on the aforementioned definition, the subject of trade secret infringement is a broad one. Infringers can be natural persons or legal persons, current or ex-employees of enterprises or other third parties. Generally, these can include:

(a) employees, lawyers, business consultants or accountants that need to know a trade secret for their work;
(b) business partners such as suppliers, agents, manufacturers and banks;
(c) transferees and licensees having the right to the use of a trade secret;

3. See Article 10 of the Law against Unfair Competition of the People's Republic of China (1993).

(d) state agencies and state personnel who learn a trade secret in the execution of their legal duties;
(e) partners, co-investors and business associates of trade secret holders.

Trade secret infringement can only take place if the information disclosed has been confirmed to be a trade secret. It must contain the elements of a trade secret as defined by law. Normally, protected information must exist under conditions of confidentiality and security.

Objectively, perpetrators of these types of infringement resort to behaviour that is prohibited by law. In addition, infringers must act with bad intent. They must have deliberately or negligently disclosed or used the secrets of another without authorization.

However, the elements of infringement of trade secrets under Chinese law have certain differences from those contained in the laws of some other countries. For example, the German Law against Unfair Competition places emphasis on punishing infringement of trade secrets under criminal law and on protecting trade secrets involved.[4] Thus, the intent of wrongdoing is required and it must be determined that the infringement was committed for the purpose of:

(a) illegal competition;
(b) seeking profits for the infringer himself or for others; or
(c) harming an enterprise owner.[5]

China places emphasis on protecting trade secrets by civil remedies, so the laws in countries employing criminal law remedies have stricter requirements with regard to subjective wrongdoing. In addition to wilful acts, negligent conduct may be sufficient to constitute infringement of the trade secrets of others. For example, according to Chinese law, if a third party obtains, uses or discloses the trade secrets of others and they knew or had reason to know that said trade secrets were obtained by improper methods, their actions constitute trade secret infringement. Furthermore, no matter for what purpose, whether deliberately or negligently, if one uses or discloses the trade secrets of another in breach of an obligation to maintain confidentiality, their behaviour constitutes infringement.

In this aspect Japanese law is slightly different, too. According to Japanese law,[6] if a person uses or discloses the trade secrets of another in breach of a confidentiality obligation, then his behaviour constitutes infringement only when his subjective intent includes one of the following:

(a) an act of illegal competition;
(b) seeking profit for himself or for others; or
(c) harming an enterprise owner.

---

4. Shao Jiandong, *Study of the Law against Unfair Competition of Germany* (Beijing, People's University Publisher, 2001), p.296.
5. See Article 17 (2) of the Law against Unfair Competition of Germany.
6. See Article 2 (1) items 4 to 9 of the *Unfair Competition Prevention Law* of Japan. <www.wipo.int/clea/docs_new/en/jp/jp005en.html >, 5 January 2008.

Based on this, infringers (in particular employees of enterprises) bear no legal liability for negligent use or disclosure of the trade secrets of another. At the same time, the elements of third-party infringement include intent or gross negligence.

II. CIVIL REMEDIES FOR TRADE SECRET INFRINGEMENT

According to Chinese tort law, damages are a constitutive requirement in order for the courts to uphold that an act of infringement, whether deliberate or inadvertent, has occurred. In substance, damages are a consequence resulting from an act of infringement. Such consequences may include death of the victim, personal injury, loss of social prestige, mental suffering, pain or pecuniary losses of various forms. Article 134 of the General Principles of the Civil Law of PRC provides ten main remedies to victims of infringement:

(a) cessation of infringement;
(b) removal of obstruction;
(c) elimination of danger;
(d) restitution of property;
(e) restoration to original condition;
(f) repair, re-working, or replacement;
(g) compensation for loss;
(h) payment of liquidated damages;
(i) elimination of ill effects and rehabilitation of reputation;
(j) apology.

The above remedies may be applied individually or collectively.

In addition to these remedies, the courts in China may also impose an admonition order, repentance, or confiscation of property used in illegal activities as well as illegal gains, or may impose a fine or detention pursuant to law. Payment of compensation for damages is one of the most important remedies provided under Chinese tort law. Generally, payment of damages means civil liability assumed by one party to another for losses incurred through an act of tort or non-performance ofan obligation. For trade secret holders, payment of damages is an important means for protecting civil rights and for parties obligated to confidentiality, it is an important mechanism for assuming civil liability.

Chinese academics generally hold that civil remedy for infringement of trade secrets is a remedy acquired by trade secret holders only by petitioning the court for intervention, and that it is a form of judicial remedy falling within the scope of public authority.[7] In China, to protect legal rights and interests a trade secret holder can file an application with the court for some form of remedy prior to or during

7. According to the general understanding of Chinese academics, public remedy refers to measures that, when an obligee's rights have been infringed upon, the obligee involved is entitled to ask the

civil motions (e.g., preservation of evidence, measures of advance execution and the like) whereby the court will examine a case in accordance with civil procedure law and then decide if a petitioner ought to be provided with such provisional remedies. At the end of the hearing the court will determine the civil liability of the infringer in accordance with civil law, such as an order to cease infringement or payment of damages under the substantive civil law.

With a view to complying with the requirements covering the measures of advance execution in Part §3 of the TRIPS Agreement,[8] China has amended most of its major regulations that cover intellectual property rights.[9] On the basis of existing remedial measures contained in its rules of civil procedure, such as attachment, preservation of evidence and measures of advance execution, measures such as preliminary injunction and ancillary preservation of evidence have been added in the newly-amended patent, copyright and trademark laws in China.[10] Regrettably, however, the original provisions of the Civil Procedure Law enacted in 1991 remain as they were with no new measures added vis-à-vis civil remedy for trade secrets.

A. Preliminary Execution in China

Preliminary execution is a measure by which the court decides or rules on the basis of urgency following the reaching of but prior to issuing its decision in a civil case. Imposition of pre-emptive or ancillary measures must be based on urgency and necessity for the holder's business needs. Such measures allow judges to order the cessation or prohibition of certain activities. China's Civil Procedure Law provides that the court may impose advance execution in the following cases:

(a) For the recovery of alimony, maintenance or education expenses, pension for the disabled or for the family of a decedent or of medical expenses.
(b) Recovery of wages for labour.

State to use its authority to eliminate the infringement and to realize its rights; private remedy refers to measures that, when an obligee's rights have been infringed upon, the obligee is entitled to act in its own capacity to eliminate the infringement and to realize its own rights. See Lian Huixing, *Introduction of Civil Law* (Law Press, Beijing) (1996), at p.65.

8. Part, Section 3 of *the Trips Agreement: Provisional Measures.* <www.wto.org>, 5 January 2008.
9. In August 2000, the seventeenth Session of the Ninth National People's Congress Standing Committee adopted a decision on an amendment of the *Patent Law*, achieving the second amendment of the *Patent Law of the People's Republic of China*, which became effective on 1 July 2001. In October 2001, the twenty-fourth Session of the Ninth National People's Congress Standing committee adopted a decision on an amendment of the *Copyright Law* and *Trademark Law*, achieving the second amendment of the *Copyright Law of the People's Republic of China* and the *Trademark Law of the People's Republic of China*, which became effective in October and December 2001 respectively.
10. Please refer to Article 61 of the Patent Law of the People's Republic of China, Article 57 of the Trademark Law of the People's Republic of China and Article 49 of the Copyright Law of the People's Republic of China.

(c) The existence of circumstances that require certain measures of advance execution on the basis of urgency.[11]

Pursuant to the judicial interpretation of the Supreme People's Court 'urgent circumstances' include circumstances that require the immediate cessation of infringement and the elimination of obstructions as well as the immediate prohibition of an act.[12]

Premises for the issuance of measures of preliminary execution by the court include:

(a) A clear and definite set of rights and obligations between the parties have been established.
(b) The petitioner must have an urgent need for imposing his rights and must have made an application to the court.
(c) The person against whom a petition is brought must be capable of fulfilling the obligations.[13]

The court may order a petitioner to provide security, failing which the application may be denied. If the petitioner loses the lawsuit, he must compensate the person against whom the application is made for any loss of property incurred as a result of advance execution. If a party is not satisfied with a decision or an order regarding preliminary execution, he may apply for review that can be granted one time only. Enforcement of the order will not be suspended during the review process.[14]

Therefore, when a trade secret holder finds that his rights are being infringed or being threatened with infringement, he can petition the court for issuance of measures of advance execution based on the abovementioned rules for implementation of protective measures such as cessation of infringement or elimination of the obstruction.

B. Preservation of Evidence in China

According to principles of evidence in China, preservation of evidence refers to an act whereby the court takes measures at the request of a litigant or according to its faculties and functions to secure and protect evidence in order to prevent it from becoming lost or difficult to obtain later.[15] According to Chinese law and

11. See Article 97 of the Civil Procedure Law of the People's Republic of China (2007).
12. Items (1) and (2) of Article 107 of the Opinions Concerning Several Questions on Application of the Civil Procedure Law of the People's Republic of China issued by China's Supreme Court (14 July 1992); Article 162 of the Opinions Concerning Several Questions on Implementation of General Principles of the Civil Law of the People's Republic of China (26 January 1988) issued by China's Supreme Court.
13. See Article 98 of the Civil Procedure Law of the People's Republic of China (2007).
14. *Ibid.* See Article 99.
15. Chang Yi (Ed.), *Theory of Civil Procedure Law* (Beijing, China University of Politics and Law Press, 1999), p.208.

provisions of judicial interpretation, the following requirements ought to be met for a court to take measures to preserve evidence:

First, the evidence for which a party is applying to the court for preservation is related to the facts to be proven, (i.e., said evidence may influence the court's decision in respect of the case in question). However, it does not necessarily follow that the preserved evidence has any causal link to the claim of said party. Second, only under circumstances where there exists the likelihood that evidence may be lost or become difficult to obtain later may the court take measures to preserve that evidence.[16] Third, applications for preservation of evidence must be filed no later than seven days prior to the expiry of the term for adducing evidence. The limitation of abatement not involving issues of suspension, discontinuation or extension is 'seven days prior to the expiry of the term for adducing evidence'. In providing a time limit for applying for the preservation of evidence, the intention of the law is to encourage parties to apply for preservation of evidence concurrently with their application for investigation and collection of evidence, so that the court can take all of the facts of a case into consideration.[17]

In China, litigants may voluntarily petition the court for preservation of evidence while the court may also, at its own discretion, take measures to preserve evidence. In the event that a petition is filed by a litigant, the court may require said litigant to provide corresponding security.[18] In general, the court will consider the type and value of evidence along with other factors to decide if security is required. The form of security is dictated by that provided in the Guarantee Law of the PRC.[19]

The methods adopted by the Chinese courts for preservation of evidence include: sealing-up, detainment, taking photos, making audio or visual recordings, duplication, authentication, investigation and making written records.[20] When preserving evidence, the court may require interested parties or their legal agents to be present. In practice, when the court preserves evidence by visual recording, it will try to arrange for both interested parties to be present in order to avoid doubt as to the integrity of the visual recording. However, failure of the interested parties or their legal agents to appear does not affect the preservation of evidence by the court.

---

16. See Article 74 of the Civil Procedure Law of the People's Republic of China (2007).
17. Huang Songyou (ed.), *Comprehension and Application of Judicial Interpretation on Civil Litigation Evidence* (Beijing, China Legal Publishing House, 2002), p.138. In China, the interested parties may reach a consensus for the time limit for providing evidence, which shall be confirmed by the courts and the court may also affix the time limit for providing evidence. If the court affixes the time limit, it should not be less than 30 days, which is counted from the second day after receipt of the notice of acceptance of a case and notice of defence in court by the interested parties. Please also refer to Article 33 of the *Several Regulations of the Supreme Court on Civil Litigation Evidence* (effective 1 April 2002).
18. See Article 74 of the Civil Procedure Law of the People's Republic of China (2007).
19. The methods of guarantee provided for by the *Guarantee Law of the People's Republic of China* include surety, mortgage, lien and pledge.
20. See Article 24 of Certain Provisions of the Supreme People's Court on Evidence in Civil Procedures (effective 2002).

Preserved evidence is not limited to use by the applicant alone. Both parties enjoy equal rights to the use of preserved evidence. Furthermore, preserved evidence must be formally entered into evidence before it can be relied upon to decide a case (i.e., it must be examined before it can be used to decide a case.)[21]

C. Attachment of Property in China

Attachment is a system by which the court takes protective measures prior to issuing its decision in a case, regarding disputed property or subject matter. This can restrict the right of a litigant to dispose of or transfer property within a specific period pursuant to the application of an interested party or another litigant or by direct order of the court. The objective of attachment is to ensure that the final decision of the court in a pending lawsuit can be successfully enforced. The attachment system is provided under the Civil Procedure Law of the PRC, according to which attachment is only available upon petition in connection with specific property related to a case. Attachment can be carried out via sealing-up, detainment, freezing or other measures prescribed by law. Should the court freeze property, it must notify the owner and property that has already been seized or frozen cannot be seized or frozen again.[22] Before taking attachment measures, the court may require a petitioner to provide security. If the petitioner fails to do so, his application will be rejected.[23] Where a relevant party is not satisfied with an attachment order, they may apply for a review but enforcement of the order will not be suspended during the review.[24] However, if a petition for attachment is wrongfully made, the petitioner must compensate the person against whom the application is made for any loss incurred as a result of the attachment.[25] After the court has ruled on attachment, unless it is rescinded by the same court or by a superior court, no entity may rescind the attachment measures.[26]

In China, attachment may be classified as pre-litigation attachment or in-litigation attachment.

According to the Civil Procedure Law of the PRC, where under urgent circumstances an interested party's lawful rights and interests would suffer irreparable damage if attachment were not adopted promptly, said party may apply to the court for attachment prior to litigation. After receiving the application, the court must decide within forty-eight hours in respect of such application. If it grants attachment, the implementation thereof will begin immediately. If the petitioner

21. Huang Songyou (ed.), Comprehension and Application of Judicial Interpretation on Civil Litigation Evidence (Beijing, China Legal Publishing House, 2002), p.143.
22. See Article 92 of the Civil Procedure Law of the People's Republic of China (2007).
23. See Article 92 of the Civil Procedure Law of the People's Republic of China (1991).
24. *Ibid.* See Article 99.
25. *Ibid.* See Article 96.
26. See Article 109 of the Opinions of the Supreme People's Court on Several Issues on Application of the Civil Procedure Law of the People's Republic of China Court (effective 1 April 2002).

fails to bring an action within fifteen days after the court imposes attachment, the court must rescind the attachment.[27]

During the proceedings, in cases where the enforcement of a judgment may become impossible or difficult because of the acts of either party or for other reasons, the court may, upon application by the other party, rule on attachment. In the absence of such application, the court may also issue attachment orders when necessary. After receiving a party's application, if the case is urgent, the court must decide in respect of attachment within forty-eight hours. Once granted, attachment must be promptly implemented.[28]

The relief of attachment of goods available to trade secret holders is only a provisional remedy prescribed by China's procedural law. Ultimately, remedies are made available through civil liability for infringement under substantive law as decided by the court.

Civil remedies provided in China's General Principles of the Civil Law of the PRC for infringement of trade secrets include cessation of infringement, elimination of effects and compensation for losses.[29]

D. Cessation of Infringement

An order to cease infringement is a form of civil remedy available under China's civil law.[30] According to Chinese law, a petition for cessation of infringement requires two preconditions:

(a) A claim must be brought by a plaintiff. In China, assumption of civil liability is based on claims made by a plaintiff, (i.e., not until a plaintiff's claim has been accepted by the court can a defendant be ordered to assume such liability).[31]

(b) The infringement is ongoing or is likely to recur. After hearing a case, if the court decides that the act of the defendant constitutes infringement and the infringement is ongoing then, upon petition by the holder the court usually orders the infringer to cease the infringement, or when the victim has obtained an order for advance execution, the court may, upon the request of the holder, order the defendant to permanently cease the infringement.

27. See Article 93 of the Civil Procedure Law of the People's Republic of China (1991).
28. See Article 93 of the Civil Procedure Law of the People's Republic of China (2007).
29. See Article 118 of the General Principles of the Civil Law of the People's Republic of China (1986).
30. See Article 134 of the General Principles of the People's Republic of China.
31. Pursuant to the provisions of Article 156 of the Opinions of the Supreme People's Court on Several Issues regarding Application of the Civil Procedure Law of the People's Republic of China (effective 1 April 2002), the plaintiff shall file its additional litigant claims at the time when the court debate is finished.

E. Obtaining Compensation for Damages

1. General Introduction

According to general interpretation in China, 'compensation for damages' refers to payment of compensation by one party that causes damage and loss to another party through infringement of that party's rights or by failing to repay a debt. To a trade secret holder, payment of compensation for damages is an important measure to protect civil rights and is a primary means of imposing civil liability.[32]

Tort damages can be divided into direct or indirect damages, pecuniary or non-pecuniary damages, and actual or future damages. The stipulation on direct damages and indirect damages in civil legislation in China is not clear. It can be found ambiguously in Article 117 of the General Principles of the Civil Law of the PRC, which states that anyone who infringes on state, collective, or personal property rights must return said property or, failing that, must reimburse its estimated value. Anyone who damages state, collective or personal property must restore the property to its original condition or reimburse its estimated value. If a victim suffers other material losses, the infringer must compensate for those losses as well. However certain departmental regulations contain definite concepts regarding direct damages and indirect damages. For example, the Opinions on Certain Issues of Administrative Enforcement in Relation to Trademarks issued by the State Administration for Industry and Commerce in 1999 points out that 'direct damages' refers to the loss or reduction of profit that a victim has suffered during the period of infringement or the estimated sales volume multiplied by the average profit margin of the victim. 'Indirect damages' consists of reasonable expenses paid by the victim, such as agency or investigation costs for investigating an act of tort.

China's civil law has no clear definition of pecuniary and non-pecuniary loss; however Articles 106 and 120 of the General Principles of the Civil Law of the PRC prescribe the scope of compensation to include pecuniary losses and non-pecuniary losses. Under these articles, any individual or legal person who deliberately infringes upon state, collective or personal property rights should restore the property to its original condition or reimburse its estimated value. Additionally, if an individual's right of personal name, portrait, reputation, or honour is infringed, he has the right to demand that the infringement be stopped, that his reputation be rehabilitated, that the adverse effects of the infringement be eliminated or that an apology be made. He may also demand compensation for losses. If a legal person's right of name, reputation, or honour has been infringed upon it has the same civil rights as an individual.

Specifically, property damage is an economic loss borne by a victim when his property or body is infringed upon. Property damage is a calculable actual loss of material wealth. Generally it appears as a change in the properties of value. For this

32. *China Encyclopaedia of Law* (Beijing, Encyclopaedia of China Publishing House, 1988), p.571.

purpose, property damage includes damage to tangible property as well as to intangible property. Normally, direct infringement upon another's property constitutes property damage, (e.g., destroying another's belongings) and this damage can be fully assessed in monetary terms. Infringement upon another's life or health, which leads to the death or disability of the victim, will give rise to relevant property damage as well, such as expenses for funeral, medical care, and nursing. In some cases, infringement upon another's right of personality, (e.g., infringement on one's reputation) will also lead to corresponding property damage.

The General Principles of the Civil Law of the PRC categorize tangible property into subject matter that can be damaged or infringed. When tangible property is infringed or destroyed, tortious liability, which is compensatory in nature, has priority. The infringer must return the property or restore damaged property to its original condition. Failing that, he must reimburse the victim for the estimated value of the property. As far as intangible property losses and other pecuniary losses combined with bodily harm are concerned, they include direct and indirect damages and are assessed based on the intent of the infringer according to principles in law.

Under Chinese tort doctrine, non-property damages can be classified into personal injury (death or injury) and other non-pecuniary damages (deterioration of social status or psychological damage). Personal injury refers to infringement upon another's right of life and health, resulting in the death or disability of the victim. Psychological damages means the psychological and physical sufferings borne by the victim as a result of the tortuous actions of an infringer. In essence, social assessment is a form of social relationship or relationship of personality. The loss of social status usually flows from an act of infringement upon one's personal rights, in particular infringement upon one's right of personal name, portrait, reputation and privacy. With regard to simple deterioration of social status, the remedial measures to be taken mainly lie in the aspect of personality, such as reputation to be rehabilitated, adverse effects to be eliminated, and an apology to be made.[33] However, if the loss of social status occurs together with other damages then, depending on the severity of those damages, civil liability will be triggered and the appropriate remedy will be applied.

The distinction between actual damages and future damages in China's civil legislation can be found in the General Principles of the Civil Law of the PRC and in certain other legislation such as the Copyright Law, the Patent Law and the Trademark Law.

Under China's civil law, actual damages refer to the reduction in value of a piece of property caused by infringement. In practice, infringement of property is

---

33. See Article 120 of the *General Principles of Civil Law of the People's Republic of China* 1986 which states that 'If a citizen's right of personal name, portrait, reputation or honour is infringed upon, he shall have the right to demand that the infringement be stopped, his reputation be rehabilitated, the ill effects be eliminated and an apology be made. He may also demand compensation for losses. The above paragraph shall also apply to infringement upon a legal person's right of name, reputation or honour.

usually the loss of the victim's property, (i.e., the loss of value of the property that constitutes actual damage). Destruction of property can be in the form of diminution and/or loss of the value of damaged property. In the case of loss, the total value of the lost property is regarded as actual damages and, in the case of diminution; the diminished portion constitutes the actual damages.

Future damages refers to the victim's loss of acquirable pecuniary interests resulting from an infringing act, specifically including loss of legal or natural benefits from the acquirable property, loss of acquirable operating profits, loss of acquirable income including salary, bonuses, and the like and possible loss or deterioration of the ability to earn money in the future. Future losses have the following characteristics: Firstly, when the rights of a victim are infringed upon, pecuniary interests do not yet exist; and secondly, under general circumstances, if the victim were free from said infringement, the pecuniary interests would certainly or most probably have been acquired.

Clause 3, Article 117 in the General Principles of the Civil Law of the PRC specifies rules for compensating future damages and loss. In practice, however, whether compensation requested by a victim for future losses will be ordered depends mainly on the possibility for the victim to obtain 'acquirable' pecuniary interests in the future. If so, then future losses will be compensated. For instance, the victim's loss of future salary and benefits are most certainly an acquirable interest and must be compensated. If the possibility is relatively small, then 'future losses' will not be supported or compensated.

2. Scope of Compensation for Infringement of Trade Secrets

Pursuant to the fundamental principle of China's civil law, the method of compensation for property damage takes restitution as the accepted form of compensation for infringement of trade secrets. If restitution of the property cannot be made, the court can grant monetary compensation.[34] However, as intangible property, restitution of trade secrets cannot be made when they are disclosed into the public domain. When the right of a holder is infringed, pecuniary compensation will be granted by the court as the main form of compensation for the damage caused by an infringer to the holder of a trade secret.

Moreover, China's courts only accept cases arising from the violation of social or public interests or social morality resulting from infringement of a person's privacy or other personal interests, and which are brought to the court by the victim as a tort for claiming compensation for emotional damages (e.g., infringement of right to life, right of health, right of personal dignity, freedom or name).[35] As a result, vis-à-vis protection of trade secrets, claims by victims for emotional damages will not be supported by the courts.

34. Wang Liming, Yang Lixin, *Tort Law* (Beijing, Law Press, 1996).
35. See Article 1 of the Interpretation of the Supreme People's Court on Problems regarding the Ascertainment of Compensation Liability for Emotional Damages in Civil Torts (2001).

The Law against Unfair Competition contains a provision that states that a party bears the responsibility for payment of compensation for damages caused by him to another as the result of infringement and that the amount of said compensation, if it is difficult to measure the actual amount of damages, should be equivalent to the profit made by an infringer during the period of infringement. Said party must also compensate reasonable costs to the damaged party if expense has been incurred investigating the activities of unfair competition conducted by the infringer.[36] Damage caused by infringement of a trade secret is defined in China as the reduction in or loss of economic benefit of a trade secret holder that would have been generated by the trade secret. The infringer must pay compensation for that portion of benefit thus reduced or lost to the damaged holder of the trade secret. However, due to the intangibility of trade secrets and the uncertainty of obtainable benefits, the actual loss of a holder of trade secrets is difficult to calculate accurately. Consequently, in judicial practice, compensation is generally determined based upon the specific conditions of a case by outlining the scope of compensation payable in accordance with legal principles. In detail, the compensation for damage caused by infringement of trade secrets focuses primarily on the following four aspects:

(a) Damage to economic interests in the current period:

This is the diminished or lost profit in a current period evidenced by the infringed holder that was caused by the infringement, which is equivalent to the difference between the expected benefit to be obtained by the holder by using his trade secret under normal conditions less the benefits obtained by using the same trade secret in the current period following the infringement. The current period refers to the period in which the infringement continues. The damage to current economic benefit is the principal part of compensation to be paid to the holder of a trade secret for the infringement.

(b) Development costs:

The creation of trade secrets usually requires certain investment in labour, material and financial resources. Such investment is recovered gradually from the future profits of the holder. Evidently, this form of investment means a consumption of property that has already taken place to the holder rather than return on investment. Generally the compensation for such investment cannot be claimed as losses against the infringer. However, the disclosure of trade secrets causes the holder to lose the possibility of recovering his development costs and to suffer the loss of property. Therefore, in cases of disclosure of trade secrets caused by infringement, a holder can file a claim for compensation for a portion of his development costs because the development costs cannot be fully recovered due to the premature disclosure of the trade secret.

---

36. See Article 20 of the People's Republic of China Law against Unfair Competition (1993).

(c) Reasonable costs of investigation:

According to the theory of elements covering civil liability in China, there should be a causal relationship between a tort and a loss. As the plaintiff's reasonable costs involved in the investigation of such 'loss' have no direct causal relation to the tort of the defendant, in judicial practice in China the court usually rejects claims made by a plaintiff for compensation for attorney fees and the like as in other civil infringement cases. Nevertheless, the Law against Unfair Competition provides that the legal liability of an infringer also includes, among other things, payment of 'reasonable investigation costs'[37] which, for the first time in Chinese law, expressly provides that an infringer is liable for payment of the costs of investigation inclusive of attorney fees.

3. Method for Computing Payment of Compensation for Losses

The damage caused to a trade secret holder by infringement is often difficult to calculate precisely. However, to the extent that the amount of compensation to be paid to said holder can be determined using an appropriate computing method, the remedy available to him is directly affected. Article 21(a) of the Law against Unfair Competition provides two computing methods:

(1) calculation based on the actual property loss of the holder; or
(2) calculation made based on the profit obtained by the infringer as a result of the infringement during the infringement period.

The courts in China have basically adopted these two types of computing methods in determining payment of compensation for infringement of trade secrets.

In addition, in Chinese judicial practice the courts use fixed-amount compensation to determine the amount to be paid in damages. Fixed-amount compensation is compensation determined by the court within certain limits in cases where the loss suffered by a holder as a result of the infringement and the illegal gains of the infringer are impossible to determine.

The concept of fixed-amount compensation first appeared in the regulations of some local courts in China. For instance, in 1995 regulations appeared in the Opinions of the Beijing Court on Several Issues in the Trial of Cases in Relation to Copyright Disputes over Computer Software.[38]

37. See Article 20 of the PRC Law against Unfair Competition (1993).
38. See Paragraph 2 of Article 7 of the Opinions of the Beijing Court on Several Issues in the Trial of Cases in Relation to Copyright Disputes over Computer Software, which states that when the actual losses of an oblige, or the benefits acquired by an infringer, are difficult or impossible to determine the infringer must pay from CNY5000 to CNY300,000 as compensation; if an infringer indeed has proof that it was unaware that his act constituted an infringement and if the consequences of the infringement are not serious, the compensation can be reduced to below CNY5000 according to specific circumstances.

In 2002, the Supreme People's Court promulgated a judicial interpretation concerning the law applicable to the hearing of patent controversies.[39] In that interpretation, the Court amended certain principles of the Beijing Higher Court, stating that the courts may determine the amount of compensation from CNY five-thousand to three-hundred thousand according to the type of right, the nature and circumstances of the infringement and other factors where the losses of the infringed or the profits of the infringer are difficult to determine. The Supreme People's Court determined that the amount of compensation should not exceed CNY five-hundred thousand.

F. Issues of Civil Procedure

A civil action is a procedure conducted before the court in which the plaintiff and the defendant participate in order to resolve civil disputes.[40] In the event of an infringement or dispute, a trade secret holder may bring an action before the court requesting that the court exercise its power of trial and order the infringer to cease its infringement and to provide remedy such as resolution of the dispute and payment of compensation for losses.

Chinese law concerning civil actions over disputes involving trade secrets mainly include the Civil Procedure Law of the PRC (2007) and the Opinions of the Supreme Court Concerning Several Issues on the Application of the Civil Procedure Law of the PRC (1992). In handling cases involving international disputes over trade secrets, apart from the aforementioned law and judicial interpretations, the Regulations of the Supreme Court on Issues Concerning Jurisdiction over Civil Cases Involving Foreign Parties (2002) are also applicable as are certain international conventions to which China is a signatory and bilateral agreements on judicial assistance concluded by China, such as the Hague Convention on Service Abroad of Judicial and Extrajudicial Documents in Civil or Commercial Matters (1965), which was ratified in 1991, and the Hague Convention on the Taking of Evidence Abroad in Civil and Commercial Matters (1970), which was ratified in 1997. Since the 1980s, China has entered into bilateral treaties on judicial assistance with thirty-two countries including France, Poland, Mongolia, Belgium, Romania, Italy, Spain, Russia, Turkey, Cuba, Thailand, Egypt, Bulgaria, Belarus, Kazakhstan, Ukraine, Greece, Cyprus, Morocco, Hungary, Kirghizstan, Tadzhikistan, Singapore, Uzbekistan and Vietnam.[41]

39. See Several Provisions of the Supreme People's Court on Issues Concerning Applicable Laws of the Trial of Patent Controversies promulgated on 19 June 2001 and effective 1 July 2001.
40. Institute of the Chinese Academy of Social Sciences, *Law Dictionary* (Beijing, Law Press, 2003), p.969.
41. Source: Webpage of the Ministry of Foreign Affairs of the People's Republic of China, <www.fmprc.gov.cn/chn/wjb/zzjg/tyfls/tfsckzlk/zgywgsbtyylb/t267986.htm>, 5 January 2008.

1. Rules on Civil Jurisdiction

The act of infringing upon trade secrets is classified as a tort in China. In accordance with the provisions of the Civil Procedure Law of the PRC, lawsuits initiated in connection with acts of infringement are under the jurisdiction of the court in the place the tort was committed or where the defendant has his residence.[42] The 'place where the tort was committed' can include the place where the consequences of a tort occurred.[43]

A lawsuit initiated over a contractual dispute involving trade secrets, including disputes over licensing agreements and contracts for technology transfer, as well as disputes over contracts for research and development of technology and secrecy agreements are under the jurisdiction of the court in the place where the defendant has his residence or where the contract is performed.[44] If a dispute over these types of contracts involves foreign parties, the parties may, through written agreement, select the jurisdiction of the court of the place that has an effective connection with the dispute.[45] If the parties fail to make a selection, the lawsuit may be brought under the jurisdiction of the court in the location of the residence of the defendant within the territory of the PRC or alternatively in the case of an action concerning a contract dispute brought against a defendant who has no residence within the territory of the PRC, if the contract is entered into or performed within the territory of the PRC or if the subject matter of the action is located within the territory of the PRC, or if the defendant has distrainable property within the territory of the PRC, or if the defendant has its representative office within the territory of the PRC. In these cases, the court in any such relevant location will have local jurisdiction.[46]

In accordance with the Civil Procedure Law of the PRC, the local courts (above the county or municipal district level) have jurisdiction as courts of first instance over civil cases while the intermediate courts have jurisdiction as courts of first instance over major cases involving foreign parties,[47] cases that have major

42. See Article 29 of the Civil Procedure Law of the People's Republic of China (2007).
43. See Article 187 of the Opinions of the Supreme People's Court on Several Issues concerning the Implementation of the General Principles of the Civil Law of the People's Republic of China (1988).
44. See Article 24 of the Civil Procedure Law of the People's Republic of China (2007).
45. According to Chinese judicial interpretation, foreign – related civil relationships refer to relationships wherein either party or both parties in a legal civil relationship is an alien, a stateless person, or a foreign legal person, and the object of the legal civil relationship is within the territory of a foreign country, and the legal facts that produce, alter, or void the rights and obligations of a civil relationship occur in a foreign country. See Article 178 of the *Opinions of the Supreme People's Court on Several Issues concerning the Implementation of the General Principles of the Civil Law of the People's Republic of China* (1988).
46. See Article 243 of the Civil Procedure Law of the People's Republic of China (2007).
47. *Ibid.* See Article 18.

impact on the area under their jurisdiction and cases under the jurisdiction of the intermediate courts as determined by the Supreme People's Court.[48] For this purpose, 'major cases involving foreign parties' refers to cases involving foreign parties with significant subject matter, complicated circumstances or the majority of interested parties residing overseas.[49]

In 1998, the Supreme People's Court issued the Summary of the National Symposium on Trial Work Concerning Intellectual Property Rights Participated in by Some Courts (the Summary), which has provided guidelines on trial procedures and application of law concerning intellectual property rights in connection with the scope and jurisdiction of cases heard by the courts in light of the characteristics of civil disputes over intellectual property rights and the actual conditions of adjudicatory personnel in China. The Summary stipulates that disputes over the ownership and infringement of trade secrets and contracts regarding trade secrets all fall within the category of civil disputes over intellectual property rights. First instance cases concerning civil disputes over intellectual property rights, including trade secret rights, are under the jurisdiction of the Intermediate Court, which is determined by the Supreme People's Court as the court of first instance for such cases according to specific circumstances of the cases with the exception of a few local courts which have set up intellectual property tribunals. Consequently, since 1998 most of these types of cases have been heard by the Intermediate Courts located in provincial capitals and in other equivalent municipalities. Civil tribunals have now been set up within the Supreme People's Court as well as within thirty-one local High Courts across the country for trial of cases involving intellectual property rights, and the Intermediate Courts in thirty-one provincial capitals and equivalent municipalities have also set up their own courts for trial of cases involving intellectual property rights. There are also four local courts that have established their own tribunals for hearing cases involving intellectual property, (i.e., the districts of Haidian and Chaoyang in Beijing, and the districts of Pudong and Huangpu in Shanghai).[50] The purpose of this is to enrich the experience of judicial personnel involved in the hearing of intellectual property cases, to improve the quality of the handling of cases and to improve efficiency in the settlement of cases.

2. Statute of Limitations

Under the General Principles of the Civil Law of the PRC, the statute of limitations stipulated by civil legislation in China (also known as 'extinctive prescription')

48. *Ibid.* See Article 19.
49. See Article 1 of the Opinions of the Supreme People's Court on Several Issues concerning the Implementation of the Civil Procedure Law of the People's Republic of China (1991).
50. Jiang Zhipei, 'China's Civil Judicial Provisions and Measures of Advance Execution for the Protection of Intellectual Property Rights' <www.chinaiprlaw.com/fgrt/fgrt119.htm >, 5 January 2006.

affects a party's right to litigation. What becomes 'extinct' is the victim's right to win a lawsuit, but not their right to sue nor their substantive rights.[51] In accordance with this principle, Chinese civil law contains regulations regarding statutes of limitation involving acts of infringement that state that if the statute of limitations is exceeded, the person entitled to bring a claim for damages will lose their right to win the lawsuit. That is, the party can institute a proceeding, but the court will not decide in favour of its claim. However, if an infringer chooses to pay compensation voluntarily, the court will permit it.[52]

There are three types of statute of limitation stipulated in China's civil legislation: general statute of limitation, special statute of limitation and the maximum statute of limitation. Under the General Principles, except as otherwise stipulated by law, the general statute of limitation regarding applications to the court for protection of civil rights is two years,[53] the special statute of limitation is one year, and the maximum statute of limitation is twenty years.[54]

In China, lawsuits concerning trade secrets involve two types of statutes of limitation, (i.e., general and maximum). The difference between these two types of statutes of limitation lies in the fact that: (a) the commencement time for each is different. A general statute of limitation commences when the entitled person knows or ought to know that their rights have been infringed upon while the maximum statute of limitation commences from the date when the infringement

51. But there are exceptions. For instance, the statute of limitation stipulated by the *Product Quality Law of the People's Republic of China* is elimination of right of claim instead of elimination of right of litigation.
52. See Article 138 of the *General Principles of Civil Law of the People's Republic of China* (1986) stating that if a party chooses to fulfil obligations voluntarily after a statute of limitation has expired, he shall not be subject to the limitation.
53. See Article 135 of the General Principles of Civil Law of the People's Republic of China (1986).
54. However, statutes of limitation in cases such as personal injury compensation, sale of below-standard commodities without proper declaration, delay or refusal to pay rental and loss or damage of consigned property apply to special statutes of limitation, which is one year. Currently in China, relevant special laws regarding statutes of limitation include the *People's Republic of China SC*, the *Product Quality Law of the People's Republic of China*, the *Contract Law of the People's Republic of China*, and the *Environmental Protection Law of the People's Republic of China*. The *People's Republic of China SC* specifies that the statute of limitation for claiming State compensation is two years, calculated from the date when the administrative act was affirmed as illegal, excluding the detaining period. This statute of limitation applies not only to personal injury compensation, but also to pecuniary damage compensation. Article 45 of the *Product Quality Law of the People's Republic of China* prescribes that statutes of limitation will be two years in cases of claims for compensation for damage caused by product defect, calculating from when the victim knew or should have known his rights and interests were infringed. Right of claim for compensation for damages caused by product defect will be valid for ten years from when the defective product which causes the damage is delivered to the initial consumer. However, this does not apply to the condition that a product's safe period of use (e.g., use by date) is greater than ten years. Article 42 of the *Environmental Protection Law of the*

begins; (b) there are differences in the provisions concerning whether the infringement should cease or be suspended. A general statute of limitation is applicable to provisions concerning cessation and suspension of infringement, whereas this is not true for a maximum statute of limitation.[55] An infringed party should exercise his right of claim within two years or lose his right to request the protection of the court. As stipulated by law, a general statute of limitation is calculated from the date when a victim knew or ought to have known that their rights were infringed.

Regarding suspension, discontinuance and extension of a statute of limitation for acts of infringement, generally they are handled in conformity with the principles contained in the General Principles of the Civil Law of the PRC which state that a statute of limitation will be suspended during the last six months of its term if a plaintiff cannot exercise his right of claim due to force majeure or other obstacles. The statute of limitation will resume on the day when the grounds for said suspension are eliminated. A statute of limitation will be discontinued when the action is brought or when one party makes a claim or agrees to fulfil its obligations. A new statute of limitation will begin from the date of the discontinuance.[56] During the last six months of the term of a statute of limitation, if an infringer is found not to be competent to participate in a civil proceeding, or if a person with limited competence who does not have a guardian or whose guardian has died or has lost his power of attorney or whose guardian has lost his competence to participate in a civil proceeding, such situations may be deemed a failure to exercise a right of claim due to other obstacles, and the relevant party may apply for a suspension of the statute of limitation.[57] If a statute of limitation is suspended because the infringed party brings an action or if the infringer agrees to fulfil its obligation and the victim makes a claim again or the infringer agrees to fulfil its obligation again during the new term of the statute of limitation, it will be regarded as a second suspension of the statute of limitation. If a victim makes a claim against a debt guarantor, an agent of a debtor or the custodian of a property, it can be considered as a suspension of the statute of limitation.[58]

People's Republic of China stipulates that statutes of limitation will be three years in cases of litigation for environment pollution damage compensation, calculating from when the victim(s) knew or should have known of the pollution damage.

55. See Article 175 of the Opinions concerning Several Questions on Implementation of the General Principles of the Civil Law of the People's Republic of China Issued by China's Supreme People's Court (1988).
56. See Articles 139 and 140 of the General Principles of the Civil Law of the People's Republic of China (1986).
57. See Article 172 of the Opinions concerning Several Questions on Implementation of the General Principles of the Civil Law of the People's Republic of China (1988).
58. *Ibid.* See Article 173.

Figure 1. Diagram of Chinese Court System

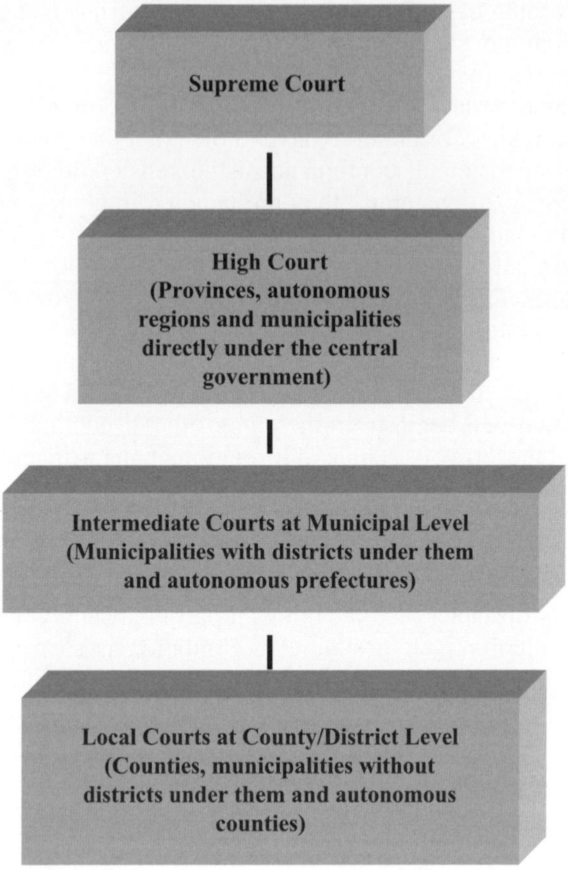

Note: The solid line represents that the relationship between a superior court and a lower court is one of guidance and supervision.

3. Burden of Proof

Assignment of burden of proof refers to an activity in which the court in a civil lawsuit assigns the burden of proof between the interested parties according to the law.[59] The direct consequence of assignment of burden of proof is that it determines which party bears the greater risk of losing a lawsuit. Moreover, the assignment of burden of proof is conducted in accordance with civil procedure law. It spans the two legal domains of substantive civil law and civil procedure law,

59. Institute of the Chinese Academy of Social Sciences, *Law Dictionary* (Beijing, Law Press, 2003), p.796.

creating a convergence of substantive law and procedural law. Assigning burden of proof between interested parties to a lawsuit is a function of the application of substantive civil law and civil procedure law. In China however, burden of proof is governed by the Civil Procedure Law of the PRC as well as by certain judicial interpretations of the Supreme People's Court.

According to the Civil Procedure Law of the PRC, parties are responsible for producing evidence to prove the facts upon which their allegations are based.[60] In 1998, the Supreme People's Court pointed out in its Summary of the National Symposium on Trial Work concerning Intellectual Property Rights Participated in by Certain Courts that the principle of the party filing a lawsuit having the burden of adducing admissible evidentiary materials as the general principle of burden of proof is applicable to cases involving civil disputes over intellectual property rights as it is to other cases involving civil disputes. Where a party cannot adduce evidence or where the evidence adduced does not support the facts upon which the allegations are based, that party bearing the burden of proof assumes the risk of an unfavourable outcome. In 2001, the Supreme People's Court in China officially issued the Provisions of the Supreme People's Court on Evidence in Civil Procedures, which fully embody the principles proposed in the Summary.

According to the general principles governing the assignment of burden of proof in lawsuits involving trade secrets, because the holder of a trade secret is the party who must exercise his right of claim in order to protect his trade secrets, he bears the burden of proof and thus cannot investigate the legal liability of an infringer until he has proven the existence of infringement. To do so, the holder of the trade secret must prove the following facts when filing a lawsuit:

(1) that they are the holder of the trade secret;
(2) that the trade secret held by the infringer is the same as that of the original holder; and
(3) that the trade secret held by the infringer was obtained by unfair means.

On the one hand, a trade secret is an unregistered intangible asset protected by security measures taken by its holder and characterized by secrecy and confidentiality; on the other hand, the infringement of trade secrets is also hard to uncover. An infringed party involved in a dispute is often only capable of providing evidence to support facts within their control, such as the trade secret itself, the legitimacy of the trade secret, and the conditions required for the infringing party to have acquired the trade secret. However, it is very difficult for a holder of a trade secret to obtain details such as the method and means by which the infringing party acquired his trade secrets. As a result, in judicial practice in cases concerning protection of trade secrets, China's courts apply the principle of the burden of proof being on the defendant. Moreover, the Intellectual Property Right Tribunal in the Beijing Higher Court has held that in lawsuits involving trade secret infringement, a holder is always in an adverse position in respect of obtaining evidence and

60. See Article 64(1) of the Civil Procedure Law of the People's Republic of China (2007).

that, consequently, if the holder is required to provide evidence, it would not be conducive to fulfilling the legislative purposes of impeding unfair competition and protecting trade secrets. Therefore, it serves the purposes of the *Law against Unfair Competition* to require an infringer, who has easier access to the evidence, to undertake the burden of proof, (i.e., the burden of proof is on the defendant).[61]

In 2001, the Supreme People's Court issued a new interpretation expressly stating that a party or its legal agent may make an application to the court to collect evidence regarding trade secrets.[62] Furthermore where there are no explicit statutory provisions and where it is not possible to determine who should be responsible for providing evidence under the existing provisions or according to judicial interpretations, the court may determine the burden of proof based on the principles of fairness and good faith and the court will take into consideration such factors as the ability of the interested parties to provide evidence.[63] The case of Foshan Ceramic, in Foshan City, Guangzhou can be used to illustrate that burden of proof is usually carried by the defendant.

In 1999, the case of *Fotao Group Joint Stock Limited Company Ceramics Research Institute v. Jinchang Ceramics Roller Factory* involving a non-patent technical secret dispute came before the court of Foshan city in Guangdong Province.[64]

The *Fotao* case was the first trade secret case heard by a Chinese court following the promulgation of the Law against Unfair Competition of the PRC at the end of 1993. In the case, the plaintiff, Guangdong Fotao Group Joint Stock Limited Company Ceramics Research Institute (Fotao), claimed that the defendant, Guangdong Nanhai City Jinchang Ceramics Roller Factory (Jinchang), had employed its ex-employees and had obtained and used its trade secret, a cold isostatic processing fine ceramic roller (the Ceramic Roller). Fotao petitioned the Court to order Jinchang to immediately cease its infringement, to compensate Fotao for economic losses and to make an apology. The defendant contended that the plaintiff had no evidence to prove that its ex-employees had disclosed its production technology for the Ceramic Roller. In addition, the technology had been disclosed by the plaintiff in the October 1990 issue, volume five of the trade

61. Intellectual Property Rights Tribunal of Beijing Higher Court, 'Several Questions on Relative Evidence in Litigation Involving Intellectual Property Rights', in *Articles on Intellectual Property Rights*, Vol. 4, Zheng Chengsi (Ed.), (Beijing, China University of Politics and Law Press, 2000) p.481.
62. In any of the following circumstances, the parties concerned and the agent ad litum thereof may petition the people's court to investigate and collect evidence: (1) The evidence petitioned for investigation and collection is archive files kept by relevant organs of the State and must be accessed by the people's court upon its authority; (2) Materials that concern State secrets, commercial secrets, or personal privacy; (3) Other materials that cannot be collected by the parties concerned or the agents ad litum thereof due to objective reasons. See Article 17 of *Certain Provisions of the Supreme People's Court on Evidence in Civil Procedures* (2001).
63. See Article 17 of Certain Provisions of the Supreme People's Court on Evidence in Civil Procedures (2001).
64. See Vol. 4 1995 of the Gazette of the Supreme of People's Court of the Peoples' Republic of China.

magazine *Ceramics.* Jinchang was established at the end of 1991 and claimed that it had invested substantial human resources, material and capital in researching available public technical information pertaining to the Ceramic Roller. The defendant contended that the technology was acquired as a result of research by its technical staff and that, therefore, Jinchang had legally acquired the technology.

After hearing the Fotao case, the Foshan Intermediate People's Court of Guangdong Province ruled for the first time in Chinese legal history that the defendant should cease its infringement in accordance with preliminary execution as provided for in the Civil Procedure Law of the PRC. During the trial, Fotao provided substantial evidence to prove that the Ceramic Roller was a technology on which it had spent a great deal of money and much time researching. The level and utility of the technology had reached an international standard and was the first such technology of its kind in China, a fact which had brought the plaintiff tremendous economic benefit. At the same time, Fotao had proved that in order to protect its technological achievement it had implemented various security measures, such as arranging for a special person to be in charge of the protection of technical information; drafting confidentiality rules and clarifying the content of its secrets such as their function, composition, prototype technology and blueprints of facilities of related workshops and oven equipment. The plaintiff had also notified its employees that they would be prosecuted if they intentionally or negligently disclosed or stole its trade secrets. The plaintiff argued that although the basic production principles and terminology regarding the Ceramic Roller had been reported in magazines, (e.g., *Ceramics*), from a technical viewpoint, such reports were a general mention or an outline of the technology which, in essence, had not disclosed the specific content of Fotao's technical secrets.

During the trial, the Court required the defendant to provide evidence of the source of its technology that was identical to that held by the plaintiff. The defendant provided technical information on the Ceramic Roller but failed to provide evidence on the type of research it had conducted. For example, which research was based on public technology, the components of the technology, and how much time the defendant had spent on its research?

In considering the evidence offered by both parties, the Court ruled that the basic production principles and terminology of the Ceramic Roller had been partly reported in some public journals, such as volume five of the October 1990 *Ceramics*, but from a technical aspect such reports were deemed only a general mention or an outline of the technology which did not result in the disclosure of the specific content of Fotao's technical secrets. Upon comparison, it was proved that the details in the report contained in volume five of the 1990 *Ceramics* magazine were not the same as those in the technical secrets of Fotao. Therefore, the production principles and technology of the Ceramic Roller could be deemed the confidential technical secrets of the plaintiff.

In addition, the Court held that in the conduct of general scientific research, even if one could acquire the same information through such means as patent documents, if he wanted to use these technologies, he would still require repeated experience and certain research. Besides, the Ceramic Roller project was based on very difficult and advanced technology, and was an innovative technology in China. If one tried to obtain such technology, he would have to invest great effort in the endeavour. The great number of research records and tentative production reports provided by Fotao had proved that it had taken dozens of its technical staff a lot of time to obtain the technology through continuous effort using good research equipment and facilities. During the hearing, defendant Jinchang had alleged that it had obtained the Ceramic Roller technology, which was identical to the trade secrets of the plaintiff, through its research of publicly available information regarding the technology. If that were true, then in accordance with subparagraph 1 of Article 64 of the Civil Procedure Law of the PRC the defendant was obliged to provide evidence that it had obtained the technology via legitimate and bona fide means, (e.g., evidence that the defendant conducted research based on information known to the public and conducted test production). However, Jinchang was able to provide only certain technical materials that it alleged it had found in publications but failed to provide the true source of those publications. On the other hand, the employees of the defendant and the ex-employees of the plaintiff were technical personnel that knew the technical secrets of the plaintiff. Thus, on 13 July 1995 the Foshan Intermediate People's Court ruled as follows:

(1) Upon entry of this judgment, the defendant, Jinchang Ceramic Roller Factory should immediately cease using the technology of the Cold Isostatic Processing Fine Ceramic Roller owned by the Fotao Group Joint Stock Company Limited Ceramics Research Institute to produce and sell ceramic rollers.
(2) The Jinchang Ceramic Roller Factory should compensate Fotao Group Joint Stock Company Limited for economic losses of CNY 264,019. If said payment is delayed, the Jinchang Ceramic Roller Factory must pay a penalty for delay of performance at twice the rate of commercial bank loans of the same duration.
(3) Upon entry of this judgment, the Jinchang Ceramic Roller Factory should within ten days make an apology to the Fotao Group Joint Stock Company Limited Ceramics Research Institute in a newspaper. The content of the apology must be examined and approved by the Court.
(4) The Jinchang Ceramic Roller Factory shall be held to an obligation of confidentiality to the Fotao Group Joint Stock Company Limited Ceramics Research Institute's technical secrets regarding the Cold Isostatic Processing Fine Ceramic Roller. The Jinchang Ceramic Roller Factory should not expand the scope of persons knowing said technology without authorization.

Neither party appealed the decision of the Foshan Intermediate People's court.

In the *Fotao* case, the court reversed the burden of proof and required that the defendant provide evidence which could identify the confidential technique at issue as a result of defendant's research, which has since been considered a great breakthrough in the assignment of burden of proof under the Chinese civil procedure regime. In addition, in responding to the plaintiff's request the Court initially granted an order temporarily halting defendant's infringement in accordance with preliminary execution as provided in the Civil Procedure Law, establishing a precedent which may be used as a standard in intellectual property disputes including infringement of trade secrets.

III. ANALYSIS AND BRIEF SUMMARY

Chinese law provides the holders of trade secrets with remedies to secure prompt and adequate protection. Current measures in China include preservation of evidence, preemptory action, and attachment of goods and cessation of infringement, among which attachment of goods is frequently applied. There are similar measures in other countries, such as the United States where ex parte injunction, temporary restraining order, permanent injunction and payment of compensation for losses can be imposed. However, remedial measures in the PRC and in the US differ greatly in their legal characteristics and remedial power.

In the United States and in other countries as well, injunctions are directed at acts of a defendant and are applied to restrain those acts or to govern the acts of a defendant, such as forbidding a defendant's use or disclosure of trade secrets, returning trade secret documents to a plaintiff or destroying duplicates of original documents.[65] However, the subject of attachment of goods under PRC law includes the property of the defendant and property belonging to the plaintiff but under the control of the defendant. The property must be tangible, as intangible property is not entitled to be preserved as property. Court orders regarding property are issued to confiscate, seize or freeze certain property, rather than to order a party to do or not to do something.[66]

Following the issuance of an injunction, in the US a defendant becomes an obligee of the injunction. If the defendant fails to abide by the injunction, he can be held in contempt of court.[67] When a Chinese court issues an order regarding attachment of goods, the court enforces the order itself. In accordance with the Civil Procedure Law of the PRC, the court can issue an order to preserve property and immediately impose enforcement of its order.[68] A defendant in China has no obligation to provide the court with security. If the court fails to confiscate, freeze or seize property pursuant to its own order it cannot charge the defendant with the offence of refusing to carry out an order of the people's court.

In the US, injunctions are also intended to forbid the disclosure and use of trade secrets by defendants so as to avoid the dissemination of information and the extension of losses.[69] In China, the measures of good attachment are designed to

65. See the US Federal Rules of Civil Procedure, Rule 65 (c).
66. See Article 94 of the Civil Procedure of People's Republic of China (2007).
67. Douglas Laycock, *Modern American Remedies, Cases and Materials*, (Beijing, CITIC Publishing House, 2003), p.237.
68. See Article 92, 93 of the Civil Procedure of People's Republic of China (2007).
69. See Restatement (Third) of Unfair Competition, 1995, (US), §44, comments b and c.

control the property of a defendant so as to secure the enforcement of pending judgments. The Civil Procedure Law of the PRC stipulates that in cases where the execution of a judgment may become impossible or difficult because of the acts of either party or for other reasons the people's court may, pursuant to petition of the defendant or the plaintiff, order the adoption of measures for the preservation of property.[70] It is clear that attachment of goods is intended for the purpose of securing enforcement of future decisions.

In the US, injunctions can directly order a defendant to cease infringing acts so as to provide the holder of a trade secret with prompt and reliable relief. In this aspect, an injunction can provide a holder with high-level protection. On the contrary, in China, because the court is unable to confiscate, seize or freeze the secret information itself, attachment of goods cannot prevent the disclosure or use of a trade secret by a defendant. Indeed, the confiscation of a defendant's property, (e.g., production facilities or technological materials) can only temporarily prevent acts of infringement. A defendant is permitted to continue to use a trade secret during civil proceedings. Consequently, attachment of goods currently available in China does not provide plaintiffs with strong and effective protection.

Furthermore, as provided by the Civil Procedure Law of the PRC, the effectiveness of preliminary execution in cases involving trade secrets and other kinds of intellectual property rights is poor. There is little precedent for the application of preliminary execution in trade secret cases in China.[71] These shortcomings arise from the fact that the prerequisites for applying preliminary execution do not suit the characteristics of trade secrets. Paragraph 1 Article 98 of the Civil Procedure Law of the PRC stipulates that in order for preliminary execution to be imposed by the people's courts, the relationship of rights and obligations between the parties concerned must be clear and definite and denial of preliminary execution would seriously affect the livelihood or operations of the petitioner. Thus, the stipulation requires petitioners to prove and judges to interpret why the failure to stop the acts of a defendant will seriously affect the livelihood or operations of the petitioner. However, trade secret cases are usually complicated because disputes regarding the existence of rights to trade secrets are usually heated. (e.g., whether information used by a defendant in his activities derives from general knowledge, experience or technology rather than from the use of plaintiff's trade secrets). This makes it difficult to determine the rights and obligations of parties. In addition, many trade secrets have low development costs and little novelty. Some trade secrets have not been put into use, while other trade secrets are, in essence, negative information. In short, even when trade secrets are disclosed or used by others, said disclosure or use will generally not have a serious effect on the livelihood or operations of a trade secret holder. As a result, under Chinese law it is always difficult for a plaintiff to justify his claim for preliminary execution.

Moreover, there are some differences in civil remedial measures in the PRC and in other countries after judgment is rendered. The purpose of imposing

70. See Article 92 of the Civil Procedure of People's Republic of China (2007).
71. Zhang Guangliang, *Remedies for Intellectual Property Rights*, (Beijing, Law Press, 2003), p.62.

cessation of infringement in Chinese law is similar to that of permanent injunction in common law countries.[72] By judgment and order of the court, a petitioner can prevent a defendant from continuing to obtain, disclose or use his trade secrets so as to prevent increased damage and to minimize losses. The aim of these remedial measures is to prevent the occurrence of infringement rather than to provide remedy for damages. The difference lies in the fact that an order for cessation of infringement is permanent while a permanent injunction under US laws is of limited duration. The duration of a permanent injunction is designed to balance the interests of the parties and the public interest and to suit the characteristics of trade secrets.[73]

When computing losses, PRC law and other countries law apply the principle of full compensation, which means that an infringer must compensate a trade secret holder for the actual losses caused by his acts. Only when it is difficult to determine the losses of an infringed party can the courts use the profits that an infringer earned during the period of infringement as the amount on which to base compensation.

According to Chinese legislation, 'bearing reasonable costs of investigation'[74] and 'payment of damages' can be combined. In accordance with judicial practice, 'reasonable costs of investigation' always refers to reasonable costs paid by an infringed party for investigating and stopping acts of infringement. Reasonable costs always include lawyer's fees, cost of buying infringed goods for use as evidence, notary fees incurred for preservation of evidence, equipment bought for examining evidence, cost of advertising for eliminating the negative effects of infringement and reasonable travel fees.[75] Payment of compensation for damages does not include reasonable costs of investigation. The payment of reasonable costs of investigation is punitive in nature because it exceeds the amount of actual damages to be paid by the infringer to the infringed party.

However, in Chinese judicial practice, the courts usually regard costs of investigation as direct damages. Whether the courts apply the principle of payment of compensation based on 'loss to a business operator caused by infringement' or the principle of 'profits earned by an infringer during the period of infringement' to determine losses and to compute compensation, infringers coming before the court in China also bear reasonable costs of investigation.[76] American legislative and judicial practices are different from those in China. The Uniform Trade Secrets Act

72. 'Permanent Injunction' means a writ or an order made by a court at the end of a lawsuit, forbidding or requiring parties to do certain things. See Peter. G. Renstorm, *The American Law Dictionary*, translated by He Weifang, et al. (Beijing, China University of Politics and Law Press, 1998).

73. See Restatement (Third) of Unfair Competition, 1995, (US), §44 comment c.

74. It means that an infringer must pay reasonable costs to a damaged party who has incurred expense to investigate the activities of unfair competition conducted by the infringer. See Paragraph one Article 20 of the *Law Against Unfair Competition of the People's Republic of China* (1993).

75. See Judge Jiang Zhipei, 'Judicial Protection of IPR in China', <www.chinaiprlaw.com/english/default.htm>, 5 January 2008.

76. *Ibid.*

not only addresses the attorney fee issue but also proposes that the court, under certain conditions, may order infringers to pay punitive damages. The Uniform Trade Secrets Act suggests that if wilful and malicious misappropriation exists, the court may award punitive damages in an amount not exceeding twice the actual losses or profits earned through the act of infringement. The court may also order infringers to pay attorney fees.[77] It is apparent that malice is an important factor in determining the awarding of attorney fees and punitive damages in cases of infringement.

The awarding of punitive damages has not been broadly adopted in the Chinese legal system and the scope of application of punitive damages is quite limited. At the present time, punitive damages are only explicitly provided for in the Law of the People's Republic of China on the Protection of the Rights and Interests of Consumers and in the Contract Law regarding the fraudulent conduct of business operators when supplying goods and services to consumers. The two laws stipulate that where a business operator has committed fraud when supplying goods and services to a consumer, he must, upon the consumer petitioning the court, pay increased compensation for losses incurred by said consumer. The amount of increased compensation will be calculated based on the price of the commodity purchased or the fee paid for the service received by the consumer.[78]

In drafting the Civil Code of the PRC, a majority of academics have proposed the adoption of a punitive damage system. They have also suggested two prerequisites for the application of punitive damages, namely the intent to infringe and that the infringed property comprises another's life, health, body, or liberty. However, certain other academics hold a different view. In their minds, punitive damage is a public liability in essence and a private liability in form. They believe that punitive damages have the characteristics of both private and public law, but

---

77. See *Uniform Trade Secrets Act*, 1985 (US), Section 3 [Damages].

(a) In addition to or in lieu of injunctive relief, a complainant may recover damages for the actual loss caused by misappropriation. A complainant also may recover for the unjust enrichment caused by misappropriation that is not taken into account in computing damages for actual loss.

(b) If wilful and malicious misappropriation exists, the court may award exemplary damages in an amount not exceeding twice any award made under subsection (a).

78. *Law of the People's Republic of China on the Protection of the Rights and Interests of Consumers*, Article 49: 'A business operator that practices fraud in providing a commodity or a service must, at the request of the consumer, increase the compensation for losses incurred by said consumer. The amount of the increase in compensation shall be the price of the commodity purchased or the fee for the service received by the consumer'.

The *Contract Law of People's Republic of China*, Article 113: 'Where one party fails to perform contractual duties or the performance fails to conform to the agreement and thereby causes losses to the other party, the amount for losses compensated shall be equal to the losses caused by the breach of contract including possible profit realized if contract duly performed but shall not exceed the possible loss caused by breach of contract which can be foreseen by the breaching party at the time of contract formation. Where the business operator has committed fraud in supplying goods and service for consumers it shall take liability for compensation according to the provisions in the *Law of the People's Republic of China on Protection of the Rights and interests of Consumers*'.

that the public law characteristics should prevail. Whether to employ the dual characteristics of private and public law in the Civil Code of the PRC, they say, should be determined by whether it is necessary or not to separate private law from public law. In other words, to focus on the private characteristics of the Civil Code of the PRC or to emphasize the functional characteristics of civil code shall determine whether to incorporate a system of punitive damages into the Civil Code. It can be seen from the history of the Chinese legal system that the negative effects of not separating private law from public law remain a great obstacle to the modernization of the Chinese legal system. Therefore, when drafting the Civil Code, it will be better to apply the recent theory that private law and public law should be strictly separated. In this aspect, it is unwise to adopt such a hybrid liability system into the Civil Code and it is better to preserve the private characteristics of the Civil Code.[79] This view reflects the concerns of quite a number of legal academics.

79. Jin Fuhai, 'It is Inappropriate to Adopt a Punitive Compensation System into Civil Code' (2003) 2 *Journal of Yantai University*, 157.

Chapter 3

Criminal Law Remedies for Trade Secret Infringement

Criminal punishment can be imposed by the legal authority of the criminal courts on an offender for perpetrating certain types of offences. Characterized by the infliction of certain suffering upon an offender (the deprivation of life, liberty or property),[1] criminal punishment is the severest form of punishment that a court can impose in the name of the state against criminal violators.[2] In China, criminal law remedy is generally imposed by the Public Security Administration, the procuratorates or the courts with the objective of investigating criminal liability and of punishing offenders.

Protection of intellectual property under criminal law was initiated in China in 1979 with the promulgation of the Criminal Law of the PRC (the 1979 Criminal Law)[3] the provisions of which, including the provision that trade secret infringement can be prosecuted as theft or as disclosure of state secrets, remained in force until 1997.

Article 186 of the 1979 Criminal Law made the disclosure of important state secrets a crime.[4] In 1989 the Standing Committee of the National People's

1. Zhang Shangzhuo, 'Law of China' in *Encyclopaedia of China*, Zhang Youyu (ed.) (Beijing, Encyclopaedia of the China Press, 1984), p.648.
2. *Ibid.*
3. The 1979 *Criminal Law of the People's Republic of China* (which has since been abolished) provides for criminal responsibility for the crime of counterfeiting registered trademarks. Article 127 provides: 'Where an industrial or commercial enterprise violates the laws and regulations on trademark administration and counterfeits the registered trademark of another enterprise, the person directly responsible shall be sentenced to a term imprisonment of not more than three years, criminal detention, or a fine'.
4. Article 186 of the 1979 *Criminal Law of the People's Republic of China* provides: 'Any State functionary who divulges important State secrets in violation of State laws and regulations on the protection of secrets, if the circumstances are serious, shall be sentenced to fixed-term

Congress promulgated the Supplementary Provisions on Punishment of the Crime of Disclosing State Secrets, which specifies the charge of (as well as the penalties for) 'stealing, espionage, buying or illegally providing state secrets to an overseas agency or person'.[5] Those legal provisions and judicial interpretations form the legal basis for prosecuting and punishing acts of trade secret infringement because scientific and technological secrets deemed 'state secrets' often have the characteristics of trade secrets. However, the 1979 Criminal Law does not provide penalties for the infringement of trade secrets other than state secrets.

In 1992 the Supreme People's Court and the Supreme People's Procuratorate jointly issued a judicial interpretation that specifically extended the application of the crime of theft to include intangible property such as technological achievements. In the judicial interpretation, the crime of theft is defined as stealing public or private property of certain value with the intent of illegal possession.[6] The term 'property' therein refers to tangible and intangible property including, among other things, electric power, gas, natural gas and important technological achievements.[7] In June 1994, the Supreme People's Procuratorate and the State Commission of Science, Technology and Industry jointly promulgated the Opinion on Treatment of Cases of Economic Crime in Technological Activities which defines the term 'technological secret' for the purposes of the PRC Criminal Law as technological information, computer software or other unpatented technological achievements that are not in the public domain, are of practical use, that can bring economic benefit or competitiveness to the owner and that are held in confidentiality by the owner.[8] On the other hand, the Opinion provides that where the circumstances are serious, an offender who steals technological secrets may be prosecuted for theft.[9]

---

imprisonment of not more than seven years and criminal detention or deprivation of political rights; a person who is not a State functionary who commits such crime mentioned in the preceding paragraph shall be punished in the light of the circumstances and in accordance with such provisions'.

5. The third session of the Standing Committee of the Seventh National People's Congress of the People's Republic of China promulgated the *Supplement of the Standing Committee of the National People's Congress on Punishment of the Crime of Stealing State Secrets* on 5 September 1988, providing 'Anyone who commits the crime of stealing, spying, purchasing or illegally providing State secrets for overseas organs or persons shall be sentenced to a term of imprisonment of not less than five years and not more than ten years; if the circumstances are not serious, the offender shall be sentenced to a term of imprisonment of not more than five years, criminal detention, or deprivation of political rights; if the circumstances are particularly serious, the offender shall be sentenced to a term of imprisonment of more than ten years, life imprisonment or to death and deprivation of political rights'.
6. See Article 1 of the *Interpretations of Certain Issues on Application of Laws to Cases of Theft* jointly promulgated by the Supreme People's Court and the Supreme People's Procuratorate on 11 December 1992.
7. *Ibid.*
8. See Section 1 of Article 5 of the *Opinion on Treatment of Cases of Economic Crime in Technological Activities* (abolished) jointly promulgated by the Supreme People's Procuratorate and the State Commission of Science, Technology, and Industry on 17 June 1994.
9. *Ibid.* See Section 2 of Article 5 Such definition is generally similar to that made in the *Law against Unfair Competition of the People's Republic of China* (1993) regarding trade secrets.

In September 1994, the Supreme People's Court also promulgated the Notice on Further Strengthening Judicial Protection of Intellectual Property, which reiterates that when hearing cases of theft of important technological achievements, the courts may impose sentence by reference to the crime of theft.[10] Therefore, it is obvious that prior to 1997, as a criminal law remedy, protection against trade secret infringement was made available primarily by prosecuting offenders under relevant provisions in connection with the crime of theft in China's criminal law. However, since 1997, that situation has changed.

The Criminal Law was amended by the Fifth Session of the Eighth National People's Congress in 1997. The amended Criminal Law, effective 1 October 1997 (the 1997 Criminal Law), put in place for the first time the crime of infringement of trade secrets. The crime of trade secret infringement is set forth in the section titled 'Intellectual Property Right Infringement Crimes' in the chapter titled 'Crimes Undermining the Order of the Socialist Market Economy'.

I. CRIME OF TRADE SECRET INFRINGEMENT

The elements of the crime of trade secret infringement as provided in the 1997 Criminal Law are substantially consistent with those for acts of trade secret infringement set forth in the Law Against Unfair Competition in such aspects as the type of act, subject matter infringed and other subjective elements. They are different only in the degree of damage incurred by an owner of a trade secret. Pursuant to Article 219 of the 1997 Criminal Law, an act of trade secret infringement is a criminal offence only when such an act has incurred or may incur material loss to the person who owns the rights to the infringed trade secret, otherwise it will be considered a general tort. The elements of the crime of trade secret infringement are as follows:

(1) The normal conduct of competition in a country is disturbed and a holder's right to keep trade secrets is diminished, (i.e., the economic benefit derived from the exclusive right to keep trade secrets is affected).
(2) In fact, a perpetrator has committed one of the following acts:
  (a) Illegally obtaining trade secrets, as provided in Article 219 of the 1997 Criminal Law, including acquiring a rightful owner's trade secret by theft, enticement, duress or other illegal means:
  In China's criminal law, 'theft' is defined as 'acquiring illegally by stealth', including stealing confidential business documents or obtaining trade secrets by covert means including wiretapping, simulation, photographing, or copying.[11] 'Enticement' refers to obtaining trade secrets by offering some benefit as a lure. 'Duress' means making or

10. See Section 2 of Article 3.2 of the *Notice on Further Strengthening Judicial Protection of Intellectual Property* promulgated by the Supreme People's Court on 29 September 1994.
11. See Article 287 of the *1997 Criminal Law*.

exercising an actual, potential, psychological or physical threat or coercion against another so as to force them to disclose a trade secret. 'Other illegal means' refers to other acts of illegally obtaining trade secrets apart from those previously mentioned above. China's existing laws provide no interpretation of the term 'other illegal means', but in judicial practice and in academic circles it is accepted that it refers to any act contrary to the civil law doctrine of good faith used to obtain trade secrets, excluding 'obtaining a trade secret by virtue of independent research and development' or 'obtaining a trade secret by virtue of reverse engineering'.

(b) Using illegally obtained trade secrets in an abusive manner, as provided in Article 219 of the 1997 Criminal Law by disclosing, using or permitting another to use an illegally obtained trade secret:
Provision (b) is actually a necessary supplement to provision (a) because an infringer will not be able to derive any benefit if he does not disclose, use or permit another to use an illegally obtained trade secret. Article 219 defines the term 'disclose' as making a secret public by oral or written means or otherwise enabling persons who should not know a secret to know the secret, thereby destroying its confidentiality. 'Use' refers to using a trade secret in production or operations for the purpose of unfair competition or personal profit. The phrase 'to permit another to use' refers to an act committed by an infringer who has obtained a trade secret by illegal means who permits another to use said trade secret.

(c) Illegally disposing of trade secrets obtained legally from another party, as provided in Article 219 of the 1997 Criminal Law, or disclosing, using or permitting another to use a trade secret acquired contrary to an agreement or to the confidentiality requirements of the owner of the trade secret;

(d) Indirectly infringing upon a trade secret, as provided in section 2 of Article 219, (i.e., a person who knows or should know that a trade secret has been obtained illegally nevertheless uses or discloses said trade secret).
In trade secret infringement, there is always a recipient, (i.e., the next person in the chain of infringement) whose existence enables the infringer to achieve his purpose and to secure illegal proceeds. Under the law, the acts of this 'recipient' may also constitute trade secret infringement. This is known as 'trade secret infringement by a third party'. In said provision, the phrase 'knows or should know' is a test determined on the basis of objective inference or objective foresight rather than on the infringer's own admission.[12]

---

12. Hu Kangsheng & Li Fucheng, *Interpretation of the Criminal Law of the People's Republic of China* (Beijing, Law Press, 1997), pp.309–310. The author of this book participated in the work to amend the 1979 *Criminal Law of the People's Republic of China.*

(3) With respect to subjective elements, the crime of trade secret infringement is an intentional offence, whether such intention is direct or indirect. Disclosure of a trade secret due to negligence does not fall under Article 219.[13]
(4) The subject of this crime may be a legal person, an unincorporated association or a natural person.[14]
(5) The crime of trade secret infringement must incur material losses to the person who has the rights to the trade secret, which draws the important distinction between guilt and innocence.

As provided in the Regulations on Standards for Prosecution of Cases Involving Economic Crime jointly promulgated by the Supreme People's Procuratorate and the Ministry of Public Security on 18 April 2001 (the 2001 Regulations), 'material loss' refers to:

(a) direct economic loss of more than CNY five-hundred thousand to a person who has rights to the trade secrets;
(b) causing bankruptcy of a person having the rights to the trade secrets or causing other serious consequences. Falling short of the above criteria, the infringement may constitute a general tort.

On 8 December 2004, the Supreme People's Court and the Supreme People's Procuratorate jointly promulgated the Interpretation Concerning Certain Issues on the Specific Application of Law in Handling Criminal Cases of Infringement of Intellectual Property Rights (the 2004 Interpretation). Under the 2004 Interpretation, if any of the acts listed in Article 219 of the 1997 Criminal Law causes losses of more than CNY five-hundred thousand to persons who have the rights to trade secrets, such acts will be deemed to have 'caused material loss to the owner of trade secrets'; if said loss exceeds CNY 2.5 million the acts will be deemed to have caused 'particularly serious consequences' as contained in Article 219 of the 1997 Criminal Law.[15] The 2004 Interpretation contains additional detailed provisions regarding relevant articles of the 1997 Criminal Law, providing a basis for court decisions and sentencing in criminal cases of trade secret infringement.

---

13. Some Chinese academics consider that the crime of trade secret infringement provided in China's *Criminal Law* must be an intentional act but, as provided in section 2 of Article 219 of the 1997 *Criminal Law*, 'Whoever acquires, uses or discloses the trade secrets of others when he knows or should know that the trade secrets were acquired through the aforementioned means shall be regarded as a kind of crime of negligence'. See Zhao Bingzhi, *Judicial Countermeasures to Difficult Issues of the Crime of Infringement upon Intellectual Property Rights* (Chang Chun, Jilin University People's Press, 2000), p.412.
14. Hu Kangsheng & Li Fucheng, *Interpretation of the Criminal Law of the People's Republic of China* (Beijing, Law Press, 1997), pp.309–310.
15. See Article 7 of the Interpretation of Certain Issues of Application of Laws to Treatment of Criminal Cases of Infringement upon Intellectual Property Rights promulgated by the Supreme People's Court and the Supreme People's Procuratorate on 8 December 2004 and effective 22 December 2004.

However, neither the 2001 Regulations nor the 2004 Interpretation contain specific provisions in respect of the method for computing losses. In practice, some courts compute the losses of victims in accordance with Article 20 of the Law against Unfair Competition, (i.e., if the loss incurred by the victim is difficult to calculate, compensation will be equivalent to the proceeds obtained by an infringer during the period of infringement). If the infringer has not received proceeds from the infringement, the court may have the losses of the trade secret owner professionally assessed and use said assessment as the basis for judgment. Regarding this issue, experts within criminal law circles in China hold varying opinions.[16]

Under the 1997 Criminal Law, the penalty for engaging in infringement of trade secrets is not to exceed three years imprisonment or criminal detention and a fine. In particularly serious cases of infringement, the penalty for infringers is imprisonment for a minimum three years and a maximum of seven years in addition to a fine.[17] When an entity commits the crime of trade secret infringement, its directly responsible person in charge and other personnel bearing direct responsibility will be punished in accordance with the same provisions as for natural persons under the Criminal Law.[18]

II. PUBLIC PROSECUTION AND PRIVATE PROSECUTION

In China, public prosecution refers to lawsuits lodged by special authorities which have been granted that right by law. Under the provisions of the Criminal Procedure Law of the PRC, the authority that is entitled to exercise the right of public prosecution on behalf of the state is the People's Procuratorate[19] which investigates crimes, maintains state security and social order and safeguards citizens. With respect to major cases of trade secret infringement turned over by the public security administration that involve damage to social order or the interests of the state or wherein an infringer is likely to be sentenced to a term of imprisonment of not less than three years, the People's Procuratorate can initiate public prosecution of said infringer before a people's court[20] provided, however, that the facts of the crime have been verified through investigation and that adequate evidence has been gathered to support criminal prosecution.

According to criminal law theory in China, private prosecution refers to cases wherein a victim or his legal representative or a victim's close relative files a lawsuit before the court in oral or written form in order to hold a defendant

16. This issue is discussed in detail in the next section in this Chapter.
17. See Section 1 of Article 219 of the Criminal Law of the People's Republic of China (1997).
18. *Ibid.* See Article 220.
19. See Article 137 of Criminal Procedure Law of the People's Republic of China (1996).
20. See Articles 138 and 141 of the Criminal Procedure Law of the People's Republic of China; Section 2 of Article 1 of the Explanations on Several Problems with respect to the Implementation of Criminal Procedure Law of the People's Republic of China promulgated by the Supreme People's Court in 1998.

criminally liable which will be directly accepted and heard by the court.[21] The Criminal Procedure Law of the PRC provides that cases of private prosecution include the following:

(1) Cases to be handled only upon complaint of victim;
(2) Minor criminal cases which the victims have evidence to prove and
(3) Cases where the victim has evidence to prove that the accused has committed a criminally punishable act of infringement upon the victim's personal or property rights, but in which the public security administration or the procuratorate has refused to prosecute the accused.[22]

In 1998, the Supreme People's Court promulgated the Explanations on Several Problems with Respect to the Implementation of Criminal Procedure Law of the PRC, containing further explanation and provisions with respect to the scope of private prosecution cases that may be directly accepted by the courts, which include:

(1) Cases to be handled only pursuant to complaint, which include:
  a) insult or libel with the exception of those materially damaging social order or state interests;
  b) interfering in the free choice of marriage with violence;
  c) maltreatment or
  d) infringement.
(2) Minor criminal cases in which a victim has evidence to prove, but in which the People's Procuratorates will not investigate, the criminal liability of the accused, including cases of:
  (a) intentional injury;
  (b) trespassing upon residential property;
  (c) infringement upon the freedom of correspondence;
  (d) bigamy;
  (c) abandonment;
  (f) production or sale of fake or inferior commodities with the exception of those that materially damage social order and state interests;
  (g) infringement upon intellectual property rights with the exception of those that materially damage social order and state interest or
  (h) infringement upon the body or democratic rights of a person or infringement upon property where the offender is likely to be sentenced to imprisonment of not more than three years.[23] Minor cases of infringement upon intellectual property wherein an offender can

21. Zhang Zipei, 'Law of China', *Encyclopaedia of China*, Zhang Youyu (ed.) (Encyclopaedia of the China Press, Beijing, 1984), p.834.
22. See Article 170 of the Criminal Procedure Law of the People's Republic of China (1996).
23. See Article 1 of Explanations on Several Problems with Respect to the Implementation of Criminal Procedure Law of the People's Republic of China promulgated by the Supreme People's Court in 1998.

be sentenced to imprisonment of not less than three years are also deemed cases eligible for private prosecution.

III. JURISDICTION AND STATUTES OF LIMITATION

A. Jurisdiction

Under the Criminal Procedure Law of the PRC, the local courts in China have jurisdiction as the courts of first instance over ordinary criminal cases.[24] The intermediate courts have jurisdiction over such first instance criminal cases as those concerning political subject matter and those endangering state security, ordinary criminal cases punishable by life imprisonment or by death, cases involving death sentences with a two-year reprieve and criminal cases in which the defendant is a foreigner.[25] In accordance with the 1997 Criminal Law, if anyone infringes upon a trade secret and thereby causes particularly serious consequences, he can be sentenced to not less than three years but not more than seven years of imprisonment and payment of a fine. Thus, first instance trade secret infringement cases fall under the jurisdiction of the local courts. According to relevant judicial interpretations and provisions, minor criminal cases of infringement upon trade secrets should be filed by infringed parties and may summarily be heard by the court.[26]

Under the Criminal Procedure Law, criminal cases of trade secret violation come under the jurisdiction of the people's court in the place where the crime was committed. If it is more appropriate for a case to be tried by the court in the place where the defendant resides, then that court may have jurisdiction over the case.[27]

B. Statutes of Limitation

A statute of limitations is the limited time period set forth in the criminal law within which offenders should be prosecuted. The 1997 Criminal Law determines statutes of limitation based on the maximum statutory sentence for each criminal act. Where the maximum statutory prison sentence is less than five years, the crime cannot be prosecuted after five years have elapsed; where the maximum statutory sentence is more than five years but less than ten years, said crime cannot be prosecuted after ten years have elapsed.[28] Therefore, the statute of limitations for ordinary crimes of infringement upon trade secrets is five years whereas if

---

24. See Article 19 of the Criminal Procedure Law of the People's Republic of China (1996).
25. *Ibid.* See Article 20.
26. *Ibid.* See Article 174 In China, a single judge tries cases that apply summary procedure.
27. See Article 24 of the Criminal Procedure Law of the People's Republic of China (1996).
28. See the Sections 1 and 2 of Article 87 of the Criminal Law of the People's Republic of China (1997).

an infringer's crime causes serious consequences to the holder of a trade secret, the statute of limitations is ten years.

IV. CIVIL SUITS COLLATERAL TO CRIMINAL PROCEEDINGS

Civil suits collateral to criminal proceedings are a means by which, while holding offenders liable for their criminal acts in the course of criminal proceedings, the public security administration, the procuratorate, and the courts can also settle the claims of victims for compensation of material losses caused by an infringer's criminal acts on the basis of the claim lodged by the procuratorate or by the victim.[29]

In private prosecution cases where a victim has suffered material loss as a result of the criminal acts of a defendant, the victim may lodge a collateral civil suit after the criminal case is accepted but prior to the decision of the court of first instance being handed down. If the victim fails to lodge its collateral civil suit prior to the judgment of the court of first instance being handed down he may lodge a separate civil suit following the outcome of the criminal case.[30]

In public prosecution cases, a victim may claim compensation with the public security administration or the procuratorate during the period of criminal investigation, preliminary hearing and review or prosecution. If a collateral civil suit has been filed with the public security administration or the procuratorate, the court will hear it as a civil suit collateral to the criminal proceedings following prosecution of the criminal case. If the victim insists on lodging a collateral civil suit with the court after the public security administration and the procuratorate have conducted mediation, the parties concerned have reached agreement, and compensation has been paid, the courts may accept the collateral civil suit.[31] In cases of public prosecution where loss has been incurred to state or collective property and the entity suffering said loss does not lodge a collateral civil suit, the procuratorate may lodge a civil suit collateral to criminal proceedings concurrent with the public prosecution, and the court will accept it.[32]

Civil suits collateral to criminal proceedings will be tried together with the criminal case. Where the material loss of a victim or a defendant's ability to compensate is difficult to determine in a short period of time, or if a party to a collateral civil suit fails to appear before the court for certain reasons, the collateral

---

29. See Sections 1 and 2 of Article 77 of the Criminal Procedure Law of the People's Republic of China (1996).
30. See Article 89 of the Explanations on Several Problems with Respect to the Implementation of the Criminal Procedure Law of the People's Republic of China published by the Supreme People's Court in 1998.
31. *Ibid.* See Article 90.
32. See Article 77.2 of the Criminal Procedure Law of the People's Republic of China (1996).

civil suit may be heard by the same trial organ after the criminal case is tried so as to avoid undue delay in the hearing of the criminal case.[33]

V. ANALYSIS AND BRIEF SUMMARY

Compared with civil law remedy, criminal law remedy is a more severe and possibly a more effective form of remedy involving not only economic punishment of a defendant (i.e., payment of fines) but also deprivation or restriction of the personal freedom of a defendant. Additionally, the application of a criminal law remedy can reduce litigation costs of the victim of an offence and relieve the victim of the burden of proof, thus effectively deterring infringement upon trade secrets. Therefore, it has been widely accepted and adopted by most countries to protect trade secrets with criminal punishment.

At the same time the international community has recognized the protection of intellectual property rights by means of criminal penalty and such method has also been accepted in international treaties. Article 61 of the TRIPS Agreement provides that:

> Members must provide for criminal procedures and penalties to be applied at least in cases of wilful trademark counterfeiting or copyright piracy on a commercial scale. Available remedies include imprisonment and/or fines sufficient to provide a deterrent consistent with the level of the penalty applied for crimes of similar gravity. Where appropriate, remedies also include the seizure, forfeiture or destruction of infringing goods and of any materials and implements that have been used in the commission of the offence. Members may provide for criminal proceedings and penalties to be applied in other cases of infringement of intellectual property rights, in particular where they are committed wilfully and on a commercial scale.

This is the general principle of criminal law remedy adopted by TRIPS. Notably, it is not compulsory for members to provide for criminal procedures and penalties to be applied in cases of trade secret infringement within member states.

Criminal law remedy for infringement of trade secrets is provided in the law and regulations of many countries so as to enhance the protection of trade secrets and to effectively punish infringement. Nevertheless, trade secrets play different roles in the economic development of different countries, trade secret holders at various levels of society do not share the same understanding of the protection afforded them under the criminal law. In addition, due to different degrees of economic development and diversified cultural backgrounds, legislation regarding criminal law remedy varies from country to country.

---

33. See Article 97 and 99 of Explanation on Several Problems with respect to the Implementation of Criminal Procedure Law of the People's Republic of China published by the Supreme People's Court in 1998.

In their early legislation, some countries applied the crime-of-theft principle to address infringement of trade secrets. Unfortunately, infringement of trade secrets could not be effectively prosecuted under traditional criminal law as a crime of theft. In general, the prosecution of the crime of theft usually requires public or private property of relatively high value being stolen for the purpose of illegally possessing it. However, what infringers of trade secrets are always concerned with and try to obtain is the value of a trade secret in and of itself and, in many circumstances, perpetrators do not need to remove the medium on which a trade secret is stored when they illegally use or disclose the trade secret. Moreover, certain other countries require that the value of stolen property must be of a certain sum in order to prosecute it as a crime of theft. However, trade secrets exist in the form of information and are intangible, thus making their value difficult to assess. Further, the intrinsic value or potential value of a trade secret usually exceeds the value of the medium on which it is stored. The courts find it difficult to charge those who steal the medium on which a trade secret is stored with theft in cases where the value of that medium is not high enough to meet of the legal criteria for the crime of theft. Consequently, the misuse of trade secrets often does not warrant a charge of theft.

Since the 1960s, with the increased understanding of trade secrets as well as the rise of their importance in economic life, a new set of criminal remedies has gradually been established in some countries, which is embodied mainly in the following changes of legislation:

(1) In addition to criminal law, laws against unfair competition and laws regulating market activities have been promulgated to enhance the protection of trade secrets from criminal infringement. In many countries, (including Germany, Japan, Austria, Denmark and Portugal among others) the infringement of secret information including trade secrets is punishable not only under criminal law but in order to effectively maintain order in market competition laws against unfair competition and laws regulating market activities have been enacted and amended that clearly provide that the infringement of trade secrets is to be prosecuted.[34]

(2) Special laws for the protection of trade secrets.

Some countries or regions have promulgated and enforce special laws for the protection of trade secrets. For example, the Economic Espionage Act was passed in the United States in 1996, Sweden promulgated the Act on the Protection of Trade Secrets in 1990,[35] the Act regarding Business Secrets was passed in Taiwan in 1996 and Thailand passed its Trade Secrets Act in 2002. These special laws all provide that offenders of trade secrets bear criminal liability and are subject to criminal punishment.

---

34. See Marketing Practices Act of Denmark (2000).
35. See Act 1990:409, of May 31, 1990, < www.wipo.int/clea/en/fiche.jsp?uid=se005>, 5 January 2007.

(3) The addition of the separate offence of infringement of trade secrets in the current criminal codes.

Some countries and regions have amended their criminal codes to include criminal liability for infringement of trade secrets. The law of these countries, including Italy, Belgium and Finland, now provides for the separate offence of infringement of trade secrets.

Although specific provisions and methods for the prosecution of certain offences vary from country to country due to their diverse legal systems, many countries still follow the basic principle of defining crimes of infringement of trade secrets according to the characteristics of the infringed subject matter, the perpetrator of the act, intent of the act and the conduct of the act.

Continental Law countries employ rigorous logic and theoretical application in codifying their criminal law and the establishment of offences in those countries depends more upon the subject matter and the severity of the damage to society caused by the crime.

French criminal law is a good example. Criminal acts concerning the infringement of trade secrets in French criminal law include violations of confidentiality, crimes of supplying information to foreign states and violations of confidentiality which endanger state defence secrets. The subject matter of the first includes rights of person while the latter two are essential to state interests.[36] In the latter two crimes, if the perpetrator of the crime is a French citizen or a soldier their acts are considered treason while if conducted by an alien constitute the crime of espionage. The objects violated under the crime of infringement of trade secrets committed by employees are limited under French labour law to the employer's right to trade secrets and bona fide employment relationships. Due to the differences between the charges and their impact on society, the French Penal Code also differentiates in its scope of criminal punishment. For example, perpetrators guilty of supplying information to foreign countries or of endangering state defence secrets can be sentenced to ten years imprisonment in addition to imposition of a fine of one-hundred thousand euros (EUR),[37] while perpetrators guilty of violations of professional secrets can be sentenced to one year of imprisonment in addition to imposition of a fine of EUR fifteen-thousand.[38]

The US Economic Espionage Act (1996) provides for two offences concerning secrets, namely crimes of economic espionage and theft of trade secrets. The prosecution of these two offences is determined by the intent of the perpetrator and by the degree of damage to society caused when trade secrets are infringed. The crime of economic espionage is the infringement of trade secrets with the intent to

36. 'Essential State interests' refers to State independence, integrity of territory, security, republican systems, means of defence, foreign affairs, protecting French people within and outside of France, protecting the natural environment and environmental balance, science and technology of states, basic elements of economic potentials and cultural properties. See *Nouveau Code Penal*, Article 410-1.
37. See *French Penal Code*, Article 411-7, 411-8.
38. *Ibid.* See Article 226-13.

benefit a foreign government, foreign institution or foreign agent. These acts cause great harm to society since they not only concern the intangible property rights of the holder but also directly endanger the interests of the state. In order to be charged with theft of trade secrets, a perpetrator must intend to use them for his own benefit or for the benefit of others (except for the benefit of the holder of the trade secret, foreign governments, foreign institutions or foreign agents). The harm caused to society by the theft of trade secrets is minor compared to that of the crime of economic espionage. According to the different characteristics of and the degree of harm caused to society by the two crimes, the Economic Espionage Act provides different criminal liability. Those who commit economic espionage can be sentenced to fifteen years in prison, be fined USD five-hundred thousand or both;[39] while those who commit theft of trade secrets can be sentenced to ten years in prison, fined or both.[40] Any institution committing the crime of economic espionage can be fined a maximum of USD ten million while for theft of trade secrets the penalty can be a fine of no more than USD five million.[41] Any party found guilty of violating the Economic Espionage Act must forfeit all direct or indirect illegal income derived from their illegal activities.[42]

Current Chinese criminal law classifies crimes into ten specific types depending on the object of the crime[43] and particular offences are charged based on the specific subject matter of the violation based on these classifications. The criteria for the definition of certain offences in China are derived from the commonly held theory of four criminal elements (subject, subjective, object, and objective requirements of a particular crime) and on the particular charges listed in the criminal law. Based on these principles, crimes involving trade secrets stipulated in Chinese criminal law include the crime of infringement of trade secrets; the crime of stealing, secretly gathering, purchasing, or illegally providing state secrets or intelligence to an organization, institution, or person outside the country; and the crime of intentionally or negligently revealing state secrets.

According to the Chinese Criminal Law and the State Secret Protection Law, the difference between the crime of trade secret infringement and the crime of stealing, secretly gathering, purchasing, or illegally providing state secrets or intelligence for an organization, institution, or person outside the country, and the crime of intentionally or negligently revealing state secrets lie in the different objects of the criminal act. The object of the crime of infringement of trade secrets can be any number of different trade secrets while the objects of the crime of stealing, secretly gathering, purchasing or illegally providing state secrets or intelligence for an organization, institution, or person outside the country, and the crime

39. See *Economic Espionage Act* (1996), section 1831(a)(5).
40. *Ibid.* See section 1832 (a) (5).
41. *Ibid.* See section 1831 (b) and section 1832 (b).
42. *Ibid.* section 1834.
43. Crimes of endangering national security, endangering public security, undermining the order of socialist economy, infringing upon the rights of a person and democratic rights of citizens, infringing on property, disrupting the order of social administration, endangering the interests of national defence, graft and bribery and crimes of dereliction of duty.

of intentionally or negligently revealing state secrets, are state secrets. State secrets can also include trade secrets that concern state security and state interests that have been determined by special legal procedures and that have been acknowledged by certain persons at a particular time.[44] The holder of state secrets is the state alone. Only through the conduct of certain legal procedures can any secret information, including technical information, be classified as a state secret. Therefore, in China, if a trade secret that does not meet the criteria of a state secret is stolen or disclosed, the act will be punished as a crime of infringement of a trade secret even if the perpetrator had the express intent to serve the interests of an extraterritorial organization or institution. In addition, Chinese criminal law regarding infringement of trade secrets does not differentiate in the identity or the intent of the subjects. The crime of infringement of trade secrets will be charged for all acts of infringement of trade secrets and the criminal penalty imposed will be the same for each.

Upon investigation of various sections of Chinese criminal law regarding the elements of the crime of infringement of trade secrets, the following similarities can be found among them:

First, except for the crime of disclosure of state secrets, intent is an element of the crime of infringement of trade secrets in all countries. Most countries do not punish infringement of trade secrets caused by negligence.

Second, though the legislative approach may vary in different countries, their legislation regarding infringement of trade secrets contains similar provisions regarding the elements of the crime. Generally, those elements include three types of acts: obtaining trade secrets by illegal methods, making use of or disclosing trade secrets without authorization, and malicious infringement by third parties.

Third, due to the particularities of trade secrets, provisions regarding the elements of the crime of infringement of trade secrets always adopt the principle of action, which means that damages are not a necessary requirement for prosecution of the crime and that criminal penalties are directed at the act of infringement of trade secrets.

Fourth, because the crime of infringement of a trade secret violates the rights of the holder of the trade secret, regarding methods of prosecution many countries allow the conduct of private prosecution along with public prosecution. In many criminal laws, it is left to the discretion of victims to decide whether to prosecute perpetrators of ordinary infringement of trade secrets while it is the procuratorates that initiate public prosecution against acts of infringement of trade secrets concerning the interests of the state.

Compared to provisions in other countries regarding the elements of infringement of trade secrets, Chinese criminal law has the following characteristics:

First, Chinese criminal law provides that there must exist certain legal consequences for all crimes of infringement of intellectual property. Consequently, in the case of trade secret infringement when a holder's legal rights are infringed but

44. See Article 2 of the Law on Protecting State Secrets of the People's Republic of China (1989).

the damages caused by said infringement do not amount to a certain sum or when infringers have not profited or if there are profits but they do not meet the standard for prosecution, it is not possible to criminally prosecute such infringers. Only when an act of infringement has caused great loss to the holder of a trade secret can perpetrators be criminally prosecuted.

Second, current Chinese criminal law does not provide for private prosecution in cases concerning infringement of trade secrets. Consequently, only procuratorates have the power to initiate prosecution in the courts regardless of whether a victim wishes to take action to protect their trade secrets rights in the criminal courts.

Third, as to the crime of infringement of trade secrets, current Chinese criminal law does not completely eliminate the possibility of prosecution of infringement caused by negligence and does not contain restrictive regulations regarding criminal intent.

Article 61 of the TRIPS Agreement for the first time in history established basic procedures for the protection of trade secrets under criminal law. However, it was left for members to decide how to execute those procedures. As a result, the various existing criminal penalties for infringement of trade secrets have significantly local characteristics.

In summary, the imposition of criminal penalties for the infringement of trade secrets is based on two theories: the protection of private property and the maintenance of competitive order.

Although there exist different legal systems among different countries, they all tend to provide for the protection of the rights of individuals (e.g., trade secret holders) as measured against the public interest in their laws. It can be said that contradicting views and value standards in different countries have given rise to different legal systems for addressing issues related to infringement of trade secrets which impose themselves on the societies of those countries.

Chapter 4

Administrative Protection of Trade Secrets

To hold back the flood of intellectual property infringement in international trade, all countries in the world emphasize the administrative protection of intellectual property rights as well as the enhancement of legislative and judicial protection. The so-called administrative protection of intellectual property rights refers to the state intellectual property administrative authorities, subject to their administrative responsibilities, applying administrative measures to regulate and handle intellectual property disputes and to sanction acts of infringement of intellectual property. Administrative protection is represented in three aspects:

(1) granting intellectual property rights (e.g., patents and copyrights)
(2) providing administrative remedies for intellectual property infringement and
(3) providing customs protection at the borders.[1]

However, current legislation in many countries seldom provides administrative relief for infringement of trade secrets. One of the reasons for this situation is that trade secrets differ from other kinds of intellectual property rights. The acquisition of trade secrets does not need publication or permission. Furthermore, in practice, it rarely happens that goods carrying trade secrets are moved across borders. Judicial relief for the infringement of trade secrets is generally provided through civil and criminal procedures in many countries.

Unlike many other countries however, this is a unique characteristic of the Chinese intellectual property system, which provides administrative legislation and enforcement for violations of intellectual property rights including trade

1. Customs are government departments supervising and regulating imported and exported goods, which play a very important role in checking and banning counterfeit goods.

secrets. According to statistics, government authorities at various levels handling intellectual property issues accepted 68,535 patent, trademark and copyright infringement cases across the country through 2004. In 2004, the courts throughout the country tried and concluded 8,332 civil intellectual property cases at first instance and 385 criminal intellectual property cases at first instance.[2]

Obviously, Chinese intellectual property administrative authorities play a very important role in solving intellectual property disputes.

I. GENERAL INTRODUCTION

Chinese law protects intellectual property, including trade secrets, mainly by two means: First, by judicial remedy including criminal and civil remedies as discussed above, and second through administrative measures.[3] In Chinese legal circles, this is called the 'dual-track system'. In ordinary cases of trade secret infringement which are not serious enough to give rise to criminal prosecution, a victim may resort to civil remedy or administrative remedy to request that the state administrative authorities investigate an infringer for its infringement of trade secrets and to protect its legal rights and interests.

As defined by legal scholars in China, 'administrative responsibility' refers to obligations imposed by administrative law for the harm done to the legal rights and interests of an individual or entity protected by administrative laws or to state or social public interest by a party due to its violation of administrative laws and regulations or its failure to perform its obligations under administrative laws and regulations.[4] Administrative responsibility in China includes administrative sanctions and administrative penalties. 'Administrative sanctions' refers to sanctions imposed by a superior administrative authority or relevant authorities on the directly responsible person-in-charge and other responsible persons in the event of administrative malfeasance committed by a government administrative authority, a civil servant, an organization authorized by law and administrative regulations to exercise the state's administrative powers or an organization or individual entrusted by an administrative

2. 'White Paper on Intellectual Property Right Protection in China (2004)'. <www.gov.cn/zwgk/2005–05/27/content_1605.htm>., 5 January 2008.
3. The term 'administrative remedy for trade secret infringement' used herein is a corresponding concept of civil remedy and penal remedy. The concept means the owner of the trade secret applies to administrative organs for administrative protection measures when his trade secret right is infringed upon by others. So this administrative remedy for trade secret infringement is not an administrative remedy in the general sense which refers to various legal measures prescribed by the State's administrative law in order to prevent administrative acts taken by the State or its administrative organs from infringing upon the lawful interests and rights of citizens, legal persons or unincorporated organizations.
4. Law Institute of Chinese Academy of Social Sciences, *Law Dictionary* (Beijing, Law Press, 2003), p. 1684.

authority to exercise that administrative authority.[5] Administrative sanctions include several types:

(1) disciplinary warning,
(2) a demerit for the record,
(3) relegation,
(4) demotion in official post and
(5) dismissal.

'Administrative penalty' means a sanction imposed on a citizen, legal person or other organization whose acts violate administrative laws, regulations or rules but are not considered a crime by the state administrative authorities and organizations that have the right to duly exercise the imposition of administrative penalties.

Administrative penalties mainly include:

(1) disciplinary warning
(2) fine
(3) confiscation of illegal gains or confiscation of illegal property or things of value
(4) order for suspension of production or business
(5) temporary suspension or revocation of permit or temporary suspension or revocation of license
(6) administrative detention.[6]

In China, administrative protection has the advantage of lower cost and higher efficiency than civil remedy. Its main functions include promptly and quickly preventing tortious acts, and preventing damages from occurring or increasing. In protecting trade secrets by virtue of administrative measures, administrative penalties are the main method for investigating infringers for administrative responsibility. Compared with civil remedy, administrative penalties in China have the following basic characteristics:

(1) Administrative penalties are imposed pursuant to legal procedures prescribed by PRC law.[7]
(2) Administrative penalties can only be imposed by administrative authorities that are vested by law with administrative and judicial powers, namely the State Council or an administrative authority determined by the government of a province, autonomous region or municipality directly under the central government that is empowered by the State Council. However, the power to impose administrative penalties involving restriction

5. See Article 55 of the Law of the People's Republic of China on Administrative Penalty (1996).
6. *Ibid.* See Article 8.
7. The laws herein include the Law of the People's Republic of China on Administrative Penalty which became effective in 1996, the Law of the People's Republic of China on Administrative Reconsideration which became effective in 1999, and the Law of the People Republic of China on Administrative Permission which became effective in 2004.

of personal freedom can only be exercised by the public security authorities.[8] Additionally, depending on the types of administrative regulations that are violated by a punishable act, administrative penalties may be imposed by various administrative authorities. For example, an act in violation of the Law against Unfair Competition can be punished by the Administration for Industry and Commerce above the county level while the customs establishments can impose punishment for acts in violation of the Customs Law of the PRC. Punishment imposed ultra vires is deemed a violation of the law.

(3) Administrative penalties may be imposed either in response to requests made by victims or by a relevant administration according to law.

(4) The primary objects of administrative penalties are civil and economic disputes subject to administrative law arising generally from acts of natural persons, legal persons or other organizations in violation of administrative rules.

(5) Administrative penalties are binding to a certain extent, but they may not be final in the solution of a dispute. After a decision has been made to impose an administrative penalty in accordance with law, the relevant party within the time limit set forth in the decision must enforce it.[9] If the party fails to enforce the administrative penalty within the time limit, the administrative authority making the decision may impose enforcement measures as permitted by law or request that the order be enforced by the court. If a party refuses to accept an administrative penalty, he may apply to an authority for administrative review or request administrative litigation.[10] During the period of administrative review or administrative litigation, however, the enforcement of the administrative penalty will not be suspended unless the law provides otherwise.

(6) The imposition of administrative penalties by administrative authorities does not limit the right of victims to file civil lawsuits with the courts. Administrative penalties do not include compensation for damages. Individuals, legal persons and other organizations that are subject to administrative penalties as a result of violations of law must assume civil liability for harm caused to others by their illegal acts.[11] Victims may file their claims for damages with the courts. Similarly, if an illegal act is found to constitute a crime, the administrative authority must transfer the case to a judicial authority for investigation of criminal liability according to law.[12]

---

8. See Article 15 of the Law of the People's Republic of China on Administrative Penalty (1996).
9. See Article 44 of the Law of the People's Republic of China on Administrative Penalty (1996).
10. *Ibid.* See Article 45 For administrative reconsideration, the Law of the People's Republic of China on Administrative Reconsideration shall apply; for administrative litigation, the Administrative Procedure Law of the People's Republic of China that became effective in 1990 shall apply.
11. *Ibid.* See Article 7.
12. See Article 22 of the Law of the People's Republic of China on Administrative Penalty. Article 3 of the Regulations on Transfer of Cases of Suspicion of Crime by Administrative Organs for

II. JURISDICTION AND AUTHORITY OF ADMINISTRATIVE COURTS AND AGENCIES

Most acts of infringement of trade secrets are acts of unfair competition and the harm caused by such acts lies in their direct disturbance of normal social economic order and fair market competition. Consequently, the Law against Unfair Competition bestows upon governments at all levels the authority to take appropriate measures to prevent unfair competition and to create sound conditions and an environment for fair competition.

As stated in the Law against Unfair Competition, acts of unfair competition fall under the jurisdiction of the Administration for Industry and Commerce where the violation occurred or where the infringer resides. The Administration for Industry and Commerce at the county (district) and municipal (prefecture) levels must handle cases occurring in their jurisdictions while branches of the Administrations for Industry and Commerce at the provincial, autonomous region and municipal levels directly under the central government must handle those sets of circumstances or complicated cases which are within their authority occurring within their jurisdictions.[13] In short, ordinary acts of infringement of trade secrets must be handled by the Administration for Industry and Commerce above the county level.[14]

III. EVIDENCE AND BURDEN OF PROOF

When a trade secret holder as a petitioner believes that his trade secrets have been infringed upon and he subsequently makes a claim to the Administration for Industry and Commerce for an investigation into the act of infringement, he will be required to provide relevant information regarding said infringement.

Law Enforcement promulgated by the State Council in July 2001 provides: 'Where administrative organs of law enforcement, in the course of investigation into acts of violation of law, finds evidence of malfeasance constituting a suspected crime they shall investigate for criminal responsibility in terms of sums involved, circumstances and consequences of malfeasance in accordance with provisions of the Criminal Law regarding crimes of undermining of the order of the socialist market economy and crimes of disrupting the order of social administration and regulations on standards for investigation into cases of economic crime made by the Supreme People's Court, the Supreme People's Procuratorate, and the Ministry of Public Security, and it shall transfer such cases to the public security organs'. The Regulations also make provisions where cases of acts in violation of law are not transferred and for corresponding responsibility, so as to ensure that cases of infringement upon intellectual property which constitute a suspected crime will be transferred in a timely manner from administrative organs to judicial organs for enforcement.

13. See Articles 4 and 5 of the Interim Regulations on the Procedure of Administrative Penalty of the Administration for Industry and Commerce promulgated by the State Administration for Industry and Commerce (2000 Revision).
14. See Article 4 of the *Several Regulations on Forbidding Infringement of Trade Secrets* promulgated by the State Administration for Industry and Commerce (1995).

The petitioner must also provide evidence for the existence of the subject trade secret and the suspected act of infringement. Meanwhile the entity or individual under investigation must provide relevant evidence on the basis of facts to the Administration for Industry and Commerce.

If the holder can prove that the information used by the accused is in conformity with or identical to his trade secret and that the accused had access to the trade secrets, whereas the accused fails to or refuses to provide proof that the information he used was obtained or used lawfully, the Administration for Industry and Commerce may find that the accused has committed acts of infringement.[15] This provision follows the principle of 'reversal of burden of proof'.

IV. TEMPORARY MEASURES

In an emergency, in order to prevent an infringer from illegally disclosing, using or permitting others to use a trade secret and from causing irreparable loss to the holder of the secret, the Administration for Industry and Commerce may, at the request of the holder, take the following measures provided that the holder voluntarily provides a written guarantee stating that it will assume responsibility for the consequences of said measures:

(1) to order the infringer to discontinue selling products manufactured using the trade secret of the holder;
(2) to withhold drawings, software or other related materials which contain the trade secrets of the holder and have been improperly obtained by the infringer.[16]

V. ADMINISTRATIVE PENALTY

When a party has made a request for an investigation into an act of infringement, he will be required to submit a written application. The Administration for Industry and Commerce decides whether or not to accept the application within ten days after receiving it. If the application is accepted, the administration will conduct an investigation and determine the facts in accordance with the administrative procedure provided by law and make a determination in respect to any penalties. If the facts of the violation are clear and corresponding legal provisions can be applied, the Administration for Industry and Commerce can announce its decision, provided that the penalty is a warning or a fine of less than CNY fifty for an individual and CNY one-thousand for a representative, otherwise penalty decisions may be handed down within seven days.

---

15. See Section 3 of Article 5 of the *Several Regulations on Forbidding Infringement upon Trade Secrets* promulgated by State Administration for Industry and Commerce (1995).
16. *Ibid.* See Articles 6 and 7.

The following administrative penalties may be imposed for infringement of trade secrets:

(1) Order to discontinue trade secret infringement;
(2) Imposition of a fine from CNY ten-thousand to CNY two-hundred thousand depending on the circumstances;
(3) Ordering and supervising the return by the infringer of drawings, software or other materials containing trade secrets to the holder;
(4) Supervising the infringer in its destruction of products that were manufactured using the trade secret of the holder and that would lead to disclosure of said trade secret if they are allowed to enter the market, except where the owner consents to another means of disposal such as purchase or sale.

Where an infringer refuses to accept the decision of the Administration for Industry and Commerce and continues its infringement, such act will be deemed a new violation and will be addressed with heavier punishment.[17]

VI. ADMINISTRATIVE MEDIATION

Although administrative penalties do not include compensation for damages, the Administration for Industry and Commerce may, when dealing with disputes concerning trade secrets, conduct mediation in respect of compensation on a voluntary basis at the request of victims. But neither mediation nor decisions reached thereby are binding. If mediation fails, the infringed party may bring a lawsuit before the court to recover compensation for damages.[18]

VII. REVIEW OR LITIGATION

Any party who is dissatisfied with an administrative penalty imposed by a local Administration for Industry and Commerce above the county level may apply for an administrative review within sixty days upon learning the decision. The application for an administrative review may, at the option of the applicant, be filed with the Administration for Industry and Commerce that made the decision or with the Administration for Industry and Commerce of a higher level.[19]

Administrative review applications are reviewed by the Administration of Industry and Commerce within five working days of receipt and an administrative review decision will be issued within sixty days from the date of receipt of the

17. *Ibid.* See Article 8.
18. See Article 9 of the *Several Regulations on Forbidding Infringement upon Trade Secrets* promulgated by the State Administration of Industry and Commerce (1995).
19. See Article 12 of the Law of the People's Republic of China on Administrative Reconsideration (1999).

application regarding acceptance or rejection, unless the statutory period for review stipulated by law is less than sixty days. If circumstances are complicated and it is impossible to make a decision within the stipulated time, the period may be extended and the applicant and the accused must be notified of such extension. In any event, extensions may not exceed thirty days.[20]

Chinese law and regulations provide that parties must first apply for administrative review with an administrative review authority. If dissatisfied with the decision thereof, they may file an administrative lawsuit with the court. In the event that an administrative review authority rejects an application or fails to reply after accepting an application, the citizen, legal person or organization may bring an administrative lawsuit before the court within fifteen days from the date of receipt of the rejection or expiry of the period for administrative review.[21]

If an individual, a legal person or an organization that is dissatisfied with an administrative penalty decision wishes to bring a suit directly before a court, they must do so within three months from the date of the administrative decision, unless the law provides otherwise.[22]

VIII. ANALYSIS AND BRIEF SUMMARY

Part III of the TRIPS Agreement contains specific requirements for the enforcement of protection of intellectual property rights which provide guidelines for administrative and customs enforcement in addition to clear criminal and civil enforcement systems for the protection of intellectual property rights.[23] TRIPS permits members to establish domestic administrative procedures for enforcement of intellectual property protection enforcement and requires members to follow the established procedures for ascertaining facts and enforcing specific remedial measures, so as to ensure fair and equitable administrative enforcement.

Pursuant to TRIPS, each member must ensure that domestic enforcement procedures are available under their laws so as to permit effective action against any act of infringement of intellectual property rights and must also ensure that enforcement procedures be applied in such a manner as to avoid the creation of barriers to legitimate trade and to provide for safeguards against their abuse. Procedures for enforcement of protection of intellectual property rights must be fair and equitable. They should not be unnecessarily complicated or costly, and it is preferred that decisions regarding the merits of a case should be in writing and based on applicable laws and regulations. All decisions made by enforcement authorities, including administrative enforcement authorities, must be based on

20. *Ibid.* See Article 31.
21. See Article 31 of the Law of the People's Republic of China on Administrative Reconsideration (1999) and Article 38 of the Administrative Procedure Law of the People's Republic of China (1989).
22. See Article 39 of the Administrative Procedure Law of the People's Republic of China (1996).
23. See Article 41 of *TRIPS Agreement*,< www.wto.org >, 5 January 2008.

all of the evidence and all parties to a dispute are entitled to present relevant evidence.

In relation to containing administrative enforcement procedures for intellectual property protection, TRIPS also expressly stipulates that members must provide the opportunity and a procedure for judicial review. Administrative reviews can be divided into two sections:[24] One is the judicial review for granting of intellectual property rights. The other is the judicial review of administrative enforcement procedures for intellectual property. The first power of review can be extended to quasi-judicial bodies while the latter is confined to judicial bodies. The TRIPS Agreement emphasizes the critical role of judicial review in final administrative decisions.

As mentioned above, the administrative enforcement of intellectual property protection is an important aspect of the Chinese intellectual property legal system and has contributed much to intellectual property protection in China. However, in recent years quite a number of academics have expressed doubts about the effect of administrative enforcement of intellectual property protection in theory as well as in practice. In their common opinion, intellectual property rights have been broadly accepted as private rights.[25] Consequently, they hold that the Chinese judicial system should be more in line with the trend in other foreign countries, which means that judicial protection must be strengthened while administrative protection should be gradually weakened until the jurisdiction of administrative authorities over intellectual property infringement is relinquished. Compared to administrative protection, judicial protection employs better standards and better procedures and includes a more comprehensive range of protection.

Nevertheless, many academics recognize the necessity of preserving administrative remedies for intellectual property right protection at this present stage of China's development. Administrative settlement of intellectual property disputes is a critical and important form for enforcement of intellectual property protection in China. It remains necessary to maintain decision making at the current administrative levels since China is at a critical turning point in its economic reform and is undertaking heavy enforcement responsibilities. In addition, Chinese individuals and businesses lack sufficient information regarding the legal protection of their intellectual property to which they are entitled and are hesitant to initiate complex lawsuits. Judges also need to improve their enforcement capabilities regarding protection. Under these circumstances, administrative enforcement and judicial protection of intellectual property protection will continue to coexist for quite a long time. The academicians believe that the implementation of a conservative attitude toward penalties in intellectual property administrative enforcement will ensure that the level of intellectual property protection in China is raised to meet the requirements of the TRIPS Agreement.

---

24. See Article 41 of TRIPS, < http://wto.org >, 5 January 2008.
25. Recognizing that intellectual property rights are private rights, the preface to the TRIPS Agreement discloses one aspect of such intangible property and explains that intellectual property rights are in essence specific property rights belonging to private persons only.

Though the latter view currently prevails among the legal community in China, many academics and judges also agree with the concept of improvement of administrative enforcement for the protection of intellectual property. While continuing to preserve administrative enforcement of intellectual property protection, it is also important to ensure that administrative decisions comply with the law and that there are fair and equitable procedures in place to enhance the governing authority of the people's courts over intellectual property so as to support appropriate administrative enforcement and to correct wrongs or improper administrative enforcement.[26] In addition, with respect to the private nature of intellectual property, it is necessary to mitigate certain administrative remedy powers, such as determining compensation for infringement, which overlaps with the authority of the courts.

In order to establish realistic and effective legal protection for intellectual property, prior to and following its entry into WTO China thoroughly modified its laws, regulations, and judicial interpretations regarding intellectual property protection. In order to comply with TRIPS and with other international intellectual property protection rules, China has modified its legislative principles and the definition of intellectual property rights, as well as the standards for their protection and legal remedies to promote the advancement and innovation of science and technology.

Based on the model of improving the judicial and administrative systems so as to achieve a situation of 'two paths co-existing and coordinating for intellectual property protection', the newly-revised Patent Law has adopted the following important modifications:

First and foremost, the new Patent Law contains an improved judicial review system.

The original Patent Law of the People's Republic of China (1992) provides that decisions of the Patent Re-examination Board regarding any request for re-examination made by an applicant, a patentee or a person who makes a request for revocation of a patent right concerning a prototype or design are final.[27] Decisions of the Patent Re-examination Board in respect to requests to declare invalid a patent right for a prototype or design are also final.[28] Thus, decisions of the patent authority in cases of ownership disputes concerning prototypes or designs dealt with by the patent authority are final and are not eligible for judicial review procedures. At the same time, when the courts find it necessary to receive confirmation of the patent authority, the Supreme People's Court of China stipulates that the people's courts should, when dealing with infringement disputes, suspend proceedings until the patent authority issues a decision. Such provisions deprive the parties of the opportunity for judicial review. It is an unusual phenomenon that

26. Jiang Zhipei, Legal Studies on Intellectual Property Protection in China Following Entry into WTO (Beijing, People's Publishing House of China, 2002), p. 287.
27. See Subparagraph 3 of Article 43, the 1992 *Patent Law of the People's Republic of China* (Revised in 1992 and 2000).
28. *Ibid.* See Subparagraph 3 Article 49.

the courts have to wait for the decision of the patent authority while the courts are trying claim confirmation cases involving utility models and designs.

In addition, Article 60 of the 1992 Patent Law stipulates that any party that is dissatisfied with decisions of patent administrative authorities for patent infringement disputes should file a claim with the people's court. However, when a claimant to a dispute over a patent right for a design wants the court to find that the defendant has committed an act of infringement, if the defendant in the lawsuit counterclaims that the patent is void, then the people's court must suspend its proceedings and wait for the patent administrative authority's decision. As a result, the court's judicial review becomes nearly useless and the decision of the administrative authority becomes, in essence, final and binding.

There are corresponding provisions for the above-mentioned situations in the new Patent Law. All administrative decisions made by different levels of local patent administrative authorities for patent infringement or counterfeiting must be reviewed by the people's court, which means that any party that is dissatisfied with a decision of the administrative authorities may file a suit in the people's court pursuant to the Administrative Procedure Law of the People's Republic of China.[29]

In order to provide a guide for proper application of the revised patent law in trials, in June 2001 the Supreme People's Court circulated the Several Rules on the Application of Laws in Handling Patent Dispute Cases. The Rules point out that:

> When the people's court considers a patent infringement dispute case which has already been reviewed by the patent authority regarding whether or not infringement exists, it must fully examine the claims of the parties.

This interpretation provides the people's courts with the legal basis for the application of the law for the complete safeguard of the parties' rights to administrative judicial review.

Second, the new patent law has established a more reasonable system for fixing patent infringement compensation. According to the 1992 Patent Law,[30] the administrative authority for patent affairs handling a matter has the power to order an infringer to cease an infringing act and also has the power to determine compensation for damages. The 2001 Patent Law changed that provision to read that the administrative authorities for patent affairs may mediate the amount of the damages of patent infringement at the request of both parties and if mediation is not successful, either party may file a lawsuit in the people's court pursuant to the Civil Procedure of the People's Republic of China.

The above-mentioned modification and changes referred to existing legislation of the time to confirm the necessity of continuing administrative enforcement to make good use of the prompt, efficient, direct and low-cost function of the administrative authorities in dealing with intellectual property infringement.

29. See Article 57 of the 2001 *Patent Law of the People's Republic of China* (Revised in 1992 and 2000).
30. See Article 60 of 1992 Patent Law of the People's Republic of China (Revised in 1992 and 2000).

On the other hand, such provisions ensure the efficient execution of administrative judicial review which can gradually undermine the power of administrative authorities dealing with civil remedies in cases concerning protection of intellectual property rights.

Compared to traditional protection of intellectual property rights, Chinese legislation regarding administrative remedy for infringement of trade secrets is just at a starting point. However, the effective judicial remedy measures applied in judicial practice in the traditional intellectual property field, particularly legal principles applied by administrative authorities to deal with infringement disputes, can be applied to administrative rulings regarding trade secret protection.

Chapter 5
Arbitration Proceedings in Labour Law

In China, arbitration is an important method for resolving labour disputes concerning trade secrets. Labour dispute arbitration is a system by which disputes are dealt with by local labour dispute arbitration committees and this process enjoys a special status.

The Labour Law of the People's Republic of China provides that labour disputes may be resolved through mediation, arbitration, litigation or consultation.[1] In labour dispute cases, however, the parties should first attempt to find a solution through negotiation. If the parties are unwilling to negotiate or if negotiation fails, they may apply for mediation with the labour dispute mediation committee of the employer with whom they are having the dispute. If mediation fails, the case may be submitted to the labour dispute arbitration commission for arbitration. The parties may also apply directly to the labour dispute arbitration commission for arbitration. If dissatisfied with an arbitration award, either party may bring a lawsuit before the court.[2] According to provisions contained in the Regulations of the People's Republic of China on the Settlement of Labour Disputes in Enterprises, it can be concluded that, in China, labour dispute mediation is an optional rather than a compulsory procedure. However, labour dispute arbitration is a compulsory procedure and the courts will not accept a case that has not yet gone through the process of arbitration.[3]

1. See Section of the Article 77 of Labour Law of the People's Republic of China (1994).
2. See Article 6 of the Regulations of the People's Republic of China on the Settlement of Labour Disputes in Enterprises promulgated by the State Council through Order No.117 (1992).
3. See Article 6 of the Regulations of the People's Republic of China on the Settlement of Labour Disputes in Enterprises promulgated by the State Council through Order No. 117 (1992).

If all of the following three prerequisites are met, a labour dispute case may be filed with the court by the parties concerned:

(a) If the relevant labour dispute arbitration committee has conducted arbitration of the labour dispute between the parties concerned and made an award according to law;
(b) If any one of the parties concerned is dissatisfied with the award made by the labour dispute arbitration committee or
(c) If the lawsuit is brought before the court within fifteen days from the date of receipt of the arbitration award. In the absence of any one of the above prerequisites, cases will not be accepted by the courts. Therefore it can be concluded that labour dispute arbitration is compulsory prior to the filing of lawsuits concerning labour disputes.

According to the Explanations of the Supreme People's Court on Certain Issues of the Application of Law in Trial of Labour Dispute Cases promulgated in 2001 and implemented by the Supreme People's Court, labour disputes include the following types of disputes:

(a) Disputes arising between employees and employers in the performance of employment agreements;
(b) Disputes arising between employees and employers who have not entered into written employment contracts but have formed an employment relationship and
(c) Disputes between retired employees and former employers that do not participate in a unified social insurance plan[4] regarding pension claims, medical expenses, work injury insurance benefits or other social insurance payments.

Therefore, in labour disputes where an employee has failed to comply with a confidentiality clause specifically agreed upon by the parties thereto and infringes upon the trade secrets of an employer, the employer must first file for arbitration with an arbitration committee, and the labour arbitration committee must accept the application and render an award in accordance with provisions of the employment contract or other relevant provisions.[5] In the absence of an employment contract, if a dispute arises out of an obligation to confidentiality and a restriction on competition created on the basis of an employment relationship, or out of trade secret infringement between an employer and an existing or former employee, the above provision also applies.

---

4. See Article 1 of the Explanations of the Supreme People's Court on Certain Issues of Application of Laws in Trial of Labour Dispute Cases issued by the Supreme People's Court on 22 March 2001.
5. See Letter of the General Office of the Ministry of Labour and Social Security on Issues concerning Infringement upon Trade secrets in Labour Dispute Cases promulgated and effective 7 July 1999.

I. MEDIATION UNDER LABOUR LAW

Established as an internal organization of an enterprise, a labour dispute mediation committee consists of representatives of employees, representatives of the enterprise, and representatives of the labour union. Employee representatives are nominated and elected by a general meeting of employees, the general manager or a person of similar capacity appoints enterprise representatives, and labour union representatives are appointed by the labour union committee.

The number of members on a mediation committee is proposed by a general meeting of employees and determined through negotiations between the general meeting of employees and the general manager. The number of enterprise representatives must not exceed one third of the total members. A representative of the labour union must assume the position of chairman of the mediation committee. An office of the labour dispute mediation committee must be maintained at the labour union. In the absence of a labour union, the establishment and composition of the labour dispute mediation committee should be determined through negotiations between employee representatives and enterprise representatives.

A labour dispute mediation committee must complete mediation within thirty days following submission of a dispute by the parties, otherwise the mediation will be deemed unsuccessful. Mediation must be conducted on the basis of free will of the parties. If successful, a mediation agreement will be constructed and should be conscientiously performed by the parties. If unsuccessful, the labour dispute arbitration committee, within a set time limit, may submit the dispute for arbitration.[6]

II. LABOUR LAW ARBITRATION

A. Nature of Labour Arbitration and Composition of Arbitration Organs

In China, counties, municipalities and municipal districts maintain labour dispute arbitration committees consisting of representatives of competent labour administrative authorities, representatives of labour unions, and representatives of integrated economic administration authorities designated by the government. The arbitration committee must be composed of an odd number of members, and the official in charge of the government labour administrative authority will act as its chairman. The section of the labour administrative authority that handles labour disputes is the executive branch of the arbitration committee and is responsible for handling its day-to-day work. The arbitration committee operates according to the principle of decision by majority vote.[7] Thus, it can be seen that labour

---

6. See Articles 6, 7, 8, 9, 10 and 11 of the *Regulations of the People's Republic of China on the Settlement of Labour Disputes in Enterprise* promulgated by the State Council through Order No. 117 (1992).
7. *Ibid.* See Articles 12, 13 and 14.

dispute arbitration in China is conducted through administrative arbitration, not private arbitration.

Arbitration committees, in the settlement of labour disputes, can employ arbitrators or arbitration tribunals. An arbitration committee may engage personnel from the labour administration authority, or from other relevant government departments and labour unions, or may engage experts, academics and lawyers as full-time or part-time arbitrators. Part-time and full-time arbitrators enjoy equal rights in arbitration.

An arbitration tribunal consists of three arbitrators but a single arbitrator appointed by the arbitration committee may hear a simple labour dispute. An arbitration tribunal may submit major or complicated labour dispute cases to the arbitration committee for deliberation and decision. An arbitration tribunal must implement the decisions of the arbitration committee.

B. Jurisdiction and Limitation

Labour dispute arbitration is conducted under the auspices of the arbitration committee agreed upon by the parties in an employment contract. In the absence of such an agreement, the dispute will be heard by the labour dispute arbitration committee of the place where the employer is located or where the employment agreement is performed or executed. If the place where the employment agreement is performed is unclear, the labour dispute arbitration committee of the place where the employer is located will conduct the arbitration. When an enterprise and an employee involved in a dispute are not located in the same jurisdiction of an arbitration committee, the arbitration committee located at the place where the employee in question has 'wage relations' should handle the dispute.[8]

8. *Ibid.* See Article 17 The arbitration committees set up in counties, cities and city districts should be in charge of handling labour disputes in their respective administrative areas. The scope of jurisdiction of arbitration committees in cities with districts, and in such districts handling labour disputes, should be decided by the People's governments of the provinces and autonomous regions. Additionally, with respect to the scope of jurisdiction of arbitration committees, there are several special provisions as follows:

First, Article 18 of the *Regulations of the People's Republic of China on the Settlement of Labour Disputes in Enterprises* contains these provisions: 'When the enterprise and the worker(s) or employee(s) involved in a dispute are not located in areas under the jurisdiction of the same arbitration committee, the dispute should be handled by the arbitration committee located at the place where the worker(s) or employee(s) in question have wage relations'. The *Explanations of Certain Issues of Regulations of the People's Republic of China on the Settlement of Labour Disputes in Enterprises* (1993) published by the Ministry of Labour (now the Ministry of Labour and Social Security) makes such provision in its Article 14: 'The place of wage relations of employees refers to the place of the enterprise which provides wages for the employees'.

Second, the *Reply on the Scope of Jurisdiction over Labour Dispute Cases* issued by the former Ministry of Labour (1995) provides: 'According to the principle of facilitating employees and workers, we may comply with the relevant provisions of the *Civil Procedure Law of the People's Republic of China'* whereby disputes arising from performance of contracts may be governed by the courts of the place where contracts are signed or performed, or may be governed by the labour dispute arbitration committee agreed upon by both parties of the employment relation in relevant arbitration articles of their employment agreements.

The party applying for labour dispute arbitration must file a written application for arbitration with a labour dispute arbitration committee within sixty days from the occurrence of a labour dispute. The arbitration committee should accept an application when a party fails to observe the limitation stipulated in the aforesaid clause due to force majeure or for other justifiable reasons.[9]

C. Conciliation and Award

In handling labour disputes, an arbitration tribunal should first mediate and try to bring the parties to reach an agreement on a voluntary basis. If an agreement is reached through mediation, the arbitration tribunal should produce a mediation document in accordance with the content of the agreement which becomes valid as of the date of service. If no agreement is reached through mediation or if one party changes its mind before the document is served, the arbitration tribunal should proceed promptly with a ruling.[10]

Figure 1. Arbitral Procedure for Labour Disputes Involving Trade Secrets

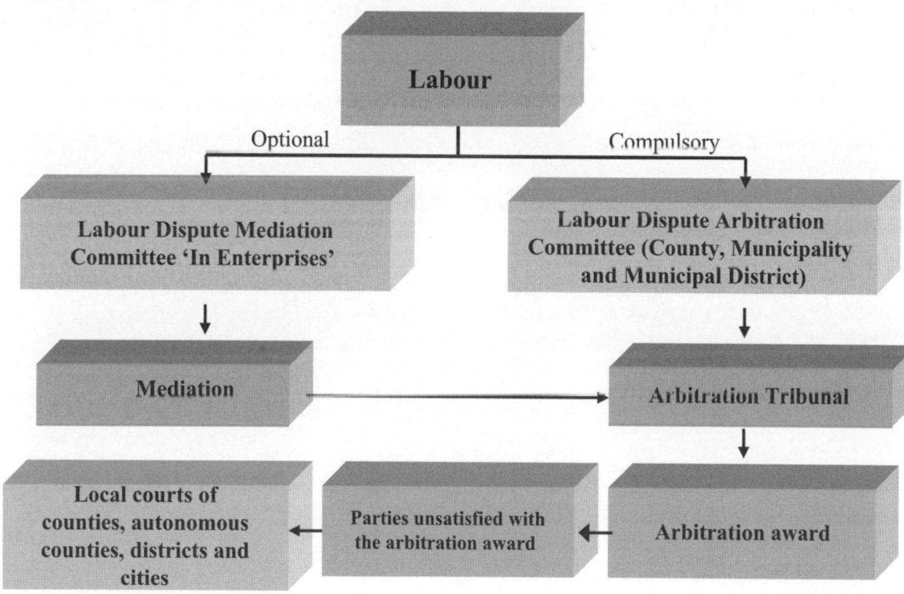

Third, the *Reply on Issues of Collective Labour Disputes of Qian'an Mine of Shougang Co.* (1999) issued by the general office of the Ministry of Labour and Social Security provides: 'Where collective labour disputes arise from employees outside Beijing when they are performing employment agreements in Beijing, such disputes should be governed by the labour dispute arbitration committee of the place where the enterprise is located'.

9. See Article 23 of the Regulations of the People's Republic of China on the Settlement of Labour Disputes in Enterprises (1992).
10. *Ibid* See Article 27.

An arbitration award will usually be rendered within sixty days from receipt of an application for arbitration. If a party refuses to accept an arbitration award, they may bring a lawsuit before the people's court within fifteen days of receiving said arbitration award. If neither party brings an action or if a party implements payment of the award or implements performance of the decision of the arbitration tribunal within the prescribed period, the other party may apply to the court for enforcement of said decision or award.[11]

11. See Articles 82 and 83 of the Labour Law of the People's Republic of China, and Article 30 of the Regulations of the People's Republic of China on the Settlement of Labour Disputes in Enterprises.

Part IV

Employment Relations and Trade Secret Protection[1]

1. The viewpoint generally accepted by Chinese labour law scholars is to divide labour relationships into those in a narrow sense and those in a broad sense. The labour relationship in a narrow sense refers to the relationship between the worker (employee) and the labour force user (employer) in a specific enterprise or employer. The labour relationship in a broad sense means the socio-economic relationship constituted by worker, labour force user and related social organization during the actual employment. See Chang Kai (editor), Labour Relations Science (China Labour and Social Security Publishing House, Beijing) (2005), at p.11. Therefore, in theory, the labour relationship in a narrow sense is the employment relationship recognized in other countries.

Chapter 1

Transformation of the Chinese Planned Economy System and the Market Reform of Its Labour Force

In terms of their characteristics, trade secrets display two basic forms: material property and personal property. Material trade secrets are referred to as the property of the trade secret holder and remain comparatively stable while personal trade secrets require that the employee is the medium that carries the secret. Thus, personal trade secrets are in constant flux. Generally, physical security measures can maintain confidentiality of material trade secrets. Physical security measures include monitoring the life cycle of a product (development, introduction, growth, maturity and termination) and full use (creation, use, storage, transfer and disposal) of trade secrets.

However, economic globalization has made it much harder to manage personal trade secrets. The personal freedom of movement that is one of the symbols of a mature market economy increases the outflow of such trade secrets and reveals the inherent contradiction between an employee's right to labour and restrictions not to compete. Employers have no right to deprive their employees of their skills and technological know-how. Furthermore employers do not have the ability to remove information, personal contacts or customer lists from the memories of their employees. What's more, the available judicial remedies for preventing disclosure of trade secrets are very weak. Therefore, when an employment relationship exists or has existed, the risk of infringement of trade secrets is higher and its consequences more severe. Infringement nowadays concerns failure of the duty to protect secrets not only during but also following employment. That is the reason why trade secret disputes arising from employment relationships are more complicated than those found outside of employment relationships.

This chapter will examine several main factors affecting the protection of trade secrets in China when employment relations are involved, including but not limited to the employment system and market reform of the labour force, the legal system for the protection of trade secrets in employment relationships and the public interest.

I. CHARACTERISTICS OF LABOUR FORCE ALLOCATION UNDER THE CHINESE PLANNED-ECONOMY SYSTEM

For the first thirty years following the establishment of the People's Republic of China in 1949, the allocation of the labour force in China was determined by means of the planned economy. This meant that the state used its administrative powers to allocate the labour force in accordance with centralized planning.

There were three significant characteristics of this system. First, it embodied the fundamental socialist principle that 'everyone has the right to work'.[1] The objective of planned allocation was to ensure that every citizen in the cities and towns obtained work. Second, owing to deficiencies in acquiring and processing data, the system could not effectively nor accurately match a worker's skills to an appropriate job. Third, allocation of jobs occurred through administrative order and left the worker with no choice.[2]

These three characteristics of labour force allocation created a unique framework for the Chinese employment system. First, the unified employment system operated under the planned allocation of the labour force. The government allocated all individuals of statutory age to state-owned enterprises without considering differences in the capabilities of workers, their work ethic or their personal characteristics. In essence there was one centralized employment system.

Second, the goal of the system was complete employment of all workers who were of statutory age in cities and towns. In relation to the public element of the enterprises, workers would simply be divided into several categories according to their qualities. Most workers who were residents of a city or town and who had reached the statutory age to work were dispatched to state-owned enterprises or to collective-owned enterprises of the towns for employment. The comparatively lesser-skilled labour force and weak and disabled individuals were allocated to affiliated departments of enterprises or were allocated to undertake temporary posts in state-owned or collective-owned enterprises.

---

1. In China, socialism includes scientific socialism, socialist systems, and the beginning stage of communist society. In a socialist country, the working classes are the master of State sovereignty and the form of ownership consists of mainly ownership by the people and through collective ownership. It applies the distribution policy of '[f]rom each according to his ability, to each according to his work'. The essence of the socialist expectation is the desire to liberate productivity, to eliminate exploitation and social and economic disparity, and to attain common wealth in the end. See China Social Science Academy Linguistics Research Institute Lexicography Editorial, *The Modern Chinese Dictionary*, (Beijing, Commercial Press, 2002), p.1116.
2. Xu Yafei, 'On the Dual Allocation of the Labour Force'(1998) *Open Times Journal.*

The third principle was that workers were assigned to employers and could not transfer among units without the approval of the government planning department and labour management supervision. There was, in fact, no free movement of the labour force.[3]

Allocation of labour was one of the most important aspects of the planned-economy system and it had to be aligned with the goals of the entire planned-economy system.[4] To meet the government's economic development targets, administrative directives allocated workers as well as funds, production processes and raw materials. Enterprises functioned passively as units of production and had no autonomous right to allocate the above-mentioned resources or to obtain profits. As a result, worker productivity and enterprise efficiency were greatly constrained due to the conflict between the centralized allocation of the labour force and the diversity of workers, as well as that between the public ownership system and the private characteristics of business unit productivity, which led to unsatisfactory results. This ultimately had a negative effect on the operating efficiency of enterprises.

Under this economic system, workers were required to make the greatest contribution that they could to the public-owned enterprise to which they had been assigned (i.e., their *danwei*) and were paid for their labour based on the number of years that they had served in that enterprise, regardless of their ability, skill or attitude toward their work. On the other hand these enterprises, in theory, exercised control over their employees and sought to obtain the greatest output from them. These two contradictory factors would inevitably lead to increased friction between the goals of the enterprise and the means it had to achieve those goals. Workers with little ability and those lacking a strong work ethic or who were unable to adapt to the planned-economy system or to the state-owned enterprise system were all included in the planned allocation and assigned to state-owned enterprises. Their lack of skill and their inability to fit into the system would cause discrepancies between the allocation of the labour force and the allocation of the means of production. As a result, the 'average doctrine' gave rise to inefficiency of the entire system of production.

On the one hand, enterprises were state-owned and the central government treated the labour force as public property. Under the public ownership system, the products generated by each sector of the labour force were allocated to the state. This, however, was over-simplified, as the system was unable to take into consideration the differences between the human resources – the workers.

On the other hand, workers used equipment that was privately owned. In essence, the production costs of the labour force were borne by the workers themselves and by their families. Those costs included expenses associated with raising

---

3. Chang Kai (ed.), *Labour Relations Science* (Beijing, China Labour and Social Security Publishing House, 2005), pp.128–129.
4. Su Chan, 'Study of the Allocation of the Labour Force in China',(2000) 1 *Theory and Reform Journal*, 59 *et seq.*

and educating their children and the expenditure of energy in physical labour resulting in aging and injury to the bodies of those workers.

The employment regime of that period was constrained by the planned-economy system and the administrative aims of the government that were reflected in three aspects:

First, the system defined the responsibilities of employers and employees. According to the definition of the socialist society during the period of the planned-economy system, people were masters of the state and were obviously and inevitably the owners of state-owned enterprises. Technically, under the Communist planned-economy system, every worker of an enterprise was, by definition, the owner of that enterprise, which meant that enterprises were comprised of employees functioning as masters and owners also acting as the means of production. Once a worker left his enterprise he was a master no longer, and that status was withdrawn accordingly. When a worker occupied a position within an enterprise and became an element within the means of production by implementing his ownership rights and privileges, management (who were also 'masters' of the enterprise) then had no right or authority to remove any worker with the same status. These were the systemic and moral difficulties that a public-owned enterprise confronted when it tried to resolve problems, for instance, regarding the issue of redundant workers.

Second, the system promised workers life-long employment. The planned-economy system for labour force allocation engendered an implied promise to the workers that the government would not only be responsible for allocating the labour force but also for guaranteeing permanent employment of workers. This meant that workers would work with the same enterprise until their retirement. The planned-economy system deprived workers of the right of free choice of employment and the government acted at its own will regarding employment and transfer of the labour force. Theoretically, this system benefited the planned-economy system that was being promoted at that time. The planned-economy system intended to ensure that every person had a career and that the population would be fully employed. As a result of the controlled assignment of work combined with dogmatic propaganda, workers generally believed in the system and also believed that the state had given them a promise of life-long employment. If the government or if an enterprise fired workers and caused unemployment, it would mean that they had violated that contract, which would not be accepted by workers from a legal or a moral perspective.

Third, the aim of the government was to maintain social stability. The ultimate aim of the government during the planned-economy period was to achieve a certain development of society and to stabilize the political system. Public-owned enterprises were not permitted to autonomously dismiss workers, neither for reasons of industry adjustment nor for reasons of technological innovation. Such dismissals could create a crisis in society as a result of the dissatisfaction of the unemployed and also because such acts could harm the stability of the government. Thus, public-owned enterprises were required to abide by the government's aim of achieving social stability, but at the cost of their own profitability.

II. MIGRATION AND DISPERSAL OF THE LABOUR FORCE DURING LABOUR MARKET REFORM

In the ten years following the decision in 1992 to establish a market economy in China, the creativity of the Chinese people was greatly inspired, economic expansion and social development were accelerated and the living conditions of its citizens were drastically improved. However, the social cost of that economic transformation and rapid economic development has been a very heavy burden that has resulted in multiple pressures related to re-prioritizing goals and remodelling social structures, and has introduced severe market competition in the re-formulation of economic rules.[5]

Following the advent of market reform, planned-economy enterprises were pushed out into a free market system they encountered other enterprises with much stronger competitive advantages. These included domestic private enterprises, foreign-invested enterprises (FIEs), and enterprises with investment from Hong Kong, Macao and Taiwan. Though the enterprises under the planned-economy were gradually market-reformed, progress was typically slower than for those of the newer, non-state-owned enterprises.[6] A number of conditions determined the fate of enterprises previously under the planned economy which could not reform. First, their products were unmarketable and performed poorly in sales, creating redundant workers due to a lack of work assignments once production of the goods had ceased. Second, the utilization of human resources was poorly managed which caused the means of production and financial support to flow to the newly-created, post-planned-economy enterprises that could generate greater value and provide better services. As time went on, older enterprises were faced with production shrinkage, operating losses and even with bankruptcy.[7]

In addition, the progress made by introducing a market for the re-assignment of the labour force accelerated the movement of labour away from the former planned-economy enterprises to the new market-economy enterprises and differentiated the labour force into several tiers. Many persons moved from the planned-economy system to the market system in which both workers and employers were able to set their own goals to obtain results that were best for them. All now pursued

---

5. Quan Heng, 'Chinese Society Transformation: Rethinking from the Political Economy, an interview with Professor Anthony Saich' (2005) 3 *Exploration and Free Views Journal* (Shanghai), 4 *et seq.*
6. Li Xingshan, 'Great Creativity – Review and Prospects for Establishment of a Socialist Market Economy in China' (13 October 2003) *Jiefang Daily* (Shanghai). According to related materials, until 2003 the percentage of 'marketized' enterprises was 55% and approximately 56.4% of management personnel were designated by the Government. Designated management personnel in State-owned enterprises accounted for 80.7%, with only 0.6% chosen from the market. Designated personnel in non-public enterprises were 28.9%, compared with 4.1% that were chosen from the market.
7. Liu Haifan, 'Deepening the Reform of State-owned Enterprises, Upholding the Direction of Socialism' (14 November 1996) *People's Daily*.

a more efficient and satisfying assignment of labour. Workers opted for employers that could offer the best pay while employers also wanted to recruit the most talented staff. The market gradually abandoned those workers and enterprises that were deemed unsuitable. The more clearly differentiated labour force was more easily connected with the positions available to them through the choices made by both employees and employers in the labour market. Diligent and more highly skilled workers from the former planned-economy enterprises adapted quickly to the market system, found re-employment and obtained positions that matched their abilities. Workers and employers took advantage of a certain degree of freedom during this shift in labour conditions. Having used their free will to achieve their respective aims, both worker and employer undertook their respective obligations in accordance with the contract between them.

In the course of this transformation, the labour force began to disperse between the former planned-economy enterprises and post planned-economy enterprises. Skilled workers (having greater ability and a better work ethic) quit the planned-economy enterprises and sought employment with various post planned-economy enterprises simply because they could achieve better living conditions and have more influence and opportunity there. This mobility was closely related to the difference in the levels of income between the former planned-economy enterprises and post planned-economy enterprises, including remuneration, benefits, social insurance and social status.

The difference in income between employees of the two types of enterprises was exaggerated by the following factors, which led skilled workers to transition to new careers and opportunities:

First, salaries were higher within post planned-economy enterprises. Enterprises with strong market competitiveness and those planning to improve their market competitiveness increased remuneration for valued workers. They started paying much higher wages than the former planned-economy enterprises so as to attract more highly skilled and competent workers.

Second, due to the 'average distribution policy', skilled workers could not obtain higher salaries at the former planned-economy enterprises based on their skill level. The market-economy enterprises paid much more to workers with higher skills. This salary policy led to a condition wherein the salaries of skilled workers at the former planned-economy enterprises were much lower than for those at market-economy enterprises while the salaries of low-skilled workers of the former planned-economy enterprises were equal to or even higher than those of the market-economy enterprises. Even after market reform, the difference in the wages of highly-skilled workers and low-skilled workers in the former planned-economy enterprises was not as great as between those of market-economy enterprises. The result was that the difference in the wages between skilled workers in the two different types of enterprises was much greater than between middle and lower-skilled workers.

Third, average salaries increased along with the efficiency of production and higher product prices while the former planned-economy enterprises had no capability to increase their salary levels.

Fourth, the government changed its policies. During the reform of social benefits, the government ordered that all enterprises gradually improve the social benefit system that enabled the labour force to gain the same security within market-economy enterprises as they had enjoyed in former planned-economy enterprises. However, due to heavy financial losses, some planned-economy enterprises could not afford to maintain a fund for the payment of social benefits and, as a result, the workers in those enterprises could not obtain social benefits. In addition, the government stipulated that enterprises should pay housing allowances and heating allowances to workers and to contribute to a housing fund for them.

Many planned-economy enterprises were not able to implement such policies while more and more post planned-economy enterprises could. One of the reasons for this was the heavy financial burden caused by the obligation of planned-economy enterprises to pay social benefits such as retirement pensions and child support as well as by their generally poor management.

The disparity in income caused by the above-mentioned factors was a strong motivation for skilled workers to seek new employment. Four choices existed for workers who chose to leave: Those possessing skills, a positive work ethic, and the ability to raise capital became entrepreneurs and established their own private enterprises; those with certain operational abilities and a work ethic, but lacking the ability to obtain start-up funds, set up sole proprietorships;[8] most of those with skills and a work ethic that were unable to raise capital to become investors became the managers of post planned-economy enterprises and the remaining workers that had technical or professional skills became technical personnel or workers at post planned-economy enterprises.[9]

The movement of skilled workers from planned-economy enterprises to post planned-economy enterprises increased the competition between these two types of enterprises. The reduced efficiency of planned-economy enterprises encouraged and accelerated the outflow of skilled workers which eventually caused a shortage of qualified labour. In addition, the competitiveness of planned-economy

---

8. In China, 'sole proprietorship' refers to farmers or industrial and commercial individuals. See China Social Science Academy Linguistics Research Institute Lexicography editorial, *Modern Chinese Dictionary* (revised 2002). 'Sole proprietorship' generally refers to individual enterprises and individual workers. Individual enterprises refer to enterprises invested in by individuals such as stores run by spouses, restaurants run by individuals, family farms, etc. Owners and their family members usually having no employees, conduct the work and management of the business. Individual enterprises are generally small and diversified in their business and have no legal person status. They are the most basic type of enterprise organization. Individual workers are also called individual operators, referring to those who make use of their own means of production and depend on themselves and their family members to conduct small-scale production and operation. These individuals include town and city residents and farmers. They are spread throughout the service industries such as agricultural services, barbers, grocery stores and handicraft industry. At the necessary time, they may also employ one or two helpers or hire several apprentices'. See *Lexicography* (Shanghai Lexicography Publishing House, 1999), pp. 843–844.
9. Chang Kai (ed.), *Labour Relations Science* (Beijing, China Labour and Social Security Publishing House, 2005), pp.165–166.

enterprises, as well as the level of their internal management and new product development were reduced as a result of the outflow of workers. Ultimately, the existence of these two different enterprise systems and the disparity in income between their labour forces, caused by the disparity in their efficiencies, brought about the displacement and relocation of a large part of the labour force as well as the decline of the traditional public-owned enterprise and the emergence of 'employees without work'.

Workers in planned-economy enterprises could be classified into two categories. The first category consisted of workers with no or low skills and a lack of work ethic. The second category consisted of workers with a certain level of ability and a work ethic. Some of them lacked knowledge and technological ability and their profiles did not meet the requirements of market-reformed enterprises. They lacked professional morals, discipline and obedience to regulations. Regarding employees without work, government departments at that time accepted the concept of life-long employment promised by the state and transferred these redundant workers to other planned-economy enterprises that could sustain their operations. Even those enterprises, however, lacked efficiency due to the above-mentioned factors. The addition of such workers increased labour costs but could not increase the efficiency of their production. These two factors together hastened the decline of such enterprises and caused a chain reaction among the remaining planned-economy enterprises. With an increase in the number of failed enterprises and employees without work, fewer and fewer planned-economy enterprises were able to sustain their operations. In addition to the reform of leading state-owned enterprises, the responsible government departments lost, in the end, the possibility of re-assigning employees without work to other enterprises. Eventually, this type of re-allocation of labour had to come to an end.

III. THE EMPLOYMENT SYSTEM DURING THE PERIOD OF TRANSFORMATION

The new employment system that marked the dawn of the labour market began in 1986 with reforms that permitted the expansion of an employment contract system and the establishment of a nationwide unemployment benefits system. In July 1986, the State Council promulgated four provisional regulations regarding labour system reform including the Provisional Regulations on the Establishment of the Employment Contract System in State-Owned Enterprises, the Provisional Regulations on Employing Workers in State-owned Enterprises, the Provisional Regulations on the Dismissal of Disobedient Workers in State-owned Enterprises, and the Provisional Regulations for Payment of Unemployment Benefits in State-owned Enterprises. These regulations created a framework for market reform of the labour force that occurred in four stages. Beginning in 1985 the employment contract system was applied to new employees of public-owned enterprises. In 1995 the system was applied to the remaining workers of state-owned enterprises. Then in 1998, a system was developed to deal with unemployment and re-assignment of redundant workers in state-owned enterprises. In 2002 re-assignment service centres and a support system for unemployed and redundant workers of state-owned enterprises were established.[10]

China adopted a progressive strategy for economic reform characterized by a reform of the planned-economy system and of former state-owned enterprises that simultaneously preserved the public ownership system while allowing the development of non-state-owned enterprises. There existed two methods of market reform.[11] One was the establishment of a planned economy system alongside a system of market-reformed enterprises that were allocated funds, labour and other means of production through market transactions.

The second method was to gradually introduce market reforms to public-owned enterprises under the planned-economy system, including market reform of labour force allocation, product sales, supply of equipment and raw materials, as well as capital. As a result, the operation of enterprises according to market forces in the post planned-economy took hold and developed due to the profit drive of the government as well as of other participants in the post planned-economy seeking profit. The movement of planned-economy enterprises toward market reform began late and moved slowly due to the hindrance of the government and activists who had a vested interest in the planned-economy system. Thus, in the 1980s and 1990s, there existed in China a dual-track system in which a quickly developing market system co-existed beside a dominant planned-economy system.

This strategy of reform led directly to two different systems of employment in the cities and towns, referred to as the 'dual-employment system'. One applied to state-owned enterprises directly controlled by the government and the other was applied to non-public enterprises guided by the market. In the non-public system, labour relations from the very beginning were regulated by the market and were sharply different from those of the planned-economy employment system:

(1) Market-reformed labour relations were created through market forces while labour relations under the planned-economy system were established by government allocation of labour.[12]
(2) As a result of the market reform of labour relationships, the subjects of labour relations (e.g., workers and employers) evolved into two independent interest groups, each having its own self interests which created conflict between them, while under the planned-economy system (wherein there were no clearly defined subjects of labour relations) there had existed no obvious difference between the interests of these groups.

---

10. From 1978 to 2001, employment in State-owned enterprises decreased from 78.3% of total employment in the cities to 31.9%, while employment in collective enterprises decreased from 21.5% to 5.4%. On the other hand, employment in the town and city non-public economy increased from zero to 62.7% in 2001. See (6 April 2003) *Wen Hui Daily*.
11. Li Xingshan, 'Great Creativity – Review and Prospects for the Establishment of a Socialist Market Economy in China' (13 October 2003) *Jiefang Daily*.
12. Labour contracts and collective bargaining will be discussed in Chapter 2 of this Part.

(3) Market-reformed labour relationships were contractual relationships which were established on the basis of the personal equality and liberty of workers. In theory, workers had full and complete rights and the freedom to control their own labour. They were free from personal bondage and the constraints of rank or status.[13] By contrast, labour relations under the planned economy system were established on the basis of rank, identity and administrative subordination.

Twenty years of growth and development later, various non-public companies had become important drivers of Chinese economic development and employed many more workers than the state-owned enterprises.[14] Market-reformed labour relations had gradually become prevalent in Chinese society. By the end of 2002, the contribution of the non-state-owned economy had reached two-thirds of China's GDP, among which non-public commercial entities (including private enterprises, individual businesses, foreign-invested enterprises, and enterprises with investment from Hong Kong, Macao and Taiwan) contributed one-third. Non-public investment reached 43.5% of total investment in 2002 and exports from the non-public economy increased to 62.3% of total exports.[15] According to the *2003 China Labour Statistics Yearbook*, in 2002 there were 247,800,000 workers in the towns and cities, out of which 71,629,000 (28.91%) were working in state-owned enterprises and the rest in various non-state-owned enterprises.[16]

Together with the development of the private economy, the reform of state-owned enterprises focused on two aspects: the strategic withdrawal of the state from the economy through privatization of a large group of small and mid-size state-owned enterprises via their sale, transfer or re-organization into joint ventures.

13. *Ibid.*
14. In terms of the Constitution of China, the economic system of public ownership includes the State-owned economy and the economy of collective ownership (Article 6). The state-owned economy is owned by the People (Article 7). The various forms of cooperative economy in cities and towns such as those in the handicraft, industrial, building, transport, commercial and service trades, all belong to the collective ownership economy. In rural areas, the responsibility system, the main form of which is the household contract that links remuneration to output, and other forms of cooperative economy such as credit and consumer cooperatives, belong to the economy of collective ownership (Article 8).
15. Labour Science Research Institute of the Ministry of Labour and Social Security, 'The Current Situation and Model Choice of Regulating China Labour Relations' (2004) 15 *Economic Material* (Beijing, Economic Material Editing Department of the State Council Development Research Centre) 17 *et seq.*
16. The Department of Population, Social Science and Technology Statistics of the National Bureau of Statistics of the People's Republic of China, the Department of Planning and Finance of the Ministry of Labour and Social Security (Compiled) *China Labour Statistical Yearbook* (Beijing, China Statistics Press, 2003), p.3. According to statistics published in *China Labour Statistics* (Beijing, China Statistics Press, 2005) which were compiled by the Department of Population and Employment Statistics, the National Bureau of Statistics of the People's Republic of China, the Department of Planning and Finance, and the Ministry of Labour and Social Security of the People's Republic of China, in 2004 there were 247,800,000 employees in the towns and cities, among which 71,629,000 were employed in State-owned enterprises.

The second aspect was the joint stock reform of mid-size and large state-owned enterprises to establish the modern company system in these enterprises. Accompanying the process was a complete shift in labour relations within the millions of state-owned enterprises. A huge segment of state-owned enterprise workers were thrown out of the old system by either 'passive' or 'active' job-loss. 'Passive job loss' meant a partial or complete halt in production or bankruptcy, with workers consequently losing their jobs as a result of the financial collapse of their employers. 'Active job loss' meant layoffs that occurred when mid-size and large enterprises with sound operations implemented the policy of 'Reduce Workers and Improve Efficiency'. Both of these groups of unemployed persons gradually entered the market-reformed employment field. From 1995 to 2002, the total number of workers in state-owned enterprises fell from seventy-five million to 33,830,000, leaving thirty million workers unemployed or underemployed. On the other hand, quite a number of state-owned enterprises that were privatized retained their workers. The number of state-owned enterprises decreased by more than thirty thousand in five years, from 74,388 in 1997 to 42,696 in 2002. By the end of 2003, over eighty per cent of small state-owned enterprises had been privatized and all mid-size state-owned enterprises around the coastal provinces had basically completed their reorganization.[17]

Through their continuing development, non-state-owned enterprises had become the crucial impetus to the growth of the labour market. The employment systems of state-owned enterprises were also on their way to market reform, but issues remaining from the planned-economy system were still constraining the growth of the labour market and market reform of the employment system. For example, employers were officially divided into government agents, public institutions and enterprises. The labour force was categorized into highly skilled workers and ordinary workers subject to different personnel and labour management systems.[18] Under the household registration system, individuals who came from other cities or from rural areas and did not have a local registered domicile had to get permission from the city government in order to work. Faced with the migration of the labour force in a developing economic environment, local governments had to divide suppliers of labour in accordance with relevant labour and personnel laws and regulations into different types (e.g., town and city labour; rural labour; labour from other jurisdictions; labour from Hong Kong, Macao, and Taiwan; and foreign labour.). A typical example was the Shanghai Bureau of Labour and Social Security that created the market admission standard of 'local first' (i.e., Shanghai residents) and 'others later' (i.e., non-residents) and 'urban first and rural later' for the labour force.[19]

17. Labour Science Research Institute of the Ministry of Labour and Social Security, 'The Current Situation and Model Choice for Regulating China Labour Relations' (2004) 15 *Economic Material*(Beijing, Economic Material Editor Department of the State Council Development Research Center) (2004) 17 *et seq.*
18. The difference between the personal management system and the labour management system is discussed at Chapter 4 of this Part.
19. Zhu Junyi, Yuan Zhigang, *Shanghai Employment Report 1995–2000* (Shanghai People's Publishing House, 2001), p.38.

In July 1994, in order to ensure that these reforms were not only incorporated into existing practice but also implemented on the basis of social justice and economic efficiency, the Labour Law, the first in China, was promulgated (albeit following twenty-nine revisions). The Labour Law is composed of four parts: labour relation regulations, the establishment of labour standards, social insurance issues, and administrative implementation. Following the promulgation of the Labour Law, the former Ministry of Labour and its successor, the Ministry of Labour and Social Security, gradually abolished the labour regulations from the era of guaranteed employment and published more than thirty related regulations. Three hundred fifty-eight regulations were abolished, half of which dated from between 1949 and 1986.[20] On 6 October 2001 administrative regulations promulgated prior to 2000 were abolished by State Council Decree 319.

With the implementation of the Labour Law and its related administrative regulations and departmental rules, there was put in place a comprehensive and improved employment contract system that created a unified and consistent set of legal labour rules and a fair, competitive labour market for state-owned enterprises, collective-owned enterprises, joint-stock enterprises, foreign-invested enterprises and private enterprises.[21]

---

20. In August 1952, the Government Administration Council of the People's Republic of China (now the State Council of the People's Republic of China) promulgated the *Decisions on the Issues of Labour Employment*, which provided that all public and private enterprises should follow a policy of 'being responsible for all employees' made redundant by innovation of production or improvement of production efficiency and should not fire any redundant employees but pay them their original salaries (calculated as enterprise cost). In July 1957, the State Council of the People's Republic of China circulated the *Ministry of Supervision's and the Ministry of Labour's Report on the Current Situation of Privately Recruiting Employees in Enterprises, Public Institutions, and Government Organs* and the *Dealing Opinions*, which required the immediate cessation of private recruiting. These temporary regulations, which met the needs of that era, gradually became the fixed labour employment system in China which, in fact, turned into a life-long employment system. The Ministry of Labour began in 1953 to extend the fixed-term employment system across the nation. The characteristic of the fixed-term labour employment system was that government allocated through administrative means all town and city labour forces to State-owned enterprises and then used fixed-term employment to establish a life-long labour relationship between enterprises and workers.
21. Private enterprises are also known as private ownership enterprises operated by private persons who have invested in them. The enterprise property belongs to those private persons. These enterprises recruit employees to conduct independent production and operations. In capitalist countries, private enterprises are the most common form of enterprise. In China, the term 'private enterprises' means profit-making organizations with more than eight employees and with property belonging to private persons. Private enterprises take three main forms, (i.e. sole proprietorships, partnerships and limited liability companies. See *Lexicography*(1999 Colour photo version) (Shanghai Lexicography Publishing House) (September 1999), at p.4673. The All China Federation of Industry and Commerce Private Economy Development Situation Analysis Group provided a definition for private economy in its *2003 Chinese Private Economy Development Situation Yearly Analysis*. Its broad definition of private economy includes all non-State-owned or non-State-controlled enterprises, including the domestic private economy (including individual business, private enterprises and collective-owned

The labour market established on the basis of labour law-based legislation consists of 'core content and four supporting systems'. The core content is that labour should be allocated by the market. The supporting systems are the employment system, the social security system, the supervisory system and the management service system which, taken together, constitute the function of the government within the market economy.[22] The employment system is the heart of the labour market system, functioning as the mechanism for allocation of the labour force. The basic theory of the employment market system was that a group of enterprises and individuals would constitute the supply and demand sides of the labour market and would achieve a proper balance via an efficient salary system. Features of the employment market system are autonomous decision-making by enterprises, normative employment and dismissal of workers, workers' having a sense that they have a choice of employment and active market competition. The employment system was the main vehicle by which the government hoped to reach its (goal of full employment aims, which included government responsibility for the creation of jobs and a proactive policy regarding the labour market.

The social benefits system is the basis for the effective operation of the modern labour market, which includes as its main components unemployment insurance, pensions and medical insurance. The supervisory system secures the normative operation of the labour market. It focuses on codification and is composed of unemployment alerts, a government policy system, a labour supervision system, a labour dispute arbitration system and a supervision system for wages.[23]

IV. THE EMPLOYMENT RELATIONSHIP UNDER THE MARKET SYSTEM

With the promotion of the market economy system and the employment system, labour relations in China have become complicated and diverse. In the field of labour relations the status of employees, the role of trade unions and the obligations and responsibilities of employers and the government have changed greatly and there has evolved a tri-partite coexistence of interests.[24] This situation will inevitably have a great impact on trade secret protection in employment relationships.

---

enterprises), foreign-invested enterprises and enterprises with investment from Hong Kong, Macau and Taiwan. The narrow definition of private economy excludes foreign-invested enterprises.

22. Zhu Junyi, Yuan Zhigang, *Shanghai Employment Report 1995–2000* (Shanghai People's Publishing House, 2001, p.91.
23. Bai Tianliang, 'We Have the Capability to Solve Employment Issues – Interview with the Deputy Minister of the Ministry of Labour and Social Security, Mr. Zhang Xiaojian' (9 December 2002) *People's Daily*, 5.
24. The three parties here refer to employers, employees and government. Under the new employment system, the relationship between them has changed.

A. Subjects and Participants in Employment Relationships

1. Employees

Currently in China, employees are defined as individuals with certain abilities that are of eligible age for employment and that have established a labour relationship with an employer by signing an employment contract.[25] Looking back on the history of Chinese labour relations, the status of employees has evolved from 'status to contract'. During the era of the planned-economy, labour relations in China were typically 'status relationships' and the relationship between an employer and an employee was in essence an unbreakable, lifelong and family-like relationship between the state and its citizens. This meant that the state used companies as a proxy to provide for workers from cradle to grave.[26] In essence, it became a part of their identity and was the basis for their legal status in society. These types of status relationships suited administrative management policy under the planned-economy system at that time, a circumstance that excluded employment contracts. Moreover, the relationship between enterprise and worker was maintained and monitored by the government. For example, in the 1990s in order to reduce the number of redundant employees in state-owned enterprises, the government implemented a new policy under which a state-owned enterprise could ask redundant employees to leave and suspend the payment of their salaries, but was required to retain their names in their employment rolls. These employees were allowed to work for another employer, for example a private company or a joint-venture company, and even to open their own companies. In China, this policy was called *Liu Zhi Ting Xing*, which means 'retained in one's position without pay' (unpaid job-retention). Even today, the practice of unemployed workers being paid basic living fees by their former state-owned employers persists. This phenomenon is a manifestation of the status relationship[27] that has greatly hindered the free movement of workers and the best

25. The Modern Chinese Lexicography defines an employee in China as a person employed by a unit or a temporary worker in a unit. See China Social Academy Linguistics Research Institute, *Modern Chinese Lexicography* (Beijing, Commercial Press, 2002), p.4567. Chinese labour law provides no definition for the term 'employee' but provides that it applies to all enterprises and individual economic organizations ('employment units') within the borders of the People's Republic of China and to all workers who form labour relationships with government organs, public institutions and societies as well as workers who form employment contract relationships (Article 2 of the *Labour Law*).
26. Dong Baohua, *Introduction to the Social Law*, (Beijing, China University of Politics and Laws Press, 2001), p.78.
27. In the middle of the 1980s, the Chinese government instituted a policy wherein employees retained their jobs but their salaries were suspended. The policy was a form of labour legislation that allowed the labour relationship to continue but according to which an employer permitted redundant workers to leave and stopped paying their salaries. Generally, employers signed contracts with workers which provided for retention of jobs but suspension of salaries so as to determine the rights and obligations of the parties to such agreements. This policy only applied to fixed-term workers. According to the *Regulations on the Arrangement of Redundant*

allocation of resources. In the 1990s, certain enterprises, particularly private, village, township and foreign-invested enterprises began to regard the labour relationship as purely contractual, a change that has contributed greatly to economic development in China.

Since then, however, more legal disputes between enterprises and workers have arisen, mainly concerning such issues as employment, income allocation, social security, welfare benefits and labour safety and health. According to statistics provided by twenty-one provincial and city trade unions and the All-Railway Federation of Trade Unions, from 1999 to 2001 the number of labour disputes concerning payment of wages, insurance and welfare benefits and other employment contract disputes rose twenty-nine per cent, twenty-eight per cent and twenty-one per cent respectively. Disputes caused by enterprise reorganization and unemployment were very common as well. From 2001 to 2003, 150,000, 186,000 and 226,300 cases were heard respectively by all levels of labour dispute arbitration committees, an annual increase of twenty-three per cent. The number of labour dispute cases heard by the courts at all levels increased from 54,797 in 2001 to 98,112 in 2003, an annual increase of twenty-eight per cent. In 2003 alone, labour dispute cases dealt with by labour dispute arbitration committees at all levels involved 801,000 parties.[28] The main reason for the increase in the number of labour disputes was the conflict of economic interests between the parties involved in them. In a market economy, enterprise owners and management pursue the highest possible profit but workers in those enterprises also seek to achieve the greatest personal benefit. During the period of economic transformation, the social contradictions inherent in employment relationships were exacerbated by a variety of factors: the asymmetry between enterprises and their employees in terms of their information resources and economic strength; imbalance between labour supply and demand; and especially, the weakening of the ability of trade unions to regulate collective labour relations.[29]

Workers in State-owned Enterprises promulgated by the State Council (State Council Decree 1993) and the *Circular on Issues arising When Workers Request to Retain Jobs but Suspend Salary* promulgated by the Ministry of Labour and Personnel, during the period of job retention without salary, workers were still considered staff of the original enterprises. During that period, if workers planned to sign employment contracts with other units and take paying jobs, they needed to negotiate with their original employing units and get their permission. When the employment period ended, however, if those workers continued to work with other units, they were required to terminate their labour relationships with their original units. When labour disputes occurred, if the disputes were regulated by the *Regulations on Labour Dispute Settlement of the People's Republic of China*, the Labour Dispute Arbitration Committee would hear such disputes. The duration of a period of job retention without pay could, in principle, be no more than two years. During that period, workers could not receive promotions, allowances, remuneration, labour protection or social welfare. When workers earned income during that period, they were required in principle to pay monthly social insurance to their original units.

28. Zhang Qiujian, 'Pondering the Harmonization of Labour Relations' (2005) 6 *Chinese Workers' Movement 6 et seq.*

29. <www.molss.gov.cn/index/index.htm> 18 August 2006.

2. Trade Unions

Trade unions are collective organizations formed by the working classes of their own free will[30] with the basic responsibility of protecting the legal interests of workers.[31] As the Chinese economic system has developed, trade unions in China have evolved from being simply a '[b]ridge and bond linking the Party and staff members'[32] to becoming one of the strongest pillars of government. According to Chinese law, trade unions should have the following six functions: a representative function, organizing individual workers to be a collective organization with social influence; an economic function, through collective negotiation improving workers' salaries as well as their social security and welfare; a political function, influencing political decisions and legislation and mobilizing workers to participate in enterprise management and industrial democracy based on equal negotiation so as to advance social development through pluralism and the rule of law; a regulatory function, using their autonomy and collective agreements to guide the behaviour of both employees and enterprises; an educational and training function, providing trade union members with basic, necessary cultural and vocational training; and a service function, providing trade union members with legal, economic, communal activity and social benefit services.[33]

By the end of September 2004, the level of trade union membership had increased by 1,020,000 to 136,940,000 members, covering 193,500 companies. The percentage of workers that became trade union members had reached sixty-three per cent.[34] By the end of 2003, vocational placement and training service institutions organized by the trade unions above the county level had found re-employment for a total of 2,049,000 unemployed workers and had trained 5,147,000 unemployed workers. These basic level trade unions had also established 3,972 help centres for workers in difficult circumstances.[35]

Within the market-reformed labour system in China however, the use of collective bargaining is in its nascent stage. The existence of active trade unions has not changed the inherent imbalance between workers and owners of capital.

---

30. See Article 2 of the *Trade Union Law of the People's Republic of China*, Adopted on 3 April 1992 at the fifth Session of the seventh National People's Congress and revised in 2001.
31. See the General Principles of the Constitution of the Trade Union of the People's Republic of China.
32. Article 5 of the *Trade Union Law of the People's Republic of China* (1992, Revised) 'Trade unions shall organize and educate workers to exercise their democratic rights pursuant to the provisions of China's Constitution and laws, give full play to the nation's role as master, participate through various channels and formats in the management of national affairs, economic and cultural institutions, and social matters, assist the people's government to develop employment opportunities, uphold the leadership or the working classes and support the worker-peasant alliance which forms the basis of the People's democratic dictatorship of socialist State power'.
33. See Articles 6 and 7 of the *Trade Union Law of The P.R.C.* (1992, Revised).
34. Zhang Junjiu, 'With Great Effort to Improve Trade Union's Work under New Conditions: Pondering the Harmonizing of Labour Relations' (2005) 3 *Chinese Workers' Movement* 6 *et seq.*
35. *Ibid.*

At present, employers control the majority of the trade unions established in all enterprises including in private enterprises as well as in small and mid-sized enterprises with Hong Kong, Macao or Taiwanese investment. Given that, it is very hard to expect trade unions to represent and protect the interests of workers. Indeed, collective employment contracts and collective salary agreements signed in accordance with current labour law and regulations are simply the product of formalism.[36]

3. Employers

Employers are the owners of the means of production and the suppliers of job opportunities. In China, they can be either individuals or organizations. However, the Labour Law used the term 'employing unit' to define a user of labour. The use of this term reflected the status of the employment relationship in the former planned-economy. In the public-owned, post planned-economy, users of labour such as enterprises, public institutions[37] and social organizations are all termed 'units' without exception. Nevertheless, with market reform of the employment relationship, among non-public-owned companies, especially among individual enterprises, there are a number of different types of users of labour (e.g., family enterprises.) The employing party there is not a 'unit' but a 'boss'. The term 'employer' is more frequently used in recent writings and legal documents concerning labour law, indicating that in academic circles as well as in society the concept has gained acceptance. For instance, since 1983 the China Enterprise Confederation has participated as a representative of Chinese employers in various activities organized by the International Labour Organization. In 2003, the Confederation was admitted as an official member of the International Organization of Employers. In 2001, the Employer Department of the China Enterprise Confederation was established to guide and coordinate local confederations to participate in the improvement of employment relationships. In addition, Article 45 of the Several Opinions on the Application of Civil Procedure Law of the People's Republic of China, promulgated by the People's Supreme Court in 1992 provides, 'When a person who is employed by an individual business, a lease-holding rural

36. At the present stage, considering their operation and structure, trade unions in China perform more like government organs or units, or agents of the employer.
37. In China, the term 'public institutions' refers to organizations established by State organs or other organizations. These organizations are established for the purpose of bringing social benefit, conducting educational, scientific and technical, cultural, or hygienic businesses such as educational institutions, science and technology institutions, public cultural institutions, public physical education and social welfare institutions. Please see the *Provisional Regulation on the Registering of Public Institutions* published in 1998 and revised in 2004 by the State Council (Decree 252 of the State Council) (Article 2). The term 'public institutions' as mentioned in the present *Regulation* refers to the public service organizations that are established by State organs or other organizations by using the State-owned assets for the purpose of engaging in activities of education, science and technology, culture, and hygiene. According to statistics, there are over 1,400,000 public institutions with over 29,220,000 employees. The professional and technical personnel in public institutions comprise 64% of all professional and technical personnel in China.

household or a partnership causes damage to other persons in the course of production or operations as stipulated in an employment contract, the employer will be the party (to the dispute)'. Though the application of the term 'employer' here is very narrow, it demonstrates that the legal expression for users of labour has followed that of international practice in labour legislation. In this thesis, the terms 'employer' and 'employing unit' have the same meaning and refer to all legal and natural persons that are responsible for managing employment matters and dealing with disputes regarding labour contracts.

At present, in their capacity as the owners of the means of production, employers can be categorized as state employers, joint-stock enterprise employers, private enterprise employers and individual employers. They are defined as follows:

(1) The state employer. The state functions as an employer in state-owned enterprises. The state authorizes the government to manage the enterprise and managers to operate the enterprise.
(2) The joint-stock company employer. The joint-stock system is the main form of ownership of the means of production in the Chinese market economy. In joint-stock companies, employers are shareholders. The chairman of the board of directors is the legal representative of the joint-stock company while the board hires and authorizes a manager, designated as a senior employee.
(3) The private enterprise employer. Following economic reform, private enterprise boomed in Chinese towns and villages. In accordance with the Provisional Regulations of the PRC on Private Enterprises,[38] private enterprises are divided into three types:
    (a) sole proprietor enterprises
    (b) partnership enterprises and
    (c) limited liability companies.[39]

    In private enterprises, property ownership of the company is clear and definite and the nature of the employment relationship within this type of enterprise is also quite distinct. It matters not whether employers are Chinese or foreigners, they are the owners of the enterprise and they have a leading and dominant status in the company. However, there exist differences between private enterprises with domestic capital and those with foreign capital. Though there are a significant number of large-scale, well-capitalized and domestically funded private enterprises, most private enterprises with domestic capital are smaller and usually located in the small to mid-size cities, towns and villages. Many of them have preserved the model of the family business and clan ownership and lack regulations regarding employment relations.[40] Private enterprises with

38. See the Provisional Regulations of the People's Republic of China on Private Enterprises promulgated by the State Council of China in 1988.
39. *Ibid.* See Article 6.
40. Luo Lei, 'Comparative Study from an International Perspective on the System of Succession and Cultural Basis of Clan Enterprises' (2002) 5 *Southeast Asia Study*.

foreign capital normally sign employment contracts with employees. The rank and responsibilities of employees are clear and distinct and the disparity in salaries is also quite wide.

(4) Individual employer. In 1999, China promulgated the PRC Law on Sole Proprietorships which encourages individuals to become registered sole proprietorships. There is no restriction on the number of employees that a sole proprietorship can recruit. The status of workers in sole proprietorships is raised from that of helper or apprentice to employee when they sign an employment contract with an employer.

4. Government

Regarding employment relationships in the market economy system, the government has three roles to play. First, the government has promulgated appropriate and relevant administrative rules and regulations regarding its involvement and influence in employment relationships. For instance, the Provisions on Collective Contracts promulgated by the Ministry of Labour and Social Security in 2004 stipulate the requirements for the qualifications of negotiating subjects and organs; the responsibility of negotiators, negotiating procedures and content; and the binding force of collective contracts. Second, in order to advance the harmonious development of employment relationships, the government acts as the guardian of the public interest by supervising the enforcement of labour law and regulations. Third, the government plays a role as the employer of public agencies and state-owned enterprises and, as such, is required to act as a model employer and to participate in and influence employment relationships.[41]

B. The Classification of Employment and Other Relationships from a Legal Perspective

In other nations, though called by various names (e.g., employment relations, labour relations or industrial relations), the meaning is certain and clear that they refer to the relationship between capital owners who are users of labour and employees. For example, in New Zealand employment relationships include relationships between an employer and an employee, a union and an employer, a union and a member of that union, a union and another union that are parties bargaining for the same collective agreement, a union and a member of another union where both unions are parties to the same collective agreement or an employer and another employer where both employers are bargaining for the same collective agreement.[42] In Russia, a labour relationship is a relationship

41. Wang Hemin, 'On the Reform of Supervisory Models under the Aims of a Government of the Law' (27 November 2004) *People's Daily*, 6.
42. See Article 4 of the New Zealand Employment Relations Act (2000).

based on an agreement between an employee and an employer in the performance by the employee of work for pay (i.e., certain specialized work which the employee has been qualified to do) pursuant to the employee's compliance with the internal work rules of the enterprise wherein the employer provides working conditions that comply with the labour law, collective contracts, labour contracts and any other agreements.[43]

A legacy of China's former planned economy is the continued existence in the labour sector of the employment relationship, the personnel relationship and the labour service relationship, each of which has its own peculiar characteristics and is subject to different laws and regulations.

1. Labour Service Relationships

In China, the employment relationship and the labour service relationship are two completely different legal concepts. An employment relationship is the legal relationship between an employee and an employer established through an employment contract that must be constructed in accordance with China Labour Law.[44] Where certain issues are not addressed by labour law and regulations, an employment relationship is regulated by other civil law.[45]

According to the Labour Law, an employer must sign a written employment contract with a worker so as to establish an employment relationship and to define the rights and obligations of each party. An employment contract must contain the nature of the work as well as provisions covering work safety, working conditions, pay, discipline, conditions for the termination of the employment contract and penalties for violation of the employment contract.

In labour service relationships, parties can conclude an agreement to define the rights and obligations between them. The content and form of the agreement can be more flexible because it is constructed in accordance with the Contract Law and the General Principles of the Civil Law of the PRC, rather than the Labour Law, which deals only with employment relationships.

According to the Contract Law, labour service agreements can be concluded in oral form. In addition, the employing party in a labour service relationship does not carry a mandatory obligation to offer its workers social security insurance or social benefits. If a worker dies or is injured, the worker or his family can only demand civil

43. See Article 15 of the Labour Code of the Russian Federation (2001).
44. The *Labour Law of the People's Republic of China* stipulates that an employment contract must be concluded where an employment relationship is to be established. An employment contract is an agreement reached between a worker and an employing unit for the establishment of the labour relationship and the definition of the rights and obligations of each party. See Article 16 of the *Labour Law of the People's Republic of China* (1994).
45. The current labour laws and regulations in effect include the Labour Law of the People's Republic of China (1994), the Regulation on Labour Security and Supervision (1994), the Regulation on Collective Contracts (1994), the Provisional Measures on Collective Negotiation of Salaries (2000), and the Trade Union Law of the People's Republic of China (1992).

remedies according to the Contract Law or according to the General Principles of the Civil Law of the PRC for breach of contract or for tort damage.[46]

With regard to disputes in labour service relationships, parties can file a lawsuit directly with a people's court without first pursuing labour dispute arbitration. Consider, for example, the case of Chen Weili (the plaintiff) and Lai Guofa (the defendant).[47] Mr. Chen was employed by Mr. Lai in August 1996 to work on a sand-carrying truck operated by Mr. Lai. Mr. Chen's duties were to change tires, to insert bolts into the coupling tripod links when backing up the truck, and to remind drivers of safety. The parties orally agreed that Mr. Lai would pay CNY 300 per month to Mr. Chen as salary and provide Mr. Chen with free food and housing. On 7 October 1996 the sand-carrying truck was being used at a site in Chengdu, the provincial capital of Sichuan. As a general practice, the insertion of a bolt into a tripod can only be accomplished when certain bolt holes are lined up. Mr. Chen jumped onto the tripod in order to insert a bolt during the operation of the truck. Mr. Chen lost his balance when the truck was backing up, and his left leg was fractured when it slipped into the moving tripod. The plaintiff claimed that while in the employ of the defendant, his leg was broken by defendant's truck. The injury was determined to be a level five disability by a local medical institution. The plaintiff requested that the court order the defendant to compensate him CNY 111,760 for medical fees, ward fees, hospital stay, nursing fees and a lump sum payment for his disability as a result of the injury. He further requested the court to order the defendant to bear the expense of the proceedings. The defendant claimed that the case was a labour dispute and that, according to related laws and regulations, the people's court had no jurisdiction over the case prior to the completion of labour arbitration. The court ruled that the oral agreement between the plaintiff and the defendant, which provided that Mr. Chen would provide labour service to Mr. Lai and that Mr. Lai would pay Mr. Chen, constituted a labour service contract and should not be subject to the *Labour Law*. The court reasoned that all enterprises and individual economic organizations could enter into employment contracts, but that the defendant was not a legally formed business because it had never received a license from the Administration of Industry and Commerce,[48] meaning that the defendant was not eligible to be the subject of an employment relationship. Therefore, the case was not an employment contract dispute but a labour service dispute that fell under the jurisdiction of the people's court and could be heard in the absence of prior arbitration.

46. If an employment relationship is established, under labour law a worker is entitled industrial injury insurance if he or she is injured or killed.
47. See Announcement of the Supreme People's Court of the People's Republic of China (Supreme People's Court, Vol.1, 2001), p.32.
48. Article 1 of the Circular of the Ministry of Labour about Several Issues of Executing the Labour Law of the People's Republic of China provides that individual economic organizations referred to in the Labour Law are individual businesses which employ no more than 7 employees and which should register and obtain a business license from the Administration of Industry and Commerce.

From the above, it can be concluded that employment relationships in China are usually subject to mandatory rules while labour service relationships are based on the free will of the parties to enter into a contract.

2. Personnel Relationships

A personnel relationship is an ambiguous concept peculiar to China and introduced during the era of the planned economy. There is no clear definition for a personnel relationship in Chinese law or regulations although certain academics hold that the personnel relationship reflects, in essence, the relationship between public servants, cadres and their employing units, (e.g., state organs, public institutions and social organizations).[49] Others believe that the personnel relationship is an administrative relationship between state personnel administrative organs and other state organs, public institutions and their staffs. Obviously, the personnel relationship differs from the employment relationship.[50]

Personnel relationships arose from the old management system of the labour force under the highly centralized planned-economy system which divided citizens into two groups: general workers and cadres. The latter included management staff; technical staff in state-owned enterprises; teachers, professors, doctors, and other staff working in schools, universities and hospitals; certain public institutions and staff of state organs. There existed a differentiation in status between general workers and cadres in the old system regarding salary and benefits. In addition, the personnel relationship was regulated by the personnel departments of the government through the establishment of specific personnel dispute settlement organs and through special human resource service markets. Thus, it can be concluded that personnel relationships under the old economy system in China were very comprehensive, including not only relationships between government agencies and their employees but also relationships between certain state-owned enterprises, public institutions and their respective cadres (e.g., management staff or professional and technical staff).

With the development of a market economy, government agencies, enterprises and public institutions have come to differ more distinctly from each other in their human resource management. The relationship between state-owned enterprises and their cadres has been defined as an employment relationship and subject to the *Labour Law*. The relationship between public institutions and their staffs is gradually being changed from a personnel relationship to an employment relationship that is established by an employment contract. Relations between government agencies and their staff members are now regulated by the Civil Servant Law as well as by certain other administrative laws and regulations. Disputes between

49. Xu Jianyu, 'On the Readjustment of Hearing Scope of Personnel Disputes in China' (2005) 9 *National Judge's College Law Journal*, 8.
50. Zhang Yanhua, Wang Dongwei, 'On the Differences and Definitions of Labour Relationships, Labour Service Relationships and Personnel Relationships' (2003) 1 *The Social Science Journal of Jiamusi University*, 37.

departments of municipal government, agencies, public institutions and their staff regarding resignation, dismissal or enforcement of employment contracts are settled in accordance with the provisions of the Labour Law. However these types of disputes must be brought to a personnel dispute arbitration institution rather than a labour arbitration committee. If one party to the dispute refuses to accept the arbitration award of a personnel dispute, they may file a lawsuit in the people's court within fifteen days of the receipt of said arbitration award.[51]

C. Regulatory Models for Employment Relationships

Over the past 300 years, the regulatory model for employment relationships has undergone three stages of development including the 'free contract model' prior to the mid-nineteenth century, the collective negotiation model and the human resource management model.[52]

In the free contract model which prevailed in the initial stage of industrialization, the employment relationship was established solely on the basis of contract and free competition. The relationship between employees and employers was regulated mainly by the market and the government rarely, if ever, intervened. Employers dominated this primitive labour relationship and had an unfettered right to hire or fire employees. Under this regulatory model, employers and employees often experienced sharp conflict.

Collective bargaining is the process through which workers negotiate with their employers or employer organizations through their own organizations or their representatives in order to reach a collective agreement. Generally speaking, these types of negotiations commonly include covenants regarding working conditions and terms of employment, the relationship between employee and employer, and the relationship between an employer or an employer organization and one or more worker organizations.[53] Under the collective bargaining and collective contract systems, individual contracts are concluded in accordance with the labour standards stipulated in a collective contract. Consequently, under collective bargaining employers no longer unilaterally determine working conditions and labour standards but instead the equal bargaining status of employees in their negotiations with employers is safeguarded.

Initially in Europe, the collective bargaining and collective contract systems consisted simply of an amicable agreement between workers and their employers,

---

51. Article 2 of the Provisions of the Supreme People's Court on Some Issues Concerning the Trial of Cases by the People's Courts over Personnel Disputes in Public Institutions.
52. Labour Science Research Institute of the Ministry of Labour and Social Security, 'The Current Situation and Model Choice of Regulating China Labour Relations' (2004) 15 *Economic Material* (Beijing, Economic Material Editor Department of the State Council Development Research Centre) 17 *et seq.*
53. International Labour Organization, Article 2 of *R91 Collective Agreements Recommendation* (1951).

and had no legal status. The courts did not accept cases regarding collective agreement disputes. It was not until the mid-nineteenth century that the collective bargaining model for settlement of disputes between workers and employers become gradually recognized by some courts. For example, the British Trade Union Act (1871) recognized the individual's right to association. The British Employers and Workmen Act (1875) permitted workers' associations to sign contracts with employers. At the beginning of the twentieth century, some countries passed laws recognizing the right of collective bargaining. For example, in 1919, the Law on Labour Contracts was passed in France and later adopted into its labour code, and in 1935 the National Labour Relations Act was passed in the United States. These laws established that workers had a right to elect representatives to sign collective agreements with their employers. From the 1930s to the 1940s, the International Labour Organization passed or published certain conventions and recommendations for collective bargaining such as the Collective Agreements Recommendation (1951) and the Convention Concerning the Promotion of Collective Bargaining (1981), which had a positive influence on the promotion of collective bargaining in all countries.

In the course of its use in regulating labour relationships, collective bargaining has also been referred to as an 'investment output' recycling procedure, through which rules and systems arise from the settlement of disputes. According to the various characteristics of the labour relationship, different interests, contradictions and even conflicts between employers and employees are regarded as 'investment' or 'input' of the recycling procedure while agreements, rules and systems by which the parties should abide are regarded as 'output' that results from the co-ordination, negotiation and asymmetrical strengths of the parties. This process, generally accepted under a market economy and prevailing in the regulation of employment relationships in market economy countries, has contributed much to social stability, productivity of society and social fairness and justice.

While collective bargaining was widely accepted, the human resource management model was also implemented by some enterprises, which enhanced the development of collective bargaining agreements and consequently improved employment relationships.

Human resource management appeared at the advent of the Information Age that began in the latter part of the twentieth century. Developed countries had by then evolved into post-industrial societies,[54] bringing about profound changes in

54. 'Post-industrial society' is American socialist Daniel Bell's term for current American society. In his opinion, the US has experienced the 'prior-industrial society' stage of 'fighting against nature' and the 'industrial stage' of 'fighting against processed nature', and has entered a 'post-industrial society' stage of 'service – the service of mankind as well as occupational and technical service'. Please refer to Daniel Bell, *The Cultural Contradictions of Capitalism*(NY, BasicBooks, 1978), pp.147–149. The famous Belgian economist Ernest Mandel points out that this society has experienced an industrial situation inclusive of everything that has ever been seen in history, such as mechanization, standardization, excessive profession, and assembly labour. All of these have entered into every aspect of social life. See Ernest Mandel, *Late Capitalism* (Schocken Books, 1975), p.387. While American Marxist cultural commentator

modes of production and labour relationships. On the one hand, many employees were no longer manual labourers but white-collar workers playing an increasingly important role in the growth of the economy. These factors made the model of employers controlling the labour of their employees outdated because it was ill-suited to the management of knowledge-based labour. On the other hand, the influence of hi-tech enterprises in industrial development has created a situation wherein while historically capital has controlled labour, knowledge has begun, to an extent, to control capital.

American academician Gary Dessler is of the view that the term 'human resource management' refers to practices and policies related to the management of people which includes recruiting, screening, training, providing incentives, conducting performance appraisals and providing a safe environment for employees to work in.[55] The goal of human resource management is to reach an agreement between employers and employees not only regarding written contracts (including, among others, labour contracts and management rules) but also psychological contracts and unspoken mutual expectations such as the expectation of a corporate culture in which the achievements of employees are recognized by their companies thereby improving the employment relationship.

The advantage of human resource management is the synthesis of the development of both employee and enterprise based on the common interests of employers and employees and the common interests of capital and labour. Employers inspire the creativity of employees while satisfying the needs of employees so as to improve the efficiency of production. Consequently, employees will base their expectations of improved salary levels and professional advancement on the success of the enterprise. Creating a balanced relationship between capital and labour under such conditions cannot be based on conflict but rather on a coordination of strengths. Because of the obvious advantages of the human resource management model, it is gradually becoming more influential in labour management than collective bargaining and is becoming the regulatory model for labour relationships.

With the gradual introduction of foreign management concepts, the introduction of human resource management has been applied in many Chinese enterprises, with the push coming from foreign-invested enterprises.[56] In terms of social development however, China is still at the mid-stage of industrialization. It can be estimated that for quite a long time to come, mass production and the assembly

---

Fredric Jameson further explains and comments that the symbol of this society is the establishment of technology priority, the birth of technical officers, and the transfer from traditional technology to new information technology. See Fredric Jameson, Jean-Francois Lyotard, *The Postmodern Condition: A Report on Knowledge* (University of Minnesota Press, 1984), p.99.

55. Gary Dessler, *A Framework for Human Resource Management* (Beijing, People's University of China Publishing House, 2004).
56. Some academics think that the introduction of human resource management into China can be attributed to the cooperation between British and American management schools and some Chinese universities. They have conducted joint projects to introduce and promote foreign management education. HRM is one of those projects. See Chang Kai, *Labour Relations Science*(Beijing, China Labour and Social Security Publishing House, 2005), p.368.

line will remain the prevailing means of industrial output. The long-term goal of many lower-level private enterprises is to evolve from family management to modern management. Furthermore, there still exist deficiencies in the Chinese labour law system such as the low-level of legislation, the narrow scope of its application, and outdated provisions[57] that impede the development of the sort of employment relations appropriate to the current moment of social transformation. Consequently, both the free contract model and the collective bargaining model will continue to co-exist and to prevail. The first model is applied mainly in the majority of small and mid-sized private enterprises while the latter exists in certain state-owned enterprises that have reorganized and have established good performance and healthy mechanisms for operating as a modern enterprise. In addition, they are able to produce goods that meet domestic and international standards.

The establishment of a collective bargaining system for labour relations that is in accord with the needs of a modern market economy has been a fundamental and important reform in labour relations in China. Collective bargaining has been highly valued because it has been closely associated with the evolution of the economic system and the reform of the political system in China. The establishment of this system is also obligatory due to the ratification by China in 1990 of the Convention concerning Tripartite Consultations to Promote the Implementation of International Labour Standards and the signing in 2002 of the Labour Administration Convention[58] Regarding the Labour Administration Convention, according to which each signatory is obligated to create domestic conditions appropriate to secure consultation, co-operation and negotiation between the public authorities and the most representative organizations of employers and workers, or employers' and workers' representatives within their systems of labour administration.[59]

---

57. The author of this article is of the view that there are three problems caused by the *Chinese Labour Law* that currently regulates Chinese labour relationships. (1) The level of legislation is quite low and has a quite weak legal effect. The legal system is composed of one law, several administrative regulations and many departmental rules. (2) The scope of application is quite narrow and cannot adapt to changes in and development of the labour employment relationship. The system has not included all employing units and their employees into the application scope of the law, which will not protect the interests of workers based on employment relationships or labour service relationships under the *Labour Law*, which has the legal force of public law. (3) The content of the *Labour Law* is outdated. With the maturity of the labour market, several important concepts (such as employing unit, workers, labour relationships, equal pay for equal work) and some basic principles (such as safeguarding rights, bone fide, fairness) need to be defined in the *Labour Law*. In addition, there is lack of related provisions on quite a number of issues such as flexible employment (also called non-full time employment mode), punitive measures regarding an employer's improper dismissal of employees, the operation of non-competition constraints and the sensitive issues of labour strikes and delinquency.
58. The *Labour Administration Convention* was adopted by the International Labour Organization at a session of Conference 64 in 1978 and became effective in 1980. The *Convention concerning Tripartite Consultations to Promote the Implementation of International Labour Standards* was adopted by the International Labour Organization in 1976 and became effective in 1978, <www.ilo.org/ilolex/english/convdisp1.htm>, 6 January 2008.
59. See Article 5 of Labour Administration Convention. <www.ilo.org/ilolex/english/convdisp1.htm >, 6 January 2008.

Following promulgation of the Labour Law in December 1994, the PRC Ministry of Labour promulgated the Regulations regarding Collective Contracts and in 1995 the All China Federation of Trade Unions published the *Opinions of the All China Federation of Trade Unions on the Work of Trade Unions in the Establishment of Collective Bargaining and Collective Contract Systems* to provide specific guidelines for the promotion of a collective contract system in China. Following that, in 1996 the Ministry of Labour, the All China Federation of Trade Unions, the State Economic and Trade Commission of the PRC, and the China Enterprise Directors Association jointly published the Circular on the Gradual Establishment of Collective Bargaining and Collective Contract Systems. The Circular makes clear that collective bargaining and collective contract systems are effective means to coordinate labour relations in the market economy, but it also emphasizes that the focus is on promoting the tentative application of a collective contract system within non-state-owned enterprises as well as within certain state-owned enterprises that have undergone reorganization, have established good mechanisms for operation as a modern enterprise and have maintained good operational performance. In 2000, the Ministry of Labour and Social Security promulgated the Tentative Regulations for the Collective Bargaining of Salaries, which contains regulations regarding the content of and legitimate parties to collective contracts; procedures for concluding, approving, filing and registering such contracts; the consequences of collective contracts; liability and obligations of parties; and the settlement of disputes. These provisions constitute an embryonic legal system for collective bargaining and collective contracts. Subsequently, collective bargaining and collective contracts are gradually being utilized by many enterprises.

By June 2002, collective contracts had been entered into by 630,000 enterprises, of which 375,000 were private enterprises and 260,000 were state-owned enterprises. More than eighty million employees were party to those contracts.[60] At the same time, the Ministry of Labour and Social Security, the All China Federation of Trade Unions (representing employers), and the China Enterprise Confederation and Enterprise Directors Association (representing employees) jointly established a tripartite mechanism to promote effective consultation at the state level and to promote the implementation of labour laws.

In 2003, in response to changes in labour relations taking place under the new market economy, the Ministry of Labour and Social Security promulgated the Regulations on Collective Contracts (the 2004 Regulations)[61] which were, in essence, a revision of the Regulations on Collective Contracts promulgated by the former PRC Ministry of Labour in 1994. The 2004 Regulations became

60. The Labour Science Research Institute of the Ministry of Labour and Social Security of the People's Republic of China, 'Research on Chinese Labour Relationships during the Transformation Stage' (7 January 2005) *Workers' Daily*, January, 7.

61. In December 2003, the Ministry of Labour and Social Security of the People's Republic of China promulgated the *Regulations on Collective Contracts*, which became effective on 1 May 2004.

more complete, more applicable, and easier to implement than the previous version.[62] The scope of their application was expanded,[63] the concept of special purpose collective contracts was added,[64] and the legal consequences of collective contracts were emphasized. The 2004 Regulations also explicitly required that the working conditions and levels of pay stipulated in labour contracts between employers and employees not be lower than those in collective contracts or in special purpose collective contracts. Once a collective contract becomes effective, all parties to it should scrupulously carry out the contract. Any party violating the contract will be liable for breach of the contract. The 2004 Regulations also contain detailed and specific provisions concerning the process for collective bargaining and for concluding contracts.[65] In addition, the 2004 Regulations provided for the examination of collective contracts by administrative organs of the government[66] and facilitated the settlement of collective contract disputes.[67]

---

62. The original *Regulations on Collective Contracts* contained 5 Chapters and 41 articles. The content of the original *Regulations* was quite general and abstract and lacked operational provisions. There have arisen many issues in the process of concluding collective contracts for which there are no correspondent legal provisions to depend upon. On the other hand, the new *Regulations* contain 8 chapters and 57 articles.
63. The original *Regulations on the Collective Contract* applied only to enterprises within the territory of the People's Republic of China (see Article 2). The new *Regulations on the Collective Contract* expands the collective contract system to cover all public institutions that have adopted a management system for enterprises (See Article 2).
64. The original *Regulations on the Collective Contract* contained only a basic explanation of the collective contract. The new *Regulations on the Collective Contract* added the concept of special purpose collective contracts and also provided a clear definition for the new concept, stating 'The so-called special purpose collective contract refers to a written agreement between an employing unit and its employees on certain collectively bargained issues in accordance with provisions of relative law, regulations, and rules'. (See Article 4).
65. A party can issue a written request to a counterparty demanding collective bargaining of collective contracts, special purpose collective contracts and related issues. The counterparty should give a written reply within twenty days after receiving the requirement on collective bargaining and should not refuse to conduct collective bargaining without due cause. The *Regulations* also provide express provisions on the procedures of bargaining meetings, how to deliver a draft of a collective contract or a draft of a special purpose collective contract at representative meetings of workers or at assembly meetings of workers, how to report to labour and social security administrative departments for review. These provisions have enhanced the operation and utility of the *Regulations*.
66. *The Regulations* clearly provide that the labour and social security departments above county level shall supervise within its jurisdiction the negotiating, signing, and performance of collective contracts between employing units and their employees and shall be responsible for reviewing collective contracts and special purpose collective contracts. Within 10 days after the chief representatives of both parties have signed the collective contract or the special purpose collective contract or the modification of the collective contract or special purpose collective contract, the employing unit should send three copies of the document to the labour and social security administrative department for review. *The Regulations* also contain provisions on such items as examination, examination duration, the content of the *Examination Opinions*, the effectiveness and publishing of collective contracts and special purpose collective contracts.
67. Chapter 7 of the new *Regulations* especially provides equal treatment of disputes involving collective agreements, expressly stipulating that, 'When disputes arise during the process of

The collective contract system is being promoted in China as it continues to progress from a planned-economy to a market economy. Hence, compared to other countries, the collective contract system in China has its own unique characteristics and deficiencies. For example, it was the Chinese government that first initiated collective bargaining and the collective contract system in legislation. With the enforcement of the Labour Law, it did not take long for collective contracts to be implemented in the majority of enterprises and regions. The hierarchical approach has led some enterprises to treat collective bargaining and collective contracts in a formalistic way. It is well known that the key element of the collective contract system is bargaining. Employers and workers must be represented on an equal footing in any bodies through which consultations are undertaken. The representatives of employers and workers must be freely chosen by their representative organizations for the purpose of collective negotiation.

In China, however, parties to employment relationships and their organizations are not experienced and are ineffective in representing the interests of employers and workers. Particularly, trade union representatives at many different levels were not chosen directly by employees but were selected in a hierarchical manner. In addition, trade union members within enterprises, institutions or government organs are organized into local trade union committees.[68] Because employees have no opportunity to organize other forms of trade unions, so that there might be separation between the trade unions and the employees they ostensibly represent, there is no real 'bargaining' taking place in the course of negotiation of collective contracts. As a result, the majority of employees in quite a number of enterprises do not even know whether they have signed collective contracts with their employers. Furthermore, many collective contracts with local private enterprises are not concluded through bargaining at all. Private enterprises permit the formation of trade unions by employees in a perfunctory manner under the supervision and insistence of the government. The form of the collective contract is standard and its content is simply a copy of the model contract. Employees (or their representatives) and leaders of trade unions (most trade union leaders are appointed by employers) simply sign the contract and submit it to the government, which is all they need to do to show that they have performed their duties.

---

collective bargaining, if the two parties cannot settle the disputes through negotiation one party or both parties can submit a written application to the department of labour and social security for coordination. In the absence of such application, if the labour and social security department thinks it appropriate it can arrange for trade unions of the same level and workers to coordinate the settlement of disputes. The coordinated settlement of disputes should be completed within 30 days after the acceptance of application. When the term expires if the dispute is not settled, the coordination term can be reasonably extended, but the extended term should not be more than 15 days'. The new *Regulations* also expressly stipulate that, 'When disputes arise during the performance of a collective contract, if the parties fail to settle disputes through coordination the parties may apply to a labour dispute arbitration committee for arbitration'.

68. See Article 5 of the Constitution of the Trade Unions of the People's Republic of China.

Without the participation of trade unions that truly represent employees in collective bargaining, the bargaining process and the signing of collective contracts has turned into a formality, indeed sometimes into just another governmental activity. It appears that China still has a long way to go in establishing a true collective bargaining system.

Chapter 2

Key Issues of Trade Secret Protection in Employment Relationships: Conflict and Balance of Interests

In a market economy workers are normally at a disadvantage in employment relationships, especially when the supply of labour exceeds the demand of the market. Because labour is not simply a commodity but requires the use of knowledge as well as a physical body to provide a service or produce goods, employees must perform the contractual obligation to work of their own accord. Thus the employee becomes a party to the employment relationship as a person. Consequently, many current labour laws emphasize the protection of workers and stipulate special rules to protect the legal rights and interests of workers. It has become a common characteristic of labour law around the world to favour the protection of workers.

Labour legislation in China has leaned toward the protection of workers' legal rights and interests since its earliest days. Article I of the Employment Contract Law explicitly states that its purpose is to protect the legitimate rights and interests of employees.[1] The inclusion of such a clear statement reflects the nature of contemporary labour relations in China. Due to the ineffectiveness of trade unions in China and the shortcomings of collective contracts, the basic rights and interests of workers in employment relationships are not sufficiently or effectively protected. As a result, the government must rely on legislation to raise the basic standard

1. This is a new law that became effective 1 January 2008. There are quite a number of arguments among Chinese academics regarding this type of provision. Many of them are of the opinion that the *Employment Contract Law* should govern the rights and obligations of employers and employees and perform a balancing act regarding employer/employee relationships.

for the protection of workers in order to strengthen the protection of their rights and interests.

Trade secrets, on the other hand, are a resource on which companies have expended much time, manpower, material and effort to develop or to purchase. The disclosure of a trade secret can cause not only an irrecoverable loss to a company but can also create unfair competition within an industry. Thus, finding a way in which to protect trade secrets is an unavoidable and critical issue facing enterprises in China. In addition, a trade secret is a form of intellectual property and the majority of trade secrets, in reality, belong to employers. It is therefore inevitable that trade secret laws incline toward the protection of the interests of trade secrets holders.

Nevertheless, certain trade secrets are comprised of the sum knowledge, experience, and skills learned and obtained by workers during the course of their work. Not only is this knowledge essential to the livelihood of employees, it is inseparable from the essence of the worker himself. If such knowledge, experience and skills are protected as the trade secrets of employers, the basic rights and interests of employees will unquestionably be harmed. Therefore, the legal protection of trade secrets within employment relationships gives rise to a conflict between theories that favour the protection of employers' interests and those that favour the protection of the interests of employees. This question has spurred great debate within legal circles in China. If trade secret law leans toward the protection of the interests of employers, certain rights of employees will inevitably be infringed upon, such as their right to a livelihood and their right to work. Likewise, if the law is inclined to protect the interests of employees, certain legal rights and interests of employers might not be safeguarded and the economic order of the market may be disturbed.

In view of the fact that the law is an effective means to balance various interests and benefits, any trade secret laws regarding employment relationships should first fully acknowledge the existence of a conflict of interest between employers and employees and, in legal theory, these laws should concentrate on the protection of the trade secrets of employers as well as the need of workers for a livelihood and the freedom to work. In addition, the law should maintain a balance between the monopoly interests of trade secret right holders and the public interest in the development of science, technology and culture. In the process of drafting and enforcing relevant laws, it is necessary to consider and then to establish reasonable legal systems in accordance with the nature of labour relations. The law should become a mechanism for reconciling conflicts among various interests regarding trade secrets. As a famous scholar once said, 'When determining whether trade secret protection is warranted, the courts must strike a balance between the conflicting social policies of freedom to contract, business ethics and private economic freedom'.[2]

---

2. Wheeler, 'Trade Secrets and the Skilled Employee in the Computer Industry' (1983) 61 *Wash. U.L.Q.* 823, referring to Paul Lavery, *Commercial Secrets: Actions for Breach of Confidence in Ireland* (London, Round Hall Sweet and Maxwell, 1996), p.149.

This chapter will begin with an introduction to the understanding and the study of our Chinese academic research regarding the issues of trade secret protection in the employment relationship, which includes the analysis of conflicting interests of parties, the ethical dimensions as well as the effect of labour law. An analysis of the current situation in China will follow in each section.

I. CONFLICTING INTERESTS OF PARTIES REGARDING TRADE SECRETS

In the process of promulgating law, recognizing various social interests is an initiative for lawmakers and is an important precondition to determining which subject matter is to be protected and to reconciling those various interests.[3] So too, in order to bring into harmony the interests of the owners of trade secrets with the interests of other relevant parties, trade secret law must fulfil the same function.

Free public access to the unimpeded distribution of information is a noteworthy feature of the modern Information Age and is a fundamental precondition for the development of a democratic society. As pointed out in the Universal Declaration of Human Rights, 'Everyone has the right to freely participate in the cultural life of the community, to enjoy the arts and to share in scientific advancement and its benefits'.[4] Thus, protecting the free circulation of information and protecting the right of free access to information has universally become an important social policy in the Information Age.

Unlike patent law which is designed to promote the disclosure and broad dissemination of technological information, the law concerning the protection of trade secrets inevitably constrains the movement of information to some extent because if information is deemed a trade secret, as long as it has not been disclosed to the public it can be protected for an unlimited period of time and no one can access it without the permission of its owner. From this perspective, protection of trade secrets runs contrary to accepted social policy and for this reason is debated by certain academics and legal practitioners. However, as further stated in the Universal Declaration of Human Rights, 'Everyone has the right to the protection of the moral and material interests resulting from any scientific, literary, or artistic production of which he or she is the author'.[5] There must exist some special legitimate reason for the protection of trade secrets. Considering the inherent economic soundness and social reasonableness of the concept of trade secrets as property[6] and the application of trade secret law in legal practice, the legitimacy of

3. Sun Guohua, Zhu Jingwen, *Jurisprudence* (Beijing, People's University Press, 2004), p.78.
4. See Article 27 of the *Universal Declaration of Human Rights* adopted and proclaimed by General Assembly Resolution 217 A (III) of the United Nations on 10 December 1948.<www.un.org/Overview/rights.html>, 6 January 2008.
5. *Ibid.*
6. The issue of the economic soundness and social appropriateness of trade secrets rights and the ethical dimensions of trade secret protection shall be discussed in following sections of this Chapter.

trade secret protection epitomizes the advantage gained by not only empowering the owner of business information with property rights, but also preserving a standard of morality in the commercial marketplace while promoting technological research and innovation.

From the aspect of interests, trade secret laws can be regarded as a mechanism for finding a balance between the monopoly interests of trade secret holders and the interests of the public, which include the right of the free circulation of information and the right of free access to information. The establishment of trade secret protection within employment relationships is a systematic attempt by a nation through its legislation to strike a balance between the exclusivity of trade secret owners and an employee's right to work. Further, on the basis of the aforementioned, trade secret law can serve the public interest regarding scientific, technological, cultural and economic development.

In light of the trade secret legislation of many other countries, the right to maintain trade secrets is confined to a limited right rather than an absolute and exclusive right. Trade secret law provides a proper and reasonable scope of protection so as to remedy its intrinsic defect of restricting the dissemination of information. For instance, trade secret law allows for multiple right-holders of a trade secret. In reality, it is common that different individuals may create the same trade secret, as competitors are not aware of the content of each other's research or plans. Consequently, the same trade secret can be possessed by different individuals at the same time. In contrast to other intellectual property law, trade secret law normally accepts independent research on identical trade secrets based on considerations of social policy. To some degree, the conduct of identical research is a waste of resources. However, the fact that different subjects may develop the same trade secret can mitigate the fact that only one holder can make use of confidential information, thus satisfying the public interest in the unimpeded dissemination of information. However, if multiple holders are not recognized, it is sometimes impossible for the court to determine the initial right-holder of a trade secret. Exclusivity would, in essence, result in harm to the normal dissemination of information within society.

In addition, trade secret law entitles an owner of a trade secret to a limited property right. Trade secret law in other countries prohibits only misappropriation of the trade secrets of another, (i.e., illegally disclosing, revealing or using the trade secrets of another.) However, trade secret law does not prohibit the acquisition of trade secrets through reverse engineering or independent research and even allows for patent application for trade secrets obtained in such manner. If the application is successful, a party obtaining trade secrets through reverse engineering or independent research can be granted patent rights based on that trade secret while the original holder will permanently lose the trade secret as a result of its dissemination into the public domain. By recognizing the legitimacy of trade secrets obtained through reverse engineering, trade secret law fosters a balance between the interests of the original inventor and the later inventor. Thus, the defect in trade secret law that limits the dissemination of information may be remedied.

The granting of limited exclusivity to the holder of a trade secret is another feature of trade secret law that benefits market competition and promotes the transmission of information. The exclusive right to a trade secret can preserve its use and benefit as well as prevent its misappropriation. Exclusive trade secret ownership ensures greater longevity of the monopoly of its holder than that of a patent, which can be regarded as a stimulus for further innovation.

However, because trade secret law does not prevent individuals from legally obtaining identical information through processes such as reverse engineering or independent research, the prospective interest in a trade secret stimulates more innovation and development of technology. Furthermore, if numerous individuals can easily obtain the same trade secret through independent development or reverse engineering, each could only make a small profit from the ownership of their trade secret and consequently there would be a little motivation to invest excessively to maintain it. The original holder might then be encouraged to publicize his trade secrets in exchange for patent protection. Consequently, trade secret information could be more widely disseminated and used in society.

II. THE ETHICAL DIMENSIONS OF TRADE SECRET PROTECTION

The law shows what would seem to be the universal tendency of the ethical system of a society to produce a legal order to enforce its ethical and social mandates.[7] In this view, laws should also promote the development of virtuous characters by citizens. Compared to other systems, the property right system is deeply rooted in certain ethical concepts. Without ethics, there would be no property rights. Especially in the field of intellectual property, law and ethics are entangled with each other, making certain legal issues more complicated. A trade secret is a very special form of intellectual property the protection of which depends very much on ethical conduct. Therefore, one of main purposes of trade secret law is to maintain ethical standards in commerce.[8]

Historically, trade secret law has generally been guided by the principles of property right and secrecy-obligation. Though these two principles have co-existed since the early days of trade secret protection legislation, they have been used to place special emphasis on certain aspects at different stages in the development of trade secret law.[9] The idea of trade secrets as property was not a popular concept and had even at the initial stages of thinking about trade secrets been denied as

7. Edgar Bodenheimer, *Jurisprudence: the Philosophy and Method of the Law* (Chinese version, Den Zhenlai, translators) (Beijing, China University of Political Science and Law Press, 1998), p.386.
8. Catherine L. Fisk, 'Working Knowledge: Trade Secrets, Restrictive Covenants in Employment, and the Rise of Corporate Intellectual Property 1800–1920' (2001) 52 *Hastings Law Journal*, 446.
9. The issue of the theoretical basis of the trade secret protection system is discussed in Chapter 1, Part III.

legitimate. Whether property rights are respected or confidentiality obligations are observed depends on the ethical choices of individuals, which reflects the basic recognition by society of certain ethical standards. The emphasis placed on the principle of obligation in trade secret legislation is thought to have derived from the essence of justice and the ethical considerations of trade secret protection. The ethical argument for acceptance of trade secrets as property is founded upon its economic soundness and social rationale.

A. The Economic Soundness of Protection of Trade Secrets

Scarcity of resources is a common constraint confronting mankind. People cannot freely obtain nor indiscriminately use economic resources. As the fruit of intellectual activity, trade secrets are not exempt. Due to limitations on physiology, aptitude, longevity and energy, individuals in society have a limited ability to store and process information. They are also ignorant of certain information. With the development of the division of labour and professional specialization, knowledge too has become increasingly specialized and the cost of obtaining knowledge has risen. As a result, trade secrets have become scarce, causing a series of socio-economic problems and raising certain moral issues.

The property right system is designed to resolve the inherent conflict between the scarcity of resources and the unlimited personal needs of individuals in society and to resolve issues of production, distribution and use of those limited resources. Apparently, previous attempts at finding legislative solutions have been based on different private interests and the tactics inspired by them, which has had an impact on the behaviour of individuals in society.

The economic soundness of trade secret property rights is based on the following:

Firstly, because property rights are guaranteed by law they have a predictable effect on resources. In theory, property rights encourage property holders to efficiently allocate resources based on the operation of the market. A property right can be defined as control over a resource based on the practical inability of another to contradict the ends of the possessor. In a market characterized by high mobility and flexibility, it is important to define the means and scope of control over resources through property rights. Property rights establish certain expectations within transactions. People can exchange their goods without fear of the interference of others and can prevent the possession or parasitic use of their goods without their permission. The more specifically that property rights are defined the less possible it is that the property of an owner can be damaged. On the contrary, if the scope of one's property rights is not able to accurately measure the contribution of every worker and if labour is not sufficiently compensated no one would invest in the development of that property, including taking the trouble to process or handle the information which is the subject of the holder's property right. Individuals would lose their motivation and be disposed to take a free ride. When the ownership of resources, including useful information, cannot be determined, individuals have unrestricted access to it resulting in the excessive use of that information. As the Chinese saying goes, they would 'kill the goose that lays the golden egg' because the future is unknown and no one can predict whether the future fruits of those resources would belong to him.

Secondly, the treatment of trade secrets as property encourages trade secret holders to develop such information. The key issue regarding the value of information is not the accumulation of it but rather how to make it valuable to society by innovatively collecting and processing it. Without proper innovation, information would be worthless. Although society possesses more information than ever before, the amount of information that is yet to be known or that cannot be utilized has also increased greatly. The danger of the modern age is the deluge of information that is more difficult to turn into knowledge.[10] In addition, the cost of maintaining the confidentiality of information can be high because trade secrets are easily disseminated. If disclosed, anyone can freely access them and become a potential competitor of the original holder. Without proper and reasonable property right protection of trade secrets, there would be little motivation for investment in trade secrets and scant legal guidance for innovative individuals to be compensated if their trade secrets are illegally disclosed. The recognition and safeguarding of trade secrets as property is, in fact, an acknowledgement of the correlation between investment and return on investment in the process of innovation, which has resulted in those factors becoming more closely correlated and internalized. When the possibility of secure ownership and financial return is assured, individuals are motivated to undertake the high risk and cost of developing intellectual property and to put limited resources to their best and most profitable use.

Thirdly, the acknowledgement of trade secrets as property encourages its holders to generate wealth and advances the development of social welfare. When trade secrets are acknowledged as private property, the possibility of others sharing benefits without cost is eliminated. Furthermore it will inspire trade secret holders to consider their costs of development vis-à-vis their return on investment and to apply their resources to the development of information that will bring them the greatest profit. For society, when a great number of individuals are simultaneously seeking the best use of resources, it will lead to competition for scarce resources. When all people are working hard at innovation, holding onto a technological lead depends on remaining one step ahead of competition. If one wants to successfully gain high profits, one must continuously invest resources in innovative intellectual areas. As a result, resources will be consistently used with high efficiency. Furthermore, commercial transactions are facilitated through the transfer of property rights. The movement of goods in the marketplace is, to a great degree, determined by the exchangeability of rights. When there is no means by which to turn trade secrets into property, the interests of trade secret holders are protected only by the recognition of those rights by other parties to the transaction.

10. George Friedman, Meredith Friedman, Colin Chapman and John Baker, *The Intelligence Edge: How to Profit in the Information Age* (Shanghai People's Publishing House,1999), p.5.

If every right in transactions concerning trade secrets must be determined by a covenant with others, the resulting high transaction cost would hinder the realization of increased value of the property. When too many uncertainties exist in the conduct of commercial transactions, enterprises will keep their intellectual property under their close control and consequently will not realize the value of their assets through market transactions. Ultimately, the best use of intellectual property will be constrained.[11]

B. THE SOCIAL REASONABLENESS OF TRADE SECRET RIGHTS

As a legal means for determining the relationship between parties with regard to assets, property rights can be described as having two fundamental characteristics. The first is possession, which can be defined as control over an asset based on the practical inability of another to contradict the ends of the possessor. The second is title, which is the expectation that others will recognize the right to control an asset even when it is not in direct possession. This recognition on the part of others is a kind of social respect and support that is backed by a set of values and ethical concepts. If the law entitles individuals to certain rights but the recognition of those rights is resisted by others, then those rights become merely illusion rather than a real benefit to society. It is the concept of justice arising from the ethical conduct of the marketplace that ensures the entitlement and use of rights as well as the imposition of obligations. Justice is the ethical basis for rights.[12] A right is a qualification based on ethical principles such as fairness or justice.[13]

Respect for one's labour constitutes the just and ethical basis for trade secret law. The term 'labour' is normally can mean the effort invested in performing a task as well as the actual workers engaged in that activity. According to classical economic theory, labour is one of the four factors of production (the others being land, capital and enterprise). It is a measure of the work done by human beings and is also the primary channel through which human beings obtain property. According to property right theory, every worker is entitled to a certain ownership of his labour because labour is an indispensable component of one's being, so that people

11. Japanese scholar, Mitsuharu Ito, points out thatif an enterprise wants to keep its trade secrets it should not sell t hem. The only possible way to do this is for the enterprise to establish a factory in a selected country and receive direct benefit through selling its products. Transnational enterprises do just that, which is a phenomenon at the heart of industrial confidentiality. Please refer to Mitsuharu Ito, 现代经济の变貌 (Chinese version) translated by Zheng Haidong (Shanghai University of Finance and Economy Publishing House,1999), p.26. Originally published in Japanese by Iwanami Shoten, Publishers, 1997, Tokyo.
12. A. J. M. Milne, *Human Rights and Human Diversity: An Essay in the Philosophy of Human Rights* (Chinese version) translated by Xia Yong and Zhang Zhiming (Beijing, Encyclopaedia of China Publishing House, 1995), p.150. Originally published in the UK by Macmillan Press Ltd, 1986.
13. Richard A. Spinello, *Ethical Aspects of Information Technology* (Chinese Version), translated by Liu Gao, (Beijing, Central Compilation and Translation Press, 1999), p.242. Originally published by Prentice Hall Inc, 1995, New Jersey

undoubtedly enjoy the right to the fruit of their labour. In his Second Treatise of Civil Government, John Locke points out that, '[f]or this labour being the unquestionable property of the labourer, no man but he can have a right to what that is once joined to'.[14] It is apparent that labour theory provides the legal basis for trade secret law because labour is the means by which individuals obtain property through the use of information in their endeavours. Trade secrets become valuable information by being processed, selected, preserved and handled. The confidential nature of trade secrets reflects the results achieved through labour and creativity in the endeavour to explore new fields. The value of trade secrets is a reflection of the true value of the fruits of one's labour and the combining of commerce with intellectual activity. Because trade secrets are developed at great cost, there exist a great number of unforeseeable risks in doing so. For instance, if an endeavour fails, the expenditure on research and development of a trade secret will return nothing to investors who must deal with the question of how to balance or even reduce their risk. They must use the knowledge gained in their attempt to eliminate the risk caused by errors and ignorance, and must exploit any possible success to offset their loss of investment. It is rational for a fair legal system to strike a balance between the cost of and compensation for one's labour and to bestow legal rights on individuals regarding their creative labour. Trade secret rights should be regarded as encouragement and compensation for labour as well as a right of the secret holder to secure income. In order for individuals to enjoy the fruits of their creative labour, be it intellectual or physical, trade secret rights should be recognized by society.

A transaction is a mutual activity conducted according to the self interests of the parties to it, a precondition of which is a mutual respect for the labour of others. Trade secret rights engender a positive externality which conforms to the doctrine of Pareto Optimality, which is to enable an entire society to benefit from the protection of trade secrets without increasing social burdens.[15] On the one hand

14. John Locke, *Second Treatise Of Civil Government (book II)* (Chinese version) (Beijing, the Commercial Press,1964), p.19.
15. The Theory of Pareto Optimality or Pareto Efficiency of Vilfredo Pareto (1848–1923), an Italian sociologist and economist. He was of the view that when economic resources and output have been allocated in such a way that no one can be made better off without sacrificing the well being of at least one person, that resource allocation is the best choice. This is the so called Pareto Optimality. In plain language, during the process of allocating resources, among all aspects of economic activities no individual should be harmed and the social welfare should be maximized. It is then that social development will reach an optimal level. Pareto's resource allocation efficiency includes two layers of implication. The first is the resource allocation efficiency of micro-economies. This refers to how a production unit, a region or a department organizes and makes use of limited resources and takes ultimate advantage of those resources so as to avoid any waste of them. It also refers to a certain number of production factors that should produce commodities while optimizing value. The second layer is the resource allocation efficiency of macro-economies. This refers to how limited resources are allocated among different production units, regions and industries. If an economic system can efficiently distribute and make use of resources, then that system is regarded as efficient. In other words, efficiency embodies Pareto Optimality.

as mentioned previously, trade secret rights are not exclusive. The possession of certain trade secrets does not exclude the possibility that other individuals will obtain the same information by legal means so that the possession of the trade secret will not become an obstacle to the creative labour of others. On the other hand, knowledge has the quality of being easily disseminated which can produce positive externalities and engenders a trickle-down effect so that other people can further develop it and can also spread and enhance knowledge through legally studying, imitating, and duplicating information.

III. EFFECT OF LABOUR LAW ON THE AUTONOMY OF PRIVATE LAW

There are no compulsory rules regarding confidentiality agreements and covenants not to compete between employers and employees in current Chinese legislation. There is also no statutory obligation for employees to keep the trade secrets of their employers confidential in the absence of an agreement between them or in the absence of the requirement of the employer for its employees to maintain confidentiality.[16] Thus, in practice, confidentiality agreements and covenants not to compete are entered into between employers and employees in accordance with the principle of freedom to contract contained in private law. However, there can exist a variety of different situations in the conduct of concluding confidentiality agreements and covenants, not to compete between employers and employees. In general, employers enjoy a more powerful position than do their employees and sometimes employers use that position to abuse the rights of those employees. In addition, it has become common for employers to ask their employees to sign a standard contract that is prepared by the company in advance. Particularly due to the pressures of the labour market, employees are sometimes hesitant to negotiate with employers regarding their contracts. Therefore, labour law proscribes certain compulsory provisions in order to keep the content of labour contracts reasonable and fair. By these compulsory provisions, the government can involve itself in the protection of the lower socio-economic strata of the population for the purpose of implementing social policy.

It has become a common characteristic of current law regarding labour contracts to regulate conduct within employment relationships based on principles of private law. On the one hand, this preserves the autonomy of parties to labour relationships as the core content of labour law while, on the other hand, labour contracts have evolved based on the right to work and the possibility of the government involvement. This means that the primary principles of labour contract law are based on principles of private law while the nature of labour relationships and the right to work are in turn determined according to the principles of labour contract law.[17] This characteristic of labour law will profoundly impact the

16. Please refer to the detailed introduction in Chapters 3 and Chapter 4 in this Part.
17. Current German labour law provides that labour contracts are concluded in accordance with the principle of autonomy of private law, collective contract, constitutional norms, single acts and

establishment of a system for the protection of trade secrets within the context of employment relationships.

A. Labour Contract Law Based on the Principle of Autonomy of Private Law

The establishment of the concept of private law in certain countries has raised the curtain on a new era of law on rights. Relationships that are established according to principles of private law are special social relationships between subjects having equal status (mainly property relationships and personal relationships). Equality, freedom and the sanctity of private rights are the basic principles of private law. Autonomy of private law refers to the basic principle and rule of civil law that individuals should determine their rights and obligations in private law according to their own free will.[18] The concept of autonomy of private law emphasizes that in relationships that are protected by private law, each party is both the subject of right on the one hand and the subject of obligation on the other hand. The realization of one party's right is the creation of another party's obligation. The law protects the individual's right to freely conduct economic activity and the protection of individual rights is central to the principle of autonomy of private law. Supporting private law is the theoretical concept of respect for mankind.

The principle of the autonomy of private law is embodied in various tenets, such as freedom of ownership, freedom of testament and the freedom of contract – which is the most important. Freedom of contract means concerned parties obtain rights and undertake obligations in accordance with the mutual consent of the parties given of their own free will. Freedom of contract includes the freedom to conclude contracts, which means parties have the freedom to decide whether to conclude a contract with others. In addition, parties have the freedom to decide who counterparties to a contract will be, to determine the content of the contract and to choose the form of the contract. All of these factors are important core content of the freedom to contract.

The principle of freedom to contract emphasizes that the formation of social relationships arises naturally out of the conduct of parties in that process and proposes to treat contracts in terms of personal autonomy. This has tremendously inspired individual creativity in society. It may be said that the freedom to contract is in fact the freedom to conduct personal actions that may bring legal consequences. Hence, as one academician has commented, it is a wonder in the history

---

the court's specific application of the law. Please refer to Zhang Guowen (translator), Wilhelm Dütz, *Arbeitsrecht*, (Beijing, Law Press, 2005), p.2. The German version was published by Verlag C.H.Beck, Munchen in 2003.

18. Law Dictionary Editorial Board of the Institute of Law of the Chinese Academy of Social Sciences, *Law Dictionary*, (Beijing, Law Press, 2003), p.1341.

of human culture that at the same time capitalism prospered in the nineteenth century, the freedom to contract in private law was emerging as the prevailing principle in human relationships. The freedom to contract can be considered a safeguard for contracting parties as well as for personal property. The freedom to contract has been recognized and guaranteed in the constitutions of many countries and China is no exception.[19]

The labour contract is the core of the labour relationship. All labour relationships are established by a labour contract and develop based on that contract. The development of labour relationships has been a process of historical development and has evolved according to concepts and principles of private law. These principles form the basis for labour contracts that is embodied in the concept that parties to a labour contract have equal status in private law and that they have independent personalities in private law. The Prussian Common Law (1794), the Austrian Civil Law (1811), the German Civil Law (1896), and the Swiss Code of Obligations (1911) all contain provisions on labour contracts, illustrating that labour relations had entered an era of relationship established by means of employment contracts. Prior to the twentieth century, there existed an almost complete freedom of contract within employment relationships. At that time, employers and employees concluded contracts based solely on their mutual consent. For example, it was not until the end of the nineteenth century that American law had generally been developing or would inevitably develop in the direction of individual autonomy through freedom of contract.[20] The United States Supreme Court held that a person's right to sell his labour under conditions that he believes to be reasonable is, in essence, tantamount to the right of a purchaser of labour to accept the conditions of suppliers of labour. Therefore, an employee's right not to work for an employer without explanation was equal to an employer's right to refuse the continued service of an employee without explanation. In all of these situations, employer and employee enjoy an equality of rights. Consequently, any legislation tending to harm that balance would be arbitrary interference in the freedom of contract.[21]

The advent of labour relationships based on contract enabled workers to free themselves from subordinate relationships with their employers and provided safeguards for the labour force to enter into a market that provided adequate possibilities for employment.

19. See the *Amendment to the Constitution of the People's Republic of China* (2004), Article 33 provides, 'Every citizen is entitled to the rights and at the same time must perform the duties prescribed by the Constitution and the law'. Article 4 of the *Contract Law of the People's Republic of China* (1999) provides, 'Contracting parties are free to enter into a contract according to law. No organization or individual may illegally interfere in this right'.
20. Bernard Schwartz, *The Law in America: A History* (Chinese version translated by Wang Jun), (Beijing, China University of Political Science and Law Publishing House, 1997), p.134.
21. Zhu Jingwen, A Challenge to Traditional Western Law: The Critical Legal Studies Movement in America (Beijing, China Prosecution Publishing House,1996), p.283.

B. The Right to Work as the Essence of the Labour Contract Law

The autonomy of private law places the rights of the individual at its centre, implying that people as subjects of private law are equal, free and sensible. What lies behind these individual rights at the heart of private law, however, is the concept of mutual respect and of all persons being equal. However, the term 'people' as mentioned here refers to a form of 'abstract person'[22] with an abstract legal personality. All persons are regarded by the law as equal subjects without distinction. Therefore, the prerequisite of freedom of contract must be the equal status of two parties. If one party is superior to another party in the law, the content of a contract will not embody mutual consent and will be decided only by the willingness of the superior party.

In modern labour relationships, each worker is the owner of his own labour and he can freely sell his labour to anyone who desires to employ him in exchange for remuneration. From the beginning, the implication of private law was that laws should respect the free will of parties to contract. However, the subordinate position of employees dictates that they are the weaker party in labour relationships. Employers always play a decisive and leading role in employment relationships and they can sometimes coerce employees by dint of their superior position.[23] The prima facie equality of employment relationships can mask certain inherent inequalities beneath the surface. In this situation, if the mutual rights and obligations of employment contracts are decided by the parties themselves, some unfairness must inevitably occur within employment relationships. For example, at present in China, in order to save time on the negotiation of individual labour contracts many employers provide a standard employment contract to their employees. To these employees, the content of these contracts appears to have been pre-determined and there is no room for them to bargain with their employers. All an employee can do is to make a choice between 'agree – sign' or 'disagree – no contract'. In the absence of negotiation and bargaining, the employment relationship is established with this type of contract. Nevertheless, what is at stake is not just a matter of simple choice. The fact is that one party to the contract (the party who prepares the 'standard' contract) is generally the economically superior party while the other, whose only realistic choice is to sign it, is always the economically weaker party. This is especially true in the case of non-competition agreements that generally directly constrain the right to work, post-employment. Even when an employee signs and agrees to such a standard contract, it usually contains clauses that are inherently unfair, (e.g., adding employment duties and obligations, unfairly reducing or exempting an employer from its obligations, restricting or depriving an employee of his rights, unduly changing an employer's obligation to

---

22. Dong Baohua, *A General Introduction to the Social Law*, (Beijing, China University of Political Science and Law Publishing House, 2001), p.68.
23. The subordinate nature of the employment contract shall be discussed in the Chapter 3 of this part.

provide evidence and forcing employees to undertake unfair risks). Employees normally would bear great loss or harm due to the unfair content of such contracts.

The appearance of the sociology of law in the twentieth century[24] changed the orientation of legislation from being centred purely on the rights of the individual. Instead, the sociology of law was socio-centric and stressed a jurisprudential concept of law stemming from the achievement of social aims and service to society.[25] As to the relationship between society and the individual, the sociology of law focused on the collective interests of the society, emphasizing the balance of individual interests and social interests and making the security of the weaker elements of society its central theme.

Concerning the evolution of the private law relationship, the sociology of law emphasized state involvement in the restriction of private rights such as ownership, freedom of contract and the autonomy of parties, so as to positively create conditions for the security of socio-economic rights such as the right to health, the right to work, the right to material assistance, the right to rest, the right to education, the right to a healthy environment and so on. For example, the state can stipulate certain legislation (such as the basic Labour Law) to restrict the content of contracts through compulsory obligation of employers or to amend unfair labour contracts so as to achieve genuine equity.

The sociology of law places social interests at its centre and seeks the optimum benefit for the public interest and the maximum social stability through sociological mechanisms. The sociology of law contains certain unique principles (e.g., the principle of protection of the weak within society). Influenced by the sociology of law, most nations have promulgated compulsory regulations orientated towards protecting the legal interests of employees, restricting the autonomy of labour contracts and protecting the public interest. All of these provisions have become critical content within modern labour law.

Due to the elements of personality, property, equality and subordination inherent in labour relationships, legislators in most countries consider the following aspects when making labour contract law:

(a) There should be an easily identifiable basic law on labour standards for the protection of workers as well as labour contract law that is beneficial for coordinating and stabilizing labour relationships.

---

24. Chinese academics define social law as legislation through which a government may intervene in the activities of a society so as to secure the interests of that society. See Dong Baohua, *A General Introduction to the Social Law* (Beijing, China University of Political Science and Law Publishing House, 2001), p.11. The view of Japanese academics on the social law is that social laws are an academic categorization of laws that can help to maintain the subsistence of economically inferior persons and enhance their welfare. See (Japan) 星野英一, translated by Wang Chuang, 'The Person of the Private Law', Liang Huixing (ed.), *Civil and Commercial Law Review* (Beijing, Law Press, 1997), p.186.
25. German academic Rudolf Thering (1818–1892) promoted the view that legal philosophy should have a core purpose of all working for the good of the whole society.

(b) The law should recognize and maintain the authority of enterprise labour rules and should also prevent the abuse of those rules.
(c) The law should emphasize the flexibility of individual contracts and should also make good use of collective contracts.
(d) In order to realize the right to work on the basis of securing the right to a livelihood, there should be an integrated system composed of the right of association, the right of associations to bargain and the right of complaint.

Upon examination of current labour legislation in certain countries, it can be seen that, in contrast to ordinary civil contracts, labour contract law exhibits the following characteristics:

Firstly, although labour contract law also values the autonomy of parties to labour contracts, it contains certain restrictions on the content of the contracts concluded by those parties. For example where labour protection and labour conditions are concerned, some countries provide minimum standards in their basic labour laws and parties freely entering into labour contracts may not include agreements that fail to meet those minimum standards. Meanwhile, labour contracts between two parties should not contradict the content of collective contracts and contradictory clauses in individual labour contracts will be deemed void.[26] Therefore, while the law provides certain latitude for party autonomy in labour contracts, the law inclines to protect workers.

Secondly, in addition to emphasizing the performance of labour service and the payment of remuneration for labour, the Labour Contract Law also stipulates special obligations for parties to labour contracts. For example, in addition to the obligation of paying salaries to workers, employers have a duty of care concerning their employees and, in addition to accepting the obligation to perform labour services, employees must accept the obligation of loyalty to their employers, must diligently perform their work and must protect the trade secrets of their company.[27] In this instance, a close personal relationship is formed within the labour relationship and it becomes a relationship that protects the common interests of employer and employee. A typical and intrinsic characteristic of relationships based on common interest is the loyalty of the parties to each other. The impact of loyalty on the performance of contractual obligations by the parties greatly surpasses that of the binding force of the law. The obligation to provide employees with protection and care on the part of employers, and the obligation of loyalty and diligence on the part of employees are as important as their respective obligations to of pay remuneration and to provide labour.

---

26. Article 9 of the *Labour Code of the Russian Federation* (2001) states that '[c]ollective contracts, agreements and labour contracts may not contain terms or conditions which reduce the rights and guarantees of employees established by labour law. Should such terms or conditions be included in a collective contract, agreement or labour contract, they shall not be applied'. The same principles in the labour law can also be found in a great number of other countries.
27. See section 2 in Chapter 2, the Belgian Law on Contracts of Employment (1978) (loi du 3 juillet 1978 relative aux contrats du travail).

Thirdly, according to the principle of fairness contained in contract law, consideration is a necessary element to the creation of a contract. The consideration must result from bargaining by the parties and must be the thing that induces the mutual promises. However, when certain causes that could not be attributed to any contractual parties result in the non-performance of labour obligations, an employer still has the obligation to pay salaries to their employees.[28]

Fourthly, as a result of the establishment of a social benefits system in certain countries, employees can seek relief for their personal injuries from their governments. This system has developed and integrated various elements inspired by the idea of solidarity or shared risk at the national level in certain countries. As a result, the payment of compensation for personal injury that occurs during the performance of an employment contract has become one of social obligation rather than simply the legal duty of an employer and insures that workers are sufficiently compensated for injuries sustained during the course of their employment.

The aforementioned characteristics of the Labour Contract Law illustrate that current labour law is developing a strong orientation towards the protection of the interests of workers. The aim in doing so through labour law is to make up for defects in the principle of equity in contract law, to correct the de facto inequity within labour relationships and to achieve fairness in the application of the law. Legislatures endow workers with statutory rights to ensure the realization of their rights and the performance of obligations by their employers.

The applicability of labour law in the conduct of labour relationships demonstrates that most countries have paid close attention to the individual within employment relationships and also reflects the legal precept that the law should serve society. As a result of social and economic development, labour relationships have moved beyond the scope of private law and have entered the realm of socialization. The socialized common interest has given rise to the concept of the worker-centric employment relationship, enabling employees to obtain advantages under the protection of labour law. This will profoundly impact the establishment of a system of protection for trade secrets within employment relationships.

28. *Ibid.* See article 27.

Chapter 3

Duty of Confidentiality and Non-Competition during the Term of Employment[1]

As mentioned above, an employment relationship is a legal notion widely employed internationally to refer to the relationship between a person called an 'employee' (frequently referred to as a 'worker') and an 'employer' for whom the employee performs work under certain conditions in return for remuneration. It is through this employment relationship, however defined, that reciprocal rights and obligations are created between the employee and the employer.[2] Employees bear many obligations to their employers, but none is more important than the duty of loyalty, which demands that employees diligently perform their jobs under the instruction of their employers. In addition, employees cannot be delinquent in their duty or infringe on the interests of their employers. This includes not disclosing the trade secrets of their employers without permission as well as not engaging in competition with their employers without permission. The question of whether it is a mandatory duty or a contractual obligation for employees to maintain the confidentiality of the trade secrets of their companies during employment must then be answered. If there are no explicit provisions regarding non-disclosure of trade secrets contained in their employment contract, the issue of whether an employee may disclose, use or permit others to use the trade secrets of their employer, remains a question. Can an employer sue or prosecute an employee for violating their obligation of loyalty? And finally, the question of whether

1. The definition and theories of non-competition shall be discussed in the next chapter.
2. International Labour Office, 'The Employment Relationship', Report V given at ninety-fifth session of the International Labour Conference (Geneva, 2006), <www.ilo.org/ilolex/english/convdisp1.htm>, 6 January 2008.

employees bear any duty of loyalty to their employers following termination of employment is of great importance.[3]

The focus of the abovementioned conflicts is mainly concentrated on the following issues:

1) the legitimatization of trade secret protection;
2) the boundary between trade secrets and skill and experience;
3) statutory obligations and contractual obligations for the protection of trade secrets;
4) the validity of non-compete agreements following employment.

I. CURRENT LEGAL SITUATION IN CHINA

In 1998, the Shanghai Pudong New Area People's Court heard the case of *Shanghai Yikeyi Clothing Ltd. v. Zhou Baojun, and Shanghai Zhongyuan Commercial Company Ltd.*[4]

The facts are as follows: On 31 December 1994 following a registration of change of shareholders with the State Administration of Industry and Commerce of Qingpu district, the defendant Zhou Baojun, became the majority shareholder of the Shanghai Zhongyuan Commercial Company Ltd. (Zhongyuan), owning 60% of the shares of the company and becoming its legal representative and general manager. From December 1996 to September 1997, Zhou was employed by the plaintiff, Shanghai Yikeyi Clothing Ltd. ('Yikeyi'), as division head of its technology and quality inspection division. Prior to December 1996, Zhou had become acquainted with the general manager and the chairman of the board of the plaintiff Yikeyi when Zhou repaired machines for the company. In December 1996, the plaintiff began to conduct business with Zhongyuan.

In February 1997, the plaintiff signed a contract with Zhongyuan to produce shoulder pads for clothing. The contract was endorsed by the chairman of the board and the general manager of the plaintiff and signed by the general manager of the plaintiff and the factory manager of the defendant Zhongyuan. The two individuals signed as each party's respective representative and officially chopped the contract using their company seals. Zhou participated in negotiating the contract as division head of the plaintiff, but did not sign as either party's agent on the contract. Before signing the contract, the chairman of the board of the plaintiff went to Zhongyuan

3. The issue of duty of loyalty will be discussed at Chapter 4 of this part.
4. The case concerned whether non-competition provisions stipulated in the *Company Law* could be applied therein. The defendant, Zhou Baojun, was not a subject of non-competition provisions as contained in the *Company Law*, and as a result, the request of the plaintiff was denied. Please refer to the judgment of first instance, Shanghai Pudong New Area People's Court (1998) Pu Jing Chu Zhi No. 3526 and the judgment of second instance, Shanghai No.1 Intermediate People's Court (1999) Hu Yizhong Jing Zhong Zhi No. 485.
<www.hshfy.sh.cn/fyitw/fyitw_xxnr_view.pl?id=8627&xh=1>, 18 August 2006.
<www.chnlaw.net/lawcase/HTML/lawcase_17304_2.htm>, 6 January 2008.

to conduct on-site inspections because the subject matter of the contract involved quite a large sum of money. Subsequently, the plaintiff and Zhongyuan both performed the contract. From 1997 to 1998, the plaintiff paid Zhongyuan a total of CNY 829,909 in processing fees and Zhongyuan earned a total profit of CNY 219,801.

Concurrent to the signing of the contract with Zhongyuan, the plaintiff signed a similar contract with Shanghai Songjiang Jinxiu School Uniform Factory. In addition, Zhou represented the plaintiff when he was employed by it in the previous signing of five contracts.

In November 1998, the plaintiff sued Zhou and Zhongyuan for violation of the non-competition agreement and petitioned the Shanghai Pudong New Area People's Court to order Zhou and Zhongyuan to reimburse any illegal income. The plaintiff alleged in its complaint that the defendant Zhou had concealed the fact that he was the legal representative and majority shareholder of Zhongyuan while he was employed by the plaintiff and had deceived the plaintiff in signing the processing contract with Zhongyuan on 27 February 1997. Based on the duty of loyalty and the duty of directors, supervisors, and managers not to compete, as stipulated in Articles 59 and 61 of the Company Law, the plaintiff petitioned the court to order the two defendants to return the profit of CNY 21, 9801.

Zhou and Zhongyuan admitted the fact that Zhou was the legal representative and general manager of Zhongyuan and that he also owned 60% of the shares of Zhongyuan. However, the two defendants argued, Zhou worked only as chief of technology and not as head of the production department of the plaintiff. As such, the defendants contended, Zhou was only the head of a department and not a manager as set forth in the Company Law and, as such, had no authority to run the company and that he therefore should not bear the responsibility of a director, manager or supervisor of a company. Thus, the defendants held, Zhou participated only in the contract negotiation and did not represent any signers of the contract and the contract itself contained no provisions that were unfair to the plaintiff. Consequently, they concluded, defendant Zhou should not be held to the duty not to compete with his company, which is, according to PRC law and regulations, a compulsory obligation of directors or managers of a company.

The court of first instance, the Shanghai Pudong New Area People's Court, finding for the plaintiff, held that although Zhou had signed five contracts on behalf of the plaintiff during his employment, said authority could only be regarded as plaintiff's specific authority to Zhou as he was only a department head and not a manager as defined by the Company Law. Zhongyuan provided shoulder pads to the plaintiff, which used the shoulder pads to produce clothing. The court held that because the products of the two parties were not identical that the relationship between Zhongyuan and the plaintiff was only a form of cooperation rather than a competitive relationship within the same industry. Thus, the court found that Zhou should not be held to the obligation not to compete with the plaintiff that was stipulated in the company's rules. Regarding the 27 February 1997 contract between the plaintiff and Zhongyuan, the court further found that due to the fact that the content of the contract was approved by the plaintiff's chairman of the board and the contract was signed by the general manager of the plaintiff, that Zhou had only participated in the negotiation and did not sign the contract as the plaintiff's agent.

Further, the court said, prior to the cooperation between the plaintiff and Zhongyuan, the general manager and the chairman of the board of the plaintiff had known Zhou and the chairman of the board of the plaintiff had also conducted on-site inspections of Zhongyuan. Because the contract involved a large sum of money and three months elapsed from the initial intent to cooperate to the signing of the contract, it was obvious that there was no issue of unfairness in the course of completing the contract. As to the content of the contract, certain clauses were quite strict and they were, on the whole, identical to those contained in the contract between the plaintiff and the Songjiang Jinxiu School Uniform Factory. Because the content of the contract was basically the same as that in contracts between the plaintiff and other co-operators, there should have been no significant misunderstandings in the contract between the plaintiff and Zhongyuan. Thus, the court determined that there was no factual or legal basis for the plaintiff's petition and it was subsequently denied.

The plaintiff refused to accept the decision of the court and filed an appeal, contending that Zhou had concealed his status as the legal representative of Zhongyuan while working as production manager of the plaintiff. The plaintiff contended in its appeal that Zhou had taken advantage of his office and had lured it into signing the contract with Zhongyuan, thereby violating relevant law and regulations, and that the profit earned by Zhongyuan should be refunded to the appellant.

The appeals court, the Shanghai Intermediate People's Court, rejected the appeal and affirmed the original judgment stating that the ascertainment of facts in the original judgment was found to be clear.

During the civil trial and in the appeals process, both the courts and the parties to the case focused on Zhou's status regarding whether in his position as department manager of an enterprise he should be subject to the non-competition provisions of the Company Law. The first important reason for the court to deny the plaintiff's request was that it held that the plaintiff and Zhongyuan had a cooperative relationship, which did not constitute competition within the same industry. Thus, the acts of the defendants did not violate the duty not to compete with the plaintiff.
Secondly, subparagraph 1 of Article 59 of the Company Law provides that:

> The directors, supervisors or managers shall abide by the company's articles of association, faithfully execute their official duties and protect the company's interests. They shall not exploit their position and power in the company to advance their own private interests.

Subparagraph 1 of Article 61 further provides that:

> The directors or managers shall not engage on their own behalf or on behalf of others in any business similar to the business of the company in which they hold office or in activities harmful to the company's interests. The proceeds from such business or activities shall belong to the company.

And Subparagraph 2 stipulates that:

> Unless otherwise provided in the company's articles of association or with the consent of a shareholders meeting, a director or manager shall not enter into any contracts or transactions with another company.

The court held, however, that Zhou was just a department head in the employ of the plaintiff and did not perform the role of manager as stipulated in the Company Law. Therefore, the court concluded, he did not enjoy the statutory authority provided by Article 50 of the Company Law. Thus, Zhou should not be held to the duty not to compete as stipulated in the Company Law.

Nevertheless, this case gives rise to an issue worthy of investigation. As a senior employee of the plaintiff, the defendant Zhou concealed his status as the largest single shareholder of Zhongyuan. The issue raised is whether Zhou should be held liable because he had concealed his position when he encouraged the plaintiff to do business with Zhongyuan (in which he owned shares) or because in the course of that business relationship he had inevitably disclosed the plaintiff's trade secrets and other secret information. In this case, neither the parties to the suit nor the courts gave attention to such issues.

As mentioned above, presently, Chinese law explicitly provides that board directors and managers should refrain from engaging, independently or together with others, in any business similar to that of their current employers or in activity detrimental to that employer. This is a compulsory duty stipulated by law when directors and manager sign non-competition agreements with their companies.[5] However, the regulations are silent regarding the non competition obligation of regular employees, including technical staff. Supervisory departments in certain industries have promulgated administrative regulations that contain clauses permitting enterprises to prohibit their employees from competing with them through non-competition agreements. However, these rules are only general internal rules of certain ministries/departments and carry no legal weight. For example, the Scientific and Technical Section of the State Construction Materials Bureau published the Notice on the Protection of Intellectual Property Achieved from Key National Scientific and Technological Research Projects and the State Science and Technology Commission published the Several Opinions on Strengthening Administration of Know-how during the Transfer of Scientific and Technological Personnel. These regulations apply only to certain industries (usually state-owned enterprises) directly supervised by those state ministries/departments.

The Shenzhen Special Economic Zone and the Zhuhai Municipality were leaders in adopting local regulations for the protection of trade secrets in promulgating the Regulations for the Protection of Enterprise Know-how which include regulations regarding non-competition agreements. Article 16 of the Shanghai Regulations on Labour Contracts enacted by the Shanghai People's Congress in 2001 provides that parties to employment contracts may incorporate

5. See Article 61 of the Company Law of People's Republic of China, and Article 30 of the Law of the People's Republic of China on Partnership Enterprises.

non-competition clauses or confidentiality agreements into those contracts and may agree upon payment of compensation following termination of employment for employees who have the duty to maintain the confidentiality of the trade secrets of the employer. The Shanghai Regulations on Labour stipulate that the scope of non-competition agreements is limited to employees not engaging, by themselves or for others, in any business that competes with their former employers for a certain length of time after leaving that employer. The duration of such non-competition agreements is subject to negotiation by parties to employment contracts but may not exceed three years unless otherwise provided in PRC law or administrative regulations.

While the scope of certain ministerial/departmental rules and local regulations has been extended to cover normal employees, these regulations are not universally applicable. Furthermore, they contain no explicit provisions regarding competition by employees with their employers during their term of employment.

As far as the duty of employees to confidentiality and non-competition is concerned, the main difficulty met by Chinese courts in the hearing of disputes and by academics in research is whether that duty is a statutory obligation or one that is only based on a contractual agreement and must be clarified. During a term of employment, if an employment contract does not contain an explicit agreement regarding the confidentiality of trade secrets, whether employees can neglect professional ethics and disclose, use or permit others to use the trade secrets of a legal holder which they may come to know becomes an issue. Furthermore, during the term of employment, in the absence of explicit agreements, the issue of whether employers can forbid their employees to have a part-time job is also questionable. The question of whether an employee's duty to maintain the confidentiality of his employer's trade secrets during his employment is statutory or contractual has been vexing to those within China's judicial circles and has directly influenced the fair hearing of these types of cases. If no clear reference has been made in an employment contract to the obligation of confidentiality, can an employee then, in the breach of his professional code of conduct, disclose, use or allow others to the use trade secrets of his employer which may come into his possession?

As mentioned above, for historical reasons, the employment regime in China had been for a long time subject to highly centralized state administration under which the labour force had been allocated according to central planning and under which all employees were at the same time the 'masters' of the enterprise that they were working for. However, with the reform of the economic regime and the establishment of a free labour market, the employment relationship in China has changed dramatically. This change is manifest not only in the allocation of labour by the market, but also by employment based upon hiring directly by enterprises and the regime of collective employment contracts established in 1999.[6]

6. Dong, Baohua, *Theory of Labour Law* (Beijing, World Books Press, 1999), p. 63.

Currently however, legislation in China (including the Labour Law dedicated to the regulation of employment relationships) does not provide a clear legal definition for the nature of employment relationships. Consequently, an employee's obligation of confidentiality lacks a logical legal foundation. Furthermore, the wording of related provisions in certain regulations is ambiguous. For example, Article 3 of the Several Regulations on Forbidding Infringement of Trade Secrets, adopted by the State Administration for Industry and Commerce, provides that activities which infringe trade secrets and which are prohibited include, inter alia:

> to disclose, use or allow others to use trade secrets of the right holder by its employee in breach of the contractual agreement entered with or the requirement of confidentiality imposed by the right holder.

It is not clear whether 'the requirement of confidentiality imposed by the right holder' mentioned here is statutory in nature. Another example is Article 22 of the Labour Law which provides:

> The parties to an employment contract may agree in the employment contract upon issues such as the duty to maintain trade secrets of the employer. An employee who fails to fulfil such duty and causes economic loss to his employer shall be liable for payment of compensation.

Article 1 of the Letter on Infringement of Trade Secrets Involved in Labour Disputes enacted by the Secretariat of the Ministry of Labour and Social Security further provides that if terms regarding the maintenance of confidentiality of trade secrets have been incorporated into an employment contract and subsequently a labour dispute arises because the employee has failed to fulfil said obligation of confidentiality and has infringed on the employer's trade secrets, the Arbitration Committee for Labour Disputes should accept a petition for arbitration in respect of such dispute and grant an award in accordance with relevant regulations and the agreement of confidentiality contained in the employment contract'. It is not clear whether these provisions of the Labour Law are suggesting that an employee's obligation of confidentiality is based solely upon contractual agreement. If the obligation is statutory, then even in the absence of a contractual agreement an employee must observe the duty of confidentiality and be can be held liable for payment of compensation for any breach of that duty. If the obligation is only contractual, then in the absence of any explicit references in the employment contract there is no legal basis for an employer to impose an obligation of confidentiality upon its employees.

Due to the ambiguity of Chinese law, many employers have tried to protect their trade secrets by signing confidentiality agreements with their employees. Employers worry, however, that clauses within such agreements will not cover all of their trade secrets and employees worry that such agreements will not be reasonable and will infringe on their right to work.

In 2004, the Shenzhen Intermediate People's Court heard a criminal case in which the defendants Fang Shunlong, Lin Yaozhang, Huang Yingzhong, Lee

Qibing and Lee Rurun, were charged with infringement of trade secrets.[7] This was a public prosecution initiated by the Shenzhen Baoan District Procuratorate.

Pan Guoji, a businessman from Hong Kong and the owner and general manager of Shenzhen City Baoan Shucan Hardware Ornaments Factory, had invented a method for automatically producing claw chains for necklaces, bracelets, anklets, hair clips and earrings. The technology increased by ten times the production efficiency of his factory. Using this technology, within a few years the products manufactured in Pan's factory had a one-hundred per cent market share and ultimately returned a profit of approximately CNY 1,600,000 per day. In 1994, when Xiang, Huang, Lee Qibing and Lee Rurun were recruited by the factory to work as mould makers, Pan warned them verbally several times not to disclose the technical secrets of the factory. At the same time, Pan also implemented strict security measures including designating special individuals to be responsible for the safekeeping of blueprints and posting a warning sign to stop any visitors from coming into contact with said blueprints. However, from April to July 1998, one by one, Xiang, Huang, Lee Qibing and Lee Rurun left Shenzhen City and went to work at the Shanghai Chuangli Fashion Ornaments Factory, which was registered in Shanghai by Taiwan businessmen Fang Shunlong and Lin Yaozhang. Chuangli, it happened, had been a former customer of Pan Guoji. All four of the ex-employees of Baoan went to work at the Shanghai Chuangli Fashion Ornaments Factory and began to produce claw chains for necklaces, bracelets, anklets, hair clips and earrings. The Factory sold the products at only half of Pan's price. In 2000, the four left Shanghai for Yiwu City in Zhejiang Province and established their own factory to manufacture the same products. As a result of the malicious competition conducted by them, the factory of Pan lost its market share and was barely able to make a profit from the sale of its products. In July 2003, Shenzhen Baoan District Procuratorate initiated a criminal case against Fang Shunlong, Lin Yaozhang and the other four, accusing Fang and Lin of inducing Pan's technical staff to leave their former factory so as to obtain Pan's trade secrets and accusing the four ex-employees of Baoan of violating their confidentiality obligation to protect the trade secrets of their former employer. The six were all charged with the crime of infringement upon trade secrets. At the same time the infringed party, Pan, filed a collateral civil suit seeking compensation from the defendants.

The Shenzhen Baoan District People's Court rejected Pan's civil suit and found the six defendants not guilty of criminal infringement. The defendants were released immediately following the announcement of the decision. The court found that because after the Baoan Procuratorate had initiated its investigation of the case Pan had applied for two patents on his technology to produce a type of claw chain and had been awarded patents by the State Intellectual Property Office prior to the court reaching its decisions in the civil and criminal cases, the technology Pan had used was no longer a secret. Secondly, Pan had only issued a verbal warning to the four technical staff to keep secret the technology but he had

7. < www.chinacourt.org/public/detail.php?id=132079&k_title=侵犯商业秘密 >, 6 January 2008.

not required them to sign written confidentiality agreements. Therefore, the court held, the accused had no obligation to confidentiality. The People's Procuratorate protested the decision of the people's court and appealed to the Shenzhen Intermediate People's Court.

On 19 September 2004 the Shenzhen Intermediate People's Court rendered a final decision that the six defendants had indeed committed the crime of infringement of Pan's trade secrets. Defendants Fang and Lin, the two Taiwan businessmen, were each sentenced to seven years in prison, (four years of which were suspended) and fined CNY one-hundred thousand. One of the four technical staff was sentenced to two years in prison with a suspension of three years and fined CNY sixty thousand. The other three technical staff were each sentenced to one and a half years in prison and fined CNY forty-thousand. In addition, the six defendants were required to reimburse the plaintiff CNY 11,600,000 for his economic loss. The Shenzhen Intermediate People's Court affirmed that a verbal warning could be considered as legitimate as a written confidentiality agreement for holders to protect their trade secrets. In addition, the Intermediate People's Court cited that it was a mistake on the part of the court of first instance to have held that the verbal warning was not a legitimate measure for the protection of trade secrets as required by Chinese law.

Pan, the infringed party, was satisfied with the final judgment. However, this case inspires a question worthy of pondering: If Pan Guoji had not verbally warned his staff to maintain the confidentiality of his technical secrets, would his staff have been held to an obligation of confidentiality?

The statistics of trade secret cases used in the graph above were derived from eighty-two cases heard before the courts in Beijing, Shanghai and Jiangsu Province from 2001 to 2005, which were published on the China IPR Judgments and Decisions website <http://ipr.chinacourt.org>. In accordance with the facts and judgments, the graph divides the statistics into four categories: dispute categories, trial results, dispute causes of action and trade secret disputes caused by employees.

According to the statistics of the dispute categories, the largest percentage of cases involved infringement of operating confidential information (32.93%). Second were cases involving the infringement of technical confidential information (21.95%). Cases involving co-existence of infringement of trade secrets and duty of non-competition comprised 25.61% of cases heard.

The total number of rejected claims (19.51%) and partially confirmed claims (18.90%) amounted to 38.41% of total cases. Only 1.83% of plaintiff's claims were upheld by the courts. The main reasons for the high percentage of rejections of plaintiffs' claims were, first, that the plaintiff could not provide sufficient evidence to support its claims. For example, in the case of *Beijing Shihuakai Electronic Commerce Limited Company v. Nis Peter Lorentzen*,[8] the court confirmed that the customer relationships and lists as well as operating information of the plaintiff met the constitutive requirement of a trade secret, and as a senior manager of plaintiff, the defendant should have kept secret various commercial

8. < http://bjgy.chinacourt.org/public/detail.php?id=7330&k_title=商业秘密&k_content= 商业秘密 &k_author= >, 6 January 2008.

Graph 1. Trade Secrets Cases in Beijing City, Shanghai City and Jiangsu Province Published on China IPR Judgments and Decisions Website by the Supreme People's Court (from 2001 to 2005)

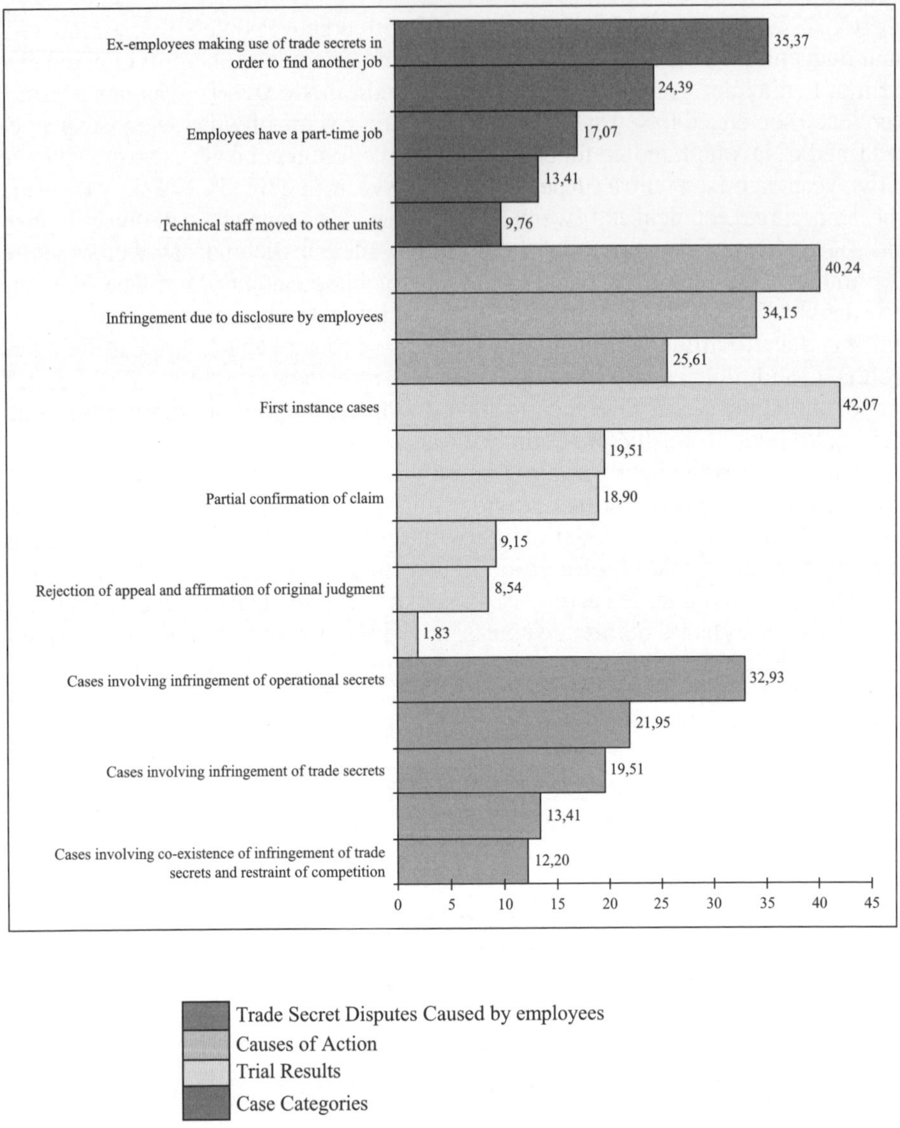

information that the defendant came in contact with while in the performance of the employment contract. While the court found that the defendant was obligated to non-competition following termination of the employment relationship, the plaintiff had failed to provide sufficient evidence that the defendant had disclosed or permitted other people to use its trade secrets. In addition, plaintiff had failed to provide proof of damages incurred to its interests resulting from the acts of the defendant.

A second reason for the high number of rejected claims was that some plaintiffs misunderstood the definition of a trade secret. For instance in *Beijing Chonghui Advertisement Limited Company v. Liu Nan, China Distance Education Journal*[9] and in Beijing *Zhongkuang Institute of Machinery and Electronic Engineering v. Zhang Wenming, Xuzhou Kuangyuan Pump Limited Company, and Xuzhou Kuangyuan Scientific and Technological Trade Limited Company,*[10] the plaintiffs deemed that their customer list and connections should be protected by trade secret law. Actually, in these cases, the subject customer information could be found in the public domain.

The statistical makes clear that, involving causes of action, the percentage of infringement due to disclosure by employees reached as high as 34.15%. However, a great number of disputes were due to misappropriation by third parties alone or in collusion with the employees of the plaintiff (40.24%).

When scrutinizing disputes involving employees, technical staff moving to other units (9.76%), technical staff and operating management staff establishing their own enterprises (13.41%) are only fourth and fifth, while ex-employees making use of trade secrets in order to find another job (35.37%) and employees having a part-time job were first and second.

II. NATURE OF AN EMPLOYEE'S DUTY OF LOYALTY IN EMPLOYMENT RELATIONSHIPS

Many Western academics hold the view that an employee's duty of confidentiality and obligation not to compete arise naturally from (the duty of loyalty to his employer. Such duty of loyalty derives from the employment relationship and is based on the nature of the employment contract.

Quite a number of academics regard modern employment relationships as a form of contractual relationship, which is a type of legal relationship established on the basis of mutual respect and mutual agreement between an employee and an employer. In this relationship, an employee provides his labour or service as his employer requires, while the employer pays the employee agreed-upon remuneration.[11] Similar to other contractual relationships, employment relationships are established by employees and employers on the basis of negotiation. Consequently, employment relationships should have a characteristic common to contractual relationships, that being the quality of equity. In practice, however,

9. < http://bjgy.chinacourt.org/public/detail.php?id=12164&k_title=商业秘密&k_content=商业秘密&k_author= >, 6 January 2008.
10. <www.jsfy.gov.cn/cpws/cpws_read.jsp?id=439>, 6 January 2008.
11. Kate Brearley and Selwyn Bloch, Employment Covenants and Confidential Information: Law, Practice and Technique (Butterworths,1999), p.6.

following the establishment of an employment relationship this equitable relationship in fact becomes a subordinate relationship. In an employment relationship, employees must meet the requirements of their employers and give their labour over to the control of the employer so that the labour of individuals is combined to become part of a collective endeavour. At the same time, in exchange for payment by their employers, workers surrender the right to their labour to their employers and enable their employers to allocate and use that labour. As each worker and his labour are combined indivisibly together, when an employer becomes the controller of the labour force it inevitably becomes the superintendent of the workers themselves. Employees must obey the instructions of their employers and as a result the employment relationship becomes a subordinate relationship. The subordination of employees to their employers is the most primary characteristic of an employment relationship.

Employment contracts differ from other kinds of contracts because, as the subject matter of employment contracts, labour is not a commodity but the processing of knowledge and the use of the physical bodies of employees. Employees must perform contractual obligations of their own free will and so the physical body of an employee is somehow a part of the employment relationship. Therefore, employers must provide employees a safe work environment[12]and are obligated to take care of their employees during the course of their employment. Specifically, it has become compulsory in modern employment law that employers are obligated tot a duty of care. As far as employees are concerned, they are obligated to faithfully carry out the instructions of their employers, to perform the contractual obligations agreed to with their employers and to work for their employers' interests. This is the so-called 'duty of loyalty' that is a prerequisite of any employer recruiting and hiring new employees.

It is generally believed that an employee's duty of loyalty originated from early law prescribing the relationship between master and servant.[13] Under the old British law regarding 'master and servant,' reinforced by the 1563 Statute of Artificers, the status of a servant determined his obligations. Servants could be punished under the old criminal law for not accepting work, for not doing work according to the directions of their master or for deserting their masters. At that time, the duty of loyalty was derived from the relationship between master and servant and entailed a restraint on personal freedom.[14] These old regulations had been in force for several hundred years in Europe until the advent of industrialization in the nineteenth century.[15] For example, with the legitimization of trade unions in the mid-nineteenth century in some countries, they began to play an

12. Manfred Weiss, 'The Duty of Employee Loyalty in Germany,' *Comparative Labour Law and Policy Journal* (Winter 1999), at p.239.
13. Benjamin Aaron, 'The Law of Employee Loyalty in the United States' (1999) 20 *Comparative Labour Law and Policy Journal*, 321.
14. Bob Hepple, 'The Duty of Employee Loyalty in English Law'(1999) 20 *Comparative Labour Law and Policy Journal*, 205.
15. Reinhold Fahlbeck, 'The Duty of Employee Loyalty in Sweden'(1999) 20 *Comparative Labour Law and Policy Journal*, 297.

important role in determining the content of employment contracts. Through the efforts of trade unions, some countries repealed or modified laws that overemphasized the status of employees and that forced employees to perform their obligations. In addition, employees were given more autonomy in negotiations regarding employment contracts with their employers, which resulted in the relative equity of employment relationships.

The modern employment contract was based on many of the principles of the master and servant contract that it replaced. Employee loyalty is one of those principles that is firmly embedded in employment law and is one of its leading principles.[16] However, one German academic is of the view that the '[d]uty of loyalty, to a great extent, was reintegrated into the general contractual framework'.[17] Modern jurists explain the logical legal basis of employees' duty of loyalty mainly based on the basic principles of contract law. For example, in Germany and Japan the duty of loyalty is defined as an accessory obligation of employment contracts that embody the value of good faith, another leading principle of contract law,[18] according to which employees should perform contracts in good faith, be loyal to their employers, subject themselves to the management of employers and work for the interests of their employers. In recent years, the British high courts have also introduced ideas such as good faith, trust and confidence (principles of the civil law system) into its Common Law.[19]

Traditionally, there have not existed many statutory regulations regarding the duty of loyalty of employees, the legal source of which generally derived from precedent and implied duty operated by law. Even now in some countries (e.g., in Germany) there is no statutory basis for this duty but rather it was developed by certain academic writings and the decisions of courts in certain jurisdictions.[20] In Common Law countries, when determining if employees were duty bound to loyalty to their employers or if they had met their duty to loyalty, the courts would apply the general principles that originated from early precedent or from modern contract law and which reflected the fundamental nature of the employment relationship. These principles imposed certain duties on parties, such as the duty of care and the duty of good faith. These duties were implied by law rather than by the consent of the parties[21] and if the parties agreed, they could exclude the application of such principles through express agreements.

---

16. Bob Hepple, 'The Duty of Employee Loyalty in English Law' (1999) 20 *Comparative Labour Law and Policy Journal*, 205.
17. Manfred Weiss, 'The Duty of Employee Loyalty in Germany' (1999) 20 *Comparative Labour Law and Policy Journal*, 240.
18. *Ibid.*
19. Bob Hepple, 'The Duty of Employ Loyalty in English Law' (1999) 20 *Comparative Labour Law and Policy Journal*, 206.
20. Manfred Weiss, 'The Duty of Employee Loyalty in Germany' (1999) 20 *Comparative Labour Law and Policy Journal*, 241.
21. Patrick Selim Atiyah, *Introduction to Law of Contract* (Chinese version) translated by Zhao Xudong, He Suailing, Zheng Xiaoxia, (Beijing, Law Press, 2002), p.209.

Nevertheless, it has become the most important form of legislation in some countries to stipulate express provisions for the duty of loyalty through statutory law. For example, in Italy, Article 2105 of the Civil Code provides an explicit definition of the duty of loyalty, which prohibits an employee from conducting any business, directly or on behalf of someone else, in competition with their employer, as well as from spreading information about the employer's organization or production methods or making use of them so as to cause any harm to the firm.[22] Further, Articles 1175 and 1176 of the Italian Civil Code require both parties to a contractual relationship to observe standards of good faith, fair dealing and due diligence in order to establish a general duty of loyalty in the field of labour law.[23]

However, regardless of codified laws or common laws, and regardless of express or implied provisions, in the course of employment, the core content of the duty of loyalty remains that employees should be under a duty not to engage in competition against their employers, not to secretly make a profit for himself from the use of assets of the company, and not to disclose information of employers.

In summary, during a term of employment the duty of confidentiality and non-competition stem from the employment relationship created by the employment contract. These duties are implied by law and are compulsory for employees. In some Continental Law countries such as Germany and Japan, said duties are regarded as accessory duties of contract. Therefore, in the course of employment, no matter whether there exist confidentiality or non-competition agreements between employers and employees, except by the consent of employers, employees should protect all information of enterprises, including trade secrets, should not engage in any competitive business against employers and should protect the interests of their employers.

III. DUTY OF LOYALTY IN CHINA

In recent years, with economic development in China, and especially with the emergence of private enterprises, the duty of loyalty of employees has become a matter of greater concern. For more than sixty years, socialist public ownership was the dominant form of corporate ownership in China. Under this old ownership system, loyalty to enterprises equated to loyalty to the state. There was no difference, in essence, between them. Influenced by the socialist indoctrination of the past, some rejected the concept of a capitalist economy and looked down on employers of non-state-owned enterprises, especially those of private enterprises. Even now it can be noted that certain younger employees are seldom of a mind to be loyal to their companies or to their employers. Some young white-collar

22. Fei Anling, Ding Mei (translator), *Civil Code of Italy* (Chinese version) (China University of Political Science and Law Press: Beijing) (1997).
23. Marco Bigi, 'The Duty of Employee Loyalty in Italian Labour Law' (1999) 20 *Comparative Labour Law and Policy Journal*, 250.

workers even claim to be loyal only to their own careers or businesses. This has resulted in a higher turnover of staff in China.

In January 2006, the Shanghai Municipal Labour and Social Security Bureau surveyed 5,112 employees online through its official web site. The Bureau published a report called the *Year-end Survey on the Employment Status of Shanghai Employees*. It was the first time that a survey had touched on issues such as year-end bonuses, career plans for the new year, changing of jobs and ongoing training in the new year. Among replies to the question 'Do you intend to change jobs?' only 10.08% of respondents indicated that they did not intend to change their jobs while 5.34% of the respondents could not change their jobs for contractual reasons, and 9.37% had changed their jobs within the last month, while 23.67% were actively preparing to change jobs and 51.51% were thinking about changing jobs. Thus, 85% of respondents had planned to change their jobs following the 2006 Chinese Lunar New Year.[24] As discussed, except for the duty of loyalty of directors, supervisors and managers of enterprises, current legislation in China does not impose any explicit duty of loyalty for ordinary employees. As a result, frequently changing employers, ignorance of the duty of loyalty and unclear laws and regulations have become, to a great extent, the main reasons for disputes regarding the protection of trade secrets between employers and employees.

With the booming private economy and the improvement of technology and scientific research in China, trade secret protection has become an important guarantee in creating competitive advantage for enterprises in the market. This, in turn, has necessitated clarification of the content and scope of an employee's duty of loyalty. Today, the juristic groundwork and legal framework for an employee's duty of protection of the trade secrets of enterprises is being studied within Chinese legal circles. Many academics are of the opinion that an employee's duty to confidentiality is an 'accessory obligation' based on an employment contract, which is a duty implied by law. Some of them explain the existence of such implied obligation using the principle of good faith stipulated in the General Principles of the Civil Law. In this respect, it is apparent that Chinese academics have accepted the view of Continental Law scholars, especially that of academics in Germany. Furthermore, the Contract Law (1999) changed the traditional Chinese theory of contract resulting from the mutual consent of parties – a great breakthrough in the concept of contractual obligations. Originally, Chinese contract law required the establishment of a contract as a prerequisite for contractual obligations, and required the consent of parties or statutory provisions to define the specific scope of those contractual obligations. In current contract law, that scope has been expanded. For example, Article 42 of the Contract Law of the PRC stipulates that a party to a

24. Please refer to the website of Shanghai Municipal Labour and Social Security Bureau, <www.12333.gov.cn/english/news/new/t20060124_10493.htm>, 18 August 2006. It can also be found in the 24 January 2006 *Oriental Morning Post*.

contract is liable for losses caused to other parties to the contract. Article 43 provides that:

> Where the business secrets of another are obtained by one party in the course of concluding a contract, whether the contract is formed or not, that party shall not disclose that information or use it improperly. Furthermore, he shall be liable for compensation where the disclosure or improper use of business secrets causes loss to the other party.

Subparagraph 2 of Article 60 further provides that:

> The parties shall perform such duties as notification, assistance and confidentiality observing the principle of good faith in accordance with the nature and purpose of the contract and trade usage.

And Article 92 sets forth that, following the termination of those contractual rights and duties, the parties must continue to perform certain duties of notice, assistance and confidentiality conforming to the principle of good faith and in accordance with trade usage. The common feature of these provisions is that the establishment of a contract is not the only prerequisite for defining the scope of certain contractual obligations. Chinese academics define such obligations as accessory obligations of contract.[25]

However, accessory obligations and implicit statutory obligations are simply the products of man-made law and the result of court decisions. The courts must determine the obligations of parties and consider the essential fairness of cases in accordance with the principle of good faith according to the specific circumstances of each case. Nevertheless, under the status quo of the Chinese legal system, decisions of the courts are not a source of law. In practice, rulings of the Supreme People's Court serve only as guidance for lower level courts. Local labour dispute arbitration committees have been the first dispute resolution organs to deal with the great number of labour dispute cases concerning trade secrets. Decisions of the court do not bind labour dispute arbitration committees. Furthermore, labour law rather than contract law must be applied in employment contract disputes. It is therefore necessary to include general principles regarding the duty of loyalty of employees, explicit and unified application standards and punishment for the violation of the duty of loyalty within the code of law. This will contribute not only to the resolution of these types of disputes but also to the education of the populace and the promotion of good faith.

---

25. Zhang Chi, Bao Zhi, 'On Accessory Obligations' (1999) 6 *Journal of East China University of Political Science and Law* 22 *et seq.*

Chapter 4
The Duties of Confidentiality and Non-Competition Following Termination of Employment

According to general principles of the Civil Law of the PRC, trade Secrets are the intangible property of enterprises and have no connection to the movement of employees. However when highly skilled workers carry their former employer's trade secrets to another enterprise, especially in cases where the second enterprise lures those employees knowing that they hold trade secrets, disputes concerning the movement of workers and trade secret protection will be greatly multiplied. These types of trade secret disputes will generally arise when employees carry away the trade secrets of their employers and subsequently engage in unfair competition against those employers.[1] According to statistics regarding cases accepted by the people's courts from 1998 to 2003, eighty per cent of all disputes regarding the disclosure of enterprise trade secrets occurred in this manner, among which seventy per cent included circumstances in which third parties illicitly obtained the trade secrets of a plaintiff from the plaintiff's employees and then used or disclosed those trade secrets. In these cases, third parties, together with the plaintiffs' employees, were found to have jointly infringed on the trade secrets of the original employer.[2]

The disclosure of trade secrets resulting from the movement of highly skilled workers can occur due to the following:

1) Scientific and technical staff leave their former employers and are re-employed by other enterprises, taking with them their scientific and/or

---

1. Zheng Chengsi, 'Anti-unfair Competition and Intellectual Property' (1997) 5 *Law Science*, 58.
2. Wang Yuxia, and Wu Wenqi of the No.2 Intermediate People's Court of Tianjing City, 'Survey and Analysis of Issues on the Protection of Trade Secrets' (2004) 4 *People's Justice*, 14.

technical knowledge or information resulting in economic loss to the former employer.

2) Scientific and technical staff or managing and operating staff leave their employers and establish their own companies, which conduct operations or offer services similar those of their former employers.
3) In the course of their full-time employment employees take part-time jobs making use of the trade secrets that they have obtained from their primary employers, thereby causing harm to said employers by acquiring a competitive advantage over them in the marketplace.
4) After employees leave their positions as the result of termination of their employment contracts or retirement, they may choose to take other employment and make use of the trade secrets they obtained when they worked with their former employers, causing that former employer to loose its competitive advantage in the marketplace.

The legitimate purpose of encouraging the free movement of highly skilled workers should be to enable them to realize their potential and to encourage the creation of additional technological enterprises and greater benefit to society through the unhindered application of their intelligence. Nevertheless, if the movement of workers destroys the trade secrets of certain enterprises, it will inevitably lead to great economic loss for those enterprises, for society and even for the state. If this happens, it will be necessary to restrict the normal movement of workers. At present, confidentiality agreements and non-competition agreements are used as preventative measures and are generally adopted by employers to defend against the outflow of their trade secrets together with the movement of highly skilled workers.

This chapter will focus on aspects of protecting trade secrets, on the duty of confidentiality of employees and on the duty of non-competition following termination of an employment relationship.

I. DUTY OF CONFIDENTIALITY OF EMPLOYEES FOLLOWING TERMINATION OF EMPLOYMENT

According to legislation in certain countries, following the termination of an employment relationship, the duty of employees to protect trade secrets is different from their duty to maintain the confidentiality of other types of secret information. Regarding the first, there exist explicit provisions for the protection of trade secrets in law which require employees to protect trade secrets that they have obtained during their employment. Such confidentiality obligations are compulsory. As for other types of confidential information except trade secrets, the obligation of confidentiality of employees following termination of their employment is based on confidentiality agreements between them and their employers. In the absence of such agreement, the obligation of confidentiality cannot be imposed on an employee following the termination of the employment relationship.[3]

As mentioned, an employee's obligation of confidentiality stems from the duty of loyalty that is based on the employment relationship. Thus, it is generally believed that the duty of loyalty also ends with the termination of the employment relationship. Following termination of employment relationships, employees can freely use any information, including trade secrets, which they have obtained during their employment unless there are explicit confidentiality agreements between the employer and employee, or work rules that restrict or prohibit the use of the employers' information.[4] However, as more countries have promulgated trade secret laws to enhance the protection of trade secrets, it has become a statutory obligation for employees to maintain the confidentiality of trade secret holders. In the absence of authority and consent being granted by the holder, all are held to the obligation to maintain the confidentiality of trade secrets. Thus, in many countries employees have the obligation to protect their former employers' trade secrets following termination of employment relationships even if there are no confidentiality agreements between them. This is why following the termination of an employment relationship, employees should continue to be held to an obligation of confidentiality regarding the trade secrets of their employers. Without the consent of their former employers, employees may not use or disclose any of their trade secrets.

Nevertheless, the scope of protection of trade secrets varies in the legislation of different countries. In addition, the elements that constitute infringement of a trade secret are different within the domestic law of each country. Consequently, following the termination of employment relationships, the obligations of employees to maintain the confidentiality of trade secrets and the legal consequences for violating that obligation vary from one country to another. For example, in Japan and in Germany, trade secret law emphasizes the motives of the wrongdoer and explicitly prescribes that 'intent' or bad faith on the part of an employee in making an unfair profit or in inflicting damages on an employer is one of the basic elements to be considered by the courts when determining if the acts of an employee have infringed the trade secrets of their employers.[5] However, these conditions do not exist in all countries, for example, in Chinese trade secret law.

In contrast to legislation that has been enacted regarding trade secrets, there is no statutory basis for protecting confidential information except for the protection of trade secrets following termination of employment relationships. The scope of this duty has been further developed through scholarly writing as well as by the decisions of the courts in certain countries. The general principle supported by

3. Bob Hepple, 'The Duty of Employ Loyalty in English Law' (1999) 20 *Comparative Labour Law and Policy Journal*, 215.
4. Takashi Araki, 'Duty of Loyalty Legal Issues of Employee Loyalty in Japan' (1999) 20 *Comparative Labour Law and Policy Journal*, 271.
5. See Article 2 Paragraph 1 of the *Unfair Competition Prevention Law* (Japan) and Article 17 of the German *Act against Unfair Competition* (1994).

certain academics and by precedent is that, except for trade secrets (for which there exists a certain expectation of confidentiality that survives the employment relationship) employers can only restrict or prohibit employees from disclosing or using their confidential information through confidentiality agreements. If the performance of such confidentiality agreements does not violate public policy, the courts of hearing will uphold such agreements. This principle is founded upon the doctrine of contracts that states that an obligation of confidentiality based on an employment relationship should end with the termination of the employment contract.[6] Secondly, as to ordinary confidential information, it remains in the employee's head and has become a part of his own skills and knowledge. Constraining the use of such information will adversely impact the life of the employee and thus should be consensual. Lastly, the free circulation of information satisfies the demands of social development in the Information Age. Internationally, it is basic national policy to encourage such free and open circulation of information. Consequently, many countries accept the abovementioned principles.[7]

II. DEFINITION AND BASIC CONTENT OF THE DUTY NOT TO COMPETE

By definition, the duty not to compete can also be construed as restraint of trade[8] in cases where enterprises attempt to restrain their business partners from engaging in certain competition against them.[9] As a statutory duty, the duty of non-competition was initially imposed by early agency law in certain Continental Law countries for the purpose of preventing agents from infringing on the interests of their principals. For example, in early cases in Germany the courts confirmed restrictive terms in agency contracts and upheld the claims of plaintiffs that commercial agents should

6. Manfred Weiss, 'The Duty of Employee Loyalty in Germany' (1999) 20 *Comparative Labour Law and Policy Journal*, 238.
7. See the series of articles in the *Comparative Labour Law and Policy Journal* (Winter 1999) which introduces in detail legislative and judicial practice in the US, Great Britain, Germany, Japan, Australia, Canada, Italy, Sweden and New Zealand. Many agree with the principle.
8. Melvin F. Jager, *Trade Secret Law* (St. Paul, Minn, West Group.,1999), p.13–7.
9. Article 46 of the *Opinions on Several Issues regarding the Application of Law In Trying Unfair Competition Cases* (advisory version), promulgated by the Supreme People's Court of the People's Republic of China, points out that restraint of competition means an enterprise's employee, whether during or following employment, should not conduct competition against the enterprise nor take a position within a competing enterprise. Article 14 of *Regulations of Shenzhen Special Economic Zone on the Protection of Enterprise's Technical Secrets*, promulgated by in 1995, provides that the contract of business restriction refers that the enterprise agrees with employee that the employee may not hold a post in other enterprises producing competing products of the same kind, and that an enterprise must pay a certain amount of compensation to said employee. The definition here is confined to the restraint of competition as accessory to an employment relationship.

not represent competitors of their principals in the conduct of similar business.[10] That concept was later extended from agency relationships to cover parties to brokerage contracts, and then to include partnerships regulated by modern commercial law. It is now also applied to the obligations of company directors. In the past, English law allowed the use of restrictive covenants in connection with the sale of a business or the formation or dissolution of a partnership to enable the buyer of the business or partnership effectively to acquire the goodwill of the business. It was not until the late nineteenth century that courts began to apply the concept of non-competition to employment relationships.[11]

There is an old proverb that is cited by businesspeople in China that says, 'When an apprentice learns the skill, his master will starve'.[12] To avoid that situation, it was commonly agreed when an apprentice learned the technology or skill of his master that in the following several years the apprentice should not conduct the same business near his master's place of business. Some Chinese academics refer to such an agreement as a customary duty of non-competition.[13]

Restraint of competition has now been broadly adopted in contract law, intellectual property law, tort law and laws regarding competition as well as in labour law. Where trade secret law is concerned, the duty of non-competition has been imposed upon all employees who have knowledge of the trade secrets of an enterprise.

In practice, subjects that can be restrained from competition can be divided into three types:

(1) commercial partners of certain enterprises or employers during the process of commercial transactions;
(2) shareholders and directors of companies;[14] and
(3) employees including management staff and technical staff. Considering the different situations of these three subjects, their obligations of non-competition also differ. For example, commercial partners are restrained from conducting certain activities only for the duration of commercial transactions while shareholders and directors, given their status within a company, are obligated not to engage in any business similar to the business of the company in which they hold office or in activities harmful to

10. Norbert Horn, Hein Kotz, Hans Georg Leser, *German Private and Commercial Law: An Introduction* (Oxford, Clarendon Press 1982); Chu Jian (translator) the Chinese version (Shanghai, Encyclopaedia of China Publishing House, 1999), p.152.
11. Catherine L. Fisk, 'Working Knowledge: Trade Secrets, Restrictive Covenants in Employment, and the Rise of Corporate Intellectual Property, 1800–1920' (2001) 52 *Hastings Law Journal*, 454.
12. 'When an apprentice learns the skill, his master will starve' is a Chinese proverb. It can be inferred from this proverb that the concept of non-competition has existed in China since early times.
13. Zheng Yubo, 'On the Constraints of Non-Competition' *Studies on Civil and Commercial Issues* (II) (Taiwan Sanmin Book Store, 1980), p.173.
14. Zhang Yurui, *Legal Protection of Trade Secrets* (Beijing, Patent Documents Publishing House, 1994), p.68.

> the company's interests on their own behalf or on behalf of others. When they cease to be shareholders or directors, they are not subject to the duty of non-competition. In employment relationships, however, employees may be subject to the duty of non-competition as stipulated in their employment contracts not only during the course of employment but also following termination of their employment. This duty often includes not working for a competing business, not soliciting or dealing with the customers of an employer, not enticing other employees and not using trade secrets or confidential information in an unauthorized manner.[15]

In practice and theory, an employee's duty of non-competition is a hot topic within the field of trade secret protection and gives rise to more debate and uncertainty regarding the nature of said duty following the termination of employment relationships.

III. THE NATURE OF THE DUTY OF NON-COMPETITION OF EMPLOYEES FOLLOWING TERMINATION OF EMPLOYMENT

In order to protect a potential profit in a commercial transaction, one party to the transaction generally tries to restrict certain business activities of another party to the transaction through a restrictive agreement so as to avoid or reduce unfair competition between them and to ensure that good will and mutual benefit arises out of the transaction. Good will between parties cannot be effectively accomplished without an enforceable non-competition agreement.[16] As long as such restrictions are not imposed for the purpose of creating a monopoly, there is no violation of the law regarding competition or of principles in antitrust law and many of the courts in various countries would uphold the enforcement of these types of agreements.[17] Regarding directors, their duty not to compete is determined by their status within the company. Directors are selected by a general meeting of shareholders and they enjoy powers authorized by law, by articles of association or by a general meeting of shareholders. They participate in all business of the company and determine the fate of the company. Directors have a special status within their companies, as well, and must therefore diligently participate in their management, must pay proper attention to the business of their companies, and must safeguard the interests of their companies. Consequently, directors must undertake the duty of loyalty to the company, work diligently for the company, and honestly carry out their obligations. When company interests conflict with the personal interests of directors, they must be loyal to the company and put the

15. Bob Hepple, 'Employee Loyalty in English Law' (1999) 20 *Comparative Labour Law and Policy Journal*, 215.
16. Harlan M. Blake, 'Employer Agreements Not To Compete' (1960) 73 *Harvard Law Review*, 646.
17. Bryan A. Garner (ed.), *Black's Law Dictionary* (US, West Publishing Co., 1999), p.1317.

company interests before their own private interests. The duty of directors not to compete is the embodiment of their duty of loyalty, which is designed to protect the interests of the company, shareholders and creditors and to protect order in commercial transactions.

Compared with directors, the duty of ordinary employees not to compete during their employment is generally regarded as the essential content of their duty of loyalty to their company. For an employee, there is an implied obligation to devote his time and best efforts to serve his employer. When an employee's personal interests conflict with the interests of his employer, he is obligated to protect his employer's interests. Loyalty to an employer is obligatory for every employee. As discussed above, the content of an employee's duty of loyalty generally includes:

(1) a duty of obedience which obligates employees to be subject to the command and supervision of their employer during the course of their work;
(2) a duty of confidentiality which requires employees not to disclose the operational secrets of employers; and
(3) a duty of enhancement, which means that an employee should work prudently during the course of his labour.[18]

Thus, based on an employee's duty of loyalty to his employer, he must not conduct any acts of competition against his employer so as to avoid any infringement of the employer's interests. In the absence of authorization or consent from their employer, an employee will be deemed in violation of his duty of loyalty if he conducts any competition against that employer for his own benefit or for the benefit of others.

How then does one justify the duty of non-competition of employees following the termination of employment relationships? In theory, following the termination an employee has no commercial partnership, economic relationship or employment relationship with his former employer. The employee's duty of loyalty to his employer should end with the termination of the employment contract, as should his duty not to compete, based on the fact that his duty of loyalty no longer exists. Nevertheless, in real life many employers require their employees to sign non-competition agreements so as to restrict their activities following the termination of their employment. Such agreements can consist of a clause or clauses within an employment contract or a supplement to the employment contract in the form of separate agreements. The validity and nature of non-competition agreements following employment inspires hot debate among academics and within judicial circles and has become a controversial topic in the area of trade secret protection.

Academics in China take a certain view of the nature of the duty of non-competition following employment. They agree that an employee's duty not to compete following the termination of an employment contract is a post-contractual

18. Shi Shangkuan, *An Introduction to Labour Law*, (Taiwan, Zhengda Publishing House, 1978), pp.24–26.

obligation.[19] A well-known Taiwanese scholar, Shi Shangkuan, holds that a contractual relationship no longer exists post-employment but that parties still have certain obligations to it (e.g., to maintain an obligation of payment or to assist a counterparty to a contract in dealing with certain issues following termination of the contract).[20] An employment contract is constituted by mutual agreement between employee and employer. Reasons for the dissolution of such relationships generally include retirement, death, and expiration of a fixed-term contract. When any one of the aforementioned situations occurs, an employee is exempted from his requirement to supply labour services and his employer no longer has an obligation to pay remuneration. But there still exist residual rights and obligations to perform, which are called post-contract obligations under the employment contract. Shi Shangkuan, along with other Taiwanese scholars, believes that the post-contractual obligations of an employment contract can be divided into statutory obligations and post-contractual obligations. Post-contractual statutory obligations are created/operated by law. For example, Article 19 of the Labour Law of Taiwan contains a provision regarding labour service that states, 'When the employment contract is terminated and the employee requests the employer to issue a labour service certificate, the employer or his agent may not refuse'. When there exist no statutory provisions in the law, parties can agree to perform certain obligations following the termination of an employment contract. Such obligations are post-contractual obligations. Shi concludes that the obligation not to compete following the termination of an employment contract is one of those post-contractual obligations. If a person violates a post-contractual obligation, he will bear liability for breach of the original contract.[21]

When it comes to interpretation of the duty of employees to confidentiality and their duty not to compete following the termination of their employment contracts, mainland Chinese academics agree on the post-contractual obligation theory. The difference is that certain mainland academics hold that post-contractual obligations are statutory duties that must be undertaken by parties following the termination of a contractual relationship. In their view, if the obligations of the parties end simultaneously with the termination of the contractual relationship, certain interests of the contracting parties would not be protected in all situations, (e.g., the obligation of confidentiality and the return of materials or data following the termination of the contract). Therefore, they hold that it is a matter of law that parties should be held to a duty to do or not to do something in accordance with the principle of good faith following the termination of a contractual relationship so as to protect the legal rights and interests of the contracting parties and are currently regarded by academics as post-contractual obligations.[22] Certain Chinese legal scholars are

19. Cui Jianyuan, *Contract Law* (Beijing, Law Press, 1996), p.72.
20. Shi Shangkuan, *An Introduction to Labour Law* (Taiwan, Zhengda Publishing House, 1978), pp.51–54.
21. Wang Zejian, *General Introduction to Obligations of Civil Law* (I) (Taiwan, San Min Bookstore, 1996), p.34.
22. Zhang Chi, Bao Zhi, 'On Accessory Obligations' (1999) 6 *Journal of East China University of Politic Science and Law*, 22.

also of the view that Article 92 of the Contract Law provides for post-contractual obligations in stipulating that:

> When the rights and obligations of contracts are terminated, the parties to the contract shall, abiding by the principle of good faith, perform such obligations as making a notice, providing assistance and maintaining confidentiality according to transaction practices.

It is obvious that mainland Chinese academics regard so-called post-contractual obligations as compulsory for parties to a contract.

Whether they are right or wrong shall not be discussed here. Their viewpoints reveal to some extent, however, the characteristics of an employee's duty not to compete following employment. First, said duties have a close connection with employment relationships. In view of the content of a covenant not to compete, these duties could be considered as the extension of the duty of loyalty during employment. Second, said duty demands that employees not conduct acts that are competitive to their former employers, which could be construed to be a duty of abstention. Thirdly, employers can remove the constraints on employees prior to the performance of said duty, while an employee has no choice but to accept the decision of his employer whether prior to or during the performance of said duty. However, as regards performance of contract, some countries have established so-called post-contractual obligations in their statutory laws. The scope of content of such obligations, however, is determined in the context of specific contractual relationships. In addition, said obligations have a certain compulsory authority which means that except for exclusions agreed to by them, the parties to a contract must perform post-contractual obligations imposed by statute. For example, in accordance with Article 92 of the Contract Law, if there are no exclusions to the covenants, the courts can directly impose the duty of confidentiality upon employees. However, if there exists no statutory law imposing confidentiality upon employees following termination of employment contracts, or if an employment contract does not contain or excludes such obligation, once an employment contract is terminated any contractual obligations (including the duty of confidentiality) shall find no ground on which to stand, which accords with the contractual doctrine of party autonomy.

In fact, there exists no statutory law that prohibits conclusion of non-competition agreements between employers and employees nor does there exist any legislation that imposes a compulsory obligation of non-competition on employees following the termination of an employment relationship. In Continental Law countries, commercial law and labour law contain only restrictive provisions regarding covenants not to compete following employment which define the scope of application of said covenants and conditions which restrict them to reasonable application. In Common Law countries, there are few statutes governing the duty not to compete of employees following the termination of their employment while increasingly more precedents involve such issues. The courts have formed certain principles in their trial practice which are similar to the provisions of the statutory laws of Continental Law countries. For example, employers and employees can negotiate and establish covenants not to compete following employment but the legal application of such covenants will be confined to a reasonable scope and may not violate public policy.

In summary, an issue exists regarding whether or not the duty of an employee not to compete following the termination of his employment can be determined by agreement with his employer. In English, such agreements are called 'non-competition agreements', 'covenants not to compete' or 'restrictive covenants'. The question remains then: Why are there so many restrictive provisions regarding the scope of application of such agreements when legislatures worldwide do not prohibit parties to contracts from reaching agreements regarding non-competition following the termination of employment?

IV. POSSIBLE IMPACT ON EMPLOYERS CAUSED BY DEPARTURE OF EMPLOYEES

There is a well-known legal principle that no employee may take away any tangible property of their employer when they leave the employ of an enterprise. However, the confidential information of the enterprise (including its trade secrets) is stored in the mind of an employee and cannot be separated from him when he leaves the employ of the enterprise. As intellectual property, trade secrets can be stored in physical media such as documents, blueprints and disks. In addition, trade secrets can also be deposited into the mind of an employee and thus will move freely with him wherever that employee goes. There is no question that employers can reach confidentiality agreements with their employees to restrict the use and disclosure of their confidential information including their trade secrets. However, when an ex-employee departs to work for a new employer who is a competitor of their former employer or when an employee departs to establish his own business which is similar to that of his former employer, it is almost inevitable that they will use or disclose the trade secrets of their former employer.

Non-competition agreements are precautionary measures designed to reduce the potential risk of losing trade secrets. One important element of trade secrets is their confidential nature. Once a trade secret loses its secrecy and becomes public information, the value of that trade secret disappears forever. To some extent, any employee who has knowledge of trade secrets can be a potential threat to the confidentiality of those trade secrets. Although the holders of trade secrets may seek civil remedies through judicial process to compensate them for monetary loss when their trade secrets are infringed, those trade secrets will never be recovered. For these reasons, in order to protect trade secrets a non-competition agreement is a precautionary measure that can be taken to overcome the deficiencies of other civil remedial measures.

In addition, there exists the potential threat that employers will lose their investment in their employees, (e.g., training fees and the cost of continuing education) when they leave the company. The essential goal of investment in human capital is the improvement of product quality, the strengthening of the competitive ability of enterprises in the marketplace, and the enhancement of the human capital of an employer. Furthermore, investment by an enterprise in its human capital can also improve the quality of labour resources and strengthen the competitive ability of employees in the labour market. Nevertheless, if employees can engage in unrestricted job-hopping, they will possibly not only infringe on the interests of their employers but will also cause their employers to hesitate to provide vocational training to employees or to invest in other human capital.

In August 2002, the Shanghai Fu He Xing New Composite Materials Company Ltd. (the 'Company') concluded a one-year employment contract with its employee Zhou and assigned him to the Company's quality control department.[23] Prior to its expiration, the employment contract was extended for one year through negotiation between the Company and Zhou, which provided Zhou special benefits such as training and a housing allowance. The new contract also stipulated that if Zhou terminated the contract prior to its expiration that he would compensate the Company for its loss. Following the signing of the contract, the Company sent Zhou to participate in a national training program for quality inspectors in the aluminium industry and the following year Zhou was sent to another training program. The company paid CNY thirty-five thousand for these training programs and also paid CNY fifteen thousand in commercial insurance fees for the duration of his training. Right after the first training program was completed, Zhou was appointed vice manager of the quality control department. Zhou later left the company without notice. Following a two-month long investigation, the Company discovered that Zhou had assumed a post in a decorating company that was a competitor of the Company. The board of directors of the Company was both shocked and angry because the Company had spent more than CNY eighty thousand over the course of two years on Zhou for salary, training fees and various other benefits.

A non-competition agreement is one of the most important measures for the protection of the interests of an employer. Especially in the Information Age, business information and effective management of human resources are critical to the development, and even to the existence, of an enterprise.

V. IMPACT OF NON-COMPETITION AGREEMENTS ON EMPLOYEES FOLLOWING EMPLOYMENT

The obligation not to compete with a former employer following employment is usually determined by an agreement between employer and employee. In view of the form, such covenants are the consequences of the mutual consent of the parties. However, non-competition agreements differ from other kinds of contracts in that the employee, a party to the agreement, performs the agreement by restricting his own employment opportunities. Therefore, in content, non-competition agreements are restrictions on an employee's right to work following employment.

23. Please refer to the China Court website. <www.chinacourt.org/public/detail.php?id=168214>, 6 January 2008.

When an employee enters into a non-competition agreement, he accepts the possibility that he may lose the opportunity to pursue a career that he enjoys or that he is good at. When he signs such an agreement, he will necessarily gradually lose his previous knowledge and skills because he will be constrained from using them in similar employment following the termination of his employment contract. In addition, non-competition agreements are always concluded prior to or during an employment relationship. As previously discussed, through the duration of employment the status of employers and employees are not completely equal. Employers are the providers of employment and the managers of their corporate businesses and thus have power over employees. On the other hand, in order not to lose present or potential job opportunities employees sign non-competition agreements with employers even though these agreements may contain stipulations that are contrary to their free will. Realistically, in the absence of an employer's requirement to do so, no employee would be willing to conclude such an agreement that restricts his job options. For these reasons, it can be said that there exists inequity in non-competition agreements between employees and employers.

In 2002, a dispute being heard in the city of Kaifeng in Henan Province over a covenant not to compete attracted broad attention on the Internet.[24] In December 2002, the China Kaifeng Instrument Factory drafted a standard non-competition agreement which contained clauses requiring that its staff maintain the confidentiality of its trade secrets and that within three years after any staff departed the employ of the Factory they could not conduct any business similar to that of the Factory, could not be an officer of an enterprise that had a competitive relationship or a conflict of interest with the Factory, and could not produce the same products or conduct the same business as the factory. If any of the staff breached the agreement, they would bear legal liability. When the Factory showed the content of this agreement to its staff and required all production, technical and operational staff to sign it, deep resentment was aroused amongst the staff. Many of the staff admitted the fact that they understood why the factory had requested its employees to sign a non-competition agreement in order to try to protect its interests in a sharply competitive market. However, they could not accept a non-competition agreement that took only the factory's interests into consideration and ignored the interests and circumstances of the workers because some of the technical staff had been working with the factory for many years, some even as long as thirty years or more. They had contributed their entire youth, wisdom and intelligence to the factory. They felt that if they were not permitted to participate in the same business as that of the Factory following their current employment that they would not be able to find another job that they were fond of or expert at. Therefore, some staff insisted that in order to ensure justice and fairness the factory should pay a certain sum of compensation as consideration for the employees accepting an obligation not to compete. To show support for the staff's proposal, the staff of the technical division of the factory signed the agreement as the factory required, but added their

24. Please refer to Xinhua website: <www.ha.xinhuanet.com/xhfu/2005-12/07/content_5762651.htm> 6 January 2008.

specific requirements according to their respective needs for economic compensation for the term of the period of non-competition. However, the factory argued that, as employees of a factory, the staff should contribute to the factory without personal consideration and should not bargain on demands from their employers including regarding the agreement. The factory then prepared a fixed term agreement and once again demanded that the technical staff sign it. The factory publicly announced that whoever refused to sign the agreement would be fired and if they had a spouse that was also employed by the factory, they would be replaced also. Under pressure from the factory all of the employees, except for one senior engineer, Wang Jianwei, signed the agreement. Soon after, the factory instructed Wang to hand over his work immediately and temporarily leave his post. Several days later, the factory announced its decision to terminate Wang's employment contract.

Obviously, this is a case in which an employer misused/abused its power and forced its employees to sign a non-competition agreement so as to restrict their options to find jobs following termination of their employment. The imposition of such agreements undoubtedly causes great economic harm to employees. The type of agreement imposed in this instance was subsequently named an 'overload agreement' by Internet users following the case.

VI. IMPACT ON PUBLIC POLICY CAUSED BY THE PERFORMANCE OF NON-COMPETITION AGREEMENTS FOLLOWING EMPLOYMENT

Performance of an agreement not to compete following employment directly affects the interests of employees and also has great impact on existing legal doctrines. The performance of a non-competition agreement will result in certain conflicts related to doctrines of freedom to contract, fair competition and appropriate protection of intellectual property rights.

A. Substantive Justice of Contracts and Agreements Not to Compete Following Employment

The doctrine of the freedom to contract has always been the theoretical pillar of non-competition agreements[25] and is cited in the statutes and precedent in some countries. It is consistently used to determine the validity of non-competition agreements. According to the doctrine of freedom to contract, whether a non-competition agreement is to be formed and what the content of such agreement shall be is decided by the mutual consent of the parties to the contract. Hence, as

25. Christina L. Wu, 'Non-compete Agreements in California: Should California Courts Uphold Choice of Law Provisions Specifying another State's Law?' (2003) 51*UCLA Law Review*, 593.

long as an agreement expresses the true will of the parties, the agreement will be legally enforceable.

As discussed above, in civil and commercial law 'contract is law'.[26] Freedom to contract is one of the basic principles of contemporary civil and economic relationships, which embodies the autonomy of contracting parties in civil and economic activities. Freedom to contract is considered the backbone of protecting the public interest in many countries so that public policy can be created based on this doctrine and the legitimate expectations of contracting parties can be satisfied. It is better for society that individuals have the intent to keep their promises so that other individuals can then feel that they can rely on those promises. The benefit gained in doing so is increased efficiency and reduced costs of trade.

The fulfilment of those expectations at the conclusion of a contract will help the contracting parties to obtain their anticipated benefit. If contracts were routinely not enforced, individuals would stop entering into them. If an employer did not feel that it could rely on the promise of its employees not to compete, the benefits of such agreements would be lost. Employers would hide confidential information from employees despite the existence of non-competition agreements and employees would not receive all the information they needed for optimal performance. Furthermore, the pay scale of employees reflects the price of negotiated non-competition agreements. Because an employee receives a wage that compensates him for entering into a non-competition agreement, the contract should be enforced as quid pro quo.

What are the expectations of employers and employees when they enter into a covenant not to compete following employment? Normally, employers anticipate that such agreements will protect the confidentiality of their business information and prevent any unfair competition against them as a result of misappropriation of their trade secrets. Employees normally enter into non-competition agreements in order to obtain more opportunities for technical training and to obtain the trade secrets of their employer so as to leverage his technical skills. Therefore, it seems reasonable for the court to uphold the enforcement of such agreements.

Nevertheless, the doctrine of freedom to contract is based on equity between parties in the form of the contractual relationship. When individual employees feel intimidated by employers (e.g., companies or enterprises have great financial power), especially when those employers offer limited compensation as consideration for the signing by employees of non-competition agreements, it is difficult for them to depend solely on the principle of freedom to contract to realize the substantive equity and justice of such agreements. Therefore, underlining the importance of the doctrine of freedom to contract, it is generally a dilemma for legislatures and courts worldwide to ensure the substantive justice of agreements not to compete following the expiration of employment contracts.

---

26. Article 1134 of the *Civil Code of France* (the same for Belgium) provides that contracts formed in accordance with the law shall have the effect of law between parties. See Luo Jiezhen (translator) *Civil Code of France* (Chinese Version, Beijing, Law Press, 2005), p.833.

B. Policies regarding Competition and Non-competition Agreements

Competition is not only a natural instinct for human beings and other living beings but it also energizes the developing market economy. Free access to the market is, in essence, the freedom of competition. In view of these factors, in earlier British and American precedents some courts have invalidated non-competition agreements on the underlying assumption that said agreements violated the doctrine of free competition in the market.[27] Until today, some legislatures still uphold this reasoning and maintain a negative attitude towards enforcement of non-competition agreements following employment. Now that the concept of non-competition has gradually been applied to employment relationships, post-employment restraint can also be thought to hinder competition in the employer's market. By preventing an ex-employee from working within the same industry or using information obtained during employment, an employer may remove a potential competitor from the marketplace or deprive an existing competitor of a valuable resource. Furthermore, an employer that enjoys market dominance could cause the cost of information capital to rise by controlling access to the use of information. This, in turn, may result in hindering the dissemination of knowledge and might easily create monopolies within certain industries.

However, in order to achieve an advantage in the technological market, some enterprises entice the skilled employees of their competitors to work for them or to obtain the technical information they possess. They try to gain and make use of the trade secrets obtained through the departing employees of their competitors. This happens all the time in the Information Age, which obviously runs counter to the morality of fair competition and will turn the market into a disorderly situation if there are no effective measures to prevent it.

In order to protect the public interest in maintaining fair and free competition and technical innovation, laws in many countries permit enterprises to conclude non-competition agreements with their employees for the purpose of protecting trade secrets. Nevertheless, the excessive protection of trade secrets, especially the market monopoly created by the abuse of post-employment constraints, will inevitably destroy the free and fair competitive environment for enterprises. How to regulate such agreements so as to achieve fair competition is a considerable problem facing legislators.

---

27. See Maureen B. Callahan, 'Post-employment Restraint Agreements: A Reassessment' (1985) 52 *University of Chicago Law Review*, 708. Professor Callahan introduced in his article that the first reported case to consider an agreement not to engage in a trade was Dyer, decided in 1414. However, it is unclear from that report whether the non-competition agreement at issue arose in the context of the sale of a business or of employment. Later, in 1602 the court in *Colgate v. Bacheler* expressly stated that the restrictions of geographic scope and duration on an ex-employee might deprive the ex-employee of his right to work and his right to a living so that such restrictions are against the benefit of the commonwealth and should be deemed void.

C. Protection of Intellectual Property and Human Rights

Confronted with the reality that in the Information Age the economic strength of a country is determined by scientific and technical advancement, many countries have proposed and implemented a strategy of 'building a country with knowledge' which regards intellectual property as the backbone of market competition. Using this strategy, all countries hope to advance their competitive capacity within an environment of increasingly globalized world trade by protecting creativity and encouraging enterprises to increase investment in scientific and technical research and development.

However, as with other intellectual property, the trade secrets of an enterprise consist not only of oral and written knowledge but also of the experience and skill of its employees that might become common knowledge or the valuable information of an enterprise through ongoing training and communication within an enterprise. However, once employees possessing such knowledge or information leave an enterprise the development of that knowledge is cut short and accumulation of common knowledge is hampered, resulting in the derogation and loss of enterprise assets. Further, turnover of highly skilled workers causes diffusion, duplication and imitation of the store of knowledge of an enterprise, which will reduce the market value of the enterprise's intellectual property. If competitors can easily obtain intellectual property from the ex-employees of other enterprises they will obtain without effort a springboard that will enable them to easily catch up with the market share enjoyed by those enterprises. Ultimately, the enterprise will lose its competitive advantage in the marketplace. For these reasons, many countries allow employers to restrain post-employment competition through agreements with their employees as an effective means to protect the trade secrets of enterprises.

Because the acquisition of work experience and skill relies on a certain corporate culture as well as on personal experience, employees, as the medium for the transmission of information in the workplace, are both beneficiaries and creators of the common knowledge of enterprises. As such, they create valuable information for their enterprises and contribute substantially to the corporate culture based on their unique personal skills and intelligence which are a means of production belonging exclusively to them. It is reasonable that employees should share the fruits of their labour within an enterprise. Based on a policy of protecting the interests of both employers and employees, as in other intellectual property law, trade secret legislation in many countries has drawn a distinct line between the trade secrets rights of employers and employees during the course of employment.

Because agreements concerning non-competition following employment do, in fact, deprive employees of the opportunity to advance to a better paying position, they will to some degree restrain the competitive ability of skilled workers in the labour market. Particularly in a society with deep divisions of labour and close professional cooperation, the latitude of employees to change jobs will be narrowed. Performance of non-competition agreements directly infringes on the basic rights of employees including their right to a livelihood and their right to work – rights that are guaranteed by the constitutions of some countries. From this point of view, as an effective measure to protect trade secrets, post-employment restraint comes at the cost of the coerced waiver of the basic rights of employees as well as hindrance of the mobility of the labour force.[28] The freedom to work and to conduct lawful competition is a principal manifestation of a worker's right to a livelihood in a market economy. The infringement of those rights undoubtedly runs counter to social policy.

VII. STANDARD FOR REASONABLENESS OF NON-COMPETITION AGREEMENTS

The previous analyses have clearly demonstrated that non-competition agreements are in essence contrary to the principles of free trade and free competition in the market economy system. When ex-employees perform non-competition agreements following employment, their freedom to work and to develop their careers is inevitably constrained, which contradicts certain fundamental principles of constitutional law and labour law in different countries. Nevertheless, non-competition agreements are still accepted by many countries and have become an important legal measure to protect the interests of employers. The primary reason for this is that agreements not to compete following employment can effectively prevent disclosure and improper use of information. They play a positive role in the protection of trade secrets as well as in the maintenance of fair market competition.

As mentioned, the constraint of competition following employment has also stirred conflict between vested interests as affirmed by contemporary law. In order to resolve these conflicts, legislators must analyze the various interests involved and act on the basis of assuring a balance among these interests. In fact, the doctrine of the balance of interests is fundamental to trade secret law. During the entire process of development of trade secret law, the balance of interests has remained a primary theme. Whether to encourage innovation or to promote the dissemination and utilization of new technologies and new knowledge, or whether to protect rights or to restrict rights, the establishment of mechanisms to balance interests has commonly been the core content of trade secret law. It is generally believed that balancing interests concerning trade secret property consists of balancing the rights of the trade secret holders and the obligation to protect trade secrets; balancing between the creator, disseminator and user of technical information and other kinds of economically valuable information; and balancing between personal interests and the public interest.

Consequently, many countries maintain a prudent attitude towards this system and treat it as a passive preventive measure and have passed laws to restrict the application of such a system to a reasonable scope with intention to strike a balance

28. The mobility of knowledge is embodied in the reality of the dissemination of technology and the application of information.

between two objects of public policy – intellectual property and the human rights of workers.

As long as non-competition agreements have been used in employment relationships, legislators have been working hard to strike a balance between various interests. For over 200 years the most cited case regarding Common Law constraint of trade has been *Mitchel v. Reynolds*,[29] believed to be the earliest report of a dispute concerning non-competition. In assigning to the plaintiff the lease of a bakeshop, the assignor, a journeyman baker, gave a bond that he would not practice his baker's art in the parish for the term of the lease by demand of the plaintiff. However, before long, the assignor violated the agreement and was sued in court. In the action on the bond, the assignor pleaded that the bond was illegal and a constraint of trade because it interfered in the practice of his craft. The court noted that there was a presumption that all constraint of trade was invalid, but held that that presumption had been overcome. The court pointed out that the presumption of invalidity stems from the 'mischief' which constraint may cause first, in the possible loss of the covenantor's means of earning a livelihood and second, in the loss of the services of a useful member of society. The court also noted that corporations might use such covenants as a means of 'monopolization'. In the meantime, the court pointed out that the agreement was reached on the basis of mutual consent. The covenantor, upon valuable consideration, by his own consent and for his own profit, gave over his trade to the plaintiff. The court stated that to refuse to enforce reasonable restraint accompanying the transfer of a business would result in unnecessary hardship or loss to a craftsman ready to retire but forced to continue in his trade or to sell out at a lower price because no one would risk the purchase of his business without the protection of an enforceable covenant not to compete. Namely if there were no restrictions, the covenantor's competitive acts would definitely harm plaintiff's livelihood, too.

While the covenant in dispute in this case was not incidental to an employment agreement but was connected to the transfer of a business, the court, in making its decision, analyzed in detail the influence of non-competition agreements on contracting parties and on social policy and recognized the reasonableness of non-competition agreements between parties.[30] In its opinion, the court thoroughly reviewed the facts of the case in search of an overarching principle to guide judicial decisions in subsequent cases where an effort might be made to enforce a covenant not to compete. Until the end of the nineteenth century, English and American courts regarded *Mitchel v. Reynolds* as the fundamental authority in constraint of competition cases.

In its modern form, the basis of the doctrine of reasonableness as applied to non-competition agreements can be found in *Nordenfelt v. Maxim Nordenfelt Guns and Ammunition Co. Ltd* (1894). In the reasoning of that precedent, the judge, Lord

29. 1 P. Wms. 181, 24 Eng. Rep. 347 (Q.B. 1711). See Harlan M. Blake, 'Employer Agreement not to Compete' (1960) 73 Harvard Law Review, 625.
30. Harlan M. Blake, 'Employer Agreements not to Compete' (1960) 73 *Harvard Law Review*, 629.

MacNaughten, put forward a set of standards to determine the rationality of a non-competition agreement:

> The public has an interest in every person freely carrying on his trade and so has the individual. All interference with individual liberty and trade, and all constraints of trade of themselves if there is nothing more, are contrary to public policy and therefore void. That is the general rule. But there are exceptions. Constraint of trade and interference with individual liberty of action may be justified by the special circumstances of a particular case. It is a sufficient justification and, indeed, it is the only justification if the restriction is reasonable – reasonable, that is, in reference to the party in whose favour it is imposed, while at the same time it is in no way injurious to the public'.[31]

Lord MacNaughten's held that the courts can constrain trade and intrude on individual liberty on a limited basis. However, there must be a prerequisite of reasonableness for such constraint or inference, namely there must exist reasonable interests that are protected by an agreement. In addition, the constraints imposed by such an agreement should be no wider than reasonably necessary to protect the interests of a covenantee and should not be against the public interest. This doctrine was pursued in many later precedents. In an article written by Robert Hepple, professor of law at Cambridge University, similar situations existing in English law are introduced.[32] He writes that contracts that prevented or restricted business competition were regarded in the formative period of the Common Law as being invariably voidable and even possibly subject to criminal sanctions. It was not until the latter nineteenth and early twentieth centuries that judicial policy came to accept that although constraints on competition were prima facie void, they could be justified if they were reasonable and not contrary to the public interest. Professor Hepple also points out that the objectives of these social policies may be said to be threefold:

> [t]o enhance efficiency, on the theory that workable competition is impeded by restrictive trade practices; to protect consumers, smaller firms and workers from large aggregations of economic power because of the threat of monopoly to civil liberty, and to protect small entrepreneurs from being devoured by larger firms; and in the context of the European Union, to promote freedom of movement of workers, goods, services and capital.

According to Professor Hepple, the European Social Charter (1961) and the Community Charter of Fundamental Rights of Workers (1989) expressly uphold the right of every individual to engage in an occupation of their choice. The European Court of Justice has also accepted that this is a fundamental right of citizens in the member states of the European Community and the European Convention on

31. Adrain Chandler, Employment Law Library Information: Protection of Ownership and Rights (Blackstone Press Limited, 1993), p.63.
32. Bob Hepple, 'The Duty of Loyalty: Employee Loyalty in English Law'(1999) 20 *Comparative Labour Law Journal*, 210.

Human Rights (1998) contains an express prohibition against any direct or indirect forced or compulsory labour.[33]

Later, the doctrine of reasonableness became the fundamental principle by which the court decided whether an employee should be held to an obligation not to compete with their former employer following employment. In Common Law countries, whether special circumstances do or do not justify constraint is a question of law for the court. When it comes time for the court to decide whether a restrictive clause is justified, an employer must affirmatively show that the constraint sought is necessary for the protection of his legal interests, and the court will take into consideration whether the constraint is so strict as to affect an employee's livelihood. In addition to those agreements whose sole purpose is to constrain employees and protect employers from future competition, the court will deem such agreements void.[34] In the United States, the Restatement (First) of Contracts also points out that in constraint of trade, the protected benefit should be greater than the loss of benefit to the restricted party and that the constraint should not impose undue hardship upon the constrained party. Furthermore, the constraint of trade should not tend to create, or have for its purpose to create, a monopoly or to control prices or to limit production artificially. The First Restatement also suggests that in employment relationships, constraint of trade should not be based on a promise to refrain from competition and should be ancillary to an existing employment relationship or employment contract. Without satisfying the aforementioned requirements, any constraint of trade will be deemed to have violated the law or to have harmed prevailing social and economic interests.[35]

In Continental Law countries, legislatures have stipulated certain restrictive norms for the application of non-competition agreements in their legislation from the aspect of reasonableness. Take Switzerland as an example. Article 340 of the Swiss Code of Obligations provides that eligible employees may sign a written non-competition covenant with their employers promising not to conduct any competitive activity against the employer following termination of employment. In particular, an employee may not conduct, participate in or benefit from any business that will compete with the employer's business for the employee's own interests. In cases where the utilization of such information might cause great harm to employers, the application of constraint must be confined to customer contacts or the employers' production or commercial secrets that employees came to know during their employment.[36]In Germany, when it concerns the duty of non-competition, the German Commercial Code stipulates restrictive provisions. The basic premise of the regulations contained in the German Commercial Code is

33. Please refer to Article 4(1) of the *European Convention on Human Rights* (1950) <www.hri.org/docs/ECHR50.html>, 6 January 2008.
34. Please refer to *Mason v. Provident Clothing & Supply Co.* and *Herbert Morris, Ltd. v. Saxelby*, cited from Harlan M. Blake, 'Employer Agreements not to Compete' (1960) 73 *Harvard Law Review*, 626.
35. Please refer to the *American Law Institute, Restatement (First) of Contracts*, 1939, (US), §515. 'When Restraint of Trade Is Unreasonable'.
36. <www.chinalawedu.com/news/2005/8/li66112036311218500291 20.html>, 6 January 2008.

that a restrictive clause must be in writing and that the duration of a constraint of freedom to compete cannot exceed a period of two years following termination of an employment contract. In addition, employers have to pay compensation to employees that are constrained by such agreements. Within this framework, a restrictive clause is valid only if employers have a legitimate business interest in said covenant and only if, considering the geographical region, the duration and the subject matter that the constraining clause does not cause excessive difficulties for the employee.[37]

For academics and judges in mainland China, the duty of non-competition is a completely new concept. With respect to research on this issue, one may refer again to the Company Law of the PRC. In order to protect the interests of investors and companies, the Company Law imposed the duty not to compete on directors and managers who hold office in a company. Even today, there are no legal stipulations in regulations regarding the non-competition obligations of employees following termination of their employment. In addition, there exist various opinions on non-competition agreements in the academic field. For example, some scholars in Taiwan hold that the main purpose of non-competition agreements is to prevent employees from engaging in malicious competition. In practice, however, some enterprises improperly apply non-competition agreements. They prevent their employees from leaving in order to keep them working in their enterprises for the long term. Some employers constrain skilled workers from moving in order to hinder their competitors. Regarding the content of non-competition agreements, some enterprises have broadened their applicable scope resulting in hardship to employees in their ability to maintain a livelihood. In recent years following more intense research by Chinese scholars and given the increase in the number of practical cases, a better understanding of the nature and function of non-competition agreements has been reached. Though related legislation still lags behind development, the standards for reasonable restrictions on the application of non-competition agreements have been explicitly put forward in certain judicial decisions.

In 2004, the Haidian District People's Court of Beijing City hearing a dispute over a non-competition agreement between Beijing Hekang Scientific and Technical Development Company Ltd. (Hekang) and Lee Zimin, an ex-employee of Hekang, held that:

> A non-competition agreement between a company and its ex-employees restricts ex-employees from conducting competitive business within a certain period and in a certain region, which objectively restricts their right to work and restricts their freedom to participate in market competition. Under the labour distribution system in a modern market economy, the right to work directly involves the basic right of employees to a livelihood that must be safeguarded. Generally, the company and its ex-employees are unequal where

37. See Article 75a and 75b of the *German Commercial Code*. Source: *Handelsgesetzbuch* (Chinese version) (Beijing, China University of the Politics and Law Publishing House, 2000), pp.29–30.

> economic status and ability to possess information are concerned. Therefore, an obligation following employment imposed on an employee by a non-competition agreement and the restriction on a citizen's basic rights such as the right to work endowed by the Constitution can gain legal effect only on a reasonable basis which must at least include that the company has a justified business interest such as protection of trade secrets and that the company pays reasonable compensation for the non-competition constraint.[38]

The facts of that case were that the plaintiff Hekang was registered and established in March 1996 and that one of the main businesses of the company was the production of clinometers and accessories. In April 1996, the defendant, Lee Zimin, began working for Hekang and assumed a post as an engineer in its sales department. Later, Lee was assigned to be district sales manager of the Central China region. On 18 December 2001 Lee resigned from Hekang and on the same day signed a non-competition agreement with the company. The agreement contained restrictive clauses stipulating that for a period of three years following termination of the employment relationship Lee could not start, participate in or be employed by any company that would produce or operate clinometers nor could he directly or indirectly contact the company's customers, its suppliers of raw materials and parts or its distributors. Further, the agreement stated, upon leaving the company Lee could not take away any trade secrets recognized by the company in any form and could not disclose them to any third party for five years. Lee also promised to pay fifty per cent of any loss to the company or CNY five-hundred thousand if he breached the agreement. Obviously, the non-competition agreement was not created for the sole purpose of protecting trade secrets and the broad scope of the agreement was extraordinary in that measure.

In November of 2001 after Lee had left the company, his wife, Chan Yanling, registered and established the Beijing Liuhe Chuangye Scientific and Technical Development Limited Company (Liuhe). From November 2001 to December 2003, Lee was the vice general manager of Liuhe. In March 2004, Lee and his wife together with another person, Chan Yanping, registered and established the Beijing Jinkehua Scientific and Technical Development Company (Jinkehua). All three were shareholders of Jinkehua and Lee took the position of executive director and general manager of the company.

In December 2004, Hekang filed a lawsuit with the Haidian District People's Court of Beijing City against Lee Zimin for his breach of the non-competition agreement. Hekang claimed that Lee was the former director and regional sales manager of the Central China region for Hekang and was in charge of sales of clinometers and their accessories. Further, the plaintiff claimed, when Lee resigned, he had signed a non-competition agreement with the plaintiff which he subsequently violated on numerous occasions by representing other companies in the signing of sales and purchase contracts for clinometers and accessories with the plaintiff's

38. Please refer to the civil judgment (2005) Hai Min Chu No. 5598 issued by the Beijing Haidian District People's Court.

customer, the China Petroleum and Chemical Corporation Zhongyuan Oilfield Company (Zhongyuan Oilfield), which had caused harm to the plaintiff's legitimate rights and interests. The plaintiff petitioned the people's court to order Lee to immediately cease any competitive activities, to cease activities that exploited the plaintiff's customers, and to cease disclosing the plaintiff's trade secrets. In addition, the plaintiff demanded compensation of CNY five-hundred thousand.

The defendant Lee contended that Hekang had failed to pay him compensation in accordance with the non-competition agreement and that Hekang had delayed payment of his salary during the course of his employment. Consequently, he did not perform the non-competition agreement. Lee also argued that the reason that he signed the covenant not to compete was to get the pay that was due to him from Hekang and that agreeing to the constraining covenant was not a true expression of his free will. Soon after his departure from Hekang, Lee sent a notice via express mail to the company and notified it that he did not accept the terms of the agreement and that believed that the covenant should not be binding upon him. Furthermore, Lee contended that Zhongyuan Oilfield was a well-known company and not a private customer of Hekang.

During the hearing, the court affirmed the fact that Liuhe and Jinkehua had signed several sale and purchase contracts with the material supply division of Zhongyuan Oilfield, the subject matter of those contracts being exclusively clinometers and accessories. However, the court held that while Hekang claimed that the customer information regarding Zhongyuan Oilfield was its trade secret, that it had only presented to the court one sale and purchase contract with Zhongyuan Oilfield dated 2 May 2001 as evidence of its assertion. The court further held that Hekang had failed to prove that it had a unique business relationship with Zhongyuan Oilfield and that had it not proved that, compared with the information in the public domain, its customer information regarding Zhongyuan Oilfield was special and that, in addition, except for a producing a general contract with Lee which included covenants on trade secret protection, Hekang had failed to prove that it had taken any measures to maintain the confidentiality of its trade secrets. As a result, the court found that Hekang had not met its obligation to provide evidence of its legal rights and interests or that its trade secrets were entitled to protection. The court also found that the sum of money that was the subject of a memorandum between Hekang and Lee was remuneration that Hekang owed Lee and that Hekang had indeed failed to prove that it had paid Lee a certain sum of money as compensation in accordance with the non-competition agreement. Therefore, the court held that the agreement between Lee and Hekang should be voided, that he should not be held to a duty of non-competition to Hekang and that there existed no facts or legal grounds for Hekang's claims. As to the confidentiality clause in the agreement, Hekang had failed to provide sufficient evidence for its claim that the customer information regarding Zhongyuan Oilfield was its trade secret. The court rejected the claims of Hekang, concluding that it lacked the legal grounds to prevent Lee from contacting Zhongyuan Oilfield.

Thus it can be concluded that many countries maintain an attitude of prudence towards non-competition agreements and regard them as a passive form of prevention, the application of which is restricted by legislation to a reasonable scope. In sum, based on the doctrines of balance of interests and reasonable requirement, enforceable and valid non-competition agreements should satisfy the following conditions, which will be discussed presently:[39]

- There is a need to prove the existence of legitimate business interests.
- There must be reasonable limits in duration and in geographical reach.
- They must be confined to a specific field of professional activities of the employee.
- Reasonable compensation must have been offered.

A. The Necessity for the Existence of Legitimate Business Interests in Non-competition Agreements

When an employer concludes a non-competition agreement with an employee, there must exist legitimate interests of the employer, which is the universally recognized basic standard to justify non-competition agreements. In the absence of legitimate business interests, there are no legal grounds to justify constraint of an employee's occupational or entrepreneurial liberty and non-competition agreements are deemed void as a result of their violation of public policy. For example, Article 74 of the German Commercial Code provides that a non-competition agreement can only be used to protect the rightful interests of an employer's business.

Nevertheless, what are legitimate interests that merit protection? The answer to that question varies greatly according to the legislation and judicial practices in different countries. Some countries explicitly provide that only the trade secrets of an employer can be protected by non-competition agreements while other countries provide that, in addition to trade secrets, customer lists and even the training fees paid by employers for their employees can be considered protected interests.[40] In fact, the scope of protected interests manifests different social policies and attitudes towards non-competition agreements in each country. Take the United States as an example. As mentioned above, California law fundamentally opposes attempts by employers to limit the mobility of their employees and provides that 'Any contract by which one is restrained from engaging in a lawful profession, trade, or business of any kind is to that extent void'.[41] The California Supreme Court has stated that covenants not to compete are unenforceable '[u]nless necessary to protect an employer's trade secrets'. Consequently, in California an employee's mobility is hindered only when necessary to protect trade

39. Please refer to the No. 3 Civil Tribunal of the Supreme People's Court of the People's Republic of China (ed.), *Guide and Reference for Intellectual Property Trials (Vol. 8)*, (Beijing, Law Press, 2004), pp.184–185.
40. John Hull, *Commercial Secrecy Law and Practice*, (London, Sweet & Maxwell,1998), p.238. The footnote has listed many English precedents which recognized customer connection as a protectable interest.
41. See California Business and Professional Code section 16600.

secrets and non-competition agreements are confined to protecting trade secrets of employers. The California stipulations reflect a public policy to enhance the mobility of employees, which is ultimately an asset to the state. In part, mobility of employees contributed to the rise of Silicon Valley which grew quickly in the early 1990s partly because of the rapid dissemination of information. As a result of limits placed on non-compete agreements, employees were able to move quickly and freely from employer to new employer, and were also able to start up their own companies. Information migrated with the employees, who passed on their knowledge to co-workers. In addition, senior employees learned from younger employees and became more productive. The rapid spread of information thus led to rapid development in Silicon Valley. Obviously, California's strong public policy toward employee mobility contributed to swift economic and technological development there.[42]

Even though there are different definitions for protected interests, the law in most countries emphasizes that non-competition agreements cannot be an instrument used by employers to protect merely an interest in avoiding competition. American professor Harlan M. Blake analyzed the issue in his article 'Employee Agreements Not to Compete', which was published in the *Harvard Law Review*. In it, he points out that the purpose of constraint on employees following the termination of employment is not intended to prevent the use of the special personal skills of employees but to prevent competitive use, for a time, of information or business relationships which pertain particularly to the employer and which the employee acquired in the course of employment.[43] Therefore, the purpose of an agreement not to compete following employment is different from that of non-competition constraints under other circumstances.

In China, certain academics propose that protected interests should include trade secrets as well as other kinds of confidential information; otherwise the burden of proof would be increased on employers to demonstrate in court hearings that the information at issue is a trade secret. The contrary view is that the scope of protected interests should be limited to trade secrets in order to hinder abuse of restrictive agreements, which used to happen all the time in China. *Beijing Hekang Scientific and Technical Development Limited Company v. Lee Zimin* is an example of such abuse.[44]

In 2004, the Supreme People's Court of the PRC published an advisory draft on its official web site entitled Certain Opinions on the Application of Laws when Dealing with Unfair Competition Disputes and in 2005, the Court published a revised version of that advisory draft. Both drafts address non-competition

---

42. Christina L.Wu, 'Non-compete Agreements in California: Should California Courts Uphold Choice of Law Provisions Specifying Another State's Law?' (2003) 51 *UCLA Law Review*, 608.
43. Harlan M. Blake, 'Employer Agreements Not to Compete' (1960) 73 *Harvard Law Review*, 647.
44. Please refer to the civil judgment in Hai Min Chu No. 5598 issued by the Beijing Haidian District People's Court (2005).

agreements but it is a pity that they offer not much more than a definition of non-competition agreements. The drafts suggest that:

> The duty of non-competition includes that during employment or within a certain period of time following employment, employees of an enterprise shall not engage in any business competing against their enterprise or hold any office in the competitors of their enterprises.[45]

However, the drafts do not provide suggestions for addressing certain fundamental issues such as interests of non-competition agreements that are entitled to protection, the issue of geographic restriction, and duration, illustrating that opinions regarding these issues have not yet been reconciled. Nevertheless, more recent court decisions affirm the principle that an employer seeking enforcement of a non-compete agreement must establish the existence of one or more legitimate business interests to justify a non-compete provision. With regard to protectable interests vis-à-vis non-competition agreements following employment, the courts in China tend to protect the trade secrets of employers.

B. The Duration and Geographical Reach of Non-competition Agreements Should Be Reasonable

Many domestic laws restrict the duration of non-competition agreements. For example, Swiss law stipulates no more than a three-year time limit.[46] German law stipulates that if the duration of a non-competition agreement is longer than two years, it shall be deemed void.[47] Italian law states that the duration of non-competition agreements for senior staff shall be no more than five years and no more than three years for general staff following employment and, if otherwise, that such agreements will be void.[48] In the United States, precedent set in different courts reflects different opinions. Some hold one year, while some two or even three years.[49] The Certain Opinions on the Enhancement of the Management of Technical Secrets among the Flow of Technical Staff published by the China State Science and Technology Commission stipulates, 'The longest duration of

45. Please refer to Article 37 of the Certain Opinions on the Application of Law When Dealing with Unfair Competition Disputes (advisory draft), which was published at: <www.chinacourt.org/public/detail.php?id=186055>, 6 January 2008.
46. See Article 340 (A) of the *Swiss Federal Code of Obligations.* Source: *The Swiss Federal Code of Obligations* (Chinese version) (Beijing, Law Press, 2002), p.99.
47. See Article 74 (A) of the *German Commercial Code.* Source: *Handelsgesetzbuch* (Chinese version) (Beijing, China University of the Politics and Law Publishing House, 2000), p.29.
48. See Article 2125 of the *Italian Civil Code.* Source: *Codice Civile Italiano* (Chinese version) (Beijing, China University of the Politics and Law Publishing House, 1997), p.528.
49. Christopher J. Soller, 'Time Period and Geographic Restrictions in Non-Compete Agreements: Understanding and Winning the Battle over Reasonabless' (2003) 74 *Pennsylvania Bar Association Quarterly*, 52. The article introduces some American precedent.

a non-competition agreement may not exceed three years'.[50] The Regulations of the Shenzhen Special Economic Zone for the Protection of Technical Secrets of Enterprises provides: 'The duration of business restriction may not exceed three years at the longest. If the duration of business restriction is not agreed on in the contract, it is three years'.[51]

Though provisions differ from one country to another, when it comes to dealing with specific cases all courts will follow the same general fundamental principles. Firstly, a restrictive covenant may only be of such length as is reasonably necessary to protect the interests of the employer.[52] As the focus of interests protected by non-competition agreements, technical secrets and operational secrets have different life cycles. Some technical and operational secrets enable an enterprise to maintain its competitive advantage for the life of the company, (e.g., the ingredients of Coca-Cola). Some technical and operational secrets can only help an enterprise to maintain a very short period of competitive advantage, (e.g., the Microsoft Windows operating system for computers is updated almost every year).[53] Thus, the duration of technical and operational secrets and the cycle of innovation of information are important factors in determining the term of non-competition constraints. Secondly, one of the purposes of non-competition agreements is to diminish an employee's memory of technical secrets that belong to their employer. Therefore, when it comes to determining a reasonable term for a specific non-competition agreement, in addition to considerations of specific industries and the status of the trade secrets, how long an employee has possessed the information and how long it will take to eliminate the ex-employee's impact should also be considered.

Due to different situations within various industries, it is very hard to provide a uniform standard to justify the duration of non-competition agreements. When it comes to determining the length of time for which it is necessary to protect a trade secret, the courts usually consider the actual facts of each case and then determine a reasonable duration in order to protect legal interests. The factors that courts usually take into consideration include, but are not limited to, the nature of an employer's business; the nature, scope and quantity of information disclosed to an ex-employee; the market; the length of the employee's employment; and the employee's pre-existing knowledge prior to employment.

There is a trend toward gradually shortening the duration of non-competition constraints. The most important reason is that hi-tech companies broadly apply non-competition agreements in order to protect their trade secrets and the technological innovation cycle of these industries is quite short. Furthermore, shortening

---

50. See Article 7 of the *Certain Opinions on the Enhancement of the Management of Technical Secrets* among the Flow of Technical Staff (the State Science and Technology Commission).
51. See Article 16 of The Regulations of the Shenzhen Special Economic Zone on the Protection of Technical Secrets of Enterprises.
52. See Christopher J. Soller, 'Time Period and Geographic Restrictions in Non-Compete Agreements: Understanding and Winning the Battle over Reasonableness' (2003) 74 *Pennsylvania Bar Association Quarterly*, 54 *et seq.*
53. David L. Gregory, 'Courts in New York Will Enforce Non-Compete Clauses in Contracts Only if they Are Carefully Contoured' (2000) 72 *New York State Bar Journal*, 34.

the duration of non-competition agreements can contribute to the social welfare of employees and reduce the wasting of the resource of highly skilled workers. For example, in 1999 the US Second Circuit Court in *EarthWeb, Inc. v. Mark Schlack*, regarding an assertion of breach of an employment contract and infringement on trade secrets, held that the speed of change in the Internet industry was quite rapid and so the duration of non-competition agreements should commensurately be no more than six months.[54] In that case the defendant Schlack was a former vice president of EarthWeb, a company that provided online products and services for information technology professionals, including content which it obtained primarily through licensing agreements and acquisition from third parties. After less than a year of employment, Schlack resigned to accept a position with ITworld.com, a subsidiary of the largest producer of print-based information for information technology professionals. EarthWeb then sued Schlack and ITworld.com and sought an injunction to prevent Schlack from being employed by ITworld.com, alleging misappropriation of trade secrets and violation of covenants not to compete and not to disclose confidential information because EarthWeb and Schlack had signed a one-year non-competition agreement and because Schlack was in charge of the company's web site content. At trial, the court found no misappropriation of trade secrets, stating that the one-year duration of the non-competition agreement was unreasonably long because of the speed of change in the Internet industry that would cause the defendants' knowledge to lose value in far less than a year.[55]

Similar to time restrictions, geographical restrictions are subject to consideration of the legitimate interests seeking to be protected. In practice, factors regarding both employer and employee will be taken into consideration when courts determine whether a covenant is reasonable as to geographic extent. Generally speaking, if there is no undue hardship to the former employee, the courts will enforce geographic limitations within the employer's primary business area and the area wherein the employee performed services during his employment. In addition, to secure enforcement of a non-compete clause within a particular territory, an employer must also demonstrate what protection the business needs in that locale.[56] Some Chinese courts have upheld in trial that geographical restrictions contained in non-competition agreements can be applied even to regions wherein the advantage of the trade secrets of the employer might reach.[57] This means that a

54. Ann C. Hodges, 'The Business Fallout from the Rapid and Planned Obsolescence of High-Tech Products: Downsizing Non-competition Agreements' (2005) 6 *Columbia Science and Technology Law Review*, 3. (Discussing the willingness of courts to enforce non-competition agreements in high technology industries).
55. 71 F. Supp. 2d 299 (So. Dist. NY 1999).
56. Emily J. Kuo, 'The Enforceability Gap of Covenants Not to Compete in Telecommuting Employment Relationships' 1996 *University of Chicago Legal Forum*, 565. This article lists quite a number of related precedents in the US.
57. See the No. 3 Civil Tribunal of the Supreme People's Court of the People's Republic of China (ed.), *Guide and Reference for Intellectual Property Trials* (Vol. 8) (Beijing, Law Press, 2004), pp.184–185.

reasonable geographical restriction should be confined to territory wherein a right-holder's business will reach because the conduct of the same business within these areas would possibly lead to disclosure or the use of the trade secrets of the right-holder, causing competition and creating obstacles for the right-holder.

Nevertheless, the traditional principle of reasonableness of geographical restrictions has been challenged by the development of the information industry and by the globalization of economies. This has caused a gradual weakening of the function of restrictive geographical standards in the determination of reasonableness of restrictions in post-employment contracts. For example, many companies now conduct business not only within the borders of their home countries but may maintain many different global operations. Under such conditions, it is very difficult to justify the geographical restriction of an employee's non-competition agreement. Employees in charge of designing, developing and selling products as well as management staff familiar with the various businesses of a company will inevitably reveal or use the trade secrets of their former employers when they take posts at any of the competitors of their former employers across the world. Considering these factors, there is judicial precedent for the disuse of geographical restrictions in some countries.[58] Scrutinizing Chinese court decisions, it can be seen that there have been few that have voided non-competition agreements due to the application of too-broad geographical restrictions because many Chinese companies generally conduct their business nationwide.

C. Restrictions on the Scope of Activities of Employees

It has been universally recognized that non-competition agreements should be confined to a certain professional field with regard to the core competitive business of enterprises. It should not be expanded to the whole professional field of competitors, which is well known to employees, and especially should not be expanded to certain businesses that employees would operate using their general knowledge, experience or skills. It is apparent that nowadays more enterprises are expanding their scope of business activities. There are a great number of technical departments within these enterprises that encompass a variety of professional fields. As a special means for protecting trade secrets and maintaining the competitive advantage of an enterprise, non-competition agreements should specify the restricted activities of employees and the scope of business within which they can participate. Employees should only be constrained from carrying out the sort of business in which they were engaged as an employee of their former enterprise. Ex-employees should not be prevented from carrying out too wide a range of activities when all of their expertise and experience lies in a restricted field.[59]

---

58. See, for example, *Med X Inc. v. Ranger*, 780 F. Supp. 398, 403 (E D La 1991), *Inc. v. Underwood*, 36 Ohio App. 3d 90, 94, 521 NE 2d 498 (1987) noting that the non-compete covenant with employee was silent as to geographical scope.
59. Kate Brearley, Employment Covenants and Confidential Information: Law, Practice, and Technique, (London, Butterworths, 1999), p.145.

For example, in the United States, the King County Superior Court in *Microsoft v. Google* granted a preliminary injunction in a lawsuit against Kai-fu Lee, a former executive of Microsoft.[60] The injunction did not satisfy the petitioner Microsoft's request to prevent Lee from working for Google. Ruling that Lee could immediately begin working for Google but that his activities should be limited, the court held that the non-competition agreement between Microsoft and Lee was authentic and valid and barred Lee from carrying out the sort of business in which he was engaged as an employee of Microsoft, including technologies concerning voice, natural languages and research engines. The court also found that Lee's preparatory work in the establishment of the Chinese R&D centre of Google had not violated the non-competition agreement and that Lee could begin recruiting employees for Google, meeting with government and university officials, and establishing a headquarters for Google's new research centre but that he was barred from hiring anyone away from Microsoft, using confidential information he learned during his employment at Microsoft or working in computer research and other specified fields for Google.

In China, the courts have also begun to give attention to the restricted activities contained in non-competition agreements and are inclined not to allow excessively restrictive agreements. In 2000, the Shanghai Pudong New Area People's Court heard the labour contract dispute between Shanghai Yamato Scale Limited Company and its ex-employee Chan Qiong in which it ultimately ruled that a non-competition agreement was void.[61]

On 7 July 1997, the plaintiff, Shanghai Yamato Scale Limited Company ('Yamato'), a company involved in the production and sale of scales and related products, signed a two-year employment contract with the defendant Chang Qiong. Chang was assigned to work in a technical section and to produce scales. In March 1998, when Yamato planned to send Chang to be trained in Japan, Chang was required to sign a written agreement that included the promise that following the completion of the training program and upon his return to China, he would provide no fewer than five years of service to the company and that if he violated the written agreement, he would be deemed to have breached his employment contract. The agreement also required that Chang maintain the confidentiality of business information of both Yamato Shanghai and Yamato Japan. If Chang resigned or terminated the employment contract for personal reasons or to take retirement, he could not join any competitive company or enterprise that produced the same or similar products of his current employer for five years after his departure. In addition, he could not conduct any business that would bring harm to the interests of his current employer. Chang also agreed that if he violated the agreement, he would be obligated to compensate his current employer for any losses caused by his breach.

---

60. <www.news.com/Lawyers-spar-at-Microsoft-Google-hearing/2100-1030_3-5851860.html>, 6 January 2008.
61. Please refer to the civil decision in Pu Min Chu No. 6776 issued by the Shanghai Pudong New Area People's Court (2000).

From 15 June to 1 July, Chang went to Japan for two-weeks of professional training. Following the completion of the training program, the plaintiff and Chang reached a new agreement to extend the duration of the employment contract to 7 August 2003. In 2000, Chang resigned from the company and paid the compensation to the Yamato as called for in their agreement. Chang promised Yamato once again that following his departure he would not disclose any technical secrets of the company, would not join any company in competition with Yamato, would not harm the interests of the company and would continue to defend the reputation of the company. Yamato agreed to terminate the employment contract with Chang and issued a notice of termination of employment to Chang.

In March 2000, Chang signed an employment contract with the Shanghai Representative Office of China International Intellect Corporation (Intellect). According to his contract, Intellect would assign Chang to work with the Anritsu Company Ltd. Shanghai Representative Office (Anitsu) from 1 March 2000 to 31 March 2001. Anritsu was registered in Hong Kong, with its main business scope being the sale of electronic products including weighing apparatus. Anritsu was a representative office in Shanghai whose business included setting up business contacts for export and import of communication instruments and mechanical and electronic equipment. In July 2000, when Yamato became aware that Chang was working for Anritsu, it wrote to Chang and Anritsu asking that Chang end his employment there as he had promised not to work with any company in competition with Yamato following his employment. The request was refused. Consequently, on 30 July 2000, Yamato petitioned for labour arbitration with the Shanghai Pudong New Area Labour and Personnel Dispute Arbitration Committee. On 30 August 2000, the Committee announced that it would not accept the case because Yamato's petition requesting that Chang cease his employment with Anritsu did not fall into any category of cases that could be heard by it. Yamato refused to accept the decision and filed a lawsuit with the court. Yamato, as the plaintiff, claimed that Chang should cease his employment with Anritsu.

After hearing the case, the Shanghai Pudong New Area People's Court issued its ruling based on the forgoing facts and on evidence that was provided by the plaintiff. The court rejected the plaintiff's claim citing however that, as an employee, Chang was obligated not only to loyalty and to diligence and to single-mindedly work for his employer during his employment, but that he also was obligated not to maliciously compete with his former employer by using its trade secrets following the termination of their employment relationship and that, therefore, the non-competition agreement between the plaintiff and Chang was legally binding. The court further held that because in employment relationships the characteristics of personality and property co-exist with those of equity and subordination, that employees should be held to the duty of loyalty to their employers during employment. If there is an agreement not to compete following employment between an employee and an employer, then employees are obligated to constrain their behaviour and not compete with their former employers. However, as a prerequisite, restrictions on an employee's right to work must be confined to a reasonable scope so as not to be a hardship on the normal conduct of the life of the employee and, if it is, such agreements will be voided. Secondly, with reference to the provisions of the Circular on Certain Issues Concerning the Implementation of Labour Contract Regulations of Shanghai Municipality (the Shanghai Municipal Regulations) issued by the Shanghai Municipal Labour and Security Bureau Division of Labour Relations, the court confirmed that there existed a duty of non-competition on the part of the defendant Chang because he had signed an agreement with plaintiff not to work with a company in the same or similar industry as that of the plaintiff following the termination of their employment relationship. The court held that:

> Employing units can stipulate in contracts that an employee who has come in contact with its trade secrets shall not be allowed to hold a position in other competing companies that produce the same products or conduct a similar business nor can they themselves produce products or conduct any business that will compete against the business of his former employer within a certain period of time (not exceeding three years) following the termination of the employment contract.

Thirdly, the court found that Chang had neither broken the agreement with plaintiff nor violated his duty of non-competition because Anitsu, the new employer of Chang, operated a business which in some small degree overlapped the plaintiff's business but did not produce the same or similar products as the plaintiff, as prescribed in the non-competition agreement between the plaintiff and Chang. In addition, Chang had taken a post only in the representative office of Anritsu. Furthermore, the plaintiff could not provide evidence that Chang knew its trade secrets.

The decision of the Shanghai Pudong New Area People's Court embodies the present attitude of the Chinese courts towards non-competition agreements. Non-competition agreements should not apply to employees within an enterprise who do not have knowledge of its trade secrets. Restrictions on competitive activities following termination of employment should be specific so as to effectively prevent the excessive application of the non-competition agreement.

D. Reasonable Compensation

It is also universally accepted by international law that employers should pay a certain sum of economic compensation to their employees as consideration for non-competition agreements. The amount of economic compensation and the means of payment can be stipulated by contract, (e.g., Article 340(A) of the Swiss Code of Obligations provides that under certain circumstances, the court has the power to order an employer to pay reasonable compensation to an employee for entering into a non-competition agreement). In Germany, payment of consideration is essential to the validity of non-competition agreements and the purpose of such a provision is to safeguard the livelihood of employees. According to Article 74 of the German Commercial Code, employees must be compensated during the period of constraint, the sum to be not less than fifty per cent of their former remuneration. Said compensation, however, may be reduced by earnings derived from any subsequent employment, depending on the level of that employment. According to Swedish law and French law, a covenant may provide for payment to a former employee during the period of constraint. For example, as to compensation for engineers in the iron and steel industry, a monthly sum of 50% of their previous monthly earnings, including usual bonuses can be paid for up to one year.

Nevertheless, there exist different opinions regarding the law and legal practice regarding the compensation issue. Some countries, such as Germany and China, regard compensation as essential to the validity of non-competition agreements. In some other countries such as Austria, it is customary but not obligatory for an employer to compensate an employee for agreeing to insertion of a non-compete clause including remuneration (usually one year's salary), payable upon termination of the contract. In addition, compensation in some countries simply evidences the reasonableness of a non-competition agreement. For example, precedent in the United States illustrates that if an enterprise pays compensation to its employees in exchange for non-compete agreements, it will strengthen the reasonableness of those agreements, which can be used to demonstrate that constraint required in the performance of an agreement will not bring undue hardship to an employee's livelihood.

In China, payment of compensation to employees by employers is a requirement for enforcement of non-competition agreements. In the opinion of many Chinese academics and legislators, if employees perform a non-competition agreement, they will lose their best job options and will be unable to make good use of their abilities in their field of expertise. Therefore, the constraint imposed by such agreements affects not only their personal development in their field of expertise but will also cause a loss of potential income. In some cases, it will cause undue hardship to their livelihood. Particularly in the hi-tech industry, new technological knowledge possessed by employees may become devalued or even vanish in a very short period due to rapid technical innovation. In the interest of justice and fairness, it is reasonable for employers to pay employees compensation for the performance of non-competition agreements so as to compensate them for the loss caused to them by the constraint on their freedom to work. Generally, in Chinese judicial practice, labour arbitration committees and people's courts also regard reasonable compensation as compulsory for the validity of non-competition agreements. In the absence of payment of compensation, an employee can refuse to perform a non-competition agreement. Take, for example, the above-mentioned non-competition dispute between the Beijing Hekang Scientific and Technical Development Company Ltd. and Lee Zimin heard before the Beijing Haidian District People's Court wherein the court ultimately ruled that the non-competition agreement was void on the ground that the plaintiff did not pay any compensation to its employee.

Because in China the payment of compensation is a prerequisite for ex-employees to be held to the performance of their duty of non-competition following employment, the people's courts and labour arbitration committees have been confronted with quite a number of related legal issues, such as the amount of compensation to be paid. In practice, when an employee quits an enterprise and when he has performed or partially performed a non-competition agreement, if the employer has not paid, or has not sufficiently paid compensation, the issue arises of whether the court should deem the agreement valid or void. The legal liability incurred as the result of a voided agreement differs from that for a breach of contract.

Regarding Shanghai New Composite Materials Company Ltd. and Zhou,[62] the court concluded that although the plaintiff and defendant had signed a non-competition agreement, they did not stipulate in the agreement that prior benefit such as payment of training fees was a prerequisite of compulsory service. Additionally the agreement stipulated only that the company would pay Zhou monthly compensation together with salary for his restraint of competition and the company did not pay any compensation until the hearing in court. In other words, the company had not performed its obligations in accordance with the agreement. The court ultimately denied the company's claim and allowed Zhou to continue working with his new employer. In its decision, the court ruled that an employer could conclude special agreements such as confidentiality agreements, non-competition agreements and necessary service agreements with its employees but that employers must perform their obligations as well.[63]

The phenomenon of insufficient payment of compensation in China is quite common at present. A majority of employers include a certain sum or a certain percentage of an employee's salary each month as compensation for their agreement to non-competition. This form of payment makes it difficult to prove whether the amount of compensation that employees have actually received is sufficient or not. Some employees leave their employment soon after they sign a non-competition agreement and consequently receive little compensation in this regard, making it difficult to determine reasonableness only through the method of payment per se. The key issue is the acceptable amount of compensation that the worker has actually obtained from an enterprise. Once it can be determined that an employee received too little compensation, the non-competition agreement or clause may be deemed void. If the compensation paid to an employee during his period of employment is not sufficient, an employer may retroactively pay the compensation in a lump sum. When the compensation paid retroactively plus the compensation paid in the past reaches a reasonable amount of consideration, the non-competition agreement shall be deemed valid. Nevertheless, in practice, when employees quit an enterprise and when they have actually performed or partially performed a non-competition agreement, if their employers have not paid or have not sufficiently paid compensation, when a dispute arises the issue will be raised of whether the court will deem the agreement valid or not. For the concerned parties, the legal consequences of a voided agreement and a breach of contract are not the same.

---

62. See IV of Chapter 4 in this part.
63. Please refer to 'A Company Sues Employee's Turnover but Loses the Suit'. <www.chinacourt.org/public/detail.php?id=168214>, 6 January 2008.

In 2005, a dispute between Shanghai Zhongyi Consulting Service Company Ltd. (Zhongyi) and former employees Wong Jianfeng, Sung Kelin, and third party Shanghai Fafu Trading Company Ltd. (Fafu) came before the Shanghai No. 2 Intermediate People's Court. In that case, the court found that there existed a confidentiality agreement between the plaintiff Zhongyi, and defendants Wong Jianfeng and Sung Kelin which stipulated:

> Within three years following expiration, termination or cancellation of this employment contract, the employee should not conduct any commercial activities competing against the business of the company. The company will pay employee monthly compensation for confidentiality equal to 20% of the employee's monthly pay.

The facts were that Wong and Sung received a fixed monthly remuneration of CNY 1,500 and CNY 3,500 respectively prior to and following the signing of the agreement. According to the agreement prima facie, the plaintiff was to pay compensation to Wong and Sung for their agreement to non-competition. However, Wong and Sung had not actually received any compensation for the agreement.[64]

Based on the facts, the court ruled that the actions of the plaintiff amounted to evasion of the law and that therefore the non-competition agreement was void. In its decision, the court also held that if an employer arbitrarily reduced the salaries of its employees and used the difference as compensation without express notification, that it would be deemed that said employer had infringed on the legal interests of its employees.

Concerning the sum of compensation to be paid, there exist only general administrative provisions in China.[65] Local regulations of Shenzhen city and

64. <www.chinaiprlaw.com/fgrt/fgrt60.htm>, 6 January 2008.
65. Article 2 of the Circular on the Several Issues of the Flow of Employees in Enterprise (Lao Bu Fa [1996] 355) promulgated by the Ministry of Labour of the People's Republic of China provides, 'When an employing unit negotiates issues with an employee possessing its trade secrets regarding the protection of trade secrets in their employment contract, it can be agreed to change an employee's post and alternate the related content of the labour contract within a certain period of time before the expiration of the employment contract or after the employee requests termination of the employment contract (no more than six months). The employing unit can also stipulate that within a certain period of time (no more than three years) after the cancellation or termination of the employment contract, the employee possessing the trade secrets of the employing unit should not hold a position at other employing units that produce similar products or conduct similar business and have a competing relationship with the employing unit, and the employee himself should not produce similar products or conduct similar business competing against the employing unit. The employing unit should pay the employee a certain sum of economic compensation'. Article 7 of the Several Opinions on the Enhancement of the Management of Technical Secrets during the Movement of Technical Staff (Guo Ke Zheng No. 19971317) promulgated by the State Science and Technology Commission of the People's Republic of China provides, 'Once there is non-competition constraint, the employing unit should pay to related staff a certain sum of compensation. If the employing unit refuses to pay or delays the payment without due cause, the non-competition constraint clauses shall automatically terminate'. Article 16 of the Labour Contract Regulations of Shanghai Municipality provides, 'For employees who have the obligation to keep the commercial

Zhuhai city provide standards for the amount of compensation to be paid, (e.g., the rule for average annual compensation in Shenzhen is no less than two-thirds and in Zhuhai it is half of one year's total salary.)[66]

Judges from different regions of China participating in the Seventh Session Seminar on Intellectual Property Trials in Certain Provinces and Cities in 2004 that were surveyed generally believe that there should be some compensation paid as consideration for non-competition agreements in China, that the amount and method of payment of compensation can be agreed upon by the parties to a contract but that it should be no less than the minimum standard, that is, at least one half of the total remuneration paid in the previous year of employment. If there is no covenant on the issue, concerned parties can negotiate the sum. If the parties fail to reach agreement, the amount of compensation to be paid will be determined based on industry standards. The payment of compensation is a prior obligation which can be used to defend against the non-performance of a non-competition agreement.[67] In January 2006 however, the People's Congress published a draft of the Labour Contract Law on the Internet. Scrutinizing the content of this draft, one finds that there existed strict consideration of the non-competition obligation because the draft suggests that when concluding a non-competition agreement, an employer should come to terms with an employee regarding the economic compensation paid by employer to employee when the employment contract has expired or is terminated. The amount of compensation may not be less than the salary of the year prior to the departure of the employee.[68] After one year of debate, the Labour Contract Law was adopted at the twenty-eighth Session of the Standing Committee of the Tenth National People's Congress of the PRC on 29 June 2007 and came into effect as of 1 January 2008. However, the rules regarding payment of remuneration in

secrets of the employing unit, the parties involved may agree upon non-competition clauses in their labour contract or in a confidentiality agreement, and the amount of compensation due thereby to the employee after the termination or revocation of the employment contract as well'.

66. Article 17 of the Regulations of the Shenzhen Special Economic Zone on the Protection of Technical Secrets of Enterprises provides, 'The compensation fees agreed on in the contract of business restriction may not be less than 2/3 of the total payment that the employee receives from the enterprise in the last year before he or she leaves the enterprise'. Article 22 of the Regulations of Zhuhai City on the Protection of Technical Secrets of Enterprises provides,

> When enterprise and employee agree on the non-competition constraint, the enterprise shall pay economic compensation to the employee during the duration of the non-competition constraint as per the non-competition agreement. If the economic compensation has not been agreed in the non-competition agreement, the annual compensation shall not be less than 1/2 of the total payment that the employee receives from the enterprise in the last year before he or she leaves the enterprise.

67. See No. 3 Civil Tribunal of the Higher People's Court of Chongqing City, *The Summary of the Seventh Session Seminar on Intellectual Property Trials in Certain Provinces and Cities*, The Guide and Reference for Intellectual Property Trials (Vol. 8) edited by the No. 3 Civil Tribunal of the Supreme People's Court of the People's Republic of China, Law Press, September 2004.

68. See Article 16 of the *Labour Contract Law* (draft). <www.npc.gov.cn/zgrdw/common/zw.jsp?label=WXZLK&id=347910&pdmc= 1503 (Last visited: August 18, 2006).

connection non-competition agreements have changed slightly, and compensation must now be paid monthly within the agreed upon non-competition period. Persons subject to non-competition are limited to senior mangers, senior technicians and other employees who have the obligation to keep the secrets of employers.[69]

69. See Article 23 and 24 of the *Labour Contract Law* (2008).

Chapter 5

Settlement of Trade Secret Disputes in Employment Relationships with Foreign Elements

Following its entry into WTO, China has attracted foreign companies to invest in China and quite a number of foreigners to work in China. According to statistics of the Shanghai Municipal Labour and Social Security Bureau, 59,348 foreigners have applied for work permits in Shanghai in recent years and, at present, there are 32,955 foreigners working in Shanghai. The number of foreigners working in Shanghai has been increasing annually. In 2002, the number increased by 51.1% over 2001, while in 2003 it increased 28.6% over 2002. By the end of September 2005, foreigners in Shanghai had applied for 11,277 work permits, surpassing the previous year's total. In the first quarter of 2005 alone, the Shanghai Municipality issued 2,500 work permits to foreigners. Eighty per cent of foreigners work in foreign-invested companies and Shanghai representative offices of foreign companies filling management and technical posts, among which 3,600 are general managers.[1] With many foreigners as well as individuals from Hong Kong, Macao and Taiwan coming to work in China, the number of foreign-related labour disputes is increasing. These disputes centre not only on labour contracts containing non-competition agreements but also on intellectual property disputes, including infringement of trade secrets.

This chapter will begin with an introduction on the current Chinese legislation regulating labour disputes with foreign elements. The understanding of Chinese academics bearing on the international legislation and practice on applicable law for foreign-related and the key issues of application of mandatory rules and public policy will be presented.

1. Statistical source: *Shanghai Statistics*. <www.stats-sh.gov.cn/2003shtj/tjnj/nj05.htm?d1=2005tjnj/C0311.htm>, 6 January 2008.

I. CURRENT CHINESE LEGISLATION REGULATING LABOUR DISPUTES INVOLVING FOREIGN ELEMENTS

In China, determining which law is applicable to foreign-related labour disputes is a very challenging issue. At present, labour dispute arbitration committees and the people's courts are quite hesitant to deal with foreign-related labour disputes. Sometimes, arbitral awards and the decisions of the courts clearly differ from each other mainly because there is a dearth of complete and available labour legislation regarding labour relations involving foreign interests. In addition the legislation on private international law is underdeveloped.

The hierarchy of the present law governing labour relations involving foreign interests consists of laws enacted by the National People's Congress and the Standing Committee of the National People's Congress. These laws include:

(1) The Contract Law of the People's Republic of China (effective 1 October 1999):

Article 126 of the Contract Law stipulates that the parties to a foreign-related contract may choose the law applicable to the settlement of contract disputes, except as otherwise stipulated by law. If the parties have not made a choice, the law of the country to which the contract is most closely connected must be applied.

(2) The Labour Law of the People's Republic of China (effective 1 January 1995):

Article 2 of the Labour Law provides that the law applies to all enterprises, employers and employees bound by a contractual relationship within the borders of the People's Republic of China.

(3) The Law of Civil Procedure of the People's Republic of China (effective 9 April 1991):

The fourth part of the law, the 'Special Stipulations for Civil Procedure involving Foreign Interests' provides procedural rules including those that the Chinese courts must abide by when dealing with foreign-related labour disputes.

(4) The General Principles of the Civil Law of the People's Republic of China (effective 1986).

Article 142 of the General Principles provides:

> If any international treaty concluded or acceded to by the People's Republic of China contains provisions differing from those in the civil laws of the People's Republic of China, the provisions of the international treaty shall apply unless the provisions are ones on which the People's Republic of China has announced reservations. International practice may be applied to matters for which neither the law of the People's Republic of China nor any international treaty concluded or acceded to by the People's Republic of China has any provisions.

Article 150 of the General Principles states that the application of foreign law or international practice must not violate the public interest in the People's Republic of China.

The administrative regulations governing labour relations include:

(1) The Provisions on Labour Management in Sino-foreign Equity Joint Ventures of the People's Republic of China (promulgated on 26 July 1980 by the State Council, the Provisions). The Provisions specify labour management issues of Sino-foreign equity joint ventures, including employment contracts, labour welfare, and social security as well as settlement of labour disputes. Article 12 of the Provisions provides that matters of employing foreign workers as well as the matter of dismissal, resignation, pay, welfare and social insurance should be specified in employment contracts with their employers.
(2) The Regulations of the People's Republic of China on Settlement of Labour Disputes in Enterprises (promulgated by the State Council on 1 August 1993).

Rules regarding labour relations promulgated by ministries or committees of the State Council as well as administrative interpretations include:

(1) The Opinions on Certain Issues Concerning the Implementation of Labour Law of the People's Republic of China (circulated by the Ministry of Labour on 4 August 1995).
(2) The Rules for the Administration of Employment of Foreigners in China (promulgated jointly by the Ministry of Labour, the Ministry of Public Security, the Ministry of Foreign Affairs, and the Ministry of Foreign Trade and Economic Cooperation of the People's Republic of China (the Rules) and effective 1 May 1996). Chapter 4 of the Rules provides specific regulations on the employment of foreigners in China, including matters of employment contracts, social insurance and welfare, and settlement of labour disputes. Articles 2 and 3 define respectively the terms 'foreigners' and 'employment of foreigners in China.'
(3) The Circular on Certain Issues Concerning the Implementation of Rules for the Administration of Employment of Foreigners in China, (promulgated by the Ministry of Labour on 19 April 1996) which provides a definition for the term 'employment in China'.
(4) The Provisions on Labour Administration of Foreign-invested Enterprises (promulgated by the Ministry of Labour, effective 11 August 1994). These provisions apply to Sino-foreign equity joint ventures, Sino-foreign contractual joint ventures, foreign-capital enterprises, and Sino-foreign limited companies established within the People's Republic of China, concerning employment contracts, staff welfare and social security, and settlement of labour disputes.
(5) The Provisions on the Administration of Employment of Taiwan, Hong Kong and Macao Residents in the Mainland (promulgated on 21 February 1994 by the Ministry of Labour).

(6) The Implementation Rules for the Provisions on Labour Management in Sino-foreign Equity Joint Ventures of the People's Republic of China (promulgated by the Ministry of Labour and Personnel with approval of the State Council and effective 19 January 1984) which modified and improved certain provisions of the Provisions on Labour Management in Sino-foreign Equity Joint Ventures of the People's Republic of China.

(7) The Circular of the General Office of the State Council on the Approval and Transmission of the Proposals Submitted by the Ministry of Labour and Personnel Concerning Further Implementation of the Policy of Granting Decision-making Power to Enterprises with Foreign Investment for the Employment of Working Personnel (the Proposals effective 25 April 1988). The Proposals modified Articles 3 and 6 of the Provisions on Labour Management in Sino-foreign Equity Joint Ventures, Article 34 of the Regulations for the Implementation of the Law on Sino-foreign Equity Joint Ventures, Article 15 of Regulations on Encouraging Foreign Investment, and Article 123 of the Implementation Rules on the Provisions on Labour Management in Sino-foreign Equity Joint Ventures of the People's Republic of China.

Judicial interpretations issued by the Supreme People's Court include:

(1) The Opinions of the Supreme People's Court on Certain Issues Concerning the Implementation of the General Principles of the Civil Law of the People's Republic of China (the Opinions (provisional) promulgated 26 January 1988).

Article 178 of the Opinions provides that, where either party in a civil legal relationship is an alien, a stateless person, or a foreign legal person, and the object of the civil legal relationship is within the territory of a foreign country and the legal facts that produce, alter, or annihilate the civil relations of rights and obligations occur in a foreign country, such relationship shall be called a foreign-related civil relationship. When hearing cases involving foreign civil relationships, the people's court shall apply the substantive law in accordance with the provisions of Chapter 8 ('Application of Law in Civil Relations with Foreigners') of the General Principles of the Civil Law.

(2) The Opinions on Certain Issues Regarding the Application of the Civil Procedure Law of the PRC (promulgated by the Supreme People's Court on 14 July 1992).

The above-mentioned laws, regulations and judicial interpretations create a legal framework for dealing with foreign-related labour disputes within which those provisions establish certain primary principles that should be applied to foreign-related labour disputes. However, there are various viewpoints in the people's courts and labour dispute arbitration committees regarding which law should apply to foreign-related employment contract disputes.

The first viewpoint is that the people's courts and labour dispute arbitration committees must apply only the Labour Law of the PRC to settle disputes regarding employment contracts between employers and employees that occur within the territory of the People's Republic of China, including foreign-related employment contract disputes. This viewpoint is based on the following:

According to its Article 2, the Labour Law applies to all enterprises and employers within the territory of China and employees who have employment relationships with said enterprises and employers. Enterprises therein include state-owned enterprises, collective-owned enterprises, foreign-invested enterprises and enterprises wholly owned by foreigners.[2] Thus, within the territory of the PRC, all enterprises, individual employers and employees must abide by the provisions of the Labour Law that govern matters including labour services, negotiation and signing of employment contracts, work hours and work content, remuneration and social insurance as well as welfare.[3]

Regarding employment of foreigners, the Rules on the Administration of Employment of Foreigners in China (promulgated jointly by the Ministry of Labour, Ministry of Public Security, Ministry of Foreign Affairs and the Ministry of Foreign Trade and Economic Cooperation of the People's Republic of China), states that foreigners wishing to work in China should conclude an employment contract with their employers in accordance with PRC law.[4] Should labour disputes arise between employers and their foreign employees, they should be settled in accordance with the Labour Law of the PRC and the Regulations of the PRC on Settlement of Labour Disputes in Enterprises.[5] 'Foreigners' here refers to individuals who are not Chinese nationals.[6] The term 'employment of foreigners in China' refers to activities of employed foreigners who do not have permanent residence in China, but engage in remunerative work[7] within Chinese territory.[8] These activities include foreigners who have signed employment contracts directly with their employers that are within the territory of China, without limitation of duration and foreigners who have signed employment contracts with foreign employers and obtain remuneration from foreign employers who are outside the territory of China, when said foreigners work in China for more than three months

2. See Guan Huai (ed.), Introduction to the Labour Law of the People's Republic of China, (Beijing, Law Press, 1994), p.38.
3. See Article 2 of the Labour Law of the People's Republic of China (1994).
4. See Article 18 of the Rules on the Administration of Employment of Foreigners in China (1996).
5. *Ibid.* See Article 26.
6. The employment in China of the spouses of personnel of foreign embassies, consulates, representative offices of the United Nations System, and other international organizations in China shall follow the Provisions of the Ministry of Foreign Affairs of the People's Republic of China Concerning the Employment of the Spouses of the Personnel of Foreign Embassies, Consulates, and the Representative Offices of the United Nations System in China. See Article 8 of the Rules For the Administration of Employment of Foreigners in China (1996).
7. *Ibid.* See Article 2.
8. *Ibid.* See Article 33.

   The rules do not apply to the employment of foreigners in Chinese Taiwan, Hong Kong or Macao.

(this stipulation does not apply to foreign technical and professional personnel who are working in China in the execution of technology transfer agreements under the assignment of foreign employers).[9]

With regard to Taiwan, Hong Kong and Macao residents, in 1994 the Ministry of Labour promulgated the Provisions on the Administration of Employment of Taiwan, Hong Kong and Macao Residents in the Mainland. According to the Provisions, when Taiwan, Hong Kong, or Macao residents are employed on the mainland, they must abide by the laws of mainland China. Mainland employers must sign employment contracts with them in accordance with all labour laws and administrative regulations. If a labour dispute arises during the course of employment, it will be settled in accordance with the Regulations of the PRC for the Settlement of Labour Disputes in Enterprises.[10] However, said residents exclude certain experts from the regions of Taiwan, Hong Kong and Macao who are invited to work in mainland China by the State Bureau of Foreign Experts, and legal representatives of representative offices set up on the mainland by Taiwan, Hong Kong and Macao enterprises, as well as some investors with legal person status who have set up enterprises on the mainland.[11]

Moreover, the Contract Law provides that the parties to a foreign-related contract may choose the law applied to a contract dispute unless the law provides otherwise.[12] In the view of Chinese academics and some judges, 'otherwise' includes provisions that apply to foreign-related employment contracts stipulated by the Labour Law and the Rules on the Administration of Employment of Foreigners in China, as well as other legislation aforementioned in this section. In addition, in China, labour laws are public laws and have binding authority over the parties to employment contracts. Labour laws may not be excluded by choice of the parties. Therefore, they conclude, employment relationships taking place within the territory of China, including foreign-related employment relationships, are subject to Chinese labour law and regulations.

An opposing opinion held by some academics and judges in China is that labour dispute arbitration committees or people's courts should, when dealing with foreign-related employment contracts, first ascertain whether the parties have reached an agreement on the application of law regarding contract disputes and whether said agreement is valid according to PRC law. If the parties to a contract have not made a choice of law for the settlement of contract disputes, labour dispute arbitration committees or the people's courts should, upon analyzing all of the facts, apply the law of the country that is most closely connected with the contract. Generally, the law of the jurisdiction wherein the labour is performed is

---

9. See Notice of the General Office of the Ministry of Labour on Certain Issues Concerning the Implementation of the Rules For the Administration of Employment of Foreigners in China (April 1996).
10. See Article 13, 14, and 15 of Provisions on the Administration of Employment of Taiwan, Hong Kong, and Macao Residents in the Mainland, promulgated by the Ministry of Labour on February 13, 1994.
11. *Ibid.* See Articles 3 and 4.
12. See Article 126 of the Contract Law of People's Republic of China (1999).

applied, which includes foreign law. When the parties choose Chinese law to be the law applicable to a foreign-related labour dispute or in circumstances where a labour dispute arbitration committee or the people's courts decide in accordance with the doctrine of closest connection if Chinese law contains no provisions for settlement of the dispute at issue, international practice may be applied. When the parties choose foreign law or in circumstances where the courts decide in accordance with the doctrine of closest connection, if said foreign law does not violate the public interests of China, an arbitration committee or the people's courts should apply foreign law to the settlement of a labour dispute. The law and reasoning supporting this viewpoint include:

Article 126 of the PRC Contract Law provides that parties to a contract involving foreign interests may choose the law applicable to the settlement of their contract dispute except if otherwise stipulated by law. If the parties to a contract involving foreign interests have not made a choice, the law of the country to which the contract is most closely connected shall be applied. This article is consistent with principles and judicial precedents in international legislation. In addition, according to the definition of foreign-related civil relations in Article 178 of the Opinions of the Supreme People's Court on Certain Issues Concerning the Implementation of the General Principles of the PRC, employment contracts concluded by employers and foreigners within the territory of China are considered contracts involving foreign interests and are subject to the Contract Law.

Even though it is obvious that the principles regarding contracts with foreign elements that were established under the Contract Law contradict provisions in the Labour Law, they are both special civil laws and they were enacted by the same legislature. According to the Law on Legislation of the PRC regarding laws enacted by the same legislative body, if a special provision is different from a general provision the special provision shall prevail; if a new provision differs from an old provision, the new provision shall prevail. It is apparent that where foreign-related employment contracts are involved, the provisions of the Contract Law should prevail over the provisions of the Labour Law because the Contract Law was enacted in 1999 and the Labour Law was promulgated in 1995. Other regulations and rules such as the Rules on the Administration of Employment of Foreigners in China are administrative regulations and their legal authority is subordinate to the Contract Law. When the provisions of administrative regulations and rules conflict with the Contract Law, the provisions of the latter shall prevail.[13]

The two viewpoints diverge on the question of whether foreign law can be applied to the settlement of disputes regarding foreign-related employment contracts by Chinese courts and labour dispute arbitration committees.

Early in 1985, the Standing Committee of the National People's Congress promulgated the Law of the PRC on Foreign-related Economic Contracts and in 1987 the Supreme People's Court issued the Answers to Certain Questions Concerning the Application of the Law of the People's Republic of China on

---

13. See Article 79 and 83 of the *Law on Legislation of the People's Republic of China*, adopted at the fifth Session of the seventh National People's Congress on 15 March 2000.

Foreign-related Economic Contracts (the Answers). The Law of the PRC on Foreign-related Economic Contracts expressly provides that the law chosen by the parties must be applied in the resolution of disputes regarding foreign-related labour service contracts.[14] Where parties to a foreign-related contract have not made a choice, the people's courts must apply the law of the country that is most closely connected with the contract. In addition, the Answers interpret, generally, that labour service contracts should apply the law of the place where the labour services were performed. However, with the promulgation of the Labour Law and the Contract Law, the issue of the application of law for foreign-related employment contracts becomes complicated and confusing.

As mentioned above, the 1999 Contract Law contained specific rules for the application of law in disputes involving foreign-related contracts. In addition, Article 2 of the Contract Law stipulates that a contract in law is an agreement through which civil rights and a relationship of obligations are established, modified or terminated between natural persons, legal persons or other associations that are subjects of equal status. It also expressly excludes certain agreements concerning personal identity relationships such as marriage, adoption, guardianship and their provisions. Other law should be applied to these agreements. It is obvious that employment contracts have not been excluded from the applicable scope of the Contract Law. However, some Chinese academics and judges are of the opinion that the Contract Law does not govern employment contracts[15] because of certain provisions in the Labour Law. Scrutinizing the Chinese Labour Law, there is no principle found to define labour/employment relationships. According to later-promulgated administrative regulations, rules and judicial interpretations, the definition of what constitutes a labour relationship is confined to relationships between enterprises and individual employees who have been providing labour to them within the territory of PRC China, and[16] contracts concluded by them in accordance with labour law are deemed employment contracts. In addition, all disputes arising in the course of the performance of contracts are labour disputes and the Labour Law must be applied.[17] Such provisions exclude the application of the Contract Law to employment contracts. The contradiction to be found here is that the Labour Law contains neither a special provision for foreign-related employment contracts nor rules for conflicts of law regarding foreign-related employment contracts which, one must conclude, results in only Chinese labour law being applied during the hearing of all disputes regarding employment contracts, including foreign-related contracts, before labour dispute arbitration committees and in the people's courts. Obviously, the viewpoint that only Chinese

14. Also translated as 'employment contract'. <www.lawinfochina.com/index.asp>, 6 January 2008.
15. Referring to the case of employment contract disputes – *Chen Weili v. Lai Guofa.*
16. See the Notice of the Ministry of Labour on Promulgating Opinions on Certain Issues of the Implementation of Labour Law of People's Republic of China (1995).
17. See Article 1 of the Supreme People's Court's Interpretations on Certain Issues Regarding Application of Laws While Dealing with Labour Disputes, adopted by Order No. 1165 meeting of Judicial Committee of the Supreme People's Court on 22 March 2001.

labour law should be applied to all disputes regarding foreign-related employment contracts does not match international legislation or legal practice worldwide.

Like ordinary employment contracts, foreign-related employment contracts are used to establish labour relationships between employers and employees, to specify the rights and obligations of parties, and to manifest the free will of the parties. However, being subject to market supply and demand as well as to the requirements of mass production, employees and employers are de facto unequal when concluding employment contracts. As well, employees are placed in a subordinate position in the course of the performance of employment contracts.[18] Consequently, depending on their specific situations, many countries have promulgated comprehensive labour laws so as to standardize the basic content of employment contracts and to emphasize the protection of workers' rights. On the other hand, foreign-related employment contacts have peculiar characteristics such as if one party or both parties to a contract are foreigners, the place of concluding the contract or the place of performance may be in a foreign country. In China, parties to labour contracts occasionally choose a litigation or arbitration forum for the settlement of disputes. However, if the law of these forums is used to settle disputes regarding foreign-related employment contracts, it will not only degrade the protection of employees' rights and benefits but will also affect the free movement of the labour force as well as the development of multilateral cooperation between countries. Therefore, given the prerequisite of not violating fundamental principles in certain domestic labour law, it has become a general practice in a great number of countries to permit the application of foreign law to some extent.

II. INTERNATIONAL LEGISLATION AND PRACTICE ON APPLICABLE LAW FOR FOREIGN-RELATED EMPLOYMENT CONTRACTS

The promulgation of the British Health and Morals of Apprentices Act (1802) signalled the birth of labour law.[19] As with many other kinds of civil relationships, when a large number of trans-boundary labour disputes arise, countries usually apply and use, on the basis of not violating fundamental principles of domestic labour law, private international law to settle foreign-related employment contract disputes. In the early legislation of private international law, forums would apply the rules of conflict for general contracts to disputes involving foreign-related employment contracts. Not until the mid-twentieth century did certain countries provide special provisions for foreign-related employment contracts in their private international law. In addition, by the end of the twentieth century, the International Labour Organization had passed a number of proposals and entered

18. See Guan Huai (ed.), *Introduction to the Labour Law of the People's Republic of China* (Beijing, Law Press,1994), p.89. Please also refer to Chapter 1 and Chapter 2 in this Part.
19. *Ibid*, p.13.

into treaties guiding labour law legislation in member states as well as in some regional organizations such as the European Community, including international treaties for supervising the legislation of private international law regarding foreign-related contracts among contracting members in which there existed detailed provisions of the application of laws for foreign-related employment contracts. Such developments and changes in legislation were designed to meet the needs of the free movement of the labour force caused by increased international trade and to effectively regulate the increasing number of trans-boundary employment contract disputes.

In reviewing international legislation and practice, it can be seen that legislation regarding disputes involving foreign-related employment contracts in different countries has the following characteristics:

(1) The law chosen by parties is subject to limited application.

It has been a universally accepted legal principle to apply the law chosen by contracting parties to settle disputes regarding foreign-related employment contracts in the courts. This principle not only embodies the original purpose of the contract but also enables contracting parties to foresee the consequences of their acts before disputes occur, which is propitious in clarifying and stabilizing contractual relationships. Once disputes arise, applying the law chosen by contracting parties enables them to accept the judgment of the court and fosters the resolution of contract disputes without delay. This principle, called in private international law the 'doctrine of party autonomy' or 'autonomy of the will of parties', has become the prevailing principle in a great amount of domestic legislation as well as in some international treaties. For example, subparagraph 1 in Article 3 of the European Community Convention on the Law Applicable to Contractual Obligations (1980) (the Rome Convention) states that, 'A contract shall be governed by the law chosen by the parties[. . .] By their choice the parties can select the law applicable to the whole or a part only of the contract'.[20] Articles 7 and 8 of the Inter-American Convention on the Law Applicable to International Contracts (1994) (the Mexico Convention) contain some of the same provisions.[21]

However constrained by factors such as legal systems and national customs, a small number of countries stipulate that parties must make an express choice of applicable law for foreign-related contracts[22] while most countries, as well as international treaties, permit the choice of applicable

20. Xu Donggeng and SHAN Hailing (eds.), *Convention on the Law Applicable to Contractual Obligations*, (Beijing, Law Press, 1998), p.225 English Source: <http://europa.eu/scadplus/leg/en/lvb/l33109.htm>, 6 January 2008.

21. The full name of the convention is the 'Inter-American Convention on the Law Applicable to International Contracts', (1994). <www.oas.org/main/main.asp?sLang=E&sLink=http://www.oas.org/DIL/treaties_and_agreements.htm>, 6 January 2008.

22. See Turkish Private International and Procedural Law (20 May 1980, No. 2675), Article 55 of the Code Civil of Gabon (1972).

law by the parties to be express or implied. For example, subparagraph 1 in Article 3 of the Rome Convention (1980); subparagraph 1 in Article 7 of the Mexico Convention (1994); subparagraph 1 in Article 116 of the Swiss Federal Code on Private International Law (1987); subparagraph 1 in Article 27 of the Private International Law of the Federal Republic of Germany (1986); subparagraph 1 in Article 20 of the Private International Law of the Federal Republic of Yugoslavia (1982); and Article 35 of the Private International Law of the Republic of Austria (1979) all contain stipulations that contracts are to be governed by the law chosen by the parties or that the agreement of the parties on said selection must be express or evident from the behaviour of the parties or from clauses contained in the contract.

As to the timing of the selection of applicable law, some countries permit parties to choose at any time before or after the conclusion of contracts, and even during the course of trial (e.g., Germany, Poland, and Switzerland) while the law of certain other countries such as the Private International Law of Hungary (1979), stipulate that the parties must choose no later than the time of the conclusion of the contract.

Legislation and practice in various countries also differ over whether or not to limit the scope of the choice of the parties regarding applicable law. Some countries emphasize that the parties' choice of law should not violate the public policies of related countries. In addition, some countries such as Poland, Portugal, Germany, and the US specify that the law chosen by parties must be the law of a country that has a certain connection with the contract. Although such differences exist, the trend indicates that international legislation inclines to reduce restrictions on the choice of law by the parties when foreign-related contract disputes are involved.[23]

The application of the principle of party autonomy to employment contracts involving foreign interests has been gradually accepted in international legislation. Most domestic legislation and international treaties that deal specifically with the issue of the application of law, (except Hungary and Tunis)[24] have stipulated that foreign-related employment should be governed by the law properly chosen by the parties. However, considering the special characteristics of employment contracts, some countries impose certain limitations in law to restrict the choice of parties.

---

23. In practice, some countries such as Australia, England and Canada do not restrict the freedom of parties to choose applicable law.
24. The official report on the Hungarian legislative decree of 1979 (Law-Decree No. 13 of 1979 on the *Private International Law of Hungary*) indicates that the decree does not allow the parties to an employment relation to choose the law governing it. See Felice Morgenstern, *International Conflicts of Labour Law* (ILO publication, 1984), p.19. Article 67 of the *Private International Law of Tunis* in *Chinese Yearbook of Private International Law and Comparative Law* (2000), Chinese Society of Private International Law and Wuhan University Research Institute of International Law (eds.) (Beijing, Law Press, 2000), p.723.

The 1987 Swiss Federal Code on Private International Law is one typical of twentieth century private international law. Chapter 9 of the Swiss Code entitled the 'Law of Obligations,' grants contractual parties quite comprehensive and active autonomy to choose applicable law.[25] However, where employment contracts are concerned, the Swiss Code explicitly provides that the scope of the parties' choice is constrained by the laws of employees' places of residence, the place of labour service performance, and the place of the employer's business. The Private International Law of the Republic of Austria permits parties to expressly or implicitly choose the law applicable to foreign-related contracts. However, subparagraph 1 of Article 44 of the Austrian Law also provides that the choice must be expressed by the terms of parties to employment contracts.

A great number of countries explicitly provide that in foreign-related employment contracts the choice of law made by the parties should not result in depriving an employee of the protection afforded to him by the mandatory rule of law that would be applicable where the employee habitually carries out his work in performance of the contract. This is designed to prevent employers from evading the mandatory rule of law of that country which has the closest connection with the contract through their choice of applicable law. The mandatory regulations of a country usually concern matters of work safety and minimum salaries.[26]

Applying certain restraints on the choice of law by the parties to settle disputes regarding foreign-related employment contracts shall, for the purpose of ensuring that a country can realize its public policy of regulating labour relations, grant parties full freedom of choice of applicable law.

(2) In the absence of choice of law by the contracting parties, many countries generally apply the laws of the country where the labour service is provided and where employers conduct their business operations.

If parties fail to choose an applicable law for an employment contract or if the law chosen by the parties violates the mandatory rules of the laws of the court, such choices are declared null and void. Under such situations, the laws of many countries generally provide that the laws of the country with the closest connection to the contract shall be applied with priority. The term 'closest connection' has different implications in

25. See Articles 18 and 19 of the Swiss Federal Code on Private International Law.
26. See Article 6 of 1980 the Rome Convention, Article 101 of the *Private International Law Relations* of Romania ([ROM] Law No. 105 of 22 September 1992), Article 3118 of the Quebec *Private International Law*, Sub-pargraph3 of Article 48 of the *Legislation on Private International Law* of Liechtenstein (1996), and Subparagraph 3 of Article 44 of the *Private International Law* of the Republic of Austria. <www.kluwerarbitration.com/arbitration/arb/country/>, 6 January 2008.

different countries, and usually refers to the laws of the place where the contract was concluded, the place where the contract is performed, the parties' respective or common nationality or residence, the place of business if parties are legal persons or the place of strongest connection to the contract.

Regarding how to deal with the issue of determining applicable law for the settlement of foreign-related employment contract disputes in the absence of choice of law by contracting parties, all countries have experienced the development and the process of perfecting their legislation and practices. As mentioned above, at the early stage prior to the 1970s, the choice of law for the settlement of foreign-related employment contract disputes was determined in accordance with general principles regarding foreign-related contracts, which meant the application of the law of the parties' common nationality or residences, or the law of the place of conclusion of the contract. With the development of international trade and improved transportation and communication, traditional principles regarding foreign-related contracts failed to satisfy the demands of employment contract relationships. Such principles did not ensure that employees would enjoy the protection of the measures being developed for that purpose. For example, the arbitrariness of the place of conclusion of contracts was becoming obvious, especially when it differed from the place of performance. Likewise, applying the law of the common nationality or residence of the parties to settlements of employment contract disputes inevitably led to a situation wherein the laws of different countries were required to be applied to settle employment contract disputes arising from the same enterprise at the same time, which increased the difficulty of the courts in dealing with such disputes.

Thus, since the 1970s, much in legislation has changed and now follows the connection between applicable law and contracts. For the purpose of effectively protecting workers' legal rights and making sure that workers enjoy effective protection, many countries and international treaties have stipulated that when parties to employment contracts fail to choose law applicable to a contract, the laws of the place of labour performance or the employer's place of business should apply.

Compared with other factors, the parties to labour contracts know or should know better the laws of the location where workers provide labour services or where employers conduct business. These laws have stronger connections to employment contracts and the application of such laws can better provide protection of workers' legal rights.

The Rome Convention, for example, provides that in the absence of choice, the laws of the country in which the employee habitually carries out his work in the performance of the contract shall be applied and if the employee does not habitually carry out his work in any one country, the laws of the country in which the place of business through which he was engaged is situated will apply.[27] In addition to the parties to the Rome Convention, Tunis, the US, Romania, Liechtenstein, Quebec and Switzerland have also included similar provisions in their legislation.

(3) Mandatory rules in the labour laws of various countries play a role when dealing with employment contract disputes.

Employment contracts have features that distinguish them from general contracts. The enforcement of workers' rights during the performance period such as professional safety, health protection, working hours, public holidays, minimum salary, industrial injury compensation, collective negotiation rights and the rights and benefits of women, children and the disabled, closely concern workers' interests and the public policies of countries.

Consequently, many countries provide specific provisions for such issues in their labour law and provide enforcement powers regarding same. There are stipulations that employment contracts performed within the territory of a country are subject to the laws of that jurisdiction so as to make sure that the basic rights and interests granted by the law are realized.

At the present stage, however, only a small number of countries make the application of their labour law compulsory for all workers including foreigners within the territory of those countries. Such provisions can be found in the Labour Code of Iraq (1970), the General Labour Code of Angora (1981), the United Arab Emirates Federal Laws of Labour Relations (1980), and the Labour Code of Ecuador (1987). Certain other countries, such as Argentina and French speaking African countries provide that employment contracts performed in their countries must apply the laws of those countries.[28]

However, many countries at present confine their mandatory rules to a reasonable and limited scope and only provide mandatory rules on certain important issues such as public policy and labour safety so as to regulate labour relations formed within the territory of those countries. Obedience to such provisions is indispensable to maintaining the political, social and economic organization of those countries. If the application of mandatory rules is arbitrarily made broader, it will inevitably deprive parties of the right to choose applicable law.

Of course due to different social systems and cultures, as well as to disparities in income between different countries, the situation vis-à-vis labour and social security systems is different, which leads to differences in the content and regimes of labour law. Some countries provide

27. See Article 6 of the 1980 Rome Convention.
28. See the 1976 Civil Code of the Argentine Republic, the 1974 Labour Law of the Republic of Cameroon, 1978 Labour Law of the Gabon Republic, 1964 Labour Law of the Republic of Cote d'ivoire, 1975 Labour Law of the Republic of Madagascar, 1963 Labour Law of the Islamic Republic of Mauritania, 1962 Labour Law of the Republic of Seychelles.

that workers should not work on statutory holidays so as to protect the health of workers, while other countries, especially developing countries, permit workers to work overtime on the condition that employers pay double-time so as to constrain employers from imposing overtime work arbitrarily and to protect the interests of workers. In addition, the labour law in some developed countries provides for paid vacations, which cannot be implemented in developing countries.

In order to balance the conflict between the labour laws of different countries and to provide sufficient protection to workers, the law in many countries stipulates that the application of foreign law should not violate mandatory rules of the domestic law of the country where workers perform the employment contract, where employers conduct business, or where employment contracts have their strongest connection. Paragraph 1 in Article 6 of the Rome Convention provides:

> Notwithstanding the provisions of Article 3, in a contract of employment a choice of law made by the parties shall not have the result of depriving the employee of the protection afforded to him by the mandatory rules of the law which would be applicable under paragraph 2 in the absence of choice.

This means that a contract of employment shall, in the absence of choice of law, be governed by the law of the country in which the employee habitually carries out his work in performance of the contract, even if he or she is temporarily employed in another country or, if the employee does not habitually carry out his work in any one country, by the law of the country in which the place of business through which he was engaged is situated.[29]

According to Article 7, when according to the Rome Convention the law of a certain country is applied, effect may be given to the mandatory rules of the law of another country with which the situation has a close connection if and in so far as under the law of the latter country those rules must be applied, whatever the chosen applicable law of the contract.[30] In addition to the Rome Convention members, some countries, especially certain developing countries, have made similar provisions in their private international law, for example Law No. 105 of the Republic of Romania on the Regulation of Private International Law Relations (1992), the Legislation of Liechtenstein on Private International Law (1996), and the Private International Law of Tunis (1997).

When a court is hearing a foreign-related employment contract dispute, it should not neglect the mandatory rules of its own laws. Therefore, it does not matter whether foreign law is chosen by the parties or determined by a court in accordance with the rules of private international law, if the application of the law contradicts the mandatory rules of the laws of

---

29. See Sub-paragraph 1 of Article 6 of the 1980 Rome Convention.
30. *Ibid.* See Sub-paragraphs 1 and 2 of Article 6.

the court the court shall exclude the application of the law. It is obvious that employment contracts should abide by the mandatory rules of the law of the place where the labour is performed and where the business of the employer is situated. Generally, the country that has the closest connection with the labour relationship is the place where the labour is performed or where the employer conducts its business.

III. APPLICATION OF MANDATORY RULES AND PUBLIC POLICY

Regarding employment contracts with foreign elements (including non-competition agreements), it is an important principle within many domestic legal regimes that the exclusion of the application of foreign law on the ground of the application of mandatory rules and protection of public policy is reasonable.

In fact, the concept of mandatory rule of law has been broadly accepted and adopted by a great number of countries and in several international communities. Paragraph 1 in Article 6 of the Rome Convention stipulates:

> Notwithstanding the provisions of Article 3, in a contract of employment a choice of law made by the parties shall not have the result of depriving the employee of the protection afforded to him by the mandatory rule of law which would be applicable under paragraph 2 in the absence of choice.[31]

If the condition of a case shows that the contract has a closer connection with a third country, the mandatory rules of that third country shall be applied. On the other hand, it does not matter what laws are applied as, in the end, the mandatory rules of the laws of the court shall not be excluded.[32] The Law Commission of Great Britain is of the view that the mandatory rule of law is '[so] important that as a matter of construction or policy it must apply in any action before a court of the forum, even where the issues are in principle governed by a foreign law selected by a choice of law rule'.[33]

The application of mandatory rules in domestic law has a long history of state intervention in national economic activity and in civil and commercial relationships through performance of relevant public policy in legislation. In the field of contract law legislation many countries try to protect special groups in civil and commercial relationships by introducing mandatory rules into their domestic law. For example, in order to protect employees – the weaker group in employment

31. Sub-paragraph 2 of Article 6 of the Rome Convention providing that the mandatory rules vested to the employees include: the law of the State in which the employee habitually carries out his work in performance of the contract, even if he or she is temporarily employed in another State; if the employee does not habitually carry out his work in any one State, by the law of the State in which the place of business through which he or she was engaged is situated.
32. *Ibid.* See sub-paragraph 1 and 2 of Article 7.
33. Law Com Working Paper No. 87(1984), Scot Law Com Consultative Memorandum No. 62 (1984), paragraph 4.5.

relationships – many countries prescribe certain rules in their labour law, such as rules regarding the notice period for the dismissal of employees and the safety and sanitary conditions of the workplace, which must be enforced. In addition, some mandatory rules concern a country's economic system and embody the will of the government to intervene in its market economy, including anti-trust law, restrictions on exports and imports, controls on prices and foreign exchange controls. Though form and content of mandatory rules differ from each other in different countries, all mandatory rules have strong binding force within the domestic law of a country which neither contracting parties nor the courts may exclude through the choice of applicable law. Some foreign academics have commented that application of mandatory rules can be regarded as an exclusionary concept since the effect of the application of mandatory rules is that a foreign domestic law, which would otherwise govern under the choice of law rules, is not applied.[34]

Whether domestic rules are mandatory should be interpreted in accordance with the law of their country of origin. In earlier codified law, the courts determined the law applicable to foreign-related civil and commercial cases in accordance with the applicable ranges provided by law. As to statutes which have not been explicitly defined as mandatory rules or which have no express provisions as to their overriding effect and no provision for their territorial scope, the construction of such statutes in order to ascertain whether they are intended to have an overriding effect in particular situations is especially difficult. The courts can only depend on the facts of a specific situation to determine whether a statute carries the force of a mandatory rule.[35] However, current statutes normally state whether they are intended to have an overriding effect and specify their applicable range, especially when domestic rules are applied in foreign-related cases. Such types of legislation will facilitate the proper application of law by the courts so as to avoid the improper expansion of the application of domestic law as well as to apply domestic law expressing a strong socio-economic policy regarding foreign-related cases. For example, English rules expressing a strong socio-economic policy are more likely to be contained in statutes which expressly provide that in various situations that statute is to have complete overriding effect, limited overriding effect or no overriding effect, such as the English Unfair Consumer Contract Regulations (1997) (the 1997 Regulations) which have limited overriding effect. The 1997 Regulations were promulgated to implement European Council Directive 93/13/EEC regarding unfair terms in consumer contracts[36] on the basis of modification of the Unfair Contract Terms Act (1977) and to provide a definition of unfair terms in consumer contracts for British judicial departments, supervisory departments and consumer protection organizations dealing with relevant disputes. The 1997 Regulations also ensure consistency regarding the issue of applicable law within other European Union member states. They explicitly stipulate that in the hearing of disputes involving consumer contracts with non-European Union

34. Cheshire and North's *Private International Law* (London, Butterworths, 1999), p.132.
35. *Ibid*, at p.579.
36. Council Directive 93/13/EEC (1993) OJ L95/29.

member states, if a contract has a close connection with the territory of the EU member states, the 1997 Regulations should be applied notwithstanding any contract term that applies or purports to apply the law of a non-EU member state.[37] The US Restatement (Second) of Conflict of Laws also suggests that the court should give local statutes the range of application intended by the legislature when that intention can be ascertained and can be given constitutional effect. On the other hand, if a legislature intended that a statute should be applied only to acts taking place within its own borders, that statute should not be given a wider range of application.[38]

In addition to mandatory rules, public policy doctrine contained in each country's law operates as well to establish exceptions to normal choice of law rules. The similarities of mandatory rules and public policies are that the content of both always concerns the significant interests of one country while differences exist only in their range of application. As an exception to the application of a provision of foreign law, public policy is usually applied to the following two situations:

(1) when the courts decide that the applicable law should be foreign law if the content of that foreign law might lead to a result that would be incompatible with the public policy of that forum; or
(2) when recognizing and enforcing the judgments or awards of foreign arbitration tribunals, if the content of the judgment or award is incompatible with the public policy contained in the laws of the country of a court.

As to disputes regarding employment contracts, the obedience to the mandatory rule of one country's law is generally embodied in the application of that country's labour protection standards as compulsory standards if the labour protection standards in the law chosen by the parties or determined by the court in accordance with the rules of private international law are lower than the standards of the law of the court. Of course, sometimes it is hard to conduct comparisons between certain bodies of law. For example, some countries provide that if an employer wrongly dismisses an employee that the employer should compensate that employee, while other countries provide that the employee should be restored to his position under such conditions. Some academics have commented that there exist certain problems in the provisions of mandatory rules of private international law and in international treaties. In practice, if such situation occurs, the courts must seriously consider the reasonable needs of employees and try to effectively protect their interests.[39]

---

37. Section 27(2) of the *Unfair Contract Terms in Consumer Contracts Regulations* (1997) Regulation 7. 'These Regulations shall apply notwithstanding any contract term which applies or purports to apply the law of a non-member State, if the contract has a close connection with the territory of the member States'.
38. Restatement (Second) of Conflict of Laws, 1971 (US), §6, comment b.
39. G.G.J. MORSE 'Contracts of Employment and the EEC Contractual Obligations Convention', *Contract Conflicts*, P.M. North (ed.) (North-Holland Publishing Company, 1982), p.152.

IV. BRIEF SUMMARY

Without doubt, a considerable number of imperfections exist within current Chinese legislation regulating disputes involving foreign elements. Certain Chinese authors believe that it is very important and necessary for China to have more foresight and to speed the development of the legislation of private international law. Since 1993, the Chinese Society of Private International Law (CSPIL), composed of professors, scholars, jurists and practicing lawyers in the area of private international law from all over China, has been in the process of drafting China's Model Law of Private International Law.[40] The most recent draft is the fifth one, which has 165 articles and includes rules regarding contract and tort issues. However, this is only a model law having no legal effect in China. In addition, certain of its content regarding labour contracts contain no detail. Consequently, the necessary force to deal with relevant disputes in legal practice cannot be met. Legislation regarding foreign-related trade secrets must be established and perfected. For example, rules regarding the choice of law applicable to foreign-related confidentiality agreements and foreign-related non-competition agreements in employment contract law must be provided. In addition, the scope of the application of labour law must be contained and specific content and scope of mandatory rules applied to foreign-related labour contract disputes must be provided as well.

40. Chinese Society of Private International Law (CSPIL) *Model Law of Private International Law of the People's Republic of China* (Beijing, Law Press, China, 2000).

Postscript

Trade secrets as important intangible assets are so highly valued by many international organizations, including the World Trade Organization and its member countries, that a great number of countries where protection of trade secrets has become one of the primary objects of the law have either promulgated trade secret laws or improved current trade secret laws so as to encourage research and innovation as well as to maintain basic commercial ethics. Meanwhile, under the regulations of the TRIPS Agreement, the definition of trade secrets, their constitutive requirements and the scope of their protection in different countries have tended to become uniform. Many countries have provided civil remedy in their domestic law to protect trade secrets from infringement and criminal penalties have been prescribed to punish serious acts of infringement of trade secrets.

The majority of trade secret disputes arise between employers and employees and they are more complicated than those occurring outside the context of employment relationships.

With the great improvement in the industrial infrastructure in many countries which began at the advent of the twentieth century, the development of enterprises has come to rely more and more heavily on intellectual property, including trade secrets. Most employees, who are now no longer traditional apprentices but well-educated workers playing a crucial role in the technological innovation and operational management of enterprises. In addition, there has been rapid progress in communications, transportation and market competition that has prompted the migration of employees to find better opportunities. Inevitably, the frequency of trade secret disputes is increasing.

When dealing with trade secret disputes involving employment relationships, the questions that present certain challenges are: Will the interests of employees be harmed when the scope of trade secrets becomes broader and when the trade secrets of employers are protected in a market economy that emphasizes fair competition and unrestricted movement of human resources? Will the public interest be harmed when it encourages fair competition and unrestricted movement of human resources? In fact, underlying these questions are the interests of employers, employees and the public and the effort to balance these sometimes conflicting interests.

Since the end of the last century many foreign scholars, especially American scholars, have been aware that ignorance of the importance of trade secret protection hinders investment in innovation by employers and insufficient protection of trade secrets harms the basic rights and interests of employees, which leads to a deterioration in the innovative capability of society in the long run. Consequently, these scholars pay close attention to issues of trade secret protection with regard to employment relationships.

In terms of the protection of trade secrets with relation to employment relationships, unlike other types of protection for intellectual property, the interests of employers, employees and the public need to be given equal consideration. Finding a balance between those interests has been a leading subject of national policy in a great number of countries and a significant requirement for the promulgation of trade secret law as well as, consequently, for resolving disputes involving trade secrets between employers and employees.

In national trade secret law and in legal practice in China, more attention should be focused on the following: First, attention to protection of trade secrets has shifted from an emphasis on its importance to its reasonableness, which means reasonable constraints on the protection of employers' trade secrets (e.g., only reasonable confidentiality agreements and reasonable covenants not to compete will be deemed valid). Second, in general, trade secret law concerns itself with the fundamental rights of employees during and following employment relationships and some countries have prescribed in their legislation that employers may not constrain the freedom of their employees to work, that the right of privacy of employees should be protected during employment and that employers should pay appropriate compensation to their ex-employees if they perform covenants not to compete following the expiration of their employment contracts. Third, the involvement of government authorities has been enhanced so as to maximize protection of the public interest. For example, the protection of trade secrets should avoid wasting the resource of skilled workers and should not violate the principles of legitimate competition and anti-trust. However, disclosure of the confidential information of employers should be protected when that disclosure serves the public interest. In short, in the process of enhancing the protection of trade secrets, an attempt is being made to harmonize public policy while ensuring that the creation and implementation of trade secret law will contribute to social progress.

In China, promulgation of trade secret legislation and research on the legal science of trade secrets began in the 1990s. The progress of establishment and development of a trade secret protection system in China has maintained a momentum similar to that being enjoyed in its economic growth and social reform. With unexpected speed and scale, China has gone through a process of 'marketization,' urbanization, diversification of economic ownership and globalization, achieving results that have attracted the attention of the world. When looking back at the development track of Chinese trade secret law, one finds that within only twenty years China has established a legal system for the protection of trade secrets with international treaties as its foundation, the Law against Unfair Competition at its centre, and the Contract Law, the Labour Law and the Criminal Law as component provisions, which is unique in the history of development of contemporary legal systems in the world. In the past one to two years, the courts in China have conducted research on trial practice regarding trade secrets as well as related policies and legal issues. At the annual National Conference on Intellectual Property Right Trials, the resolution of disputes involving trade secrets is always an important issue. In addition, the Supreme People's Court drafted a judicial interpretation of the Law against Unfair Competition that includes guidelines for the hearing of trade secret lawsuits and in November 2005 it published that draft at <www.Chinacourt.org> to solicit public opinion. In March 2006, the Supreme People's Court opened the China IPR Judgments and Decisions web site and plans to eventually publish all of its decisions, some of which concern disputes regarding intellectual property rights, on the Internet. While actively cooperating with strategic research on intellectual property rights being conducted at the state level for improving the national intellectual property right system, the Supreme People's Court is also conducting research for improving the judicial protection system for intellectual property rights, which includes remedial judicial systems. The measures taken by the courts and the legislature in China have created an environment for the improvement of trade secret protection.

Generally speaking, in these initial stages the trade secret system as constituted by current Chinese law addresses only basic issues of trade secret protection. Historically, the promulgation of certain law in China, including legislation for the protection of trade secrets, has come under a certain degree of external pressure. Customarily, however, these laws are promptly implemented via administrative authority in China. Under these circumstances, the development of a legal regime of trade secret law in China has continued to lag behind that in other countries, which to some extent has negatively affected the fair implementation of law and has given rise to legal disputes. The legal issues that need to be addressed in legislation and in legal practice include.

I. CURRENT LEGISLATION ON THE PROTECTION OF TRADE SECRETS IN CHINA MUST BE IMPROVED

First, clarify the right to protect trade secrets as a civil right in our basic civil law.

Protection of trade secrets is a kind of civil right that depends mainly on civil law such as contract law, tort law and property law. Currently, however, the principal law being applied to the protection of civil rights in China is the General Principles of the Civil Law of the People's Republic of China, which fails to clarify the legal status of trade secrets, although it has affirmed intellectual property as a property right and has recognized the civil right to three types of traditional intellectual property, (i.e., patents, trademarks and copyrights).

Second, expand subjective matter to protect trade secrets in employment relationships.

As a basic law regarding competition in the marketplace, the Law against Unfair Competition (the main source of trade secret protection in China) defines both right-holders and infringing parties as 'managers' (which includes only legal persons, economic organizations and individuals who deal with commercial business or profitable services). Consequently, the Law against Unfair Competition refrains from regulating certain types of disputes between employers and their employees regarding protection of trade secrets. Furthermore, the Law against Unfair Competition requires that trade secrets must have the nature of 'utility'. For this reason, confidential information that is at the stage of theoretical research is not protected if obtained by others without consent. In practice, there may be only one step between the 'theoretical research' stage and 'utilization'.

II. SUBSTANTIVE SUPPORT FOR PRIVATE LAW IN OUR LEGAL SYSTEM MUST BE PROVIDED

The difference between the protection of trade secrets in China from that in Western countries lies not only in their legal provisions per se, but also in a legal system supported by the rationale of private law as well as the professional quality of legal practitioners, especially of judges. Due to their unique nature, trade secrets should be protected based on traditional principles of contract law, tort law and property law and thus disputes regarding trade secrets need to be regulated in a similar manner. Effective protection of trade secrets relies upon traditional civil principles and theories.

Nowadays, it has become a preferred choice of many enterprises and technical personnel not to apply for patents but to ensure a longer period of exclusive possession by maintaining the secrecy of the know-how they have obtained. When looking at the progress of formation and development of the modern trade secret protection system worldwide, it can clearly be seen that the appropriate and efficient operation of protection mechanisms has benefited from the continuous improvement of property right theory and confidential relationship theory, as well as from the harmonization of domestic trade secret legislation including the Law against Unfair Competition, the Contract Law and the Criminal Law. When the rights and interests of trade secret holders are infringed, they can file suit and petition the court to prevent infringing parties from using or disclosing their trade secrets through legal remedial measures such as injunction. If losses occur, a trade secret holder can be compensated in accordance with express confidentiality agreements between concerned parties, de facto implied confidentiality agreements or, in the absence of contractual covenants, the obligation of confidentiality that exists in law. In addition, in order to avoid the unauthorized use or disclosure of trade secrets which have been legally obtained for personal benefit or for the benefit of others, such as in employment relationships or business relationships, the law can prescribe certain regulations to restrict intentional or negligent direct or indirect acts of infringement of trade secrets based on the theory of confidential relationships, thereby protecting the rights and interests of trade secret holders.

Though progress in establishing a system of trade secret protection law in China has been accelerated by the advocacy and involvement of the government, in respect of effective prevention of trade secret infringement and additional losses to trade secret holders, the current civil remedy mechanism has serious shortcomings. For example, the applicability and workability of the preliminary execution scheme is weak and its application is very limited in cases involving trade secrets. Also, the concept of an employee's obligation of confidentiality lacks a logical legal foundation. In addition, there are some legal blind spots in current legislation which concern the private right nature of trade secrets, the nature of an employee's obligation of confidentiality (statutory or contractual), the legal applicability of non-competition agreements, the legal definition of 'employee' and 'employment relationship' and the legal foundation for balancing the need for trade secret protection and the public interest. All of these issues arise from the lack of substantial support of private law in the current legal system in China. For example, Chinese property law, labour contract law and tort law, which are closely related to the protection of private rights, are still in the process of being drawn up. Particularly, the draft of the trade secret law has not yet been added to the legislative schedule for examination. Thus, the sum total of all current provisions directly related to trade secret protection amounts to only ten articles and several thousand words – far from what is necessary to referee the current number of disputes regarding trade secrets.

III. THE LEGAL NATURE OF AN EMPLOYEE'S OBLIGATION OF CONFIDENTIALITY IN RESPECT OF TRADE SECRETS MUST BE CLARIFIED AND LEGISLATION ON NON-COMPETITION AGREEMENTS MUST BE IMPROVED

The question of whether an employee's obligation to maintain the confidentiality of an employer's trade secrets during the period of employment is statutory or contractual has been troubling China's judicial circles and directly influencing the fair hearing of these types of cases. If no clear reference has been made in an employment contract to the obligation of confidentiality, can an employee then, in breach of the professional code of conduct, disclose, use or allow others to use trade secrets of the employer in his possession? This question has been confounding judges and legal academics in China.

For historical reasons, China's employment regime has for a long time been subject to highly centralized state administration under which the labour force has been allocated according to central planning and wherein all employees were naturally also the 'masters' of the enterprises for which they worked. However, with the reform of the economic regime and the establishment of a free labour market in China, the employment relationship has changed dramatically. This change is manifest not only in the allocation of the labour force by the market, but also in employment based upon hiring by enterprises and in the regime of collective labour contracts established in 1999.[1]

However, current Chinese legislation (including the Labour Law) dedicated to the regulation of employment relationships has not provided a clear legal definition for the current nature of employment relationships. As a result, the obligation of employee confidentiality lacks a logical legal foundation. Furthermore, the wording of related provisions in certain regulations is ambiguous. For example, Article 3 of the Several Regulations on Forbidding the Infringement of Trade Secrets adopted by the State Administration for Industry and Commerce provides that activities which infringe trade secrets and which are prohibited include, inter alia:

> [an] employee disclosing, using, or allowing others to use trade secrets of a right holder in breach of a contractual agreement entered into with the right holder or of the requirement of confidentiality imposed by the right holder.

It is not clear whether 'the requirement of confidentiality imposed by the right holder' is statutory in nature. Another example is Article 22 of the Labour Law which provides:

> The parties to an employment contract may agree in the employment contract upon issues such as the duty to maintain trade secrets of the employer. The employee who has failed to fulfil such duty and caused economic loss to the employer shall be liable to pay compensation.

Article 1 of the Letter on Infringement of Trade Secrets Involved in Labour Disputes issued by the Secretariat of the Ministry of Labour and Social Security further provides that:

> If terms regarding maintaining confidentiality of trade secrets have been incorporated into an employment contract and subsequently a labour dispute arises because the employee has failed to fulfil his obligation of confidentiality and caused infringement of the employer's trade secrets, the Arbitration Committee for Labour Disputes shall accept the application for arbitration in respect of such dispute, and give award in accordance with relevant regulations and the agreement of confidentiality contained in the employment contract.

It is not clear whether these provisions of the Labour Law are suggesting that the effect of an employee's obligation of confidence is based solely upon contractual agreement. If such obligation is statutory, even in the absence of a contractual agreement, the employee must observe the duty of confidentiality and is liable for

---

1. Dong, Baohua, *Theory of Labour Law* (Beijing, World Books Press, 1999), p.63.

the payment of compensation for any breach of said duty; if said obligation is only contractual, then in the absence of any or explicit references in an employment contract, there is no legal basis for an employer to impose the obligation of confidentiality upon its employees.

Due to the ambiguity of Chinese law, many employers have tried to protect their trade secrets by signing confidentiality agreements with their employees. However, employers still worry that the clauses within such agreements will not sufficiently protect all of their trade secrets.

IV. CURRENT LEGAL REMEDIES NEED TO BE IMPROVED

A. Existing Civil Remedies in China Need to Be Improved in Order to Effectively Prevent Damage to Trade Secret Holders

Historically, trade secret right holders have sought civil remedy based upon the following considerations:

(a) to compensate for losses suffered;
(b) to prevent imminent or further loss; or
(c) to punish infringing activity.

However, in respect of effective prevention of trade secret infringement and preventing further losses, the civil remedy mechanism has serious drawbacks.

First of all, the applicability and workability of the preliminary execution scheme is weak. The term 'preliminary execution' in China refers to a scheme under which the court, after accepting but prior to rendering its final decision in a civil case, may temporarily order a party to fulfil its obligation in order to meet the urgent need for livelihood, business operations of the right holder or the urgent need to stop or prevent certain activity. Article 97 of the Civil Procedure Law of the PRC provides that the people's courts may, at the request of the parties concerned, order preliminary execution in respect to the following cases:

(a) those involving claims for alimony, support for children or elders, pension for the disabled or the family of a decedent or expenses for medical care;
(b) those involving claims for remuneration for labour; and
(c) those involving urgent circumstances that require preliminary execution.

The judicial interpretation of the Supreme People's Court provides that 'urgent circumstances' include those wherein infringement needs to be stopped or an obstruction needs to be removed immediately and where certain other activity needs to be stopped immediately.[2] However, in cases involving trade secrets

2. Article 107(1),(2) of the Supreme Court Opinion on Several Issues Concerning the Application of the Civil Procedure Law of the People's Republic of China adopted on 14 July 1992; Article 162

and other intellectual property, the applicability of preliminary execution is weak and thus its application is very limited in such cases.[3] This is due mainly to the fact that conditions for preliminary execution are difficult to meet in lawsuits involving trade secrets. Article 98(1) of the Civil Procedure Law provides that cases in which preliminary execution is ordered by a people's court must meet the condition that the relationship of rights and obligations between the parties is definite and that denial of preliminary execution would seriously affect the livelihood or business of the applicant. This requires the petitioner, as well as the court, to explain, in order to support the adoption of a preliminary execution order, why, in the absence of such order the production or business operations of the applicant will be seriously affected. However, cases involving trade secrets are often complicated. The parties may have substantial disagreements regarding whether the trade secret of the plaintiff exists and whether the defendant's activity has been based on said trade secret or simply the common knowledge and skills of the defendant. Furthermore, the rights and obligations of the plaintiff and the defendant are not clear and many trade secrets cost little to create, contain little originality, are often not in use or belong to the category of negative information which, even if used by others, will not seriously affect the life or business of the trade secret holder. Therefore, it is difficult for a plaintiff to obtain preliminary execution in these cases.

Secondly, uneven treatment of remedies exists. In order to be in conformity with the requirements of the provisional measures contained in Part III section 3 of TRIPS (Article 50), principle Chinese intellectual property laws have been amended from 2000 to 2001.[4] On the basis of remedial measures provided by the Civil Procedure Law such as preservation of assets, preservation of evidence and preliminary execution, the newly-amended Patent Law, Copyright Law and Trademark Law have added preliminary injunction and pre-trial preservation of evidence to civil procedure.[5] Trade secrets, however, have not received the same treatment as no new civil remedy measures have been added regarding their treatment. The old regulations contained in the Civil Procedure Law (1991) have been left unchanged. Compared to remedies for infringement of traditional intellectual property, the mechanism for the protection of trade secrets is more demanding due to the fact that trade secrets are an intangible property preserved by measures of confidentiality, are easily disseminated and transferred and, once disclosed, lost forever. When infringement of trade secrets occurs, should protective measures not be taken in a timely manner, it will be difficult for the right holder to provide

---

of the Supreme Court Opinion on Several Issues Concerning the Implementation of the General Principles of the Civil Law of the People's Republic of China adopted on 24 January 1988.

3. See Zhang, Guangliang *Civil Remedies for Intellectual Property* (Beijing, Law Press, 2003), p.62.
4. The Standing Committee of the National People's Congress amended the *Patent Law* for the second time in August 2000, which became effective 1 July 2001; and amended the *Copyright Law* and the *Trademark Law* for the second time in October 2001, which became effective in October and December 2001 respectively.
5. See Article 61 of the *Patent Law*, Article 57 of the *Trademark Law*, and Article 49 of the *Copyright Law*.

evidence and impossible for the facts to be clarified. Consequently, the trade secret will be exposed. Therefore, for the purpose of providing timely and sufficient civil remedy to the right holder of trade secrets, it is necessary to provide for certain pre-trial (interlocutory) remedial measures in the procedural rule in order that a right holder can seek eventual material remedy.

B. With Respect of Jurisdiction of Trade Secret Disputes, The Hierarchical Jurisdiction for Civil and Criminal Remedies Needs to Be Improved

In the Chinese framework of judicial remedy for the protection of trade secrets, civil remedy is the basic form and criminal remedy is an ad hoc form. The basic characteristic of the first is that it applies to all activities involving infringement of trade secrets disregarding the intention of the infringer (i.e., malice or negligence) and the circumstances (i.e., serious or not). The ad hoc nature of the latter is manifest by the fact that it is not always available to a right holder. According to current law, only activities that intentionally infringe trade secrets and are serious in circumstance constitute the crime of infringement of trade secrets and individuals who engage in such activities can be held criminally liable

Article 18 of the Civil Procedure Law of the PRC provides that the basic people's courts have jurisdiction as the courts of first instance over civil cases. Article 19 further provides that the intermediate people's courts have jurisdiction as courts of first instance over:

> [m]ajor cases involving foreign interests, cases that have great impact on the area under their jurisdiction; and cases under the jurisdiction of the intermediate people's courts as determined by the Supreme People's Court.

'Major cases involving foreign interests' refers to cases with foreign elements that involve large sums of money, complicated circumstances or a majority of involved parties living abroad. In 1998, the Supreme People's Court promulgated the Memorandum of Certain National Courts' Working Conference on the Trial of Intellectual Property Cases (the Memorandum) which provides guidance (taking into account the characteristics of civil disputes over intellectual property and the professional quality of current judicial personnel) for issues regarding judicial procedure and application of law in intellectual property cases such as scope of admission and jurisdiction. The Memorandum provides that disputes over the ownership of, infringement of, and contracts involving trade secrets are all within the scope of civil disputes regarding intellectual property. In respect of civil disputes regarding intellectual property, except for a few basic courts which have established specialized intellectual property tribunals and may have jurisdiction as the court of first instance, the intermediate court, if so determined by the high court (taking into consideration the circumstances of the case) is the court of first instance for these types of cases. Thus, since 1998, the majority of civil disputes involving trade secrets have been tried by the intermediate courts of provincial capitals as the courts of first instance. However, the integrity of the entire system must be considered when considering adjustment to current policy. Inconsistency in the legal framework for the protection of trade secrets has arisen from the fact that, at present, the hierarchical jurisdiction of civil cases involving trade secrets, as well as that of criminal cases, is not synchronised. The Criminal Procedure Law in China provides that the intermediate people's courts have jurisdiction as courts of first instance over criminal cases punishable by life imprisonment or by death and over criminal cases involving foreign elements (Article 20). Cases involving trade secret infringement fall within the jurisdiction of basic people's courts as the court of first instance.

Thus, it appears that there is inconsistency regarding the trial of trade secret cases in that, while simple (i.e., civil) cases must be tried by intermediate courts more complicated (i.e., criminal) cases might be tried by basic courts. Compared to civil remedy, criminal remedy is more serious and involves not only economic punishment such as fines, but also deprivation and restriction of the personal liberty of a defendant and penalties not only for the entity which has conducted infringement, but also for its key management personnel. Therefore, the use of criminal remedy for the purpose of punishing crimes, in terms of the sum of money involved, the degree of complexity and the seriousness of the circumstances, is much more important than the use of civil remedy for the purpose of compensating a right holder. Furthermore, since difficult issues such as defining trade secrets, collecting evidence and procedural guarantees are involved, civil trade secret cases are heard by collegial panels in the intermediate courts.[6] In contrast, judges in the basic courts often lack experience. Therefore, inconsistency in respect of misplaced hierarchical jurisdiction will have a direct negative impact on the quality of the trial of criminal cases involving trade secrets, making it easier for certain parties to bring malicious lawsuits.

C. The Function and Status of Criminal Penalties in the Protection of Trade Secrets Must Be Clarified

At present, the protection of trade secrets under criminal law is one of the key issues attracting the attention of legal scholars in China. Although the number of criminal cases involving infringement of trade secrets is still relatively small, it has been rising continuously in recent years. According to statistics, from 1998 to 2002, the number of cases involving trade secret infringement investigated by the police at various levels exceeded five-hundred, accounting for nine per cent of all criminal cases of intellectual property infringement and involving CNY six-hundred million, which accounted for thirty-two per cent of all the money involved in criminal cases

6. Collegial panels are the basic units in each court. They are not permanent bodies but organized to adjudicate individual cases. A collegial panel is composed of three to seven judges, the number of which must be odd. Simple civil cases, economic cases, minor criminal cases and cases that are otherwise provided for in law can be tried by a single judge.

involving intellectual property infringement.[7] From 2000 to 2003, second only to trademark infringement crimes (75%), the courts at various levels adjudicated 1,369 criminal cases of intellectual property infringement involving 722 people, among which 8.6% were crimes of trade secret infringement.[8] Cases involving infringement of know-how comprise the majority of criminal cases of trade secret infringement.

It is necessary to protect trade secrets using the criminal law. However, criminal cases involving trade secrets in China have involved many incidents of abuse of the criminal law or arbitrary criminalization of acts of infringement. The courts in certain jurisdictions, acting as 'hit men' for business competitors, have used their authority to battle crime to promote local protectionism. In order to protect local businesses, they have been interfering in economic disputes in the name of the criminal law by bringing charges of trade secret infringement with insufficient evidence. The Criminal Law is an important tool for protecting society and for maintaining market order and fair competition which, if abused, can become a weapon for those seeking to conduct unfair competition and will have a negative impact on the healthy development of the socialist market economy.

Two factors that cause this phenomenon have been identified by scholars:

(a) the traditional trend of the wide application of the criminal law has led to the presumption that it is the cure for all sorts of problems and can be used without hesitation;
(b) the lack of independence of the judiciary from local governments has led to the abuse of criminal procedure to attack competitors or to prevent the normal transfer of personnel in order to protect local economic interests.[9]

In addition, defects in Chinese legislation, especially in provisions related to the Criminal Law, are also the cause of the above-mentioned phenomenon. These defects include:

(a) Ambiguity exists regarding the definition of 'serious losses'.

Under Chinese law, the line between general activities of infringement and the crime of trade secret infringement is drawn based upon the degree or amount of loss suffered by a right holder. The crime of trade secret infringement in the current Criminal Law refers to acts that violate the laws of the state for the protection of trade secrets by infringing on trade secrets and causing serious loss to a right holder. Since breach of the Law against Unfair Competition is a prerequisite for an act to be deemed the crime of trade secret infringement, such acts share certain common characteristics with the act of civil infringement of trade secrets.

Firstly, the perpetrators of both acts have the same characteristics, (i.e., natural persons above the age of sixteen having legal capacity and legal

7. <www.chinaiprlaw.cn/file/200412213887.html>, 6 January 2008.
8. The Third Civil Chamber of the Supreme People's Court, *Guidance and Reference for Intellectual Property Trials* (Vol. 8) (Beijing, Law Press, 2004), p.3.
9. Professor You, Wei, speech at the Conference on Application of Law on Crimes of Trade Secret Infringement, <www.sfyj.org/list.asp?unid=722>, 6 January 2008.

persons or non-legal person organizations having legal capacity). 'Natural persons' include employees of the right holder as well as experts who have acquired trade secrets through their working relationship with the right holder.

Secondly, the infringing activities conducted by these infringers are similar. They include obtaining trade secrets from a right holder through theft, enticement, coercion or other illegitimate means; disclosing, using or allowing others to use trade secrets obtained through the illegitimate means identified above; disclosing, using or allowing others to use the trade secrets in one's possession in breach of a contractual obligation of confidentiality or an obligation of confidentiality imposed by the right holder of the trade secret; and activities of third parties who acquire trade secrets and who know or should know that the illegal activities mentioned in the previous sections were used to obtain, use or disclose the trade secret of another.[10] The first three activities are direct infringement of trade secrets involving acquisition by the infringer of those trade secrets from the right holder through legitimate or illegitimate means. The latter activity refers to the acts of third parties indirectly infringing trade secrets.

Thirdly, intentional infringement as well as infringement due to the negligence of third parties constitutes a crime. Article 219 of the Criminal Law provides that whosoever engages in the abovementioned activities and infringes on the trade secrets of another, causing serious loss to the right holder of the trade secrets, shall, in cases where the loss suffered by the right holder is serious, be sentenced to probation or to a term of imprisonment of not more than three years and/or fined. In cases where the loss suffered by a right holder is extremely serious, an infringer can be sentenced to a term of imprisonment of not less than three years but not more than seven years and/or fined. Article 12(6) of the Interpretation on Several Issues Concerning the Application of Law in Trials of Theft Cases, adopted by the Supreme Court in 1998, clearly provides that the theft of trade secrets such as technical achievements shall be punished in accordance with Article 219 of the Criminal Law. Article 65 of the Regulation on the Threshold of Prosecuting Economic Crimes, adopted by the Supreme People's Procuratorate and the Ministry of Public Security on 18 April 2001, provides that infringement of trade secrets shall be prosecuted if the economic loss suffered by the right holder is estimated to be more than half a million Yuan, if the right holder has been forced into bankruptcy, or if there have been other serious consequences. However, this regulation is neither a legislative nor a judicial interpretation and, as such, the courts are not bound to follow its guidance.

Consequently, in 2004 the Supreme People's Court and the Supreme People's Procuratorate jointly enacted the Interpretation on Several Issues Concerning the Application of Law in Handling Criminal Cases Involving Intellectual Property in order to provide guidance for the procuratorates and

10. See Article 219 of Criminal Law and Article 10 of the Law against Unfair Competition of the People's Republic of China (1993).

the courts in the prosecution and adjudication of crimes of trade secret infringement in accordance with the Criminal Law. The Interpretation provides detailed explanations for related provisions of the Criminal Law. Article 7 therein explains circumstances under which infringement of trade secrets will cause the right holder 'serious losses' and 'extremely serious consequences' as provided for in the Criminal Law (i.e., if the infringement which is prohibited by law has caused a right holder to suffer a loss exceeding the sum of CNY 500,000, 'serious loss' of the right holder shall be established; if the infringement has caused the right holder to suffer a loss exceeding the sum of CNY 2.5 million, 'extremely serious consequences' shall be identified.) Obviously, the Interpretation has adopted the threshold of the abovementioned Regulation on the Threshold of Prosecuting Economic Crimes, and drawn a line between activity which is considered criminal and infringement that does not rise to the level of a crime. However, it remains unclear in the Interpretation whether a loss amounting to CNY 500,000 refers to the value of a trade secret and the media bearing said secret or to an actual loss of interest suffered by the right holder. Therefore, the question of how to establish the value of losses remains problematic in judicial practice.

(b) Assessing 'serious loss' is difficult.

Due to the special nature of trade secrets, it is hard for some right holders to establish the value of their losses. Article 20 of the Law against Unfair Competition provides that if the loss of a right holder is difficult to establish, the sum of compensation shall be equal to the profit gained by the infringer during the period of the infringement. Consequently, in the trial of criminal cases of trade secret infringement some procuratorates and courts, when the right holder cannot provide the value of its actual loss, have been using the profit gained by the infringer as the basis of assessing the loss of the right holder and deciding whether the infringement constitutes a crime. It is argued that this approach has confused criminal and civil principles. The loss of the right holder and the gain of the infringer are two completely different concepts, the scope of which is not identical. Equating the loss of a right holder to the gain of an infringer is inconsistent with the basic principle of the criminal law – *Nulla poena sine lege*. The direct consequence of this equation is that the scope of the application of the criminal law has been widened.

Traditionally, the Criminal Law in China has mainly targeted those acts that cause serious harm to society, its citizens and their property. Therefore, in the Criminal Law, many crimes are crimes of consequence. Only when a perpetrator has conducted acts prohibited by law and caused serious losses to society or others will his acts be punishable by the Criminal Law. However, it is worth considering whether this doctrine is adequate for the protection of intellectual property. Classifying trade secret infringement as a crime of consequence and the ambiguity surrounding the assessment of such consequences have caused not only undesirable flexibility regarding the key issue of differentiating crimes from general infringement, but also difficulty in determining and prosecuting crimes regarding trade secret infringement.

In conclusion, in light of the legislation of other countries, in order to improve the system of trade secret protection in China its legislature should make great effort to accomplish the following:

Firstly, improve current legislation in China regarding employment relationships and clarify the obligation of confidentiality of employees. For example, promulgate employment contract law and include explicit provisions regarding confidentiality obligations and non-competition obligations of employees during and following employment. Also, it should be expressly stated that certain obligations during employment may not be exempted except through express covenants between parties. At the same time, it should be provided that the obligation of ex-employees to keep confidential the secret information of their previous employers (trade secrets are excluded) and not to compete should be established on the basis of covenants with those employers. The Employment Contract Law should provide a reasonable basis for constraining competition following employment, which should include protected interests, reasonable duration (one year is preferred) and compensation for ex-employees if they cannot find proper employment due to such restrictions.

Secondly, accelerate the process of approving the draft of the Trade Secret Law, which should contain a definition for trade secrets, the scope of trade secrets, acts of infringement of trade secrets and the liability for infringement of trade secrets. It should also establish injunctive measures so as to prevent or stop infringement of trade secrets.

Thirdly, enhance existing criminal penalties for infringement of trade secrets. For example, differentiate crimes of infringement and general infringement from industrial espionage and simple theft of trade secrets by individuals.

Fourthly, establish and perfect legislation regarding foreign-related trade secrets. For example, provide rules for choice of law applicable to foreign-related confidentiality agreements and foreign-related non-competition agreements in employment contract law. In addition, properly confine the scope of the application of labour law and provide specific content and scope of mandatory rules applied to foreign-related labour contract disputes.

Over the past thirty years, following the country's reform and opening up to the world, China has achieved an average 9% annual economic growth. In 2004, its total import and export volume surpassed one trillion US dollars for the first time in history. With the achievements of rapid economic development brought by reform and opening up, there has arisen in China more and more doubt regarding its original economic development policy, especially the industrial development policy of 'exchange markets for technology'[11] and 'follow the ways of major industrialized countries'.[12]

---

11. On 25 March 1994, the sixteenth Executive Meeting of the State Council reviewed and passed the *Outline of National Industrial Policies* for the 1990s, which provides that '[in] order to exchange key technologies and equipment, some sectors of the domestic markets will be conditionally opened up'.
12. The comparative advantages theory of major industrial countries originated out of concern for the pattern of international trade. Impacted by the comparative advantages theory of

Previously, the industrial development of China depended more on high consumption of resources and a cheap and intensive labour force. The economic growth of China has, so far, not been achieved through technological innovation. With exports increasing annually, the exportation of low value-added products is becoming more and more constrained by factors such as energy, resources, and environment,[13] threatening further economic development. The dream of being the 'factory to the world,' however, has rapidly brought China into contact with major players in international technology circles.

The policy of 'exchange markets for technology' has resulted in China being heavily dependent on foreign technology and resources. Firstly, foreign-invested enterprises have become the major export enterprises within China's hi-tech industries. The percentage of hi-tech export products of foreign-invested enterprises increased from 70.5% in 1996 to 81.5% in 2001 and to 82.2% in 2002. Secondly, China is still lacking in technology, independent R&D and innovation. Many industrial technologies are still supplied by foreign countries and key technologies and equipment within many industries are still heavily reliant on foreign enterprises. Since China began to implement its Patent Law in 1985, the State Patent Office of the PRC has accepted over 280,000 patent applications, among which foreign applications comprise fifty-four per cent. Particularly, foreign applications for electronic technologies have reached eighty to ninety per cent.[14] Thirdly, China's economic development has come to rely more and more on the consumption of resources and imported raw materials. Though GDP increased 9.2% in 2004, the cost of that growth was consumption of thirty-one per cent of the raw coal, 7.4% of the oil, twenty-seven per cent of the iron and steel and over fourty per cent of the cement of the world. The degree of China's foreign-dependence for supply of fifteen raw materials of non-ferrous metals increased from fifteen per cent in 1995 to fifty per cent in 2003 and it is estimated that China's foreign-dependence on oil will be over sixty per cent by 2020. All developed countries have tried to keep their foreign-dependence under thirty per cent (e.g., below

---

international trade, for a long time China has regarded the 'labour cost advantage' as its 'comparative advantage' in the international trade. Subsequently, many export-oriented, labour-intensive, and capital-intensive enterprises, such as textile factories were established in China. The reason for this condition is that such products belong to the category of the manufacturing industry, which generally do not require high technology but have a strong capacity for substitution and can enhance the economic development of comparatively technologically backward countries. Please refer to Zhou Qiren 'Changes in Cost Advantages of the Chinese Manufacturing Industry', (2 May 2005) *Economic Report of the 21st Century*, 18. Or please refer to Wang Shihao 'Jump over the Trap of Comparative Advantages' (28 February 2006) *Guangming Daily*, 10.

13. China's import and export volume totalled one trillion US dollars in 2004, the third highest in the world, among which, total export of goods were USD 593.4 billion, an increase of 35.4% compared to the same period of the previous year. Source: Zhang Rui, 'From Chinese Manufacturing to Chinese Innovation' (24 August 2005) *Shanghai Security News*, A5.
14. Wang Junxiu, Liu Shuanggui and Qi Ou, 'The New Globalization: A Report on the Study of China's Strategic Criterion of Hi-tech' </www.ihns.ac.cn/zhanlue/wencong.htm>, 6 January 2008. The Authors are The Natural Science History Research Institute of Chinese Academy of Science.

twenty-seven per cent in the US and below thirty per cent in Japan).[15] Fourthly, China's investment in R&D comprises quite a small percentage of its GDP. Compared to three per cent in Japan and in the US, 4.7% in Israel and three per cent for European Union members, China's investment in R&D is only 1.32% of its GDP. Ninety-nine per cent of invention patents worldwide are, in fact, controlled by the twenty top innovation-oriented countries and, rather than falling, this percentage has been steadily increasing in recent years.[16]

In an attempt to change this situation, on 9 February 2005 the State Council promulgated the Outline of the National Program for Long- and Medium-Term Scientific and Technological Development. The general goals of scientific and technological development in China till 2020 included in the Outline can be summarized as follows: Independent innovation will be obviously strengthened and the capacity for science and technology to contribute to economic and social development and the safeguarding of state security will be enhanced so as to provide powerful support for building a moderately prosperous society in all respects. The strength of basic research and research in cutting-edge disciplines will be greatly improved and a number of scientific and technological achievements will be reached that have important impact in the world. China will thereby become a member of the community of innovation-oriented countries, thus providing the foundation for it to become a scientifically and technologically strong country by the middle of the twenty-first century.[17] As a key factor of industrial evolution and improvement of the competitive capability of the country, and also as a guideline for a new pattern for industrialization, the national policy of independent innovation has determined the strategic conversion of China's economic development from being resource-based to innovation-oriented and from foreign technology-dependent to independently innovative.

Improvement of its capacity for independent innovation and the evolution of China from the 'factory to the world' to an innovation-oriented nation, creating a social environment in which enterprises are encouraged to be independent and innovative, will be based on the accumulation of independent intellectual property and the development of an effective system for utilizing that intellectual property. Protecting intellectual property rights in China will encourage and leverage its growing capacity for independent innovation that will not only improve and upgrade its industrial structure, but will finally bring about change in its pattern of economic growth. The process of technological innovation is one from research and development to industrialization and commercialization. Independent innovation will be reflected in various products that will be pushed into the market in the long run. Effective protection of intellectual property rights is an important means to encourage market competition, and will be the basis for independent innovation.

---

15. Qiu Huihui and Lei Zhonghui, 'The Chinese Path of a scientifically and Technologically Strong Country' (13 January 2006) *Economic Report of the 21st Century*, 5.
16. Qiu Huihui, 'Two Thousand Scholars Reshape Technological Views' (20 June 2005) *Economic Report of the 21st Century*, 19.
17. <www.most.gov.cn/ztzl/qgkjdh/qgkjdhzywj/t20060209_28638.htm>, 6 January 2008.

The initial purpose of trade secret protection in China was to meet the standards necessary for entry into the WTO as well as to attract foreign investment. Nevertheless, as its pattern of economic growth changes and more and more Chinese enterprises participate in international competition, the primary goal of the protection of trade secrets will be to leverage the capacity of the nation and its enterprises for technological innovation to further raise the status of its industries and to obtain competitive advantage and profit in the international marketplace. As a nation that is becoming wealthier and stronger, China must continue to perfect its legal system for the protection of trade secrets, depending closely on technological innovation to gradually minimize its consumption of natural resources and the destruction of its ecological environment. Indeed, China should gradually break away from dependence on foreign investment and foreign technology and close the gap between regional and class differences. For all of the aforementioned reasons, the author sincerely hopes that this book will contribute to perfecting a system of trade secret protection and to the development of a culture of respect for intellectual property rights[18] in China and that it will stimulate increased communication between academics around the world and aid them in coming to a greater understanding of the trade secrets protection system in the People's Republic of China.

18. 'Culture of respect for Intellectual property rights' refers to a general psychological phenomenon of mankind with relation to intellectual property rights and issues impacting upon intellectual property rights in the course of related activities, mainly the recognition of, attitude toward, belief in and values regarding intellectual property rights and patterns of behaviour concerning protection of intellectual property rights. See Ma Weiye, 'On Culture and Intellectual Property Right Culture' <www.cnipr.com/zsyd/xslw/qita/t20051028_57686.htm> 6 January 2008.

Appendix 1

List of Chinese Research Treatises on the Science of Law on Trade Secrets from 1994 to 2005

Serial No.	***Book Name***	***Author***	***Name of the Publishing House***	***Publishing Time***	***Total Pages***
1	Legal Protection of Trade Secrets	Zhang Yurui	Patent Documents Publishing House	1994	254
2	Analyses of Status Quo of Legal System for Trade Secrets and Related Cases	Editing Committee of the Series of Books on the Legal System of Business	China Legal System Publishing House	1995	237
3	Sharp Implements for Business Warfare: Acquisition and Protection of Trade Secrets	Bai Yunfei	China Material Publishing House	1997	236

***Table** (continued)*

Serial No.	Book Name	Author	Name of the Publishing House	Publishing Time	Total Pages
4	Have Trade Secrets Stolen and Protected	Gu Min	Foreign Economic and Trade University Publishing House	1998	78
5	The Era of Trade Secrets	Li Jun	Gold Wall Press	1998	229
6	Science of Law on Trade Secrets	Zhang Yurui	China Legal System Publishing House	1999	778
7	Principles of the Law on the Protection of Trade Secrets	Kong Xiangjun	China Legal System Publishing House	1999	450
8	Analyses of Cases on the Protection of Trade Secrets	Su Huchao	Economic Publishing House of Shanxi Province	1999	224
9	A Talk about Laws on Trade Secrets	Lu Heyun	Hubei People's Publishing House	2000	421
10	A Summary of Trade Secrets and Relevant Procedural Preservation	Sun Ou	Intellectual Property Publishing House	2000	206
11	Keep Your Trade Secrets	Cai Jianwen	Economic Daily	2000	407

Table (continued)

Serial No.	Book Name	Author	Name of the Publishing House	Publishing Time	Total Pages
12	A Comparative Study of Secrecy Laws	Subject Group of the Comparative Research of Secrecy Laws	Gold Wall Press	2001	389
13	A Practical Manual for the Protection Trade Secrets	Wang Aibo	Gold Wall Press	2001	277
14	A Practical Book on the Management of the Construction of Enterprises Comparative Intelligence Systems and the Protection of Trade Secrets	Xu Yaqun	Audio and Video Publishing House of Anhui Province	2003	1454
15	Legal Practice of Enterprise Trade Secrets Protection	Xu Haifeng	China Machine Press	2004	316
16	Handling Records of Cases on Trade Secrets	Zhu Miaochun	Intellectual Property Publishing House	2004	516
17	Trade Secret Protection Law	Ni Cailong	Publishing House of Shanghai University	2005	297

***Table** (continued)*

Serial No.	***Book Name***	***Author***	***Name of the Publishing House***	***Publishing Time***	***Total Pages***
18	Comparative Studies on Trade Secrets Law	Dai Yongsheng	Publishing House of East China Normal University	2005	243
19	Trade Secrets and Commercial Bribery: Legal Risks and Solutions	Zhang Yurui	Law Press	2005	386

Appendix 2

List of Chinese Research Treatises on the Science of Law on Trade Secrets from 1994 to 2005

Serial No.	***Book Name***	***Author***	***Name of the Publishing House***	***Publishing Time***	***Related Pages***
1	Series of Treatises on Civil and Commercial Law, Volume 6.	Edited by Liang Huixing	Law Press	1996	43
2	The Application and Improvement of Unfair Competition Law	Kong Xiangjun	Law Press	1998	171
3	Practical Cases of Unfair Competition Law	Written by Cao Qunjin et al.	Hunan People's Publishing House	1998	16
4	Chinese Intellectual Property Right Issues in the Coming twenty-first Century	Edited by Kongping	Law Press	1998	21

Table *(continued)*

Serial No.	**Book Name**	**Author**	**Name of the Publishing House**	**Publishing Time**	**Related Pages**
5	Representations of Famous Intellectual Property Right Cases	Intellectual Property Right Commission of Beijing Lawyers' Association	Law Press	1999	335
6	Legal Issues in the Evaluation of the Intellectual Property Rights	Edited by Zheng Chengsi	Law Press	1999	26
7	Judges' Views on Intellectual Property Right	Edited by Chen Xu	Law Press	1999	72
8	High and New Technology and Intellectual Property Right Law	Chen Chuanfu	Publishing House of Wuhan University	2000	55
9	Knowledge Economy and Intellectual Property Right Law	Edited by Zhang Naigen and Lu Fei	Publishing House of Fudan University	2000	26
10	WTO and Chinese Judicial Trials	Edited by Cao Jianming	Law Press	2001	45
11	A New Study on the Unfair Competition Law	Kong Xiangjun	Publishing House of People's Courts	2001	96

Table (continued)

Serial No.	Book Name	Author	Name of the Publishing House	Publishing Time	Related Pages
12	An Article by Article Explanation of WTO Intellectual Property Agreements	Zheng Chengsi	Fangzheng Publishing House of China	2001	129
13	Research on Issues of WTO and Chinese Legal System	Edited by Cao Jianming	Publishing House of People's Courts	2001	23
14	Fundamentals of Intellectual Property Law	Edited by Liu Chunmao	Intellectual Property Publishing House	2002	42
15	Protection of Intellectual Property Rights and Damages for Infringement	Han Liling	China Democracy and Legal System Publishing House	2002	17
16	The Intellectual Property Right Law towards the Knowledge Economy Era	Wu Handong, Hu Kaizhong	Law Press	2002	36
17	Protection of Intellectual Property Rights and Technological Innovation	Edited by Liu Yue E	Intellectual Property Publishing House	2002	26

Table *(continued)*

Serial No.	***Book Name***	***Author***	***Name of the Publishing House***	***Publishing Time***	***Related Pages***
18	Protective System for Intellectual Property Rights	Edited by Du Wenjuan	Publishing House of Beijing University of Technology	2003	8
19	Studies on the Civil Litigation of Intellectual Property Litigation	Zhang Geng	Law Press	2004	22
20	Studies on the Hot Issues of Intellectual Property Rights	Yang Xiaochun, Yang Lihua	Publishing House of Chinese People's Public Security University	2004	63
21	Questions and Answers for the Application of Intellectual Property Right Laws	Jiang Zhipei	Publishing House of People's Courts	2004	10
22	Intellectual Property Rights and Market Competition	Edited by Zhang Yumin	Law Press	2005	46
23	Ethical Explanation of Competitive Orders: Research on the Law against Unfair Competition	Xie Xiaoyao	Law Press	2005	43

Selected Bibliography

Atiyah, P.S. *Introduction to Law of Contract*. 15th ed. Chinese version. Beijing: Law Press, 2002.

Baohua, D. *A General Introduction to the Social Law*. Beijing: China University of Political Science and Law Publishing House, 2001.

Baohua, D. *On the Labour Law*. Shanghai: Shanghai World Publishing House, 1999.

Bauner, D.L. & J.C. Poindexter. *Legal Environment of Business in the Information Age*. New York: McGraw-Hill, 2004.

Bayles, M.D. *Principles of Law: A Normative Analysis*. Beijing: Encyclopedia of China Publishing House, 1996.

Bell, D. *The Cultural Contradictions of Capitalism*. New York: Basic Books, 1978.

Bingzhi, Z. *Judicial Countermeasures to Difficult Issues of the Crime of Encroachment upon Intellectual Property Rights*. Chang Chun: Jilin University People's Press, 2000.

Blakeney, M. *Trade Related Aspects of Intellectual Property Rights: A Concise Guide to the Trips Agreement*. London: Sweet & Maxwell, 1996.

Blanpain, R. *European Labour Law*. The Hague: Kluwer Law International, 2000.

Bodenheimer, E. *Jurisprudence: The Philosophy and Method of the Law* (Chinese version). Beijing: China University of Political Science and Law Press, 1998.

Brearley, K. & S. Bloch. *Employment Covenants and Confidential Information: Law, Practice and Technique*. London: Butterworths, 1999.

Brilmayer, L. & J. Goldsmith. *Conflict of Laws: Cases and Materials*. 15th ed. New York: Aspen Publishers, 2002.

Budden, M.C. *Protecting Trade Secrets under the Uniform Trade Secrets Act*. London: Quorum Books, 1996.

Buxton, L.-A. *Employment Law in Europe: A Country by Country Guide for Employers*. Hampshire: Gower House, 1995.

Chandler, A. *Employment Law Library Information: Protection Ownership and Rights*. London: Blackstone Press, 1993.
Chengsi, Z. *One by One Explanation of WTO Intellectual Property Treaty*. Beijing: China Fang Zheng Publishing House, 2002.
Cheshire & North, *Private International Law*. 13th ed. London: Butterworths, 1999.
China Encyclopaedia Law. Beijing: Encyclopaedia of China Publishing House, 1988.
Chisum, D. & M.A. Jacobs. *Understanding Intellectual Property Law*. Matthew Bender, 1992.
Chuanfu, C. *High and New Technologies and Laws on the Intellectual Property*. Wu Han: The Publishing House of Wu Han University, 2000.
Clark, L.S., R.J. Aalberts & P.D. Kinder. *Law and Business: The Regulatory Environment*. 4th ed. New York: McGraw-Hill, 1994.
Coleman, A. *The Legal Protection of Trade Secrets*. London: Sweet & Maxwell, 1992.
The Concise Encyclopedia Britannica. Beijing: Encyclopedia of China Publishing House, 1985.
Dawei, P. & L. Wenqi. *A Guide to Common Law System*. Beijing: Law Press, 2000.
Department of Population and Employment Statistics. *China Labour Statistical 2005*. People's Republic of China: National Bureau of Statistics, Department of Planning and Finance, Ministry of Labour and Social Security, 2005.
Dessler, G. *Essentials of Human Resource Management* (second version). Beijing: People's University of China Publishing House, 2004.
Dratler, J. Jr. & D. Conway-Jones, *Intellectual Property Law: Commercial Creative and Industrial Property*. New York: New York Law Publishing Company, 1991.
Editing Committee of the Series of Books on the Legal System of Trade Secret. *Analyses of Status Quo of Legal Systems for Trade Secret and Relevant Cases*. Beijing: China Law Press, 1995.
Fraumann, E. & J. Koletar. *Trade Secret Safeguards*. American Society for Industrial Security, 1999.
Friedman, G., M. Friedman, C. Chapman & J. Baker. *The Intelligence Edge: How to Profit in the Information Age* (Chinese version). Shanghai: Shanghai People's Publishing House, 1999.
Garner, B.A. (ed.). *Black's Law Dictionary*. 17th ed. St. Paul, Minnesota: West Group,1999.
Gervais, D. *The TRIPS Agreement: Drafting History and Analysis*. London: Sweet & Maxwell, 1998.
Gorman, R.A. *Basic Text on Labour Law: Unionization and Collective Bargaining*. Chinese version. Beijing: China University of Politics and Law Press, 2003.
Government of China. *Status Quo of the IP Protection in China*. A white book. 1994.

Guangliang, Z. *Remedies for Intellectual Property Rights.* Beijing: Law Press, 2003.
Guohua, S. & Z, Jingwen, *Jurisprudence*, Beijing: People University Press, 2004.
Gurgess, P. (ed.). *Contracts and Terms and Conditions of Employment.* London: Institute of Personnel and Development, 1995.
Haibin, T. *How to Protect Trade Secrets in the US.* Beijing: Law Press, 1998.
Harrison, J.L. *Law and Economics.* 2nd ed. St. Paul, Minnesota: West Group, 2000.
Herring, J. *Criminal Law.* 3rd ed. Houndmills: Palgrave MacMillan, 2002.
Herth, C. (ed.). *Intellectual Property Law in Asia.* (The Hague: Kluwer Law International, 2003.
Heyun, L. *A Discourse on Laws Regarding Trade Secrets.* Bao Din: People's Publishing House of Hubei, 2000.
Horn, N., H, Kotz & H.G. Leser. *German Private and Commercial Law: An Introduction.* Oxford: Clarendon Press, 1982. The Chinese version of this book, translated by C. Jian, was published by Encyclopedia of China Publishing House, Shanghai, 1999.
Huai, G. (ed.). *Introduction to the Labour Law of the People's Republic of China.* Beijing: Law Press, 1994.
Huixing, L. *Introduction of Civil Law.* Beijing: Law Press, 1996.
Hull, J. *Commercial Secrecy: Law and Practice.* London: Sweet & Maxwell, 1998.
Huocan, W. *WTO and Intellectual Property Disputes.* Shanghai: Shanghai People's Publishing House, 2001.
Ito, M. *Xiandai Jingji De Tuibian.* Chinese version. Beijing: Shanghai University of Finance and Economy Publishing House, 1999.
Jager, M.F. *Trade Secrets Law.* St. Paul, Minnesota: West Group, 1999.
Jefferson, M. *Criminal Law.* 15th ed. Searson Education, 2001.
Jiandong, S. *Study of German Law against Unfair Competition.* Beijing: People University Publishing House, 2001.
Jianyuan, C. *Contract Law.* Beijing: Law Press, 1996.
Jianzhi, D. & C. Xu. *A Study on the Compensation for Damages on the Intellectual Property.* Beijing: Law Press, 1997.
Jingwen, Z. *A Challenge to the Traditional Western Laws: The Critical Legal Studies Movement in America.* Beijing: China Prosecution Publishing House, 1996.
Jun, L. *The Era of Trade Secret.* Beijing: Jincheng Publishing House, 1998.
Junyi, Z. & Y. Zhigang. *Shanghai Employment Report 1995-2000.* Shanghai: Shanghai People's Publishing House: 2001.
Kai, C. (ed.). *Labour Relations Science.* Beijing: China Labour & Social Security Publishing House, 2005.
Kangsheng, H. & L. Fucheng. *Interpretation of the Criminal Law of the People's Republic of China.* Beijing: Law Press, 1997.
Lavery, P. *Commercial Secrets.* London: Sweet & Maxwell, 1996.
Law Institute of Chinese Academy of Social Sciences. *Law Dictionary.* Beijing: Law Press, 2003.

Law of China Cyclopaedia. Beijing: China Encyclopaedia Press,1984.

Laycock, D. *Modern American Remedies: Cases and Materials.* Beijing: CITIC Publishing House, 2003.

Licheng, M. & L. Zhijun. *Confrontation – Records of the Third Time Ideological Emancipation of Modern China.* Beijing: Today's China Publishing House, 1998.

Liming, W. & Yang Lixin, *Tort Law.* Beijing: Law Press, 1996.

Locke, J. *Two Treatises Of Civil Government.* Book II, Chinese version. Beijing: The Commercial Press, 2004.

Loewy, A.H. *Criminal Law.* 4th ed. St. Paul, Minnesota: West Group, 2003.

Mallor, J.P., A.J. Barnes, T. Bowers, M.J. Phillips & A.W. Langvardt. *Business Law and the Regulatory Environment: Concepts and Cases.* 11th ed. New York: McGraw-Hill, 2001.

Mandel, E. *Late Capitalism.* London: NLB, 1975.

McAdams, T. *Law, Business, and Society.* 16th ed. New York: McGraw-Hill, 2001.

Milgrim, R.M. *Milgrim on Trade Secrets.* New York: Matthew Bender, 1984.

Milne, A.J.M. *Human Rights and Human Diversity: An Essay in the Philosophy of Human Rights.* Chinese version. Beijing: Encyclopedia of China Publishing House, 1995.

Modern Japanese Enterprise System. Chinese version. Beijing: Economic Science Publishing House, 1995.

Naigen, Z. & L. Fei. *Intellectual Economy and the Intellectual Property Law.* Shanghai: The Publishing House of Fudan University, 2000.

The No. 3 Civil Tribunal of the Supreme People's Court of the PRC (eds). *The Guide and Reference for Intellectual Property Trials.* Vol. 8. Beijing: Law Press, 2004.

Ou, S. *A Summary of Trade Secret and Relevant Procedural Preservation.* Beijing: Intellectual Property Publishing House, 2000.

PLI Course Handbook Series. *Protecting Trade Secrets.* 1981.

Ran, T. & J. Hua. *Questions and Answers on Practical Affairs about the Copyright Law of the PRC.* Beijing: Law Press, 2002.

Reed, O.L., P.J. Shedd, J.W. Morehead & R.N. Corley. *The Legal and Regulatory Environment of Business.* 12th ed. New York: McGraw-Hill, 2002.

Renstorm, P.G. *The American Law Dictionary.* Chinese version. Beijing: China University of Politics and Law Publishing House, 1998.

Schwartz, B. *The Law in America: A History.* Chinese version. Beijing: China University of Political Science and Law Publishing House, 1997.

Shangkuan, S. *An Introduction to Labour Law.* Taiwan: Taiwan Province Zhengda Publishing House, 1978.

Sinha, S.P. *Jurisprudence: Legal Philosophy.* St. Paul, Minnesota: West Publishing, 1993.

Songyou, H. (ed.). *Comprehension and Application of Judicial Interpretation on Civil Litigation Evidence.* Beijing: Law Press, 2002.

Spinello, R.A. *Ethical Aspects of Information Technology*. Chinese version. Beijing: 1999. Translated by L. Gao, Central Compilation and Translation Press.

Subject Group of the Comparative Research of Secrecy Laws. *Comparative Research of Secrecy Laws.* Beijing: Jincheng Publishing House, 2001.

Taylor, J.F.A. *The Masks of Society: An Inquiry into the Covenants of Civilization.* New York: Irvington Publishers, 1966.

Torremans, P. *Intellectual Property Law.* London: Oxford University Press, 2005.

Torremans, P. & J. Holyoak, *Intellectual Property Law.* London: Butterworths, 2001.

Walker, D.M. *The Oxford Companion to Law.* Chinese version. Beijing: The Law Press, 2003. (The English version of this book was originally published in English by Oxford University Press in 1980.)

Watal, J. *Intellectual Property Rights in the WTO and Developing Countries.* The Hague: Kluwer Law International, 2001.

Xiangjun, K. *Application and Perfection of Anti-Unfair Competition Law.* Beijing: Law Press, 1995.

Xiangjun, K. *Principles of the Law on the Protection of Trade Secret.* Beijing: China System Publishing House, 1999.

Xiaohu, Y. *Constitutionalism Road of New China.* Shanghai: Shanghai Jiao Tong University Press, 2000.

Yi, C. (ed.). *Theory of Civil Procedure Law.* Beijing: China University of Politics and Law Press, 1999.

Yurui, Z. *200 Subjects on the Application and Protection of Trade Secrets.* Beijing: People's Publishing House, 1996.

Yurui, Z. *Legal Protection of Trade Secrets.* Beijing: Patent Literature Publishing House, 1994.

Yurui, Z. *Science of Law on Trade Secrets.* Beijing: China Law Press, 1999.

Zhipei, J. *Legal Studies On Intellectual Property Protection in China after Entry to WTO.* Beijing: Chinese People's Publishing House, 2002.

List of Statutes of People's Republic of China

Archives Law of the People's Republic of China 1987 (Revised in 1996) (中华人民共和国档案法)

Accounting Law of the People's Republic of China 1993 (中华人民共和国会计法)

Administrative Procedure Law of the People's Republic of China 1989 (中华人民共和国行政诉讼法)

Amendments to the Interim Regulation on the Procedure of Administrative Penalty of Administration for Industry and Commerce promulgated by the State Administration for Industry and Commerce 2000 (工商行政管理机关行政处罚程序暂行规定)

Constitution of the People's Republic of China 1982 (中华人民共和国宪法)

Copyright Law of the People's Republic of China1990 (中华人民共和国版权法)

Civil Procedure Law of the People's Republic of China 1991 (中华人民共和国民事诉讼法)

Company Law of the People's Republic of China 1993 (Revised in 2004) (中华人民共和国公司法)

Circular on the Several Issues of the Flow of Employees in Enterprise1996 (关于企业职工流动若干问题的通知)

Criminal Procedure Law of the People's Republic of China 1996 (中华人民共和国刑事诉讼法)

Criminal Law of the People's Republic of China 1997 (中华人民共和国刑法)

Contract Law of the People's Republic of China 1999 (中华人民共和国合同法)

Copyright Law of the People's Republic of China 2001 (中华人民共和国版权法)

Certain Provisions of the Supreme People's Court on Evidence in Civil Procedures 2002 (最高人民法院关于民事诉讼证据的若干规定)

Explanations of the Supreme People's Court on Certain Issues of Application of Laws in Trial of Labour Dispute Cases promulgated by Supreme People's Court 2001 (最高人民法院关于审理劳动争议案件适用法律若干问题的解释)

General Principles of Civil Law of the People's Republic of China 1986 (中华人民共和国民法通则)

Law on Protecting State Secrets of the People's Republic of China 1989 (中华人民共和国保守国家秘密法)

Implementation Method on Law of the People's Republic of China on Guarding State Secrets 1990（中华人民共和国保守国家秘密法实施办法）

Interpretations of Certain Issues on Application of Laws to Cases of Theft jointly promulgated by the Supreme People's Court and Supreme People's Procuratorate on December 11
1992〔最高人民法院、最高人民检察院联合颁布的（关于办理盗窃案件具体应用法律的若干问题的解释）〕

Interpretation of the Supreme People's Court on Problems regarding the Ascertainment of Compensation Liability for Emotional Damages in Civil Torts 2001 (最高人民法院关于确定民事侵权精神损害赔偿责任若干问题的解释)

Interim Regulation on the Registration of Public Institutions 1998(Revised in 2004)(事业单位登记管理暂行条例)

Interpretation of Supreme People's Court and the Supreme People's Procuratorate regarding Certain Issues on the Specific Application of Laws to Treatment of Criminal Cases of Encroachment upon Intellectual Property Rights 2004
(最高人民法院、最高人民检察院关于办理侵犯知识产权刑事案件具体应用法律若干问题的解释)

Interpretation of the Supreme People's Court concerning Certain Issues on Application of Law for the Trial of Cases on Disputes over Technology Contracts 2005 (最高人民法院关于审理技术合同纠纷案件适用法律若干问题的解释)

Law against Unfair Competition 1993(中华人民共和国反不正当竞争法)

Law regarding the Protection of the Rights and Interests of Consumers1994(中华人民共和国消费者权益保护法)

Law of the People's Republic of China on Commercial Banks 1995 (Revised in 2003) (中华人民共和国商业银行法)

Law of the People's Republic of China on Administrative Penalty1996 (中华人民共和国行政处罚法)

Law of the People's Republic of China on Administrative Reconsideration 1999 (中华人民共和国行政复议法)

Law of the People's Republic of China on Lawyers 1996 (Revised in 2000,) (中华人民共和国律师法)

Law on Legislation of the People's Republic of China 2000 (中华人民共和国立法法)

Law of the People Republic of China on Administrative Permission 2004 (中华人民共和国行政许可法)

Mapping Law of the People's Republic of China 1993（中华人民共和国测绘法）

Provisional Regulations for Maintaining State Secrets 1951(保守国家机密暂行条例)

Proposals regarding Science and Technology Exchange and Maintaining Confidentiality 1962(关于科学技术交流与保密工作的若干意见)

Proposals for Science and Technology Exchange and Maintaining Confidentiality, 1965 (关于科学技术交流与保密工作的若干意见)

Provisions on Reasonable Mobility of Science and Technology Personnel 1983 (关于科技人员合理流动的若干规定)

Regulations on the Issue of Science and Technology Secrets 1958 (关于科学技术秘密问题的规定)

Regulations for Maintaining Confidentiality of Science and Technology 1978 (科学技术保密条例)

Provisional Rules for Adopting the Labour Contract System in State-run Enterprises 1986 (国营企业实行劳动合同制暂行规定)

Provisional Rules for Employing Workers in State-run Enterprises 1986 (国营企业招用工人暂行规定)

Provisional Regulations of the PRC on Private Enterprises 1988 (中华人民共和国私营企业暂行条例)

Provisions of the Supreme People's Court about Several Issues Concerning the Application of the Civil Procedure Law of the People's Republic of China 1992〔中华人民共和国最高人民法院关于实施（中华人民共和国民事诉讼法）若干问题的意见〕

Rules for Implementation of Technology Contract Law of People's Republic of China 1992 (中华人民共和国技术合同实施条例)

Regulations on Protection of Traditional Chinese Medicines 1992 (中药品种保护条例)

Regulations of the People's Republic of China on the Settlement of Labour Disputes in Enterprises1992, （中华人民共和国企业劳动争议处理条例）

Provisions on the Administration of Employment of Taiwan, Hong Kong, and Macao Residents in the Mainland 1994 (台湾和香港、澳门居民在内地就业管理规定)

Regulation on the Labour Security and Supervision 1994 (劳动保障监察条例)

Regulation on the Collective Contract 1994 (集体合同规定)

Regulations for Prohibiting Infringement of Trade Secrets 1995(关于禁止侵犯商业秘密行为的若干规定)

Rules of the Supreme People's Court on Some Issues on Hearing Cases of the Scientific and Technological Disputes 1995 (审理科技纠纷案件的若干问题的规定)

Regulations on Transfer of Cases on Suspicion of Crime by Administrative Organ for Law Enforcement 2001(行政执法机关移送涉嫌犯罪案件的规定)

Procedural Rules for Hearings on Labour Administrative Penalties 1996 (劳动行政处罚听证程序规定)

Patent Law of the People's Republic of China 1984 (Revised in 1992, 2000), (中华人民共和国专利法)

Provisional Measures on the Collectively Negotiating of Salaries 2000 (工资集体协商试行办法)

Regulations of the People's Republic of China on the Settlement of Labour Disputes in Enterprises promulgated by the No.117 order of the State Council 1993 (中华人民共和国企业劳动争议处理条例)

Rules on the Administration of Employment of Foreigners in China1996 (外国人在中国就业管理规定)

Regulations on Collective Contract 2004 (集体合同规定)

Regulations on the Control of Exports of Military Items of the People's Republic of China 1997 (中华人民共和国军品出口管理条例)

Regulations for the Protection of Traditional Arts and Crafts1997 (传统工艺美术保护条例)

Several Opinions on the Enhancement of the Management of Technical Secrets among the Flow of Technical Staff 1997 (关于加强科技人员流动中技术秘密管理的若干意见)

Technology Contract Law of the People's Republic of China 1987 (Expired)(中华人民共和国技术合同法)

The Provisional Regulations regarding the Resignation of Personnel in Specific Technical Fields and the Resignation of Managerial Personnel within State-owned Institutions (promulgated by the State Personnel Bureau and effective September 8, 1990) (全民所有制事业单位专业技术人员和管理人员辞职暂行规定)

Trade Union Law of the People's Republic of China 1992 (中华人民共和国工会法)

The Notice on the Strengthening of Protection of Trade Secrets of State-owned Enterprises 1997 (关于加强国有企业商业秘密保护工作的通知)

The Several Proposals for the Strengthening of the Management of Technological Secrets in the Movement of Scientific and Technological Personnel 1997 (关于加强科技人员流动中技术秘密管理的若干意见)

The Provisional Methods for the Management of Holders of Projects Concerning Confidential State Technology 1998 (国家秘密技术项目持有单位管理暂行办法)

The Regulations for Certified Inspectors of the State Council 1998 (国务院稽查特派员条例)

Trademark Law of the People's Republic of China 2001 (中华人民共和国商标法)

Index

D

Q

R

S

T

Max Planck Series on Asian Intellectual Property Law

1. Christopher Heath and Kung-Chung Liu (eds), *The Protection of Well-Known Marks in Asia*, 2000 (ISBN 90-411-9705-2).
2. Christoph Antons, *Intellectual Property Law in Indonesia*, 2002 (ISBN 90-411-9803-2).
3. Christopher Heath, *The System of Unfair Competition Prevention in Japan*, 2002 (ISBN 90-411-9837-7).
4. Christopher Heath and Kung-Chung Liu (eds), *Legal Rules of Technology Transfer in Asia*, 2002 (ISBN 90-411-9883-0).
5. Christopher Heath (ed.), *Intellectual Property Law in Asia*, 2002 (ISBN 90-411-9894-6).
6. Christopher Heath (ed.), *Intellectual Property Law in Korea*, 2003 (ISBN 90-411-9906-3).
7. Christopher Heath (ed.), *Intellectual Property Law in Taiwan*, 2003 (ISBN 90-411-9920-9).
8. Christopher Heath and Anselm Kamperman Sanders (eds), *Industrial Property in the Bio-Medical Age*, 2003 (ISBN 90-411-9926-8).
9. Christopher Heath (ed.), *Parallel Imports in Asia*, 2004 (ISBN 90-411-2114-5).
10. C. Antons, M. Blakeney and C. Heath (eds), *Intellectual Property Harmonisation with ASEAN and APEC*, 2004 (ISBN 90-411-2292-3).
11. Peter Ganea and Thomas Pattloch; Christopher Heath (ed.), *Intellectual Property Law in China*, 2005 (ISBN 90-411-2340-7).
12. Peter Ganea, Christopher Heath and Hiroshi Saitô (eds), *Japanese Copyright Law* Writings in Honour of Gerhard Schricker, 2005 (ISBN 90-411-2393-8).
13. SHAN Hailing, *The Protection of Trade Secrets in China*, 2008 (ISBN 978-90-411-2758-5).